Inter-Organizational Information Systems in the Internet Age

Sean B. Eom
Southeast Missouri State University, USA

IDEA GROUP PUBLISHING
Hershey • London • Melbourne • Singapore

Acquisitions Editor: Mehdi Khosrow-Pour
Senior Managing Editor: Jan Travers
Managing Editor: Amanda Appicello
Development Editor: Michele Rossi
Copy Editor: Lori Eby
Typesetter: Sara Reed
Cover Design: Lisa Tosheff
Printed at: Yurchak Printing Inc.

Published in the United States of America by
          Idea Group Publishing (an imprint of Idea Group Inc.)
          701 E. Chocolate Avenue
          Hershey PA 17033
          Tel: 717-533-8845
          Fax: 717-533-8661
          E-mail: cust@idea-group.com
          Web site: http://www.idea-group.com

and in the United Kingdom by
          Idea Group Publishing (an imprint of Idea Group Inc.)
          3 Henrietta Street
          Covent Garden
          London WC2E 8LU
          Tel: 44 20 7240 0856
          Fax: 44 20 7379 3313
          Web site: http://www.eurospan.co.uk

Library of Congress Cataloging-in-Publication Data

Inter-organizational information systems in the internet age / Sean B. Eom, editor.
       p. cm.
    Includes bibliographical references and index.
    ISBN 1-59140-318-9 (hardcover) -- ISBN 1-59140-319-7 (pbk.) -- ISBN 1-59140-320-0
(ebook)
 1. Business enterprises--Computer network resources. 2. Business information
services. 3. Information resources management. I. Eom, Sean B.
    HF54.56.I55 2004
    658.4'028'011--dc22
                                                            2004013519

British Cataloguing in Publication Data
A Cataloguing in Publication record for this book is available from the British Library.

All work contributed to this book is new, previously-unpublished material. The views expressed in
this book are those of the authors, but not necessarily of the publisher.

Dedication

This book is dedicated to the two individuals who have changed the course of my life. I am indebted perpetually to them for their influence on me.

Jong Ye Won, my mother

Dr. Sang M. Lee, my doctoral advisor and mentor

Inter-Organizational Information Systems in the Internet Age

Table of Contents

Preface

Since the U.S. Department of Defense initiated the development of networked computers in 1969, Internet technologies have rapidly advanced and revolutionized the way we communicate and conduct business. The second wave of the technological revolution came with intranet technology in the mid-1990s. With the intranet, organizations have strengthened the powers and speed of data gathering and sharing, communication, collaboration, and decision making within a firewall-protected organizational boundary. The third wave of this technological evolution, extranets, began in the second half of the 1990s. Many believe that it is the key technology enabler that is triggering a revolution in the structure and operations of many organizations in the new Internet-driven global economy. In addition to maturing Internet technologies, several technology drivers, as well as business drivers, further pushed the emergence of new types of organizations—virtual corporations, virtual organizations, extended enterprises, and trans-enterprise systems.

Since we began to study information systems, academics and practitioners have expanded the focus of information technology's role in managing organizations, from individuals to groups to functional departments to organizations to inter-organizations. In the 1980s, technology's impact on organizations has been an ongoing research theme. For example, Rockart and Short (1989, p. 7) argued that a firm's ability to continuously improve the effectiveness of managing interdependence is the critical element in responding to new and pressing competitive forces. The concept of inter-organizational systems (IOSs) emerged as a tool for achieving competitive advantages. Many well-known examples of information systems that provide competitive advantages that are discussed in the literature (Porter & Millar, 1985) are those of inter-organizational information systems (IOISs).

The Objective of this Book

The purpose of this book is to provide the readers with a guidepost that helps them understand the current state of IOS and the foundational concepts. This book aims to provide readers with a framework for IOS management, which is comprised of the management of IOS technology infrastructure and the ongoing process of IOS analysis and planning, design, implementation, and evaluation (see Figure 1). Discussed in this book are the foundational concepts of the IOIS, its typology, real-world IOS examples (supranet-based IOS and intronet-based IOS), configurations (horizontal or vertical electronic linkage) and categories, benefits, risks, corporate strategies, future trends, and a wide range of issues addressing all aspects of IOIS management, including technological and organizational issues, opportunities, and managerial issues in the processes of planning, designing, implementing, and evaluating IOISs.

In designing supranet-based IOSs, identifying the information requirements of a business or industrial association is an extremely important activity in the IOS development process. This book presents the virtual association platform model, a framework of the relationships, and the corresponding information flow. The framework provides the readers with indispensable tools with which to identify information requirements as well as the flow of information among the various entities, such as consortium members, association (consortium), government, financial institutions, customers, nonmember customers, and nonmember sup-

Figure 1: IOIS management framework

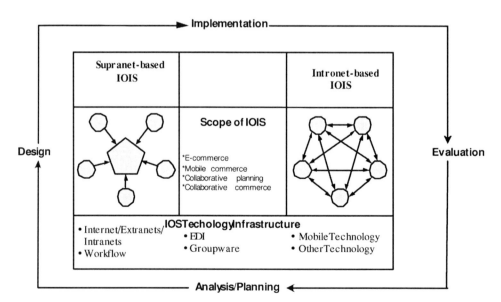

pliers. Other critically important contributions of this book are in the IOS network information management and IOS evaluations. Network information management refers to the management of IOS information resources, infrastructures, and systems to improve the management of information flows in the most efficient and effective way. Further, the book presents inter-organizational decision support systems, IOS research methods, and empirical study on how information technology encourages the creation of strategic networks.

The Structure of the Book

This book is divided into seven sections: *Foundations*, *Technology Infrastructure*, *Systems Analysis/Planning*, *Systems Management*, *Implementation and Applications*, *Evaluation*, and *Research Method and Empirical Study*.

The first section, *Foundations*, consists of three chapters. These three chapters offer a broad landscape for the rest of the book. In chapter 1, Eom provides the readers with a brief overview of foundational concepts, definitions, and information technology infrastructure. A definition of IOS is *an information and management system that transcends organizational boundaries via electronic linkages with its trading partners to share data, information, and business applications; provide the capabilities of electronic transactions, including buying and selling goods and services; and facilitate communications and decision making for the purposes of increasing efficiency, effectiveness, competitiveness, and profitability for participating organizations.* The electronic linkage is established by an information technology environment, including extranets, Internet, groupware, electronic data interchange (EDI), workflow, mobile communication technologies, and other information and communication technologies. Finally, the chapter systematically classifies the IOIS literature of 192 bibliographic items into 10 subspecialties. Therefore, along with a previous survey (Ngai & Wat, 2002) of 275 bibliographic items, readers are in a better position to comprehend the big picture of IOS.

In Chapter 2, O'Donnell and Glassberg provide a typology of IOIS to help readers understand the purpose of IOIS systems and how they are structured, in order to fill in the gaps not yet investigated by researchers. This typology not only highlights the differences and similarities among the many configurations of IOIS available today, but also contrasts this with internal Web sites (Intranets) and public (external) Internet Web sites. This approach offers new insights for both practitioners and researchers. O'Donnell and Glassberg present the background and the typology of IOIS. The two general areas in which these systems differ-the structures of the relationships and the types and formats of the information exchanged-are identified and discussed in separate sections, respectively. Each system that has features that help distinguish between it and these differences will be highlighted. Next, the benefits and risks of IOIS are discussed. Later, previous research on EDI and systems is introduced to identify exciting new areas for investigation. Finally, O'Donnell and Glassberg identify future trends for IOIS, and the implications for both researchers and practitioners are discussed.

Chapter 3 aims to develop a framework for business-to-business inter-organizational systems based on real-world IOS examples. Based upon two dimensions-role linkage and system support level, Hong proposes a new framework that classifies IOS into four basic types: resource pooling, operational cooperation, operational coordination, and complementary cooperation. He reviews selected cases that fit into each category and considers the common characteristics of systems in each category. He then draws implications for IOS planning and suggests a four-step process for creating an IOS plan. It is argued that each category of IOS needs to be linked with a specific business strategy, although each employs a common technical infrastructure.

The second section of the book is titled *Technology Infrastructure*. The first chapter in this section, Chapter 4, discusses an extranet, which is one of the information systems infrastructures on which an IOS is built. An extranet is a Web-based private network that interconnects a company's network to the networks of business partners, suppliers, customers, and others in a secure, electronic, online environment for the purpose of conducting business. The extranet is an extended corporate intranet using Internet technology operating over the Internet for a wide range of applications in the areas of sales, marketing, manufacturing, online publishing, design and development of new product, communications via videoconferencing and real-time voice conversations, business transactions, decision making, etc. Extranets are the core technology for building IOSs. There are a host of other technologies that serve as infrastructures for managing IOS. They include coordination technologies for coordinating resources, facilities, and projects, monitoring technologies, filtering and negotiating technologies (intelligent agents), and decision-making and knowledge management technologies. In this chapter, the authors provide brief overviews of each of these technologies.

Chapter 5 presents the Application Service Provision/Provider (ASP) business model, which offers a pragmatic adoption path for inter-organizations in the Internet Age. The official body of authority, ASP Industry Consortium, defines ASP as "a third party service firm which deploys, manages and remotely hosts software applications through centrally-located services in a rental or lease agreement" (ASP Consortium, 2001). Such application deliveries are done to multiple entities from data centers across a wide area network as a service, rather than as a product, priced according to a license fee and maintenance contract set by the vendor. This model enables ASPs to serve their customers regardless of geographical, cultural, organizational, and technical constraints, thereby adding value of location. Given this pragmatic adoption path, academics are beginning to question: Where are enterprises adopting ASP technology first? Why are they choosing these areas? Where will they apply the evolving Web services technology next?

This chapter's primary purpose is to point out a number of issues that concern management of inter-organizations of the Internet Age and to explore the impact of ASP on such organizations. It will examine the strategies that will enable inter-organizations to better manage ASP resources for competitive advantage. While the phenomenon of ASP is still in an embryonic stage, we draw from seminal works of IS pioneers like Markus, Porter, Checkland, Maslow, and others. Their intellectual contributions, plus findings from research work at Brunel University, provide a framework for discussion. By shedding light on patterns of ASP's trajectory, drivers, benefits, and risks, the chapter will help managers and academics reflect on determining where ASP-and associated technologies-might be deployed and define a broad implementation program to exploit the potential of an ASP business model. The chapter seeks to find if Web services architectures are distinctively able to enhance the flexible coordination of business processes, which span various enterprises and rely on inter-organizational information systems in the Internet Age.

The third section of the book is titled *Systems Analysis/Planning*. In Chapter 6, the subject matter concerns the study of information and communication technology application to improve business/industrial association environment. This chapter provides the readers with an important example of supranet-based IOS (introduced in Chapter 1). Business/industrial associations are a form of industrial aggregation that has the purpose of providing all association members with social activities and collective business services. Business associations represent the interest of their members. In pursuing consortium competitiveness and efficiency, the development of successful information and communication technology solutions is a must to create and extend value chains by improving collaboration, information sharing, and joint decision making among association members.

Pigni and others present the virtual association platform model, which is a comprehensive framework for analysis of the information requirements for the activities of business/industrial associations. They provide an assessment of the main activities of a business association and describe the relevance of relationships management within a business association. They then propose a framework for use in identifying the information requirements of a business/industrial association BA. Finally, such a framework is applied to the case of the 2Cities portal, a platform designed to deliver services to business/industrial associations in Western Australia. This global model is used for defining the information requirements for the design of a technological platform supporting its activities.

The fourth section of the book is called *Systems Management*. The IOS is created by a long-term IT-related business arrangement regulated by contract, including EDI, EFT, and Internet services. A plethora of various issues has been discussed in the literature. These issues include organizational, collaboration, technological, and other miscellaneous issues, as reviewed in Chapter 1. In Chapter 7, Klein and his colleagues discussed the specific challenges of designing and running IS in an inter-organizational setting and presented an IOIS management framework as a basis for explaining the different outcomes of IOISs. Their framework proposes that the IOS outcomes are the results of the dynamic process among several elements. The IOISs need to be strategically aligned with the purpose of the network and the strategic goals of its members. Furthermore, they need to be organizationally embedded so that they can support network relations and processes. The cases have highlighted the need to develop shared visions and incentives for the IOIS—successfully in the ONIA NET case, unsuccessfully in the DIMER example—and to build relationships and inter-organizational practices that provide initial support for the IOIS. Once in place, we observe a reciprocal relationship between the technically mediated and the social relationships: initial trust is essential for the setup of the IOIS, which then has to confirm and reinforce trust, e.g., through extended transparency among the network members.

The fifth section of the book, *Implementation and Applications*, deals with the implementation of the IOS and specific applications. The IOS can be applied in the form of transaction processing systems, management information systems, decision support systems (DSSs), etc. In this section, we include two chapters on DSS applications. Chapter 8, presented by Hope Koch, contains information about the adoption and diffusion of IOISs. Realizing the full potential of emerging inter-organizational connectivity requires understanding what facilitates its adoption and diffusion. A history of IOIS adoption research exists in electronic data interchange (EDI). Based on this work, Chwelos, Benbasat, and Dexter (2001) hypothesized that constructs at three levels (organizational, inter-organizational, and technological) influence IOIS adoption. This chapter expands Chwelos et al.'s hypothesis by looking at variables found to significantly influence adoption and diffusion of an array of IOISs. In this process, Koch reviews 25 empirical IOIS studies and lists and categorizes variables significantly influencing IOIS adoption and diffusion by IOIS type. Bringing IOIS adoption and diffusion literature together, this chapter can be a starting point for research on emerging IOISs. Koch's research supports and extends Chwelos et al.'s hypothesis. While Chwelos et al.'s hypothesis focuses on EDI adoption, her research found that variables at the adoption and diffusion stages for an array of IOISs fall into Chwelos et al.'s construct categories. However, some variables fall into multiple categories. Koch further proposes that variables found to significantly influence IOIS adoption and diffusion also facilitate adoption and diffusion of emerging IOIS forms.

In Chapter 9, Eom discusses inter-organizational DSSs (IODSSs) as a new frontier in DSSs. The focus of DSSs has been shifting from teams, work groups, and intranet-based organizational DSSs to extranet-based IODSSs. The extranets' built-in technologies are sufficient to make the extranets as rudimentary IODSS. This chapter discusses the evolution of DSSs from single-user DSSs to IODSSs. To better understand the IODSS, Eom briefly discusses two predecessors, the organizational DSS and the global DSS, followed by the IODSS definition, architecture, and its applications. With the addition of many readily available Web groupware to extranets, the IODSS is an indispensable communication/decision support tool for enhancing inter-organizational competitiveness to achieve system-wide global objectives. In doing so, costs must be minimized, and products must be differentiated. The cost minimization can be achieved by making a series of decisions in the value chains, such as inbound logistics, operations, outbound logistics, marketing, service, etc. Over the past three decades, numerous DSSs have been developed to manage each stage of the value chain. Future research is designed to develop integrated models to optimize the extended enterprise as a whole. To do so, changes in management process thinking from a discrete firm-based view to an industry-based perspective of cooperation is necessary. Furthermore, several ongoing technological developments in the DSS area can make the IODSS an effective management support tool.

Chapter 10 examines recent developments associated with building and deploying IODSSs to support external stakeholders of an organization. The IODSS concept is defined, and an information-technology architecture for such a system is explored. Examples of current implementations are categorized as communication, data, document, knowledge, and model-driven IODSSs. Further, implementations of IODSSs are categorized as customer- and supplier-focused. Advantages, disadvantages, and current issues associated with the IODSS conclude the discussion.

The sixth section of the book, *Evaluation*, has one chapter titled "Evaluating Inter-Organizational Information Systems." In Chapter 11, Drury and Scholtz describe different means of evaluating the usability and suitability of computer-based IOISs. They begin by describing why doing so is important yet difficult, and they provide an assessment of the advantages and disadvantages of the major types of evaluation. The chapter continues with a case study focusing on determining whether an application provides the necessary insight into other collaborators' identities, presence, and activities, while keeping sensitive information private from a subset of the collaborators. The goal of this chapter is to provide practical guidance to organizations seeking IOISs to help them choose (or develop) an IOIS that best meets their needs. The authors describe evaluation methods for multiuser applications, in general. One evaluation method, in particular, Synchronous Collaborative Awareness and Privacy Evaluation (SCAPE), is singled out for description. The chapter also presents a case study using SCAPE to evaluate Groove™, a popular tool that aids inter-organizational information sharing.

The seventh section of the book is titled *Research Method and Empirical Study*. The section consists of Chapters 12 and 13. Chapter 12 suggests the use of comparative pairs analysis as a method of collecting data for inter-organizational information system and chain research. It is argued that chains of organizations can be analyzed by collecting data from a focal firm about upstream suppliers and downstream customers. By comparing pairs of respondents within the focal firm, the differences between customers and suppliers can be analyzed. In addition, it is suggested that by asking each respondent to discuss two third-party organizations, differences in responses can be highlighted and explained during the data collection process. This can provide a rich source of data to explain the results obtained.

Chapter 13 analyzes how information technology fosters and supports the creation of strategic networks. The creation of strategic networks of firms has been widely studied, and there has been some work on the importance of information technology (IT) in these networks. But, there is little in the literature that explains in detail the role of IT in the formation of inter-organizational networks. There are gaps with respect to what IT actually does, and how it makes possible, or at least facilitates, the operation of the network. This chapter attempts to fill this important gap, in a literature where IT appears to be very important for inter-organizational relations, but the reason why is anecdotal. This chapter looks in detail at the reasons why strategic networks are formed, developing a theoretical framework that can explain these reasons adequately, and allows us to analyze the role of IT in the formation and maintenance of these networks. The conclusions we come to will be tested against a case study, which, as well as being illustrative, will allow us to make a theoretical generalization.

Acknowledgments

*I am deeply thankful to all authors of this book for their valuable contri-
butions. I feel very fortunate to work with them in that in addition to their
high-quality chapter contributions, many of them also served as reviewers
of other chapters, and their constructive comments resulted in the production of this fine book. I truly believe that almost all the articles in this
book will be making indispensable contributions to the inter-organizational information systems literature. The editor was very surprised to see
all of the reviewers' reports that are full of detailed, constructive, and
critical comments. I thank them again.*

*My daughter, Caroline, has done a superb job in proofreading the manu-
script. Substantial portions of a previous article published in the International Encyclopedia of Business and Management is used in a chapter of
the book. I am very grateful for the permission granted by Thomson Learning to use my earlier work. Thanks also go to Professor Mehdi Khosrow-
Pour of Idea Group Publishing for inviting me to produce this book. Last
but not least, I would like to thank Ms. Michele Rossi, Ms. Jan Travers,
and other staff members at Idea Group Publishing for their guidance and
hard work in each and every step of this long editing and publishing process.*

Section I:

Foundations

Chapter I

An Introduction to Inter-Organizational Information Systems with Selected Bibliography

Sean B. Eom
Southeast Missouri State University, USA

Abstract

One of the important roles of information technology is to permit firms to manage organizational interdependence. Over the past two decades, the concept of inter-organizational information systems (IOISs) has emerged as a strategic tool for achieving competitive advantages and IOISs have been a major research theme. Many well-known examples of information systems that provide competitive advantages discussed in the literature are those of IOISs. This chapter provides the readers with a brief overview of foundational concepts, definitions, and the information technology infrastructure of IOIS. Finally, the chapter systematically classifies the IOIS literature of 192 bibliographic items into 10 subspecialties. Therefore, along with this survey of 192 bibliographic items, readers are referred to Ngai and Wat's recent survey (Ngai & Wat, 2002) to comprehend the big picture of IOISs.

Introduction

In 1989, researchers at MIT's Center for Information Systems refocused the issue of the organizational impact of information technology. After reviewing abundant theories that had been proposed, Rockart and Short (1989) argued that information technology's most important role is permitting firms to manage organizational interdependence:

For more than two decades, the question of what impact information technology (IT) will have on business organizations has continued to puzzle academics and practitioners alike. Indeed, in an era when the business press has widely disseminated the idea that IT is changing the way business operates and the way they relate to customers and suppliers, the question of technology's impact on the organization itself has gained renewed urgency. (p. 7)

We will argue here that information technology (IT) provides a new approach to one of management's oldest organizational problems: that of effectively managing interdependence. *Our fundamental thesis is that a firm's ability to continuously improve the effectiveness of managing interdependence is the critical element in responding to new and pressing competitive forces.*

Over the past two decades, the concept of the inter-organizational information system (IOIS) has emerged as a tool for achieving competitive advantages. The IOIS has been a major research topic. Many well-known examples of information systems that provide competitive advantages discussed in the literature (Porter & Millar, 1985) are those of IOISs. The purpose of this chapter is to provide readers with the foundational concepts and a brief overview of the IOIS literature. There are few guideposts that help students and researchers understand the current state of the IOIS, partly due to the fuzzy definitions of the IOIS and the complex and evolving nature of the IOIS information technology infrastructure. For example, private network-based traditional electronic data interchange (EDI) and Internet-based EDI are examples of IOIS technologies. To study Internet-based EDI, researchers and students also need to understand ongoing changes in foundational telecommunication technologies, standards for encapsulating messages, cheaper alternative message transport mechanisms created by combining the Web, XML, and Java, and other protocols. Ideally, a comprehensive literature survey should include all these topics. However, the breadth and depth of IOIS-related topics may make it almost impractical.

Nevertheless, there is a strong need for a survey of the literature in the IOIS area. Although the introductory chapter may not be a comprehensive literature survey, I hope that this will serve a purpose of guiding researchers and students to the exciting and expanding area of academic inquiry.

The critical component of an IOIS is, needless to say, the information systems component. To organize the vast amount of IOISs literature, the chapter presents the definition of an IOIS first and attempts to systematically classify the IOISs literature into several subspecialties. Throughout this book, the terms inter-organizational systems (IOSs) and inter-organizational information systems (IOISs) are used interchangeably.

An inter-organizational information system (IOIS) is a system that contains one or more other systems of trading partners. Each system has its own structures, subsystems, strategies, technologies, and goals. An IOIS is a supra-system that consists of information systems of trading partners. Each system pursues its own goal while pursuing the supra-system's goals. An IOIS is built on the cooperative relationships among trading partners. While these two goals are consistent with each other, the cooperative relationships continue to exist and, consequently, so the IOIS exists, to achieve the goals of the supra-systems. The IOISs manage cooperative ventures between otherwise independent agents (Kumar & Van Dissel, 1996). The IOS-enabled partnerships and alliances make it possible to seek business opportunities via new organizational and market relationships.

Definition

We begin with the review of various definitions. In addition to inter-organizational systems, some other terminologies were suggested, including multiorganizational systems, inter-organizational information sharing systems, etc.

An IOS is "an automated information system shared by two or more companies" (Cash & Konsynski, 1985, p. 134).

The multiorganizational system is an information system that links one or more firms to their customers or their suppliers and facilitates the exchange of products and services (Bakos, 1991).

The essential requirement for an inter-organizational information sharing system is a computer-based, electronic link between the two organizations that automates some element of work, such as order editing, inventory status checking, or, minimally, transaction transfer, that would previously have been performed manually or through other media, such as the mail. (Barrett, 1986-1987, p.6)

An IOS is a network-based information system (IS) that extends beyond traditional enterprise boundaries. With an IOS permitting information access to other organizations, the organizational boundaries are redefined and extended to the extent that a firm's value chain needs to be redesigned (Hong, 2002).

An IOS is the information and communication technology that transcends organizational boundaries (Applegate, McFarlan, & Mckenney, 1996; Cash & Konsynski, 1985; Kumar & Van Dissel, 1996).

According to Vlosky, Wilson, and Vlosky (1997, p. 75), the IOSs are "electronic buyer–seller information exchanges that are implemented to facilitate business transactions and increase efficiency, competitiveness and profitability for participating companies."

Based on the reviews of several definitions, the IOIS is defined as follows:

An inter-organizational system (IOS) is an information and management system that transcends organizational boundaries via electronic linkages

Figure 1: IOIS management framework

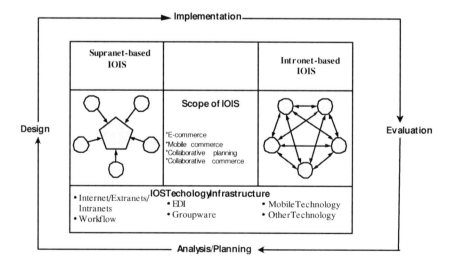

with its trading partners to share data, information, and business applications, provide the capabilities of electronic transactions including buying and selling goods and services, and facilitate communications and decision making for the purpose of increasing efficiency, effectiveness, competitiveness, and profitability for participating organizations. The electronic linkage is established by the Internet, extranets, intranets, groupware, electronic data interchange (EDI), workflow systems, mobile communication technologies, and other information and communication technologies.

The definition here is a broad one that encompasses systems that support supply chain management, electronic commerce, mobile commerce, and collaborative commerce activities. This book aims to provide readers with a framework for IOIS management (Figure 1), which is comprised of the management of the IOIS technology infrastructure and the ongoing process of IOIS analysis/planning, design, implementation, and evaluation.

One issue involved in this definition of an IOIS is the fuzzy distinction between the IOIS and electronic commerce (e-commerce). Electronic commerce is defined in Laudon and Laudon (2004) as follows:

The process of buying and selling goods and services electronically with computerized business transactions using the Internet, networks, and other digital technologies. It also encompasses activities supporting those market transactions, such as advertising, marketing, customer support, delivery and payment. (p. 24)

Other authors (Kalakota & Whinston, 1997; Turban, King, Lee, & Viehland, 2004) agreed on the narrow definition given above but expanded it by adding several more dimensions. For example, the expanded definition by Turban and others is reproduced here.

Electronic commerce (EC) can be defined from the following perspectives:

•   Communications - From a communications perspective, EC is the delivery of goods, services, information, or payments over computer networks or through any other electronic means.

•   Commercial (trading) - From a commercial perspective, EC provides the capability of buying and selling products, services, and information on the Internet and via other online services.

- Business process - From a business process perspective, EC is doing business electronically by completing business processes over electronic networks, thereby substituting information for physical business processes (Weill & Vitale, 2001, p. 13).

- Service - From a service perspective, EC is a tool that addresses the desire of governments, firms, consumers, and management to cut service costs while improving the quality of customer service and increasing the speed of service delivery.

- Learning - From a learning perspective, EC is an enabler of online training and education in schools, universities, and other organizations, including businesses.

- Collaborative - From a collaborative service perspective, EC is the framework for inter- and intraorganizational collaboration.

- Community - From a community perspective, EC provides a gathering place where community members can learn, transact, and collaborate.

We believe that the broad definition of e-commerce may need to be reexamined. Perhaps, the definition is too extravagant to justify it. I can hardly agree with the notion that e-commerce is an enabler of online education at universities. There is no doubt that inter-organizational business activities have been and will continue to be further accelerated in the future. The research in this area will be further intensified. As an academic discipline becomes a coherent and substantive field, we need to build a cumulative research tradition in which definitions and concepts are shared (Keen, 1980). In doing so, consensus building is a first step among academics and practitioners in regard to definitions of the foundational terms and subspecialties to be researched in that field. As any academic discipline becomes a mature field of study, there should be a shared and agreed-upon set of definitions, topics, concepts, and subspecialties.

Supply chain management requires the extensive use of IOISs in the process of procuring raw materials, transforming them into intermediate and finished products, and distributing the finished products to retail outlets and customers. The IOISs help participating organizations in the supply chain forecast customer demand, plan production and inventory, track shipments, and communicate with trading partners.

The core of an IOIS is to support daily transactions of buying and selling by providing electronic catalogs and other databases on the Internet and electronic payment tools in a secure business environment. A recent innovative application of IOIS support is in the area of designing, developing, manufacturing, and managing products through their life cycles with trading partners collaboratively. This is an extended application of supply chain management of the IOIS and the

CPFR (collaborative planning, forecasting, and replenishment) system. Developed in 1998, the CPFR system enables trading partners to improve business processes, customer service, and inventories. The growth of CPFR has created a demand for e-business software products to address and support collaborative commerce activities (Anonymous, 2002).

Collaborative commerce is the use of information technologies to manage product life cycle management (PLM), supplier relationship management (SRM), supply chain management (SCM), and customer relationship management (CRM), jointly by the collaborating organizations. Using workflow and other collaboration tools such as groupware, all key stakeholders can collaborate in the product life cycle, from inception (concept) through design, introduction of a salable item, and eventual product retirement (Brown & Sappenfield, 2003).

Classification Of IOIS Research

As discussed earlier in the chapter, the definition of an IOIS in this book is a broad one that encompasses systems that support electronic commerce, supply chain management, mobile commerce, and collaborative commerce activities. Depending on the definitions (narrow versus broad), there may be fuzzy distinctions between an IOIS and electronic commerce. While preparing the introductory chapter, a paper on literature review and classification of 275 electronic commerce research papers was published in 2002 by Ngai and Wat (2002). Due to the broad definition of e-commerce adopted by Ngai and Wat, a substantial portion of bibliography is overlapped, and therefore, we decided not to include that overlapped bibliography of 275 articles published between 1993 and 1999 in this chapter. The bibliography of 185 items in this chapter consists of books, journal articles, conference proceedings, doctoral dissertations, and case studies. Therefore, along with this survey of 185 bibliographic items, readers are referred to Ngai and Wat (2002) to comprehend the big picture of an IOIS. Ngai and Wat did an excellent job of compiling the literature on introduction/ foundational concepts of IOISs and e-commerce and technological issues, including network security issues. (Please note that for the numbers in brackets, complete reference information is included at the end of this chapter.)

1. Foundational

Introduction to IOISs

- Introduction to EC [4, 79, 100, 156, 181, 192]

- General introduction to an IOIS [9, 87]
- Electronic integration in various industries [54, 191]

Objectives of an IOIS

- Transforming boundaries, relations, and markets [7, 20, 28, 66, 77, 87, 176]
- Strategic control to influence behavior in the extended enterprise [12, 87]
- Operational efficiencies [87, 170]
- Interdependent benefits [30, 149]
- Collaboration and cooperation [14, 93]
- Information sharing [11, 88]
- Competitive advantages [19, 33, 38, 75, 87, 113, 114, 132, 177]
- The economics of switching costs [30]
- Global economic development [103]

Typology for an IOIS

Categorization by

- Technological and organizational dimensions [75]
- Purposes, participants, and functions [75]
- Inter-organizational interdependence [90, 93]
- The linkage of participants' roles [72]

2. Technology Infrastructure

Extranets

- IOIS infrastructure [127]
- Introduction to extranets [6]

EDI (Electronic Data Interchange)

- EDI introduction [48, 51, 57, 89]
- EDI impact on just-in-time (JIT) shipments [81, 164] and delivery performance [1], business process improvement [15], and inventory and financial performance [44]
- EDI implementation [135, 145, 155, 157]
- Risks, challenges, and vulnerability of EDI [10, 107, 150]
- Identifying antecedents of user satisfaction with EDI [78]

- EDI audit and control [64, 102]
- Determinants of EDI implementation and diffusion [67, 101, 143]
- Strategic value of EDI [13, 35, 37, 68, 122, 152, 162, 184]
- EDI use in selected industries [43, 45, 50, 86, 110, 126, 154, 160, 165, 166, 178]

Enterprise Resource Planning (ERP) Systems [18]

Delegation Technologies [47, 87]

Workflow Systems and Collaborative Technologies
- Modeling workflows crossing organizational boundaries [82, 173, 174, 185]
- Using mobile agents to manage IOIS workflow [105]
- An IOIS workflow support using XRL (Extensible Routing Language) [92]
- Workflow interoperability model (the monitor-nested model) [91]
- Workflow overview and research issues [167]

3. Design and Development of IOISs

Incentives for IOIS Development
- Process redesign [37, 80]

Five Levels of IOIS Participation [11]

IOIS Strategic Planning Framework [61]
- Planning and implementation systems of development projects [120]
- Alliance or alone? How to build an IOIS [169]
- Challenges during the development of an IOIS [22]

User Participation in the IOIS Development [23, 25, 63]

Developing a Requirements Engineering Method for IOIS [56]

4. Implementation of an IOIS
- Lessons learned from implementing an IOIS [16, 128, 182]

- Critical success factors [24, 53, 60, 97, 129, 134, 163, 187]
- Adoption model [59, 76, 151]

5. Management of an IOIS
Framework
- A multidisciplinary framework [96]

Issues that Impact IOIS Management
- Collaboration issues-IOISs are created by long-term business arrangements regulated by contract, including EDI, EFT, and Internet services. Collaboration involves economic, strategic, social [3, 94], and management [93, 189] issues [46, 117, 121].
- Organizational issues include relationships among participants [115, 133]; size of the firm and resources availability [49, 140], including skilled personnel [49, 142]; management style, such as leadership behavior [52, 147], and existence of communication channels [125]; and relationship satisfaction gap between buyer and seller and how to close this gap [180, 188].
- Technology issues [95, 190]
- Others-Influence of the external environment on the IOIS [186], the political economy of information exchange politics and property rights in the development of an IOIS [71]

6. Evaluation of an IOIS
- Multicriteria decision analysis approach [141]
- Modeling inter-organizational procedures and effectiveness [17, 161]
- Cost and benefit analysis [39, 60, 98, 116, 144, 171]
- A preliminary theory of IOIS effectiveness: A comparative study of four community mental health systems [137]

7. Examples of IOIS Applications
The following industries reported IOIS applications:
- Cotton [106]
- Airline reservation systems [31, 42, 73]
- Grocery chains [34]
- Hospital supply [179]

- Hong Kong TradeLink [83]
- Singapore TradeNet [84]
- Semiconductor [65]
- Automotive Network eXchange [85, 119]
- Japan airlines [29]
- Health care [109, 130]
- Construction [21]
- McKesson drug company: Economost [40]
- Supply chain management [136]
- Inter-Organizational DSS [118, 139]
- Use of an IOIS to support the outsourcing of logistics activities to third-party firms [104], environmental management [158], and design [74]

8. Case Study of an IOIS
- KHDS Vision 2000 engine factory [108]
- Inter-organizational technology transfer [58]
- The electronic virtual laboratory (Link.Net) [146]
- Trust, power, and the IOIS: The case of the electronic trading community Translease [2]
- From EDI to Internet commerce: The BHP steel experience [26]

9. Impact of an IOIS
- Production and logistical management [168]
- Inventory performance [183] and cycle time reduction [129]
- The property and casualty insurance market [99]
- International banking [172, 175]
- Process and structure in buyer and seller exchange [159]
- Supply chain management [27, 70, 124, 131, 138]
- On-time performance in U.S. air cargo [55]
- Market structure and corporate strategies [111]

10. Miscellaneous
- Agent-mediated inter-organizational business process coordination [69]
- Competitive growth of an IOIS [62, 148]

- Production of collective action in an alliance-based IOIS [182]
- The antecedents of an IOIS [153]
- Performance, interdependence, and coordination in business-to-business electronic commerce and supply chain management [36]
- Supplier-affiliated extended supply chain backbone [41]
- Networks and network structures for public policy and management [112]
- Cooperative and competitive strategies in an IOIS [32]
- Industrial networks: A new view of reality [5]

Conclusion

This chapter provides readers with a brief overview of foundational concepts and definitions. The chapter also systematically classifies the IOIS literature of 192 bibliographic items into 10 subspecialties. Therefore, along with this survey of 192 bibliographic items, readers are referred to Ngai and Wat's recent survey (Ngai & Wat, 2002) in order to comprehend the big picture of IOISs.

References

Anonymous. (2002). Another boost for CPFR. *Frontline Solutions, 3*(12), 51–52.

Anonymous. (2003, November 13). EDI and As2 'Can Live Together'. *Supply Management, 8*, 13.

Applegate, M. L., McFarlan, F. W., & Mckenney, J. L. (1996). *Corporate information systems management: Text and cases* (4th ed.). Chicago: Irwin.

Bakos, J. Y. (1991). Information links and electronic marketplaces: The role of interorganizational information systems in vertical markets. *Journal of Management Information Systems, 8*(2), 31–52.

Balasubramanian, S., Peterson, R. A., & Jarvenpaa, S. L. (2002). Exploring the implications of M–commerce for markets and marketing. *Academy of Marketing Science Journal, 30*(4), 348–361.

Barrett, S. S. (1986–1987). Strategic alternatives and inter-organizational system implementation: An overview. *Journal of Management Information Systems, 3*(3), 5–16.

Barshney, U., & Vetter, R. (2001). Recent advances in wireless networking. *IEEE Computer, 33*(6), 100–103.

Brown, M., & Sappenfield, D. (2003). Collaborative commerce: Not dead yet. *Intelligent Enterprise, 6*(4), 20–25.

Bushaus, D. (2000). Trade the ANX way. *InformationWeek, 776,* 93–97.

Cash, J. I., Jr., & Konsynski, B. R. (1985). IS redraws competitive boundaries. *Harvard Business Review, 63*(2), 134–142.

Gaskin, J. E. (2000, February 21). Enterprise applications—Groupware gets thin—A new generation of thin-client products proves that Web groupware can scale across an enterprise network. *InternetWeek,* 45.

Greenemeier, L. (2001, November 12). Tile manufacturer turns to Internet-based EDI system. *InformationWeek,* 79.

Hayes, M., Hulme, G. V., Kontzer, T., Whiting, R., & Colkin, E. (2002, October 14). Top of the week: News scan. *InformationWeek,* 32.

Hong, I. B. (2002). A new framework for interorganizational systems based on the linkage of participants' roles. *Information & Management, 39*(4), 261–270.

Kalakota, R., & Whinston, A. B. (1997). *Manager's guide to electronic commerce.* Reading, MA: Addison-Wesley.

Keen, P. G. W. (1980). MIS research: Reference disciplines and a cumulative tradition. In E. R. McLean (Ed.), *Proceedings of the First International Conference on Information Systems* (pp. 9–18). Philadelphia, PA.

Kumar, K., & Van Dissel, H. G. (1996). Sustainable collaboration: Managing conflict and cooperation in Interorganizational systems. *MIS Quarterly, 20*(3), 279–300.

Laudon, K. C., & Laudon, J. P. (2004). *Management information systems: Managing the digital firm* (8th ed.). Upper Saddle River, NJ: Prentice Hall.

Liebrecht, D. (1999). A TCP/IP-based network for the automotive industry. *America's Network, 103*(7), 67–69.

Margulius, D. L. (2002, April 22). Workflow meets BPM. *InfoWorld, 24,* 64–65.

Ngai, E. W. T., & Wat, F. K. T. (2002). A literature review and classification of electronic commerce research. *Information & Management, 39*(5), 415–429.

Nunamaker, J. F., Jr., Vogel, D. R., Heminger, A., Martz, W. B., Jr., Grohowski, R., & McGoff, C. (1989). Experiences at IBM with group support systems: A field study. *Decision Support Systems, 5*(2), 183–196.

Phoosuphanusorn, S. (2003, November 5). Visa to launch mobile commerce; Technology may be introduced in 2005. *Knight Ridder Tribune Business News*, p. 1.

Porter, M. E., & Millar, V. E. (1985). How information gives you competitive advantage. *Harvard Business Review, 63*(4), 149–160.

Riggins, F. J., & Rhee, H.-S. (1998). Toward a unified view of electronic commerce. *Communication of the ACM, 41*(10), 88–95.

Rockart, J. F., & Short, J. E. (1989). IT in the 1990's: Managing organizational interdependence. *Sloan Management Review, 30*(2), 7–17.

Turban, E., King, D., Lee, J. K., & Viehland, D. (2004). *Electronic commerce 2004: A managerial perspective*. Upper Saddle River, NJ: Pearson Education, Inc.

Vlosky, R. P., Wilson, D. T., & Vlosky, R. B. (1997). Closing the interorganizational information systems relationship satisfaction gap. *Journal of Marketing Practice, 3*(2), 75–82.

Weill, P., & Vitale, M. R. (2001). *Place to space: Migrating to e-business models*. Boston, MA: Harvard Business School Press.

Wheeler, B. C., Dennis, A. R., & Press, L. I. (1999). Groupware comes to the Internet: Charting a new world. *The DATA Base for Advances in Information Systems, 30*(3–4), 8–21.

Zimmerman, A. (2003, November 21). B-2-B—Internet 2.0: To sell Goods to Wal-Mart, get on the Net. *Wall Street Journal*, p. B1.

Numbered References

1.   Ahmad, S., & Schroeder, R. G. (2001). The impact of electronic data interchange on delivery performance. *Production and Operations Management, 10*(1), 16–30.

2.   Allen, D. K., Colligan, D., Finnie, A., & Kern, T. (2000). Trust, power and Interorganizational information systems: The case of the electronic trading community Translease. *Information Systems Journal, 10*(1), 21–40.

3.   Alter, C. (1990). An exploratory study of conflict and coordination in interorganizational service delivery systems. *Academy of Management Journal, 33*(3), 478.

4.   Applegate, L. M., Holsapple, C. W., Kalakota, R., Radermacher, F. J., & Whinston, A. B. (1996). Electronic commerce: Building blocks of new business opportunity. *Journal of Organizational Computing and Electronic Commerce, 6*(1), 1–10.

5. Axelsson, B., & Easton, G. (1992). *Industrial networks: A new view of reality*. London; New York: Routledge.

6. Baker, R. H. (1997). *Extranets: The complete sourcebook*. New York: McGraw-Hill.

7. Bakos, J. Y. (1991). Information links and electronic marketplaces: The role of interorganizational information systems in vertical markets. *Journal of Management Information Systems*, 8(2), 31–52.

8. Bakos, J. Y. (1991). A strategic analysis of electronic market place. *MIS Quarterly*, 15(3), 295–310.

9. Bakos, Y., & Brynjolfsson, E. (1987). *Interorganizational information systems*. Unpublished Ph.D. thesis, Massachusetts Institute of Technology, Cambridge, MA.

10. Barrett, M. I. (1999). Challenges of EDI adoption for electronic trading in the London insurance market. *European Journal of Information Systems*, 8(1), 1–15.

11. Barrett, S., & Konsynski, B. R. (1982). Interorganizational information sharing systems. *MIS Quarterly*, 6(Special Issue), 93–105.

12. Barrett, S. S. (1986–1987). Strategic alternatives and inter-organizational system implementation: An overview. *Journal of Management Information Systems*, 3(3), 5–16.

13. Benjamin, R., DeLong, D., & Scott-Morton, M. (1990). Electronic data interchange: How much competitive advantage? *Long Range Planning*, 23(1), 29–40.

14. Bensaou, M. (1997). Interorganizational cooperation: The role of information technology—An empirical comparison of U.S. and Japanese supplier relations. *Information Systems Research*, 8(2), 107–124.

15. Bhatt, G. D. (2001). Business process improvement through electronic data interchange (EDI) systems: An empirical study. *Supply Chain Management*, 6(2), 60–73.

16. Boddy, D. (2000). Implementing interorganizational IT systems: Lessons from a call centre project. *Journal of Information Technology*, 15(1), 29–37.

17. Bons, R. W. H., Lee, R. M., Wagenaar, R. W., & Wrigley, C. D. (1995). Modeling inter-organizational trade procedures using documentary petri nets. In T. Mudge, B. D. Shriver, H. El–Rewini, & J. F. Nunamaker, Jr. (Eds.), *Proceedings of the 28th Hawaii International Conference on System Sciences, January 28, 1995, Wailea, HI* (pp. 189–198), Wailea, HI. Washington, DC: IEEE Computer Society Press.

18. Buxmann, P., & Konig, W. (2000). *Inter-organizational cooperation with SAP systems: Perspectives on logistics and service management (SAP Excellence)*. Heidelberg: Springer-Verlag.

19. Cash, J. I., Jr., & Konsynski, B. R. (1985). IS redraws competitive boundaries. *Harvard Business Review, 63*(2), 134–142.

20. Cash, J. I., McFarlan, W. F., McKenney, J. L., and Applegate, L. M. *Corporate Infromation Systems Management: Text and Cases (3rd Ed)*, R.D. Irwin, Homewood, IL,1992.

21. Castle, C. M. (1999). *Construction project networks: A study of Internet-based Interorganizational information systems in the building industry*. Unpublished dissertation: Doctor of Design, Harvard University, Cambridge, MA.

22. Cavaye, A. (1997). Challenges during the development of transnational information systems. *Journal of Information Technology, 12*(2), 99–106.

23. Cavaye, A. L. M. (1995). Participation in the development of interorganizational systems involving users outside the organization. *Journal of Information Technology*, (10), 135–147.

24. Cavaye, A. L. M., & Cragg, P. B. (1995). Factors contributing to the success of customer oriented interorganizational systems. *The Journal of Strategic Information Systems, 4*(1), 13–30.

25. Cavaye, A. M. (1995). Participation in the development of inter-organizational systems involving users outside the organization. *Journal of Information Technology*, (10), 135–147.

26. Chan, C., & Swatman, P. M. C. (2000). From EDI to Internet commerce: The BHP Steel experience. *Internet Research: Electronic Networking Applications and Policy, 10*(1), 72–82.

27. Chandra, M., Cherian, J., & Saharia, A. (1995). Control and efficiency in distribution channels: The impact of inter-organizational systems. In M. K. Ahuja, D. F. Galleta, & H. J. Watson (eds.), *Proceedings of the First Americas Conference on Information Systems* (pp. 279–281). Pittsburgh, PA: Association for Information Systems (AIS).

28. Charan, R. (1991). How networks reshape organizations for results. *Harvard Business Review, 69*(5), 104–115.

29. Chatfield, A. T., & BjØrn-Andersen, N. (1997). The impact of IOS-enabled business process change on business: Transformation of the value chain of Japan Airlines. *Journal of Management Information Systems, 14*(1), 13–40.

55. Forster, P. W. (2000). *The performance impact of interorganizational information systems: An empirical study on on-time performance in U.S. air cargo.* Unpublished Ph.D. dissertation, University of California–Irvine, Irvine, CA.

56. Fowler, D. C., & Swatman, P. A. (1996). Experiences in developing a requirements engineering method of multi-organisational systems. In P. M. C. Swatman, J. Gricar, & J. Novak (Eds.), *Ninth International Conference on EDI–IOS: Electronic Commerce for Trade Efficiency and Effectiveness, Proceedings* (pp. 1–12), *Bled, Slovenia, June 10–12,* Moderna Organizacija Kranj, Bled, Slovenia.

57. GEISCO (General Electric Information Services). (1985). *Introduction to electronic data interchange: A primer.* Bridgeport, CT: General Electric Company.

58. Gibson, D. V., & Harlan, G. T. (1995). Inter-organizational technology transfer: The case of the NSF Science and Technology Centers. In T. Mudge, B. D. Shriver, H. El-Rewini, & J. F. Nunamaker, Jr. (Eds.), *Proceedings of the 28th Hawaii International Conference on System Sciences, January 28, 1995, Wailea, HI* (pp. 661–670). Washington, DC: IEEE Computer Society Press.

59. Grover, V. (1993). An empirically derived model for the adoption of customer-based Interorganizational Systems. *Decision Sciences, 24*(3), 603–640.

60. Grover, V. (1990). *Factors influencing adoption and implementation of customer-based interorganizational systems.* Unpublished Ph.D., University of Pittsburgh, Pittsburgh, PA.

61. Gupta, A. (1995). A stakeholder analysis approach for interorganizational systems. *Industrial Management & Data Systems, 95*(3), 3–10.

62. Gutierrez, T. L. (1990). *Competitive growth of interorganizational systems: A cross-industry comparison.* Unpublished M.S. thesis, Massachusetts Institute of Technology, Cambridge, MA.

63. Hallberg, N., Pileman, S., & Timpka, T. (1998). Participatory design of inter-organizational systems: A method approach. In *Proceedings of the Fifth PDC—Participatory Design Conference* (pp. 129–136), Computer Professionals for Social Responsibility, Seattle, WA.

64. Hansen, J. V., & Hill, N. C. (1989). Control and audit of electronic data interchange. *MIS Quarterly, 13*(4), 403–413.

65. Hart, P., & Estrin, D. (1991). Inter-organization networks, computer integration, and shifts in interdependence: The case of the semiconductor industry. *ACM Transactions on Information Systems*, (9), 370–417.

66. Henderson, J. C., & Venkatraman, N. (1993). Strategic alignment: Leveraging information technology for transforming organizations. *IBM Systems Journal, 32*(1), 4–16.

67. Hendon, R. A., & Nath, R. (2001). Partner congruence in electronic data interchange (EDI)-enabled relationships. *Journal of Business Logistics, 22*(2), 109–127.

68. Hendon, R. A., Nath, R., & Hendon, D. W. (1998). The strategic and tactical value of electronic data interchange for marketing firms. *The Mid-Atlantic Journal of Business, 34*(1), 53–73.

69. Hofmann, O., & Bodendorf, F. (2000). Agent mediated inter-organizational business process coordination. In R. Trappl (Ed.), *Proceedings of European Meetings on Cybernetics and Systems Conference, April 15, 2000, Vienna, Austria* (pp. 615–620), Austrian Society for Cybernetic Studies, Vienna.

70. Holland, C. P. (1995). Cooperative supply chain management: The impact of interorganizational information systems. *The Journal of Strategic Information Systems, 4*(2), 117–134.

71. Homburg, V. (2000). The political economy of information exchange politics and property rights in the development and use of interorganizational information systems. *Knowledge, Technology, & Policy, 13*(Part 3), 49–66.

72. Hong, I. B. (2002). A new framework for interorganizational systems based on the linkage of participants' roles. *Information & Management, 39*(4), 261–270.

73. Hopper, M. D. (1990). Rattling sabre—New ways to compete on information. *Harvard Business Review*, 118–125.

74. Huang, J. (1997). *Interorganizational information systems in design.* Unpublished thesis (Doctor of Design), Harvard University.

75. Johnston, H. R., & Vitale, M. R. (1988). Creating competitive advantage with interorganizational information systems. *MIS Quarterly, 12*(2), 153–165.

76. Johnston, R. B., & Gregor, S. (2000). A theory of industry-level activity for understanding the adoption of interorganizational systems. *European Journal of Information Systems, 9*(4), 243–251.

77. Johnston, R. B., & Lawrence, P. R. (1988). Beyond vertical integration—The rise of the value-adding partnership. *Harvard Business Review, 66*(4), 94–101.

78. Jones, M. C., & Beatty, R. C. (2001). User satisfaction with EDI: An empirical investigation. *Information Resources Management Journal, 14*(2), 17–26.

79. Kalakota, R., & Whinston, A. B. (1996). *Frontiers of electronic commerce*. Reading, MA: Addison-Wesley.

80. Kambil, A., & Short, J. E. (1994). Electronic integration and business network redesign: A roles-linkage perspectives. *Journal of Management Information Systems*, *10*(4), 59–73.

81. Kekre, S., & Mukhopadhyay, T. (1992). Impact of electronic data interchange on quality improvement and inventory reduction programs: A field study. *International Journal of Production Economics*, (28), 265–282.

82. Khosrowpour, M. (Ed.) (2002). *Collaborative information technologies*. Hershey, PA: IRM Press.

83. King, J., & Konsynski, B. (1990). Hong Kong Tradelink: News from the Second City (p. 14). Cambridge, MA: Harvard Business School.

84. King, J., & Konsynski, B. (1990). Singapore Tradenet: A tale of one city (p. 17). Cambridge, MA: Harvard Business School.

85. Kisiel, R. (2002). Anxebusiness links with Japan Group. *Automotive News*, 26.

86. Klein, S., & Schad, H. (1996). The introduction of EDI systems in healthcare supply chains: A framework for business transformation. In P. M. C. Swatman, J. Gricar, & J. Novak (Eds.), *Ninth International Conference on EDI–IOS: Electronic Commerce for Trade Efficiency and Effectiveness, Proceedings, Bled, Slovenia, June 10–12* (pp. 28–53). Moderna Organizacija Kranj, Bled, Slovenia.

87. Konsynski, B. R. (1993). Strategic control in the extended enterprise. *IBM Systems Journal*, *32*(1), 111–142.

88. Konsynski, B. R., & McFarlan, W. F. (1990). Information partnerships—Shared data, shared scale. *Harvard Business Review*, 114–120.

89. Kreuwels, C. M. A. (1992). Electronic data interchange: An introduction and examples of its structural impact. *Production Planning and Control*, (3), 381–392.

90. Kronen, J., & Loebecke, C. (1996). Cooperation information systems (CIS)—Typology and illustrative examples. In P. M. C. Swatman, J. Gricar, & J. Novak (Eds.), *Ninth International Conference on EDI–IOS: Electronic Commerce for Trade Efficiency and Effectiveness, Proceedings, Bled, Slovenia, June 10–12* (pp. 203–219). Moderna Organizacija Kranj, Bled, Slovenia.

91. Kuechler, W., Jr., Vaishnavi, V. K., & Kuelchler, D. (2001). Supporting optimization of business-to-business e-commerce relationships. *Decision Support Systems*, *31*(3), 363–377.

92. Kumar, A., & Zhao, J. L. (2002). Workflow support for electronic commerce applications. *Decision Support Systems, 32*(3), 265–278.

93. Kumar, K., & Van Dissel, H. G. (1996). Sustainable collaboration: Managing conflict and cooperation in interorganizational systems. *MIS Quarterly, 20*(3), 279–300.

94. Kumar, R., & Crook, C. W. (1996). Educating senior management on the strategic benefits of EDI. *Journal of Systems Management*, 42–47.

95. Kumar, R., & Crook, C. W. (1997). Using information technologies to enhance industry effectiveness: The case of the textile industry. In *Cases in the management of information technology*. Hershey, PA: Idea Group Publishing.

96. Kumar, R. L., & Crook, C. W. (1999). A multi-disciplinary framework for the management of inter-organizational systems. *The DATA BASE for Advances in Information Systems, 30*(1), 22–37.

97. Kurnia, S., & Johnston, R. B. (2001). The need for a procedual view of interorganizational systems adoption. *Communication Abstracts, 24*(5), 591–738.

98. Larson, P. D. (1994). An empirical study of inter-organizational functional integration and total costs. *Journal of Business Logistics, 15*(1), 153–169.

99. Lee, B. T. (1993). *The adoption and impact of inter-organizational information systems: An empirical study of the property and casualty insurance market.* Unpublished dissertation, thesis (Ph.D.), UCLA, Los Angeles, CA.

100. Lee, H. G., & Clark, T. H. (1996). Impacts of the electronic marketplace on transaction cost and market structure. *International Journal of Electronic Commerce, 1*(1), 127–149.

101. Lee, S., Han, I., & Park, J. S. (2000). Effects of organizational characteristics on EDI implementation in Korea. *Telecommunications Systems, 14*(1–4).

102. Lee, S., & Han., I. (2000). The impact of EDI controls on the relationship between EDI implementation and performance. *Information Resources Management Journal, 13*(4), 25.

103. Levinson, N. S. (1994). Interorganizational information systems: New approaches to global economic development. *Information & Management, 26*(5), 257–263.

104. Lewis, I., & Talalayevsky, A. (2000). Third-party logistics: Leveraging information technology. *Journal of Business Logistics, 21*(2), 173–185.

105. Liberman, M., & Ersdorf, W. L. (1997). Using mobile agents to support Interorganizational workflow management. *Applied Artificial Intelligence, 11*(6), 551–572.

106. Lindsey, D., Cheney, P. H., Kasper, G. M., & Ives, B. (1990). Telcot: An introduction of information technology for competitive advantage in the cotton industry. *MIS Quarterly, 14*(4), 347–357.

107. Lobet-Maris, C. (1993). EDI: Risks and vulnerability in the new interorganizational systems. In J. Berleur, C. Beradon, & R. Laufer (Eds.), *Facing the challenge of risks and vulnerability in an information society, Proceedings of an IFIP/Working Group 9.2 Working Conference, May 1993, Namur, Belgium* (pp. 131–144). Amsterdam; New York: North-Holland.

108. Loebbecke, C. (1996). Innovative IT-based logistics—A case study of KHDS Vision 2000 Engine Factory. In P. M. C. Swatman, J. Gricar, & J. Novak (Eds.), *Ninth International Conference on EDI–IOS: Electronic Commerce for Trade Efficiency and Effectiveness, Proceedings, Bled, Slovenia, June 10–12* (pp. 123–141). Moderna Organizacija Kranj, Bled, Slovenia.

109. Luke, R. D., Begun, J. W., & Pointer, D. D. (1989). Quasi firms: Strategic Interorganizational forms in the health care industry. *Academy of Management Review, 14*(1), pp. 9–19.

110. Maingot, M., & Quon, T. (2001). A survey of electronic data interchange (EDI) in the top public companies in Canada. *INFOR, 39*(3), 317–332.

111. Malone, T. W., & Benjamin, R. I. (1987). Electronic markets and electronic hierarchies: Effects of information technology on market structure and corporate strategies. *Communications of the ACM, 30*(6), 484–497.

112. Mandell, M. P. (2001). *Getting results through collaboration: Networks and network structures for public policy and management.* Westport, CT: Quorum Books.

113. McFarlan, F. W. (1984). Information technology changes the way you compete. *Harvard Business Review, 62*(3), 98–103.

114. McFarlan, F. W., McKenney, J. L., & Pyburn, P. (1983). The information archipelago—Plotting a course. *Harvard Business Review, 61*(1), 145–156.

115. McKinney, V. R. (1998). *The role of the partner relationship in interorganizational systems.* Unpublished dissertation, thesis (Ph.D.), University of Texas at Arlington, Arlington, TX.

116. Meier, J. (1990). *A formal analysis of costs and benefits of interorganizational systems.* Unpublished Ph.D. dissertation, University of Hawaii, Honolulu, HI.

117. Meier, J. (1995). The importance of relationship management in establishing successful interorganizational systems. *The Journal of Strategic Information Systems*, *4*(2), 135–148.

118. Meier, J., & Sprague, R. H., Jr. (2001). The evolution of interorganizational systems. *Journal of Information Systems*, (6), 184–191.

119. Messmer, E., & Greene, T. (2001). VPN woes force shift at giant e-commerce Net. *Network World*, pp. 1, 13.

120. Mokhtar, S., & Kasimin, H. (1998). Inter-organizational information system in the planning and implementation systems of development projects. In C. Avgerou (Ed.), *Proceedings of the Fifth International Federation of Information Processing Working Group 9.4 Conference on Implementation and Evaluation of Information Systems in Developing Countries, February 5* (pp. 222–233), IFIP, London.

121. Moritz, P. H. (1986). *Interorganizational collaboration in multihospital systems: An analysis using the intriligator interorganizational relationships (IOR) model.* Unpublished Ph.D. dissertation, University of Maryland, College Park, MD.

122. Mukhopadhyay, T., Kekre, S., & Kalathur, S. (1995). Business value of information technology: A study of electronic data interchange. *MIS Quarterly*, *19*(2), 137–156.

123. Ngai, E. W. T., & Wat, F. K. T. (2002). A literature review and classification of electronic commerce research. *Information & Management*, *39*(5), 415–429.

124. Nidumolu, S. (1989). The impact of inter-organizational systems on the form and climate of seller–buyer relationships: A structural equations modelling approach. In *Proceedings of the Tenth International Conference on Information Systems* (pp. 289–304), Boston, MA.

125. Nilakanta, S., & Scamell, R. (1990). The effect of information sources and communication channels on the diffusion of innovation in a data base development environment. *Management Science*, *36*(1), 24–40.

126. O'Callaghan, R., J., KANFMANN P.J., and Konsynski, B. R. "Adoption Correlates and Share Effects of Electronic Data Interchange Systems in Marketing Channels," *Journal of Marketing Research* (56), 1992, pp. 45-56.

127. Park, K. H., & Favrel, J. (1997). An inter-organizational information system infrastructure for extended (or virtual) enterprises. In J. Kim (Ed.), *Intelligent manufacturing systems—International Federation of Automatic Control Workshop, July 4, Seoul, Korea* (pp. 43–48). Oxford; New York: Pergamon Press.

128. Payton, F. C. (2000). Lessons learned from three interorganizational health care information systems. *Information & Management, 37*(6), 311–322.

129. Payton, F. C. (1997). *Uncovering the critical factors in the implementation process of interorganizational health care information systems.* Unpublished dissertation: thesis (Ph.D.), Case Western Reserve University, Cleveland, OH.

130. Payton, F. C., & Ginzberg, M. J. (2001). Inter-organizational health care systems implementations: An exploratory study of early electronic commerce initiatives. *Health Care Management Review, 26*(2), 20–32.

131. Petersen, G. (1989). Opportunities and challenges for IES in sales and marketing are substantial and growing. *Industrial Engineering, 21*(5), 52–55.

132. Porter, M. E., & Millar, V. E. (1985). How information gives you competitive advantage. *Harvard Business Review, 63*(4), 149–160.

133. Premkumar, G., & Ramamurthy, K. (1994). The impact of inter-organizational relationships on initiation of inter-organizational systems. In *Proceedings of the Annual Meeting—Decision Sciences* Institute (pp. 843–845), Decision Sciences Institute, Honolulu, HI.

134. Premkumar, G., & Ramamurthy, K. (1995). The role of interorganizational and organizational factors on the decision mode for adoption of interorganizational systems. *Decision Sciences, 26*(3), 303–336.

135. Premkumar, G., Ramamurthy, K., & Nilakanta, S. (1994). Implementation of electronic data interchange. *Journal of Management Information Systems, 11*(2), 157–186.

136. Premkumar, G. P. (2000). Interorganization systems and supply chain management: An information processing perspective. *Information Systems Management, 17*(3), 56–69.

137. Provan, K. G., & Milward, H. B. (1995). A preliminary theory of interorganizational network effectiveness: A comparative study of four community mental health systems. *Administrative Science Quarterly, 40*(1), 1–32.

138. Provan, K. G., & Skinner, S. (1989). Interorganizational dependence and control as predictors of opportunism in dealer–supplier relations. *Academy of Management Journal, 32*(1), 202–212.

139. Raghunathan, S. (1999). Interorganizational collaborative forecasting and replenishment systems and supply chain implications. *Decision Sciences, 30*(4), 1053–1971.

140. Rai, A., & Howard, G. S. (1993). An organizational context for case innovation. *Information Resource Management Journal, 6*(3), 21–34.

141. Raina, S. (1997). *Multi-criteria decision analysis approach to evalua-tion of interorganizational systems.* Unpublished Ph.D., University of Alabama.

142. Ramamurthy, K., & Premkumar, G. (1995). Determinants and outcomes of electronic data interchanges diffusion. *IEEE Transactions on Engineer-ing Management, 42*(4), 332–351.

143. Ramamurthy, K., Premkumar, G., & Crum, M. R. (1999). Organizational and interorganizational determinants of EDI diffusion and organizational performance: A causal model. *Journal of Organizational Computing and Electronic Commerce, 9*(4), 253–285.

144. Rasch, R. H., & Hansen, J. V. (1997). A design approach for analyzing interorganizational information systems. *Annals of Operations Research,* (72), 95–102.

145. Ratnasingam, P. (2001). Inter-organizational trust in EDI adoption: The case of Ford Motor Company and PBR Limited in Australia. *Internet Research, 11*(3), 261–268.

146. Redwood, M., Vigo, K., Dawe, R., & Hastings, J. (1996). Link: The electronic virtual laboratory. In P. M. C. Swatman, J. Gricar, & J. Novak (Eds.), *Ninth International Conference on EDI–IOS: Electronic Com-merce for Trade Efficiency and Effectiveness, Proceedings, Bled, Slovenia, June 10–12* (pp. 113–122), Moderna Organizacija Kranj, Bled, Slovenia.

147. Reich, B. H., & Benbasat, I. (1990). An empirical investigation of factors influencing the success of customer-oriented strategic systems. *Informa-tion Systems Research, 1*(3), 325–347.

148. Riggins, F. J. (1993). *The growth of interorganizational systems in the presence of network externalities and unequal interdependent ben-efits.* Carnegie Mellon University, PA.

149. Riggins, F. J., & Mukhopadhyay, T. (1994). Interdependent benefits from interorganizational systems: Opportunities for business partner re-engi-neering. *Journal of Management Information Systems, 11*(2), 37–57.

150. Riggins, F. J., & Mukhopadhyay, T. (1999). Overcoming EDI adoption and implementation risks. *International Journal of Electronic Commerce, 3*(4), 103–123.

151. Riggins, F. J., Mukhopadhyay, T., & Kriebel, C. H. (1994). Optimal policies for subsidizing supplier interorganizational system adoption. *Journal of Organizational Computing, 5*(3), 295–326.

152. Rochester, J. B. (1989). The strategic value of EDI. *I/S Analyzer, 27*(8), 1–14.

153. Sabherwal, R., & Vijayasarathy, L. R. (1994). An empirical investigation of the antecedents of telecommunication-based interorganizational systems. *European Journal of Information Systems*, *3*(4), 268–283.

154. Salam, A. W. (1994). Electronic data interchange and corporate EFT: A survey. *TMA Journal*, *14*(3), 59–61.

155. Saunders, C. S., & Clark, S. (1992). EDI adoption and implementation: A focus on interorganizational linkages. *Information Resource Management Journal*, *5*(1), 9–19.

156. Senn, J. A. (2000). Business-to-business e-commerce. *Information Systems Management*, pp. 23–32.

157. Senn, J. A. (1992). Electronic data interchange: The elements of implementation. *Journal of Information Systems Management*, (9), 45–53.

158. Shaft, T., Sharfman, M., & Swahn, M. (2001). Using interorganizational information systems to support environmental management efforts at ASG. *Journal of Industrial Ecology*, *5*(4), 95–115.

159. Sharma, P. (2000). *The effects of interorganizational systems on process and structure in buyer seller exchange*. Unpublished Ph.D. dissertation, University of Nebraska–Lincoln, Lincoln, NE.

160. Sheombar, H. S. (1992). EDI-induced redesign of Co-ordination in logistics. *International Journal of Physical Distribution and Logistics Management*, *22*(8), 4–14.

161. Siegel, G. B., Clayton, R., & Kovoor, S. (1990). Modeling interorganizational effectiveness. *Public Productivity & Management Review*, *13*(3), 215.

162. Sokol, P. K. (1989). *EDI: The competitive advantage*. New York: McGraw-Hill.

163. Soliman, K. S. (2000). *Determining the critical factors affecting the adoption decision of Internet-based interorganizational information systems*. Unpublished Ph.D. dissertation, University of Memphis, Memphis, TN.

164. Srinivasan, K., Kekre, S., & Mukhopadhyay, T. (1994). Impact of electronic data interchange technology on JIT shipments. *Management Science*, *40*(10), 1291–1304.

165. Sriram, V., & Banerjee, S. (1994). Electronic data interchange: Does its adoption change purchasing policies and procedures? *International Journal of Purchasing and Materials Management*, (30), 31–40.

166. Stern, L. W., & Kaufmann, P. J. (1985). Electronic data interchange in selected consumer goods industries: An interorganizatinoal perception. In R. Buzzel (Ed.), *Marketing in an Electronic age* (pp. 52–74). Boston, MA: Harvard Business School Press.

167. Stohr, E. A., & Zhao, J. L. (2001). Workflow automation: An overview and research issues. *Information Systems Frontiers*, *3*(3), 281–291.

168. Strzelczak, S. (1996). EDI, IOS and BPR impact on computer-aided production and logistical management. In P. M. C. Swatman, J. Gricar, & J. Novak (Eds.), *Ninth International Conference on EDI–IOS: Electronic Commerce for Trade Efficiency and Effectiveness, Proceedings, Bled, Slovenia, June 10–12* (pp. 68–77), Moderna Organizacija, Kranj, Slovenia.

169. Suomi, R. (1991). Alliance or alone? How to build interorganizational information systems. *Technology Analysis & Strategic Management*, *3*(3), 211–234.

170. Suomi, R. (1988). Inter-organizational information systems as company resources. *Information & Management*, (15), 105–112.

171. Talalayevsky, A., & Hershauer, J. C. (1997). Coordination cost evaluation of network configurations. *Journal of Organizational Computing and Electronic Commerce*, *7*(2&3), 185–199.

172. Toppen, R., Smits, M., & Ribbens, P. (2000). Effects of two interorganizational systems to settle cross border Euro payments between financial institutions in Europe. In R. H. Sprague, Jr. (Ed.), *Proceedings of the 33rd Annual Hawaii International Conference on System Sciences, Maui, HI* (p. 181). Washington, DC: IEEE Computer Society Press.

173. van der Aalst, W. (2000). Loosely coupled interorganizational workflows: Modeling and analyzing workflows crossing organizational boundaries. *Information & Management*, *37*(2), 67–75.

174. van der Aalst, W. M. P. (1999). Interorganizational workflows. *Systems Analysis, Modeling, Simulation*, *34*(3), 335–368.

175. Veith, R. H. (1980). *The interorganizational impact of computerized information processing networks: The case of international banking.* Unpublished thesis (Ph.D.), Syracuse University.

176. Venkatraman, N. (1994). IT-enabled business transformation: From automation to business scope redefinition. *Sloan Management Review*, *35*(2), 73–87.

177. Venkatraman, N., & Zaheer, A. (1990). Electronic integration and strategic advantage: A quasi-experimental study in the insurance industry. *Information Systems Research*, *1*(4), 377–393.

178. Vijayasarathy, L. R. (1994). *Consequences of interorganizational information systems: An empirical investigation of the effects of EDI use on interorganizational relationships in the retail industry.* Unpublished Ph.D. dissertation, Florida International University, Miami, FL.

179. Vitale, M. R. (1986). *American Hospital Supply Corp: The ASAP System*. Boston, MA: Harvard University Press.

180. Vlosky, R. P., Wilson, D. T., & Vlosky, R. B. (1997). Closing the interorganizational information systems relationship satisfaction gap. *Journal of Marketing Practice*, *3*(2), 75–82.

181. Vogel, D. (1996). Electronic commerce options and strategies in the international office of the future. In P. M. C. Swatman, J. Gricar, & J. Novak (Eds.), *Ninth International Conference on EDI–IOS: Electronic Commerce for Trade Efficiency and Effectiveness, Proceedings, Bled, Slovenia, June 10–12* (pp. 547–555).

182. Volkoff, O., Chan, Y. E., & Peter Newson, E. F. (1998). Leading the development and implementation of collaborative interorganizational systems. *Information & Management*, *35*(2), 63–76.

183. Wagner, C. (1998). Use of simulation gaming to assess impact of interorganizational information sharing on inventory performance. In E. D. Hoadley, & I. Benbasat (Eds.), *Proceedings of the Fourth Americas Conference on Information Systems* (pp. 795–797), *August, Baltimore, MD*, Association for Information Systems (AIS), Baltimore, MD.

184. Wang, E. T. G., & Seidmann, A. (1995). Electronic data interchange: Competitive externalities and strategic implementation policies. *Management Science*, *41*(3), 401–418.

185. Weigand, H., & van den Heuvel, W.-J. (2002). Cross-organizational workflow integration using contracts. *Decision Support Systems*, *33*(3), 247–265.

186. Wey, Y. J., & Gibson, D. V. (1991). Influence of the external environment on interorganizational systems: An integration of transaction costs and resource dependence perspective. In *Proceedings of Hawaii International Conference on System Sciences* (pp. 501–507). Washington, DC: IEEE Computer Society Press.

187. Whang, J. (1992). *An empirical study of factors influencing interorganizational information systems implementation: A case of the real estate industry*. Unpublished thesis (Ph.D.), University of Nebraska–Lincoln, Lincoln, NE.

188. Williams, T. (1997). Interorganisational information systems: Issues affecting interorganisational cooperation. *Journal of Strategic Information Systems*, *6*(3), 231–250.

189. Wood, D. J., & Gray, B. (1991). Toward a comprehensive theory of collaboration. *Journal of Applied Behavioral Science*, *27*(2), 163–179.

190. Wortmann, H. S., Nick. (2001). ICT issues among collaborative enter-prises: From rigid to adaptive agent-based technologies. *Production Planning and Control*, *12*(5), 452–465.

191. Zaheer, A., & Venkatraman, N. (1994). Determinants of electronic integration in the insurance industry. *Management Science*, *40*(5), 549–566.

192. Zwass, V. (1996). Electronic commerce: Structures and issues. *International Journal of Electronic Commerce*, *1*(1), 3–23.

Chapter II

A Typology of Inter-Organizational Information Systems

Joseph B. O'Donnell
Canisius College, USA

Bonnie C. Glassberg
Miami University, USA

Abstract

This chapter provides a typology of inter-organizational information systems (IOISs) in order to provide a better understanding of the purposes of IOISs and their organizational uses, and to fill in the gaps not yet investigated by researchers. It provides a comparison of IOISs in terms of network structures and type of information exchanged, covers the benefits and risks of these systems, suggests new areas for research, and describes expected trends for IOISs. This typology highlights the differences and similarities not only among the many configurations of IOISs available today, but also contrasts this with internal Web sites (intranets) and public (external) Internet Web sites. It is hoped that the typology and ideas presented here provide new insights for academics and practitioners that will be used to improve the evolving landscape of electronic commerce.

Introduction

Inter-organizational information systems (IOISs) are essential to the growth of business-to-business (B2B) electronic commerce (e-commerce). According to Forrester Research, this market segment is expected to reach $2.7 trillion in sales by the end of 2004 (Kafka, 2000). Web-based IOISs facilitate the processing of B2B e-commerce transactions and enhance the seamless communication of information between businesses. Despite the importance of Web-based IOISs, such as extranets, the majority of IOIS research has focused on older systems, such as electronic data interchange (EDI). Additional research regarding e-commerce has focused on business-to-consumer (B2C) e-commerce. To understand the purpose of IOISs and their organizational uses, and to fill in the gaps not yet investigated by researchers, this chapter provides a typology of IOIS. This typology highlights the differences and similarities not only among the many configurations of IOISs available today but also contrasts this with internal Web sites (intranets) and public (external) Internet Web sites. This approach offers new insights for practitioners and researchers.

The chapter is organized as follows. First, the background of an IOIS is presented. Next, the typology of IOISs is introduced. Two general areas where these systems differ, the structures of the relationships, and the types and formats of the information exchanged, are identified and discussed in separate sections, respectively. Each system has features that help to distinguish it, and these differences will be highlighted. Two tables (1 and 2) are provided to aid understanding and offer a broad landscape for the rest of the book. Next, the benefits and risks of an IOIS are discussed. Later, previous research on EDI and Web-based systems is introduced to identify exciting new areas for investigation. Finally, the authors identify future trends for IOISs, and the implications for researchers and practitioners are discussed.

Background

The Internet provides the backbone for high-speed communication, collaboration, and commerce. Originally designed in 1969 for the Department of Defense, the Internet now is a network of computer networks used by individuals and organizations to communicate information and process transactions. Prior to the wide acceptance of the Internet, one of the first types of IOISs to emerge was *Electronic Data Interchange* (EDI). EDI systems offered a link between two companies for the hands-off transmission of data in a fixed text-based format without the use of the Internet. As the Internet evolved, it facilitated the establishment of virtual spaces for information storage and new ways to link objects together.

As the Internet grew, individuals and firms began to create *public Web sites* for sharing information. While these types of Web sites do not technically fall under the umbrella of an IOIS, they can be used to provide data to current and potential business partners as well as customers. As the general public is most familiar with these types of Web spaces, these spaces will serve as a starting point for comparison and are included in this chapter. Another recent type of Web-based system is the *intranet*. The purpose of an intranet is to share company information with and between employees. These systems are Web sites typically created on a private local or wide area network and maintained wholly within the organization. As intranets can utilize the same Web technology as do IOISs, they also are described herein for comparison.

While the Internet handles proprietary and public information, a large share of e-commerce is accomplished using Web-based systems. Public Web sites, intranets, and several forms of IOISs use Web technology. Johnston and Vitale (1998) defined an IOIS:

...an automated information system shared by two or more companies. An IOIS is built around information technology, that is, around computer and communication technology, that facilitates creation, storage, transformation and transmission of information. An IOIS differs from an internal distributed information system by allowing information to be sent across organizational boundaries (p.154).

Using Web-based technology, IOISs incorporate Web browsers, graphical interfaces, and databases. The technology to build an IOIS is relatively inexpensive and well established. Except for security issues, such as encryption and authentication, the technology is readily available for large and small organizations. An *extranet* is an emerging form of IOIS that is expected to surpass EDI in e-commerce volume. An extranet exists when a company offers password-protected, limited access to a portion of its intranet to selective exchange partners outside the company's firewall (see Figure 1). The purpose of an extranet is to provide external communications, document exchange, and even collaborative design (Lange, 1996). It offers graphical user interface tools, greater communication functionality, low technical requirements, and relatively low adoption costs in comparison to EDI. The extranet allows companies to communicate in free-form text, graphics, sound, video, as well as standard EDI format. The term "intronet" has also been used to describe this type of IOIS (Riggins & Rhee, 1998).

In contrast, a *B2B virtual market*, also know as a "supranet," represents a consortium sponsored and controlled network that provides seamless communication across applications (Riggins & Rhee, 1998). This network provides for collaboration and transaction processing between market members (Applegate, Austin, & McFarlan, 2002). The distinction between extranets and the B2B virtual market is significant, and therefore, each appears separately in the typology that follows. In all, these vastly different types of IOISs (EDI, extranets, and B2B virtual markets) merit researcher interest, as they are poised to reshape our business world in the Internet age.

Typology of IOIS

To gain an understanding of an IOIS in relation to modern Web-based technology, it is useful to perform a comparison of Internet Web sites, intranets, extranets, B2B virtual markets, and EDI. Each type of system will be compared first by looking at the structure of the relationship. Structural characteristics include the identification of the interacting parties, which party acts as the system host, and the requirements for security. Finishing off this portion is Barrett and Konsynski's Model of Inter-Organization Information Sharing, which addresses firm participation. Then, the typology continues with a look at the level and nature of the information exchanged. Here, these relevant features are discussed: the general functions performed by each system, the format of the information that is transferred, the types of information communicated, the requirements for confidentiality of the data, and the cost of the technology and system implementation.

A Structural Comparison of Systems Types

For an overview of the structural differences between systems, see Table 1. Parties to the exchange differ between systems. An Internet Web site involves an entity and the general public, while the intranet involves parties strictly within the organization. Intranets are primarily used by companies to provide information exchange and data resources for employees. Extranets and EDIs, on the other hand, involve an entity and its business partners. Business partners can include suppliers, vendors, and business advisors. B2B virtual markets offer platforms for interactions between business partners that are members of the proprietary virtual market.

The host entity also differs among the systems. A single organization typically hosts an Internet Web site, an intranet, an extranet, and EDI. In contrast, the B2B

Table 1: Comparison of Web-based and EDI systems—structures

| | Internet Web Site | Intranet (Internal) | IOIS | | |
			Extranet	B2B Virtual Market	EDI
Interacting parties	General public	Employees	Organization with business partner(s)	Organization with virtual market business partner(s)	Organization with specific business partner
System host	Organization	Organization	Organization	Network market facilitator	Organization
Security	Data remains outside of outer firewall	Data stays inside inner firewall	Data stays between inner and outer firewalls	Inside inner firewall of network facilitator	Transactions allowed inside of inner firewall
Barrett and Konsynski IOIS level	Level 2— Application (Information) Processing Node	Not applicable	Level 4— Network Control Node	Level 5— Integrated Network Node	Level 3— Multiparticipant Exchange Node

Figure 1: Security structure

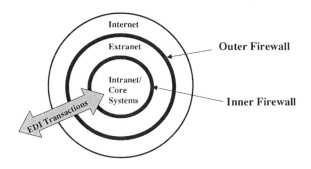

market is hosted by a network market facilitator. The facilitator may be a dominant member of the market or, more frequently, a separate company formed by a group of market members. An example of a market facilitator is Covisint, which represents a global Internet-based electronic marketplace with eight major auto manufacturers and thousands of suppliers (Applegate et al., 2002). This marketplace has the potential to dramatically reduce inefficiencies and improve productivity in the global auto industry. Covisint was formed through a joint venture between Ford Motor Company, General Motors, DaimlerChrysler, Oracle, and CommerceOne (Applegate et al., 2002).

Next, we address the structural requirements for security. Figure 1 graphically depicts where these systems are positioned relative to the inner and outer firewalls of a corporation. A firewall is a set of hardware and software components that provide security by preventing outsiders from accessing internal, proprietary corporate data. Many organizations find it necessary to create more than one level of network security to protect corporate resources and core systems from unlawful access. For an organization with two levels of network security, the intranet is the most secure Web-based system, operating inside the inner firewall. Intranet security controls restrict access to only authorized personnel. Conversely, the company's Internet Web site is the least secure, as it resides outside the external firewall. Public Web sites often have limited or no restrictions for access and most do not require passwords. For those Web sites that do, access is often free by just registering. The extranet is a more secure environment than a public Web site, as it operates between the inner and outer firewalls. Extranets maintain security controls and provide access only to authorized business partners. In contrast to the extranet, a B2B virtual market-place contains one firewall that protects the network facilitator's site. The community of business partners interacts inside the security protection of the outer firewall. The EDI systems are the most unusual IOISs, as they pass transactions through multiple levels of security in order to reach core systems. This poses an added security risk, which is mitigated by using predefined data formats and encryption technology.

The literature describes several IOIS frameworks, and each is slightly different in its focus. Barrett and Konsynski (1982) developed a model of inter-organizational information sharing that is useful here in analyzing linkage differences in Web-based and EDI systems. Other models that were identified but not described in detail are summarized below:

- Johnston and Vitale (1988) developed a classification framework based on dimensions of an IOIS business purpose, the relationship of the business partners, and the information function.

- Kumar and van Dissel (1996) provided a framework for an IOIS based on inter-organizational interdependence including information resources, value and supply chains, and networks.

- Choudhury (1997) provided a framework for classifying IOISs based on exchange relationships.

- Hong (2002) developed a framework based on the two dimensions of role linkage (horizontal versus vertical) and system support level (strategic versus operational).

The Barrett et al. (1982) model involves five different levels of information sharing and is based on the purpose and organizational objectives of the system. The levels are based on firm participation and are generally independent of the system's technology. Low-end participation involves minimal amounts of participant responsibility, cost commitment, and complexity of the operating environment. High-end participation includes significant levels for all three areas. At the lowest level, Remote I/O Node is the remote input to and output from another organization's systems with minimal firm participation. The next level, Application Processing Node, involves a firm hosting and sharing of a single application with other organizations. The third level, Multiparticipant Exchange Node, involves the development of a network linking with other organizations. This level involves an increased level of complexity and cost from the previous level, along with shared responsibility between the firm and its business partners to maintain the network. The fourth level, Network Control Node, involves the sharing of a network with diverse applications that is maintained solely by the firm and used by many different types of business partners. The fifth level, Integrated Network Node, involves a data communication facility processing transactions in real-time mode. At Level 5, the operating environment is more complex, with simultaneous processing at multiple participant sites. This mode requires significant security and coordination costs to manage communications throughout the network.

To highlight the B2B virtual market's and extranet's relative positions in the Barrett et al. IOISs model, they are compared with the other Web-based systems and EDI. The intranet is not applicable to the model, as it is not an inter-organizational system. Internet sites are considered to be at Level 2 participation, Application Processing Node, where an organization hosts the Web site to facilitate the communication of information. The "application" in this case is information processing, so the authors feel that this level could also be termed the "Information Processing Node." EDI represents a Level 3 situation, Multiparticipant Exchange Node, as it provides limited types of transmissions in a shared network that is maintained by the business partners. Conversely, extranets are at a Level 4 situation, Network Control Node, where the system is maintained by one firm and can be designed to fulfill diverse purposes with many different kinds of business partners. One benefit of the extranet is the potential for developing numerous interlocking networks. For example, a firm creates an extranet with partners for information sharing. One of the partners joins an additional partnership and creates another extranet for information sharing. As more extranets are created, a loosely linked network of real-time systems can evolve. This loose network structure is different than the Level 5 situation described by Barrett and Konsynski, because the information is not available to all parties equally. Rather, the information sharing is selectively tied to extranet nodes based on membership.

The B2B virtual markets fit Barrett and Konsynski's model as a Level 5 situation, Integrated Network Node, for the network provider. The network application is hosted by the network provider, which is typically an association of firms or an outside sponsor. The B2B marketplace involves numerous applications and parties participating in a virtual community to buy and sell goods. This software serves as the infrastructure of the marketplace, supporting several processes such as purchasing, ordering, auction bidding, collecting payments, authenticating members, and communicating technical information (such as CAD and CAM specifications). Market member applications can be linked to the virtual market. These can involve the use of intelligent agents to generate optimum bid amounts for suppliers and to optimize the evaluation of bids for the purchaser.

Barrett and Konsynski (1982) stressed that integrated network nodes require strong security and data communication capabilities. A major concern is transaction security for B2B virtual markets and extranets. Message encryption and authentication through certificate authorities are paramount to IOIS success. Advancements in data communications capabilities, especially higher bandwidths, enable the extranet and B2B markets to provide greater multimedia capabilities.

Barrett and Konsynski's (1982) taxonomy highlights the different levels of participation in maintaining an IOIS. Firms require varying levels of resources depending on the complexity of their systems and their participation in hosting their systems. Organizations should design e-commerce strategies that balance IOIS participation levels with the benefits from these systems.

An Information Exchange Comparison of Systems Types

In this section, the spotlight is on the level and nature of the information provided or exchanged in Web-based systems and EDI (see Table 2). This includes the general functions performed by each system, the format of the information that is transferred, the types of information communicated, the requirements for confidentiality of the data, and the costs of the technology and system implementation.

In general, Internet Web sites, extranets, virtual markets, and EDI function as electronic marketplaces. They all can be designed to process e-commerce transactions. Although Web sites, extranets, and virtual markets offer interactive media content, EDI transactions are one-way exchanges normally limited in scope. Intranets include interactive communication but do not involve an electronic marketplace because they involve intracompany activity. A new area of activity, called a Reverse Auction, is taking place using the B2B virtual market format. In a virtual market, many suppliers provide data and services to an array of buyers. The buyers aim to compare the offerings available on selected criteria. In a reverse auction, requirements are set by the buyer, and the sellers compete (bid against each other), attempting to win the contract.

Web-based systems are flexible, allowing designers to utilize multimedia content, including text, audio, and video components. Multiformat information transfer

Table 2: Comparison of Web-based and EDI systems—information exchanges

	Internet Web Site	Intranet (Internal)	IOIS		
			Extranet	B2B Virtual Market	EDI
Function	-Electronic marketplace	-Interactive communication	-Interactive communication -Electronic marketplace	-Interactive communication -Electronic marketplace -Reverse auctions	-Electronic marketplace
Format of information transfer	Multiformat Flexible	Multiformat Flexible	Multiformat Flexible	Multiformat Flexible	Fixed format Rigid
Types of information communicated	-Financial transactions -Product and service offerings -Advertising	-Financial transactions -Product and service offerings -Organizational data	-Financial transactions -Product and service offerings -Advertising -Organizational data (limited)	-Financial transactions -Product and service offerings -Advertising -Virtual market communication	-Financial transactions -Purchase orders or sales data
Confidentiality	Nonconfidential	Confidential	Confidential	Confidential	Confidential
Cost of technology, implementation	-Low cost -Limited changes to core systems	-Low cost -Limited changes to core systems	-Moderate cost -May require changes to core systems	-Moderate cost -Complex	-Costly -Requires changes to core systems
Global issues	-Cultural differences -Language -Foreign exchange -Technology infrastructure -Legal issues	-Cultural differences -Language -Foreign exchange -Technology— Infrastructure -Legal issues	-Cultural differences -Language -Foreign exchange -Technology infrastructure -Legal issues -Intellectual property rights	-Cultural differences -Language -Foreign exchange -Technology infrastructure -Legal Issues -Intellectual property rights -Antitrust legislation	-Language -Foreign exchange -Technology infrastructure -Legal issues

thus can occur on all four Web-based systems, but not in EDI, which is text based. The intranet, extranet, and B2B virtual market may provide additional interactive communication features such as electronic mail, videoconferencing, and streaming video. The format of Web-based systems is dependent on the designers' objectives. Internet and intranet sites are designed by the host organization. Ultimately, the extranet may be designed by the host organization, but the business partners' requirements should be thoroughly considered. The B2B virtual market systems are designed based on the needs of market members. Conversely, EDI transactions are typically in rigid, standardized formats agreed upon at the industry level. They are most often related to sales and purchase orders.

With advances in Web technology, some partners are processing EDI through Web-based technology. Still, EDI is relatively inflexible due to the industry-level standards, Many IOISs now use extensible markup language (XML), which provides a more flexible communication mechanism than EDI (Morrell & Ezingeard, 2002). The XML offers tagging of data that allows users to capture specific data for comparison (Morrell & Ezingeard, 2002). The XML tags allow for a more flexible data format than the predefined industry-level format of EDI.

A specialized form of XML, known as extensible business reporting language (XBRL), was designed to enhance reporting in the financial sector. The XBRL maintains a flexible tagging structure that has been customized for financial reporting (Greenstein & Vasarhelyi, 2001). This reporting language is designed to allow publicly traded companies to communicate detailed financial information to external auditors, financial analysts, and the Securities Exchange Commission (SEC). Thus, XBRL can be used for the transmission of nonaggregated and timely information to financial market stakeholders. This is in stark contrast to companies providing aggregated information in financial statements well after the reporting period has been completed.

Next, the type of information communicated by IOISs, Internet Web sites, and intranets is discussed. Although all may include financial transactions, intranet transactions are initiated and processed inside of the firm's boundaries, while the other systems involve outside parties at the initiation or completion of the transaction. The Internet, intranet, and extranet are similar in that their Web sites may contain organizational and product-related information. The B2B virtual market is unique in providing communication between the market facilitator and market members. This communication may involve general market announcements such as procedures for market auctions, bidding, or contract requirements. Whereas Internet Web sites, extranets, and virtual markets can contain advertising and promotional information, the intranet and the corporate Web site may post additional data, such as job openings, surveys, or statistics on firm performance.

In regard to confidentiality, each system has different requirements. Internally held data found in an intranet must provide for a high level of confidentiality. New products being developed, novel marketing campaigns, and customer data are proprietary, and this knowledge should remain under tight security with restricted access. In contrast, Internet Web sites are the least secure areas for storing information. Limitations for shared access in the public domain generally are few. Extranet, B2B virtual markets, and EDI hold a middle ground in terms of confidentiality. Extranets and B2B virtual markets contain more confidential information than the publicly accessed Internet site but less classified information than the privately held intranet. An EDI contains detailed confidential information such as purchase and sales dollar amounts and quantities but does not contain the kind of aggregated confidential information that is maintained on an intranet.

Next, the systems are compared in relation to the cost and complexity of the technology, and the effects on core systems of implementing them. Web-based technology represents a relatively low investment in hardware and software. These components are inexpensive and readily available. Internet and intranet Web sites can be designed to have a limited impact on core systems and can even be built using off-the-shelf software. Web-based transactions can be massaged for acceptance by the core systems, as in extranets and virtual markets. Transactions received in this manner, however, pose an additional security risk. Thus, the complexity required to build them is higher, as is the cost of implementing them. At the other end of the spectrum is EDI, which requires specialized software to generate and interpret transactions. Furthermore, core systems require significant modification to process these transactions, thus raising the cost. Considerable in-house training is required to implement an EDI system, and there will be a learning curve as the partners adjust to the new way of managing the exchange. To limit this cost, some organizations have implemented front-end, EDI personal computer (PC) systems or adopted the use of Web-based EDI. These front-end systems are not integrated directly with the organization's core systems and, therefore, manual intervention is required. As the purpose of EDI is to eliminate manual effort, the overall benefits of using EDI may be reduced.

Finally, global Web-based and EDI systems face unique issues not encountered by U.S. domestic systems, as shown at the bottom of Table 2. These systems must address cultural, language, currency, legal, and government differences. Web designers may have to develop systems customized for each country or language. Interestingly, a global developer of extranets estimates that it takes three times longer to develop a non-U.S. site than a U.S. site (Dalton, 1998). Although EDI must address currency and legal differences, it does not require customized formatting for cultural and language issues. Another factor of importance is the host country's technological infrastructure, which can impact the reliability of systems and the potential for different protocol standards.

In summary, IOISs (extranets, B2B virtual markets, and EDI) can be compared and contrasted with Internet (public) Web sites and intranets (internal Web sites) on two important facets of e-commerce: their structural components and types of information exchanged. Each type of IOIS evolved to manage different aspects of a firm's business, both within and outside corporate boundaries. Extranets and B2B virtual markets differ from Internet Web sites in their security capabilities, confidentiality requirements, and business partnership focus. Extranets and virtual markets are similar to EDI in their B2B focus but differ in their technological architectures, design flexibility, and multimedia communication formats. Flexible markup languages, such as XML, provide new opportunities for managing inter-organizational relationships far beyond that of EDI. Finally, the B2B virtual market differs from the extranet and EDI in that it is hosted by the network facilitator and is restricted to market members. Even though the complexity and cost of implementing an IOIS typically exceeds that of developing and maintaining corporate Web sites or intranets, the benefits of these systems can be great. In the next section, the benefits that accrue to the organization and market members are highlighted.

IOIS Benefits

Companies are looking for ways to find a competitive edge in the global marketplace. The IOISs have been embraced as strategic ways to gain that edge and provide potential benefits. Cash and Konsynski (1985) suggested that IOISs can facilitate cost leadership and differentiation. Product and service differentiation is attained through value-added components. These authors pointed out that IOISs impact business processes, skill and staff requirements, and business strategies. Cash, Eccles, Nohria, and Nolan (1994) identified the following benefits of inter-organizational systems:

- Reduced paperwork and improved transaction efficiency
- Improved control of inventories and suppliers
- Strengthened channel control
- Improved customer relationships
- Shared resources and risks

Other researchers indicated further benefits that may accrue due to the following:

- Raising or lowering barriers to entry in an industry
- Achieving network economies of scale and scope

The IOISs, including EDI and Web-based systems, improved transaction efficiency by reducing paperwork and eliminating duplicate data entry. A further benefit of the reduced data entry is fewer data entry errors. Also, integrating IOISs with an organization's core systems provides timely information for improved decision making.

Information technology advancements in IOISs have provided significant improvements to supply chain management, including improved information flows, and opportunities for process improvement through reengineering supply chains (Morrell & Ezingeard, 2002). According to Kumar (2001, p. 58), a supply chain "is a network of organizations and their associated activities that work together, usually in a sequential manner to produce value for the consumer." Web-based IOISs enable improved information flow through seamless transmission of information between buyers. These communication capabilities enable buyers and suppliers to better plan supply chain demand and to have the agility to respond quickly and effectively to fluctuations in demand. Furthermore, buyers and suppliers have reduced supply chain costs and cycle times by reengineering processes that leverage the benefit of Web-based IOISs.

More specifically, modern business practices, such as vendor-managed inventories, allow retailers to maintain lower inventory levels, while suppliers gain a better understanding of their retailers' demands. Under vendor-managed inventories, the supplier monitors the retailer's inventory levels through the IOIS and replenishes the retailer's inventory as needed. Vendor-managed inventory can be accomplished through the supplier using the buyer's extranet.

Use of an IOIS for collaborative forecasting of supply chain demand and production scheduling benefits manufacturers and suppliers (Raghunathan, 1999). This method of forecasting involves business partners working together to forecast their combined needs. Supply chain members who do not participate in collaborative forecasting and production create additional costs to the supply chain that are borne by the manufacturer or retailer (Raghunathan, 1999). In the situation of global competition, consumers are less likely to bear the excess cost of an inefficient supply chain. Therefore, manufacturers and suppliers may be forced to absorb the cost of inefficiency, which would result in reduced profitability, and in extreme cases, cause the organization to cease operations in that supply chain. A possible downside of collaborative forecasting is the potential for proprietary information to be used by the business partner in a way that harms the organization.

According to Kumar (2001, p. 59), "The availability of modern information and communication technologies [of an IOIS] make it possible to obtain an overview of the entire supply chain and to redesign and manage it in order to meet [customer] demand." This is especially true in the case of the B2B virtual market, where the transactions are going through a centralized system supported by the network facilitator. A further requirement for an IOIS is the complexity involved in global sourcing that increases the complexity and geographic distance of the supply chain (Kumar, 2001). Kumar (2001, p. 60) suggested that, "in the current environment of dynamic demand-driven supply networks temporary supply chains regularly emerge, operate for the lifetime of the opportunity, and then dissolve again. Such temporary partnerships require flexible communication and processing platforms." Both extranet and B2B virtual market IOISs provide flexible technology platforms. The extranet could quickly accommodate the creation of a supply chain through a series of partnerships between suppliers and buyers. The B2B virtual market can easily be used to create new supply chains as long as the necessary business partners are market members. The B2B virtual markets are structured so that organizations can efficiently change business members. However, inflexibility issues may arise if a nonmarket member is needed to complete the supply chain. In such cases, the organization may need to use a combination of extranet and B2B virtual market partners. Alternatively, the B2B virtual market may need to provide the agility to quickly add nonmembers to its market.

Outwardly focused organizations utilize systems that link them to other organizations. Supply chain and customer relationship management (CRM) systems provide these links (David, McCarthy, & Sommer, 2003). Improving customer relationships is accomplished through shorter product acquisition times, value-added services, and CRM capabilities. An electronic customer relationship management (e-CRM) system provides a unified view of the customer (Pan & Lee, 2003). An IOIS can be used for this purpose. Shared information can be used to build customer loyalty and to identify opportunities to increase sales through cross-selling to existing customers. Use of an IOIS, such as EDI, reduces product procurement cycle times through automated ordering of goods and electronic sharing of product designs. The IOIS can be used to electronically distribute marketing materials and product information to customers.

Another benefit of an IOIS is to share resources and risks through joint ventures such as research and development projects. An IOIS may provide integration and synergy without ownership. Ownership of assets may lead to loss of flexibility or use of resources for less profitable initiatives. An IOIS increases the capability to communicate between businesses and encourage outsourcing of noncore business operations to reduce costs. Application service providers (ASPs) facilitate outsourcing by hosting an organization's systems on its own hardware through Web-based technology. Access to ASP applications is made possible through extranets.

Firms strive to be agile in a competitive industry. A Web-based IOIS provides opportunities for an efficient and flexible supply chain, improving customer relationship management, and sharing resources across organizations. Extranets and B2B virtual markets provide capabilities to create and dissolve supplier–buyer partnerships, even for a limited one-time business opportunity. The extranet requires the organization to approach another organization for partnership, while the B2B virtual market has a readily available group of members using a common system for inter-organizational communication. Researchers should understand the advantages and disadvantage of extranets and virtual markets in creating supplier–buyer relationships. In regard to inter-organizational resource sharing, extranets support the use of ASPs. Further research regarding IOIS support of other outsourcing activities is needed.

The IOISs facilitate four types of business information partnerships in e-commerce (Applegate, McFarlan, & McKenney, 1996). The first type involves joint marketing partnerships, where companies coordinate with rivals to gain access to new customers and territories. IOIS partnerships using extranets are able to enter into these joint partnerships, while EDI would provide little assistance in this area. Second, intra-industry partnerships involve partnerships of companies providing complementary services. Take, for example, the automated teller machine (ATM) network used to process interbank transactions. The B2B virtual market creates a network for processing electronic transactions as a complementary service. Third, buyer–seller partnerships are established by sellers to service their customers. Extranets, B2B electronic markets, and EDI are structured to support this initiative. Finally, information technology (IT) vender-driven partnerships bring the vendor's technology to new markets. For example, major accounting firms and accounting software vendors partner to provide accounting package implementations to firms' customers. Covisint is an example of this type of partnership, where a software company, Oracle, an e-commerce market provider, Ecommerce One, and a major automobile company joined together to create an electronic marketplace. EDI is less capable of supporting this type of partnership. Further analysis of Web-based IOISs would clarify their roles in maintaining these four types of e-commerce partnerships.

With the origin of IOISs, companies strengthened channel control through the use of proprietary systems to raise distributor-product awareness or raise entry barriers to the industry. For example, the American Airlines SABRE reservation system was provided to travel agents for making reservations and to other carriers. American Airline controlled a direct link with travel agents. However, an Internet-based IOIS is open system architecture, rather than proprietary, thus allowing channel participants to easily move between IOISs. Some researchers suggest that channel control can be maintained through a virtual community of dominant channel members (suppliers and buyers) (Applegate et al., 2002). A B2B virtual market that includes the dominant channel members allows the IOIS to be used to differentiate the supply chain. Therefore, the IOIS should be capable of implementing proprietary strategies and capabilities for competitive advantage without having proprietary technology (Applegate et al., 2002).

Inter-organizational system processes and structures are critical to successful coordination and control of business partnerships in the B2B e-commerce environment (Applegate et al., 2002). The Internet provides a nonproprietary and networked infrastructure that significantly decreases the cost and time needed to connect, transact business, and share information (Applegate et al., 2002). The use of Internet technologies allows consortiums of organizations to achieve network economies of scale and network economies of scope. Network economies of scale are achieved when a community of firms uses a common infrastructure and capabilities to produce and distribute products and services faster, better, and cheaper. Network economies of scope occur when a community of firms uses a common infrastructure and capabilities to launch new products and services, enter new markets, or build new businesses (Applegate et al., 2002). Electronic B2B increases opportunities for research investigating adoption of electronic markets.

IOIS Risks

Differences exist among the inter-organizational partnerships that lead to varying levels of information access. The more information shared, the higher the risk of opportunism. Allowing sensitive corporate information outside the inner firewall, such as for an extranet, requires additional security software and skilled information watchdogs to protect these resources. A firm must consider the quality, quantity, and type of information that will be shared with exchange partners and should not take the decision to join an IOIS lightly.

The strength and the nature of the partnership influence the level of IOIS access. "Casual" or one-time partnerships may lead to an IOIS providing limited information. For example, Federal Express' extranet enables customers to track their shipped parcels (Senn, 1998). Customers, who are business partners, access only their parcel information and, thus, do not gain access to sensitive company information. Conversely, stronger partner relationships often involve sharing more sensitive information. For instance, partnerships that involve strategic alliances with a long-term commitment often provide increased access to partner information.

In other situations, partnerships may be based on strong alliances, but one or both of the partners could switch, with little cost, to another partnership. For example, Covisint provides a B2B market where suppliers and designers exchange product schedules, order information; computer-aided design (CAD) files for product design, purchase orders, and other financial information (Applegate et al., 2002). The suppliers and buyers must coordinate their technologies with Covisint to facilitate a seamless exchange of information. Also, because a standard approach is used for the B2B virtual market, buyers and suppliers have low technical switching costs and can easily create new partnerships with other market members.

The low switching costs of the modern IOIS potentially reduce the incentives for open collaboration. Open collaboration requires some level of discussion of proprietary information. Potentially, the business partner could obtain an organization's proprietary information and use this information opportunistically with another business partner to the harm of the organization. To mitigate this risk, organizations must understand the motivations of the business partners and weigh the risks of trusting these partners in collaboration when using an IOIS.

New Areas for Research

A major focus of IOIS research has been on the adoption of EDI. Iacovou, Benbasat, and Dexter (1995) found that small firm adoption of EDI depended on three major factors: organizational readiness, external pressure to adopt, and perceived benefits. Organization readiness refers to the firm's financial and technological resources. Financial resources relate to the availability of funds to pay for the EDI implementation. Technological readiness refers to the sophistication of IT usage and IT management. Two major sources of pressure to adopt are competitive pressure and pressure imposed by trading partners. These researchers found that management perceived EDI benefits of cost savings and improvement of business processes and relationships.

A study of financial EDI suggests that adoption of this type of IOIS is dependent on organizational factors and business environment characteristics, including coercive and normative pressures (Teo, Wei, & Benbasat, 2003). In the study by Teo, Wei, and Benbasat, coercive pressures included perceived dominance of supplier adopters and customer adopters, and conformity with the parent corporation. Normative pressures included the extent of adoption among suppliers and customers, and the organization's participation in industry associations.

Hart and Saunders (1998) analyzed the relationship between power and trust in relation to EDI use. These researchers found that a higher level of trust between partners correlated with more diverse use of EDI. These researchers suggested that a more cooperative approach will encourage diverse use of IOISs. Conversely, customer power was found to have mixed relationships with the volume of EDI use. For the suppliers of a chemical company, volume was positively correlated with the power of a chemical company, while there was a negative relationship with a retail customer.

Researchers found that IOIS benefits depend on changes in business process when implementing the IOIS. Riggins & Mukhopadhyay (1994) found that the buyer benefited when the supplier adopted an optional buyer-initiated modification to its system. In addition, Clark and Stoddard (1996) found that interorganizational process redesign through continuous replenishment (CRP) and EDI benefited suppliers and retailers. They also found that neither CRP nor EDI alone resulted in benefits to both parties.

Prior EDI research provides a solid foundation for understanding IOISs, but the emergence of new Web technology requires analysis of IOISs in the context of the Internet. Traditionally, EDI was developed under older, proprietary technologies. Underlying components of EDI adoption were the startup cost and state of organizational readiness critical to using the technology. Conversely, extranets rely on flexible, open software that is easier to use and requires fewer monetary and technical resources. Some aspects of adoption, such as the importance of process reengineering, are similar between the technologies. However, some of the characteristics that may inhibit or benefit adoption are likely to differ between extranets and EDI.

Adoption of EDI has been somewhat dependent on the relative power of the exchange partners. Some organizations were pressured to adopt EDI if they wanted to continue their relationships with larger or more powerful exchange partners. Smaller firms that complied might have considered the move as just one of the many costs of doing business. Trust influenced the use of EDI and should also be important to the use of the extranet. The flexible nature of the extranet allows organizations to easily enter, maintain, and leave inter-organizational partnerships. The level of trust in the partners, however, will affect the level of information sharing between them. Organizations are concerned that the partner will use proprietary information opportunistically, causing harm to the organization. Research on the influence of trust in extranet-based partnerships would provide further understanding of this important issue.

The B2B virtual marketplace, involving a consortium of market members, is different than EDI, which involves the interaction of two partners. The reasons for adoption, and the benefits seen, of the IOIS most likely differ. Like EDI, normative pressures such as adoption of suppliers, customers, and organizations may encourage adoption. However, the necessary levels of normative pressure may vary among the Web-based IOIS. For instance, one executive indicated that 80 percent of physical market participants are needed to make a successful electronic market (Applegate et al., 2002). Thus, for the B2B virtual markets, the majority of the physical market members must join the electronic market before normative pressures are sufficient to encourage adoption. Investigations are needed to identify the factors that encourage or inhibit membership in virtual markets.

Rayport and Sviokla (1994) suggested that information technology has changed the delivery mechanisms of products, from a place to an information space. These authors mentioned that physical products such as answering machines have been replaced by an information service such as an answering service. They pointed out that the information services can be bundled together to provide value-added services and opportunities for differentiation for customers. Researchers may be able to identify the value-added services that are more effective in enhancing the IOIS environment for business partners.

The literature on electronic markets describes an exciting and challenging business environment where organizations partner to provide goods and services. The low cost and communication capabilities facilitate the formation of virtual organizations and electronic communities that will gain a competitive advantage over competing virtual organizations and communities. The extranet and B2B virtual market comprise the backbone to this exciting environment that is of interest to the organizational theory, economics, and information systems disciplines. More research is needed to determine the factors that drive firms to engage in B2B virtual markets and what features make them more or less appealing than other forms of partnerships.

Web-based IOISs, the extranet, and the B2B virtual market maintain distinct differences from EDI that warrant further research. Research efforts should focus on areas of Web-based IOIS adoption, inter-organizational trust, virtual and horizontal partnerships supported by IOISs, and advantages and disadvantages of inter-organizational partnerships based on extranet versus a B2B virtual market.

The IOIS adoption research should focus on Web-based IOISs along with EDI. This will provide an understanding of the effectiveness of modern tools on adoption. More importantly, a comparison of the EDI and Web-based IOISs will assist researchers in identifying the adoption variables that vary by technology and those that are constant for different technologies. Focusing on the constant IOIS factors will provide a sound foundation of IOIS research that will last beyond the current state of technology.

With the recent improvements in information technology and communication capabilities, a possible inhibitor to IOIS effectiveness is the human factor of trust. The IOISs are most effective with collaboration between partners which necessitates information sharing. Trust is difficult to achieve in an environment where business partners can easily change. Research on trust building that leads to long-term strategic partnerships should be identified and evaluated so that an understanding of the determinants of these partnerships can be gained. In addition, agency theory should be applied to the inter-organizational situation. More specifically, a further understanding of methods to monitor, control, and encourage the agent (business partner organization) are needed so that its members do not act opportunistically to the detriment of the principal (organization).

Analysis of the influence of the information exchange on partner trust, length of partnership, and volume of inter-organizational transactions would shed light on the influence of IOIS capabilities on business partnerships. Web-based IOISs provide various multimedia methods, which vary in effectiveness, to use to communicate with partners. Identifying the type of information that best suits each medium would benefit practitioners through stronger partnerships. Virtual markets may also be analyzed in regard to antitrust laws, should there be unfair barriers to entering the electronic market or monopolistic activity through inter-organizational partnerships. These initiatives will provide researchers with better understanding of the influence of trust development on IOIS adoption and provide practitioners with recommended methods for fostering successful inter-organizational partnerships.

An IOIS may support horizontal partnerships, involving suppliers of complementary products, and vertical partnerships, involving buyer–supplier relationships (Hong, 2002). The horizontal partnerships involve competitors and suppliers of complementary products working together to meet current market demands or expand into new markets. IOIS support for these partnerships involves communication of general industry information while not disclosing proprietary information. Investigating IOIS support of this competitive cooperative environment will provide an understanding of the components of system support for these partnerships.

The vertical partnership focuses on the supply chain, which can include long-lasting partnerships and temporal partnerships that quickly can be created and dissolved. The IOIS is required to support these different partnerships through information sharing and management reporting. Investigation of how an IOIS can assist in strengthening these partnerships and in providing appropriate levels and types of information for the different partnerships is useful to forming an understanding in different partnership settings.

Companies interested in inter-organizational partnerships can often seek out partners through extranets and, in some cases, through B2B virtual markets. Understanding the business implications of these two approaches will help companies form business strategies. For instance, will forming a partnership using an extranet provide a stronger competitive advantage than joining in a partnership using the B2B virtual market, where the technology and the business supplier are easily accessible to your competitors? In addition, as these IOISs evolve, researchers will be able to determine the dominant platform for B2B activity and the reasons for the dominance. Through the research initiatives described above, academics and practitioners will have a better understanding of the current capabilities of IOISs that will better prepare them for dealing with future changes.

In summary, EDI research provided the first look at the nature of inter-organizational systems. Therefore, it serves as a starting point for future investigations. The emergence of Web-based technology led to the development of new forms of IOISs—extranets and B2B virtual markets—that are fundamentally different from EDI. New methods, variables, and tools are needed to study them. Existing literature on marketing, channel dynamics, networks, and joint ventures may provide clues to enhance our understanding of the competitive IOIS environment. Researchers are encouraged to find the factors leading to success with Web-based IOISs. These investigations will improve our understanding of global initiatives and provide guidance to practitioners who are empowered to utilize IOISs for competitive advantage.

Future Trends

Information technology, computing power, and communication capabilities should continue to improve at a rapid pace. As the technology for building and operating IOISs advances, an increase should be seen in the variety and number of virtual organizations. This means that opportunities to participate in different partnerships should be plentiful, and technical and economic reasons for avoiding IOISs may be moot in the near future. As the use of Web technology continues its onslaught into our everyday lives, virtual organizations may become a more dominant unit of analysis for research than the brick-and-mortar establishments we are so familiar with today.

The predicted frequency of inter-organizational partnerships will place greater demands on IOISs. As the enterprise system has done for the firm, an IOIS will need to provide management across different organizations with the information and decision support tools to manage the virtual enterprise. Current IOISs provide system connectivity but are limited in terms of management support tools. The IOISs face unique decision support difficulties in comparison to enterprise systems. For instance, inter-organizational information required for planning and decision making may be withheld by the business partner. Also, group decision support systems must assist managers from different organizations who have different perspectives. In addition, the need for intelligent agents in B2B e-commerce will most likely increase. Other benefits may be realized by expanding analysis tools for IOISs. For example, there may be difficulty in performing meaningful trend analysis, through data mining, of virtual organizations that are in existence for a short period of time and have limited historical information. Additionally, researchers may focus on effective decision-making models for IOIS environments. Little work has been done on evaluating the suitability of joining into a virtual organization and the extent of the risks incurred as a member of a virtual organization.

Improvements to the supply chain through the use of IOISs have come primarily from reducing costs and generating shorter cycle times. In the future, there will be smaller, if any, gains obtained in these areas. Future opportunities will likely focus on improving quality and providing value-added services through virtual organizations. Scientific models to evaluate quality improvement in virtual organizations and to optimize the use of value-added services are warranted.

Finally, the IOIS is expected to impact financial reporting through more timely and detailed information provided by XBRL. This will enable stakeholders in the financial community to perform analysis based on their aggregation of the financial data. Research will need to be performed to determine whether the availability of this timely and detailed data assists the financial community in reducing the occurrence of financial fraud that has rocked the U.S. financial markets.

Summary

Inter-organizational information systems are in a special class of business system. They allow the formation of partnerships between firms. Three types of IOISs were described in this chapter: extranets, B2B virtual markets, and EDI. Each type has specific features and characteristics that differentiate them from each other, and they have informational and network properties that distinguish them from non-IOISs, such as Internet Web sites and intranets. A typology of an IOIS was introduced to highlight commonalities and differences in terms of network structures and information exchanges. Structural characteristics include the identification of the interacting parties, which party acts as the system host, requirements for security, and the extent of information sharing. A comparison of systems based on information exchanges identified the general functions performed by each system, the format of the information that is transferred, the types of information communicated, the requirements for confidentiality of the data, and the cost and complexity of the technology. The benefits and risks of entering into an IOIS were described. Finally, new avenues of research are suggested and speculation on the future of IOISs were offered. It is hoped that the typology and ideas presented here provide new insights for academics and practitioners into the evolving landscape of e-commerce.

References

Applegate, L. M., Austin, R. D., & McFarlan, F. W. (2002). *Corporate information strategy and management: Text and cases* (6th ed.). Boston, MA: McGraw-Hill/Irwin.

Applegate, L. M., McFarlan, F. W., & McKenney, J. L. (1996). *Corporate information systems management: Text and cases*. Chicago: Irwin.

Barrett, S., & Konsynski, B. (1982). Inter-organization information sharing systems. *MIS Quarterly*, 93–105.

Cash, J. I., Jr., & Konsynski, B. R. (1985). IS redraws competitive boundaries. *Harvard Business Review*, *63*(2), 134–142.

Cash, J. I., Jr., Eccles, R. G., Nohria, N., & Nolan, R. L. (1994). *Building the Information Age organization: Structure, control and information technologies*. Chicago: Irwin.

Dalton, G. (1998). International innovators ready to go global? *Information Week*, (668), 48–60.

David, J. S., McCarthy, W. E., & Sommer, B. E. (2003). Agility—Key to survival of the fittest in the software market. *Communications of the ACM*, *46*(5), 65–69.

Greenstein, M., & Vasarhelyi, M. (2001). *Electronic commerce: Security, risk management, and control* (2nd ed.). Boston, MA: McGraw-Hill/Irwin.

Hart, P. J., & Saunders, C. S. (1998). Emerging electronic partnerships: Antecedents and dimensions of EDI use from the supplier's perspective. *Journal of Management Information Systems: JMIS*, *14*(4), 87–111.

Hong, I. B. (2002). A new framework for interorganizational systems based on the linkage of participant roles. *Information and Management*, *39*(4), 261–270.

Iacovou, C. L., Benbasat, I., & Dexter, A. S. (1995). Electronic data interchange and small organizations: Adoption and impact of technology. *MIS Quarterly*, *19*(4), 465–485.

Johnston, H. R., & Vitale, M. R. (1988). Creating competitive advantage with interorganizational information systems. *MIS Quarterly*, *12*(2), 153–165.

Kafka, S. (2000). eMarketplaces boost B2B trade. Forester Research. Retrieved May 27, 2003, from the World Wide Web: www.forester.com.

Kumar, K. (2001). Technology for supporting supply chain management. *Communications of the ACM*, *44*(6), 58–61.

Kumar, K., & van Dissel, H. G. (1996). Sustainable collaboration: Managing conflict and cooperation in interorganizational systems. *MIS Quarterly*, *20*(3), 279–300.

Lange, L. (1996). Engineering's next Net wave: Extranet. *Electronic Engineering Times*, (933), 6.

Morrell, M., & Ezingeard, J. N. (2002). Revisiting adoption factors of interorganizational information systems in SMEs. *Logistics Information Management*, *15*(1), 46–57.

Pan, S. L., & Lee, J. N. (2003). Using e-CRM for a united view of the customer.

Raghunathan, S. (1999). Interorganizational collaborative forecasting and re-plenishment systems and supply chain implications. *Decision Sciences, 30*(4), 1053–1071.

Rayport, J. F., & Sviokla, J. J. (1994). Managing in the marketspace. *Harvard Business Review, 72*(6), 141–150.

Riggins, F. J., & Mukhopadhyay, T. (1994). Interdependent benefits from interorganizational systems: Opportunities for business partner reengineering. *Journal of Management Information Systems: JMIS, 11*(2), 37–57.

Riggins, F. J., & Rhee, H. S. (1998). Toward a unified view of electronic commerce. *Communications of the ACM, 41*(10), 88–95.

Senn, J. A. (1998). WISs at Federal Express. *Communications of the ACM, 41*(7), 117–118.

Teo, H. H., Wei, K. K., & Benbasat, I. (2003). Predicting intention to adopt interorganizational linkages: An institutional perspective. *MIS Quarterly, 27*(1), 19–49.

Chapter III

Classifying B2B Inter-Organizational Systems:
A Role Linkage Perspective*

Ilyoo B. Hong
University of California at Los Angeles, USA

Abstract

This paper aims at developing a framework for business-to-business (B2B) inter-organizational systems (IOSs), based on real-world IOS examples. Based upon two dimensions, role linkage and system support level, we propose a new framework that classifies IOSs into four basic types: (1) resource pooling, (2) operational cooperation, (3) operational coordination, and (4) complementary cooperation. We review select cases that fit into each category and consider the common characteristics of systems in each category. Then we draw implications for IOS planning and suggest a five-step process for creating an IOS plan. It is argued that each category of IOS needs to be linked with a specific business strategy, although each employs a common technical infrastructure.

* This research was funded by a grant from Chung-Ang University.

Introduction

An increasingly large number of companies use information technology (IT) for more than operational and management support (Rackoff et al., 1985). In particular, with the rapid advance of telecommunications technology, firms have searched for strategic opportunities from computer networks linking organizations. The information and communications technology that transcends traditional organizational boundaries has been termed inter-organizational systems (Applegate et al., 1996; Cash & Konsynski, 1985; Kumar & Dissel, 1996). Inter-organizational systems (IOSs) function to blur the boundaries of today's organizations as they enable information to flow from one organization to another (Kaufman, 1966; Konsynski, 1993).

The common purpose of traditional IOSs has been to support firms' value chains, so that they can better compete in the market. The IOSs that have emerged in recent years, however, increasingly support partnering among organizations. That is, there is a shift in the role of IT—from a competition weapon to a cooperation enabler among businesses. It is necessary to view IOSs in a broader context that encompasses not only the traditional value chain but also partnerships and strategic alliances among firms within an industry. This paper addresses the need to incorporate the increasing trend of partnership formation among business firms into a framework for B2B IOSs. The existing frameworks are either too complex to be applied to IOS planning or too outdated with respect to the many forms of emerging global networks.

Related Literature

The IOS research has produced a number of articles that attempted to illuminate numerous aspects of inter-organizational networking, including the inter-organizational relationship, IOS strategic planning (McFarlan et al., 1983), and the IOS network structure (Malone et al., 1987; Marchewka & Towell, 1998).

Barrett and Konsynski classified IOSs on five levels of IOS participation. At Level 1, a firm accesses a system that is run and operated by other companies. Level 2 participants design, develop, maintain, and share a single application, such as a customer order-processing system. Level 3 participants take responsibility for a network which lower-level participants may share. Level 4 participants develop and share a network with diverse applications that may be used by many different types of participants. At Level 5, any number of lower-level participants may be integrated in real time over complex operating environments.

Johnston and Vitale (1988) developed a classification framework using three dimensions: business purpose, relationships with participants, and information function. The framework takes the form of a decision tree, where the three dimensions are sequentially interconnected. Business purpose indicates why an IOS is needed; it could be either to leverage present business or to enter a new information-driven business. Relationships refer to those linked by the system; they could be customers, dealers, suppliers, or competitors. Information function is concerned with functions that the system is intended to perform; it may process boundary transactions, retrieve and analyze shared information, or be internally used. When taken together, these dimensions produce 24 possible combinations (= 2 × 4 × 3). Thus, this framework suffers from complexity that makes it hard to analyze the characteristics of each category. It also is not so much a framework to classify an IOS as one to study the relationships among its factors.

Kumar and van Dissel present a typology for an IOS based on inter-organizational interdependence. They view an IOS as a technology designed and implemented to simplify the relationships between organizations. Based on three interdependent relationships, including pooled, sequential, and reciprocal interdependencies, their framework comprises information resources, value and supply chains, and networks. The pooled information resource IOSs involve sharing common IT resources. Examples include common databases, communication networks, and applications. These provide economies of scale with consequent cost and risk sharing. The second type, the value- or supply-chain IOS, supports customer–supplier relationships and occurs as a consequence of these relationships along the value or supply chain. These IOSs institutionalize sequential interdependency between organizations. Order-entry and processing systems and CAD-to-CAD IOSs belong to this type. Finally, networked IOSs operationalize and implement reciprocal interdependencies between organizations. They are exemplified by joint marketing programs, where firms exchange information for mutual advantage.

Meanwhile, with the growing use of the Internet by business organizations for conducting commercial transactions, IOS research is being merged with the electronic commerce (EC) area. Related literature (Sawhney & Kaplan, 1999) suggests that the B2B e-marketplace linking suppliers and buyers may be classified into two types, horizontal and vertical. Vertical e-marketplaces are organized around industries, whereas horizontal ones focus on specific business functions or processes. The Internet-based IS created by this B2B intermediary is likely to emerge as a new form of IOS in the digital economy.

As a whole, prior research on the classification of IOS lacks the perspective of the linkage of corporate value activities.1 Classification is based upon modes of IOS participation, the why–who–what of IOSs, interorganizational interdependence, etc. But, few researchers have looked at the "value activity linkage" as a way to understand IOS characteristics.

The Configuration of Inter-Organizational Systems

An IOS can be configured in various ways. It can be set up as one-to-one (a typical buyer–seller system), one-to-many (a marketing or purchasing system), or many-to-many (electronic markets), depending on the interaction patterns between the participants. The IOS can also be configured according to the type of dependence existing between the firms joining the network. Pooled interdependency requires a star-like configuration in which data movement is directed toward the central hub. With an IOS using sequential interdependency, nodes are arranged in a straight line, where the output of one node becomes the input of the next. The reciprocal interdependent system necessitates a complex IOS in which participants are interdependent. The existing views of the IOS configuration focus on the physical interconnection of, and data flows between, participating firms.

The configuration of an IOS, however, can be viewed from a different perspective—in terms of horizontal or vertical electronic linkages between organizations. As shown in Figure 1, the IOS configuration can be either horizontal or vertical. The linkage between heterogeneous value chains is vertical, whereas the linkage between firms spanning a single industry is horizontal.

Thus, the way that an IOS is configured is associated with its purpose or the strategy. For example, organizations are horizontally connected for cooperation between competitors. On the other hand, organizations seek vertical interconnection when it is important to team up with buyers, sellers, or organizations that provide complementary products or resources.

Figure 1: Horizontal and vertical linking of firms over an IOS

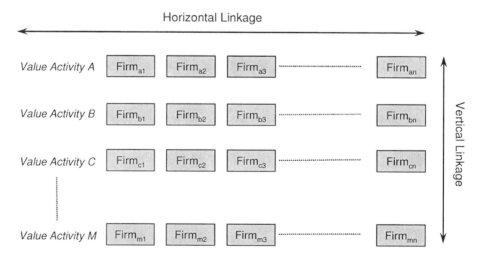

A Framework for Inter-Organizational Systems

Here, we use the concept of horizontal and vertical linkages to gain a perspective on IOS configuration and develop a new framework for classifying IOS, with emphasis upon participants: customers, suppliers, affinity organizations, or competitors (Tapscott & Caston, 1993). Meanwhile, an IOS can be viewed in terms of its system support level: operational or strategic. Farbey, Land, and Targett (1995) suggested that operational applications focus on process automation and primarily aim at saving time and costs, while strategic applications are intended to achieve strategic goals and have the potential to transform entire businesses. The system might have been motivated either by the need to impact the way that the operations are performed or by the need to utilize the resources of multiple organizations strategically. Thus, our framework consists of two dimensions, role linkage and system support level, as shown in Figure 2.

Dimensions of Inter-Organizational Systems

Herein we draw distinctions between differing values of each dimension, to provide a logical basis for our framework.

Role Linkage

(1) Horizontal - This linkage is formed via the interconnection of firms performing common value activities. It can be defined as the degree to which an IOS links a homogeneous group of organizations in order to foster their mutual cooperation. Homogeneous organizations share a common role-the contribution of identical inputs toward the augmented output.

(2) Vertical - This linkage involves different roles of participating organizations that cooperate to add value to existing products or services. The classical IOS example, America Hospital Supply's ASAP, involves electronic links between the hospital supply distributors and the health care organizations. Such buyer–seller networks are typically designed to support the value chain.

System Support Level

(1) Strategic Support - In recent years, the formation of partnerships and strategic alliances is becoming increasingly common, as it enables firms to

either pool or share resources. Gurbaxani and Whang (1996) argued that the incentives for resource-oriented cooperation include exploitation of the economies of scale in operations and transaction costs. Konsynski and McFarlan (1990) suggested that the driving force in an "information partnership" is the sharing of large investments in hardware and software to reduce potential risk as well as of training expenses. Sharing technical burden may motivate firms to join the information partnership, especially when a project demands high-level skills and expertise. In addition, interfirm cooperation can be motivated for a behavioral reason; partnering between firms can standardize on an interface so that users do not have to learn different interfaces at different firms (Applegate et al., 1996). More recently, IOSs linking firms for their reciprocal relationships are noticeable.

(2) Operational Support - The IOS can be created for the primary purpose of supporting routine operations. Firms can connect to merely share each other's information as part of their day-to-day business or to support a value or supply chain. When an IOS of this category is implemented, it fundamentally transforms the business processes of the participants to increase the operational efficiency and makes a participant operationally dependent upon the IOS. Unlike the strategically oriented IOS, the IOS for operational support causes the participants' operations to be integrated, creating exit barriers.

The Four Categories of IOSs

Depending on the role linkage and the motivator, IOSs are categorized into four types: (1) resource pooling, (2) complementary cooperation, (3) operational cooperation, and (4) operational coordination. The classification framework is shown in Figure 2.

Resource-Pooling IOS

Belonging to this category are those IOSs that link the participants performing common value activities (i.e., rival firms) in order to permit risk- or cost-sharing by pooling their resources. This type, in general, aims at forming a coalition to compete with large firms or in expanding markets.

(1) IVANS (Insurance Value-Added Network Services) - Frequently cited in the SIS literature, this is a group of independent insurance companies with thousands of agents. The system was created by the industry trade association, ACORD, to cope with their loss of market share to direct sales

Figure 2: A framework for inter-organizational systems

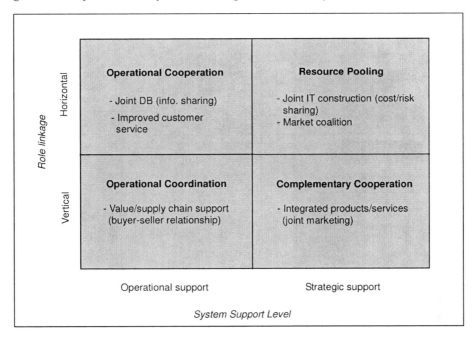

forces from State Farm Allstate. The IOS allows independent agents across the United States to access property and casualty insurance companies for policy issuance, price quotation, and other information (Newmann, 1994).

(2)   ECONOMOST - McKesson Corporation, a distributor of drugs, healthcare products, and other consumer goods, built ECONOMOST, a form of order entry and inventory management system, that interconnects the independent drug stores that exclusively sell McKesson's products. This horizontal linkage was formed by a coalition of the independent drugstores and was intended to challenge the market attack by large drug chains. This form of partnership, in which small companies seek the advantages of vertically integrated companies, is referred to as a VAP (value-adding partnership). The VAPs secure economies of scale by sharing such resources as purchasing, warehouses, research and development centers, and information.

(3)   Garden.com - More recently, Garden.com created an Internet-based IOS to respond to customer needs. It uses the Internet to interconnect over 70 flower growers and uses the network to deliver flower orders within 2 days. When a customer places an order, it is transmitted to the appropriate supplier over the company extranet. Although there are many flower growers in America at the regional level, there was no way to make their products available to national customers, because their primary target was

local customers. Thus, Garden.com used the Internet to bring together the inventories of the regional growers to buyers scattered throughout the nation. This company was able to pool together the resources of the individual flower growers to build national-level giant-volume inventories, while at the same time increasing the speed of responding to customer needs.

Complementary Cooperation IOS

This category represents a form of cooperation between firms playing different roles in an industry value chain; it allows them to expand the business capacity beyond the limit of the resources possessed by a single firm, thereby enlarging its "virtual resources." The prime purpose of this partnership is market access via complementary advantages.

(1)   UAL and SAS - Air carriers, including UAL and SAS, have attempted to offer an integrated travel service that combines the airline, car-rental, and hotel businesses using a CRS. The prime motive of the virtual vertical integration along the service value chain is to provide the traveler with a convenient value-added service.

(2)   Citibank - A global financial institution, Citibank allied with American Airlines, Mariott Hotel, and a national supermarket chain to offer the CityCard and use a computer-based network to capture the data of point-of-service (POS) transactions processed through the CityCard into a database. Citibank used this to give bonus points for purchases exceeding a certain amount, to offer product discounts by electronic coupons, to give rebates on select product purchases, and to connect the POS database to an electronic payment system so that the purchase amount charged to the credit card would be automatically withdrawn from the customer's bank account. Meanwhile, Citibank created Citisatcom, a satellite communication network to facilitate the operations of the regional credit card centers. It relied only on the Global Transaction Network to ally itself with banks in the United States and Japan.

(3)   Reuters Holding PLC - A reputed British news agency, Reuters, had been losing money in 1973. In an attempt to regain competitiveness, it used its worldwide news agency network to collect and market information of high value. The company interconnected the 127 commodity and other exchanges via a telecommunications network and built a Reuters Monitor Service (RMS) to offer commodities and financial information. In addition, they acquired a firm that owned vast databases of financial information and

constructed the Integrated Data Network (IDN) that permitted trades with 114 countries around the globe.

Operational Cooperation IOS

This type of IOS brings together firms in a common value chain primarily to improve the quality of service or to share information of common interest. Thus, by agreeing with rivals to collaborate on some common operations, firms can together create a huge virtual organization that allows them to operate as though they were a single company.

(1) AutoNetwork - Developed for a cluster of used part suppliers, AutoNetwork is a good example of using an IOS technology to create a virtual warehouse that, in fact, consists of many individual suppliers. Automobile dismantlers, often called wrecking yards, sell reusable parts to garages, body shops, insurance companies, and individuals, and it is important for them to exchange part availability information. The traditional voice hotlines (basically telephone networks of auto dismantlers) have been replaced by a computer network that interconnects the dismantlers. A parts request is sent in an e-mail message to all the parties joining the network; anyone who has the requested part replies accordingly. The virtual warehouse of user parts therefore functions as a large central warehouse to help locate parts more effectively.

(2) Sabre: The well-known airline reservation system created by American Airlines is another example in this category. While the system is typically known as a classical example of an IS used as a competitive weapon, it also allows airlines to form a horizontal partnership to enable operational cooperation via shared databases. The joint database enables inter-airline collaboration on day-to-day operations, such as exchange of frequent flyer points, and this can help to improve customer satisfaction.

(3) Travelers insurance company: This is one of the companies providing managed health care; it focuses on maintaining standards of health-care quality, as well as on controlling increases in health-care costs. The essence of managed care is information; the company created the CareOptions medical management system to provide medical personnel access to large databases with millions of case histories to guide treatment decisions for patients. The goal was to make the correct diagnosis the first time without unnecessary tests, etc. The system represented a combination of local medical expertise with the administrative resources of a national company. The providers, customers, and insurers access information on

how patients' conditions were diagnosed and treated, what each provider did, and the outcomes. This is part of a strategy to make available a huge volume of experience to make better clinical decisions.

Operational Coordination IOS

An IOS can be configured to interconnect differing roles played by firms serving an industry value chain so as to increase the operational efficiency.

(1) Nike, Inc. - This U.S.-based manufacturer outsourced athletic footwear production to contractors in Asia to focus on product design and marketing; that is, they vertically disintegrated their value chain. In the 1980s, the technicians who had been charged with control and coordination over the production process were replaced by an IOS that linked U.S. designers with Asian contractors using a CAD/CAM system. The coordination and control system built by Nike monitored each phase of the production process from design through sales.

(2) Zephyr - To decrease procurement processing time, Lawrence Livermore National Laboratory (LLNL) developed a paperless procurement system called Zephyr which improves procurement processing time by 90%. Because traditional procurement processing based on paper can create delays, LLNL designed Web pages for its engineering and procurement departments. Vendors respond to procurement's Web page with quotes, and the winning bid is then awarded the same day via the vendor's Web page on the LLNL site. Upon shipment of the item, the vendor initiates a credit card transaction that results in a transfer payment to the vendor's bank. Typically, electronic payments occur 48 to 72 hours after the shipment notification.

(3) CFAR - Wal-Mart Stores, a retailer, and Warner-Lambert Company, a manufacturer, announced that they were engaged in a pilot project initiated by Wal-Mart, known as Collaborative Forecasting and Replenishment (CFAR) (Computerworld, 1996). The CFAR system was designed to allow linked companies to collaborate on developing joint demand forecasts and production schedules through Internet and EDI networks (Raghunathan, 1999). Warner-Lambert is currently loading forecast data it receives from Wal-Mart directly into their enterprise demand planning system. Because CFAR allows exchange of complex decision support models and manufacturer/retailer strategies, the savings in inventory and manufacturing costs can be realized.

(4) Manheim Auctions - This Atlanta, Georgia-based automobile auction company recently launched an Internet-based IOS that allows retail dealers

to purchase used vehicles via electronic auctions. In the existing environment, dealers had to gather in the auction market and purchase and transport used vehicles to their lots, resulting in considerable cost. The Web-based IOS relieved dealers of the burden of paying auction costs when buying vehicles. The system now allows dealers to view a list of used cars along with related photographs by simply entering a set of conditions for a desired car. In addition, dealers no longer have to purchase vehicles in advance, thereby eliminating much of the risk (Stefanov, 1999).

Discussion

The IOS examples given for each of the four categories have been grouped as such, based on the two dimensions, including the way that they are configured and their system support levels. And, it is presumed that the examples within each category share common characteristics.

Implications for IOS Planning

Now we can examine the systems to draw useful implications for IOS planning, such as purpose, benefits, supporting strategies, etc.

Resource-Pooling IOS

Resource-pooling IOSs purport to form a coalition to create a market power or to distribute investments among the participating firms (Table 1). These systems make the separate organizations appear large, making available the resources needed to compete with a strong player or to reduce the risk or financial burden of IT construction. A growth strategy may be implemented through an IOS of this type, as the systems may help to broaden the market share by strengthening corporate competitiveness. However, the firms performing a common value activity may be confronted with conflicts of interest, unless a common set of goals can initially be anticipated and clearly spelled out.

Complementary Cooperation IOS

IOS examples in this category are shown to strongly reveal the interdependency relationships among the participants, as the firms need to depend on one another

Table 1: Characteristics of resource-pooling IOS

IOS Innovator	IOS Configuration	Purpose	Benefits
ACORD (IVANS)	Small insurance firms / Agents	To form a coalition to compete with a large insurer	Increase in market share
McKesson (ECONOMOST)	Distributor / Drug stores	To enable a VAP (value-adding partnership)	Economies of scale resulting from virtual vertical integration; improved competitiveness
Garden.com	Flower growers / Merchant / Consumers	To bring together the individual growers' inventories into a virtual warehouse	Decrease in inventory costs; increase in speed and performance

Table 2: Characteristics of complementary cooperation IOS

IOS Innovator	IOS Configuration	Purpose	Benefits
UAL & SAS	Air carriers / Car-rentals / Hotels	To provide integrated travel service	Value-added service; revenue increase
Citibank	Air carrier / Hotel / Bank / Super market chain	To share sales transaction data; to promote sales; to provide automatic payment	Increased sales; more efficient payment processing; improved customer service (from the interbank alliance)
Reuters Holding PLC	Financial DB firm / Commodity exchanges / News agencies	To collect and offer commodity and financial information	Worldwide expansion of business

for reciprocal advantages (Table 2). The airline companies or Citibank will not be able to attract a new customer segment on their own. How well related products or services are packaged into an attractive offering is likely to determine their success. Implementation of these systems would be effective when linked to a differentiation strategy aimed at creating a unique image in combination with a strategy tailored to the needs of potential customers.

Operational Cooperation IOS

The IOS examples presented above illustrate firms that aim to improve customer service by cooperating with firms performing identical value activities; they are characterized by their using joint databases to facilitate information sharing. Access to this joint database affects the ability to perform day-to-day operations in a flexible manner. This, in turn, influences the quality of customer service. For this reason, firms planning to introduce operational cooperation IOS will be better off tying it with a differentiation strategy with a focus on customer service improvement (Table 3).

Table 3: Characteristics of operational cooperation IOS

IOS Innovator	IOS Configuration	Purpose	Benefits
Incomnet (AutoNetwork)	Used part suppliers	To exchange used part availability information; to create a virtual warehouse	Easier and faster information exchange; quicker turnaround time; revenue increase; improved customer service
American Airlines (Sabre)	Air carriers / Travel agents	To share seat availability and flight information	Improved customer service
Travelers Insurance Company	Insurance company / Service providers (hospitals)	To share case history database for correct diagnosis	Provision of quality health care; health-care cost control

Table 4: Characteristics of operational coordination IOS

IOS Innovator	IOS Configuration		Purpose	Benefits
Nike, Inc.	Shoe manufacturer / Asian contractors		To facilitate communication between designers and contractors	Virtual vertical integration; control and coordination over outsourced production
LLNL (Zephyr)	Vendors / Research lab		To expedite procurement processing; to automate credit card transaction	Reduced procurement processing time by 90%; faster electronic payments
Wal-Mart (CFAR)	Vendors / Retailer		To collaborate on developing joint demand forecasts and production schedules	Savings in inventory and manufacturing costs
Manheim Auctions	Auction company / Retail dealers		To avoid face-to-face auction costs	Savings in auction and transportation costs; decrease in dealers' sale risk

Operational Coordination IOS

The primary motive for creating this type of IOS is cost efficiency enabled by effective coordination of a firm's operations through the industry value chain (Table 4). The first example is based on virtual vertical integration, while the other three illustrate the buyer–seller relationship. Planning for this type of IOS will have to center around a cost leadership strategy geared toward cutting the operational costs (ordering/inventory, shipping, production, etc.).

Comparing the Four Types of IOS

While all types of IOSs share the common characteristic of interconnecting businesses to enable dissemination of information, the above discussions on the four different types of IOSs clearly demonstrate that they differ in some ways, including the purpose, relationship among linked organizations, benefits, and applicable strategies (Table 5). Figure 3 depicts how these IOSs differ from one another.

Table 5: Comparison of the characteristics among the four IOS categories

Attribute / IOS Type	Purposes	Relationship among the Linked Organizations	Benefits	Applicable Strategies
Resource Pooling	To compete with large competitors; to form a virtual warehouse; to distribute costs or risks	Rivals (horizontal)	Increase in competitiveness and market share; decrease in cost burden	Growth strategy
Complementary Cooperation	To provide integrated service; to share sales transaction data to induce sales	Complementarily related products/ services (vertical)	Improved customer service; increased sales	Differentiation strategy and focus strategy
Operational Cooperation	To create a virtual warehouse; to share and exchange business information to help operation	Rivals (horizontal)	Decreased in stocking costs; improved customer service	Differentiation strategy
Operational Coordination	To facilitate communication for coordination; to process internal operations efficiently	Firms on a value chain (vertical)	Improved control function; improved operational efficiency	Cost leadership strategy

Figure 3: The five-step process for IOS planning

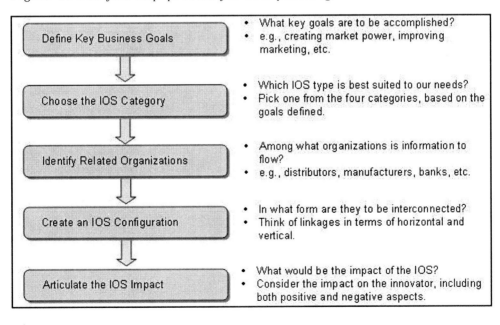

- Define Key Business Goals
  - What key goals are to be accomplished?
  - e.g., creating market power, improving marketing, etc.

- Choose the IOS Category
  - Which IOS type is best suited to our needs?
  - Pick one from the four categories, based on the goals defined.

- Identify Related Organizations
  - Among what organizations is information to flow?
  - e.g., distributors, manufacturers, banks, etc.

- Create an IOS Configuration
  - In what form are they to be interconnected?
  - Think of linkages in terms of horizontal and vertical.

- Articulate the IOS Impact
  - What would be the impact of the IOS?
  - Consider the impact on the innovator, including both positive and negative aspects.

Applying the Findings to IOS Planning

Drawing on our discussion of the examples, we can suggest a four-step process for planning for an IOS, as illustrated in Figure 3.

This step-by-step method of spelling out the configuration and impact of IOSs is based on the assumption that real-world inter-organizational systems that we create can also be classified into one of the four IOS categories. Thus, it will be much faster and easier to use the known characteristics of the chosen IOS type as a template to create an IOS plan, rather than starting from the scratch.

To illustrate an example of using the five-step model to plan for an IOS, consider a global cell phone manufacturer that wants to add speed and efficiency to the worldwide operations that presently are not responsive to the challenges of the diverse business environment.

(1)   Define Key Business Goals - Important goals of this company would probably include expediting the global operations scattered in different sites around the globe, providing tighter control and coordination over the operations, among others. These goals will become the basis for determining not only the type of IOS needed but also the system configuration.

(2)   Choose the IOS Category - The Purposes column in Table 5 may be reviewed to find the closest IOS category. The IOS type that best matches the stated goals would be operational coordination. This IOS is characterized by focusing on operational rather than strategic support, where the efficiency in day-to-day operations is the target objective.

(3)   Identify Related Organizations: As shown in Table 5, an IOS of this type is likely to involve firms on a value chain, just as Nike created a system that linked the American headquarters office concentrating on the R&D and marketing functions to the Asian production facilities. Likewise, the cell phone manufacturer may consider firms on its value chain, such as plants, part suppliers, distributors, and other related organizations. Suppose that part suppliers, plants, and distributors are chosen as potential participants in the IOS.

(4)   Create an IOS Configuration: As we saw in the previous section, the firms on a value chain are interconnected via a vertical linkage. The focal IOS may be configured in the following diagram.

The horizontal lines interconnecting part suppliers and distributors are shown with dotted lines, because they represent networks, and there is no information flow among the nodes. The individual links involved in this diagram may be examined in the following table.

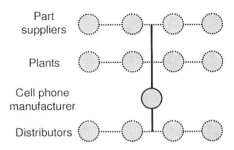

Organization #1	Organization #2	Information to Flow	Impact on the Firm
Part suppliers	Plants	• Ordering • Shipping • Payment	Improved part supply chain
Plants	Cell phone manufacturer (headquarters' office)	• Production scheduling • Inventory levels • Demand forecasts	Better production decisions; savings on storage costs
Cell phone manufacturer	Distributors	• Ordering • Shipping • Payment • Demand forecasts	Improved logistics/ distribution

(5) Articulate the IOS Impact: The system, when appropriately deployed, is presumed to have a significant impact on the cell manufacturer. The company will have better control and coordination over the activities along the value chain, thereby enabling time and cost savings involved in performing value activities. In addition, the company and its global partners will be able to operate as if they were one company. This means improved responsiveness to customer needs.

Conclusion

Inter-organizational systems emerging in recent years tend to be much more complicated than those illustrated in this paper. Their configuration is often a combination of horizontal and vertical linkages. For example, the Covisint joint electronic marketplace announced in February 2000 by General Motors, Ford, and DaimlerChrysler is an example of an IOS that goes beyond the distinctive categories depicted in the framework. The exchange formed by the Big Three automakers is expected to account for purchases of approximately $250 billion a year and involve about 60,000 suppliers (Lewis, 2001). This type of partnership provides operational support rather than strategic support. However, it is a hybrid of operational cooperation and operational coordination in that it involves horizontally linked firms (i.e., automakers) and vertically linked firms (i.e., an automaker to part manufacturers or to distributors). The vertical linkage is for the basic buy and sell functions, whereas the horizontal linkage is to create a critical mass by pooling resources, such as IT or capital, so that they can lower the costs via economies of scale.

While there is such a new trend toward industry-wide IOSs that are far more complex and larger in scale than those that appeared earlier, we need a conceptual framework that will enable us to gain fundamental insights into the way that an IOS is configured. This paper presents a new classification framework, focusing on the linkage of participants' roles. It recognizes that IOSs need to be examined in terms of how their participants' roles are linked (horizontal or vertical) and what key motivator drives the IOS development (i.e., strategic or operational). Based on these two dimensions, our framework classifies IOSs into four categories, including resource pooling, complementary cooperation, operational cooperation, and operational coordination.

Firms that consider introducing a resource-pooling IOS can rely on a *growth strategy* designed to expand the market, and can use joint databases as a key means to share business information. A complementary cooperation IOS can be implemented via a *differentiation strategy* in conjunction with a *focus strategy*, such that the existing product or service is combined with related products or services along the industry value chain to attract a specific customer segment with added values. Joint databases can be employed to provide real-time information sharing for this type of IOS. An operational cooperation IOS can be accompanied by a *differentiation strategy* to improve customer service and use a joint database as a key means to share information. Importantly, this type of IOS should be tightly integrated with existing operational systems. Finally, an operational coordination IOS can be built based on a *cost leadership strategy* designed to increase control and coordination.

References

Applegate, L. M., McFarlan, F. W., & McKenney, J. L. (1996). *Corporate information systems management: Text and cases* (4th ed.), Chicago: Irwin.

Applegate, L. M., Holsapple, C. W., Kalakota, R., Radermacher, F. J., & Whinston, A. B. (1996). Electronic commerce: Building blocks of new business opportunity. *Journal of Organizational Computing and Electronic Commerce, 6*(1), 1–10.

Bakos, J. Y. (1991). A strategic analysis of electronic marketplaces, *MIS Quarterly, 15,* 295–310.

Barret, S., & Konsynski, B. R. (1982). Inter-organizational information sharing systems. *MIS Quarterly,* 93–105.

Cash, J. I., & Konsynski, B. R. (1985). IS redraws competitive boundaries. *Harvard Business Review,* 134–142.

Clark, T. H., & Stoddard, D. B. (1996). Interorganizational business process redesign: Merging technological and process innovation. *Journal of Management Information Systems, 13*(2), 9–28.

Farbey, B., Land, F. F., & Targett, D. (1995). A taxonomy of information systems applications: The benefits' evaluation ladder. *European Journal of Information Systems, 4*(1), 41–50.

Ferguson, C. H. (1990). Computers and the coming of the U.S. Keiretsu. *Harvard Business Review.*

Gurbaxani, V., & Whang, S. (1996). The impact of information systems on organizations and markets. *Communications of the ACM,* 59–73.

Johnston, H. R., & Vitale, M. R. (1988). Creating competitive advantage with interorganizational information systems. *MIS Quarterly.*

Kaufmann, F. (1966). Data system that cross company boundaries. *Harvard Business Review.*

Konsynski, B. R. (1993). Strategic control in the extended enterprise. *IBM Systems Journal, 32*(1).

Konsynski, B. R., & McFarlan, W. F. (1990). Information partnerships—Shared data, shared scale. *Harvard Business Review,* 114–120.

Kumar, K., & Dissel, H. G. (1996). Sustainable collaboration: Managing conflict and cooperation in interorganizational systems. *MIS Quarterly.*

Lewis, I. (2001). Logistics and electronic commerce: An interorganizational systems perspective. *Transportation Journal, 40*(4), 5–13.

Malone, T. W., Yates, J., & Benjamin, R. I. (1987). Electronic markets and electronic hierarchies: Effects of information technology and market structure and corporate strategies. *Communications of the ACM,* 484–497.

Marchewka, J. T., & Towell, E. R. (1998). A comparison of market and hierarchical IOS network structures. In *Proceedings of the 1998 DSI Conference.*

McFarlan, F. W., McKinney, J. L., & Pyburn, P. (1983). The information archipelago—Plotting a course. *Harvard Business Review.*

Newmann, S. (1994). *Strategic information systems: Competition through information technologies.* New York: Macmillan.

Porter, M. E. (1985). *Competitive advantage: Creating and sustaining superior performance.* New York: The Free Press.

Rackoff, N., Wiseman, C., & Ullrich, W. A. (1985). Information systems for competitive advantage: Implementation of a planning process. *MIS Quarterly, 9*(4).

Raghunathan, S. (1999). Interorganizational collaborative forecasting and replenishment systems and supply chain implications. *Decision Sciences, 30*(4), 1053–1071.

Sawhney, M., & Kaplan, S. (1999). Let's get vertical. Business 2.0. Retrieved from the World Wide Web: http://www.business2.com

Stefanov, K. (1999). The interchain: Interorganizational systems. Working paper, Sofia University.

Tapscott, D., & Caston, A. (1993). *Paradigm shift: The new promise of information technology.* New York: McGraw-Hill.

Wisemann, C., & Macmillan, I. C. (1984). Creating competitive weapons from information systems. *Journal of Business Strategy.*

Section II:

Technology Infrastructure

Chapter IV

Information Technology Infrastructure for Inter-Organizational Systems

Sean B. Eom
Southeast Missouri State University, USA

Choong Kwon Lee
Georgia Southern University, USA

Abstract

An IOS is an information and management system that transcends organizational boundaries via electronic linkages with its trading partners. The electronic linkage is established by information and communication technologies. Extranets[1] are the core technology for building IOSs. There are a host of other technologies that serve as the infrastructure for managing IOSs. They include coordination technologies, monitoring technologies, filtering and negotiating technologies (intelligent agents), and decision-making and knowledge-management technologies. In this chapter, a brief overview of each of these technologies is presented.

Introduction

As defined earlier, an IOS is an information and management system that transcends organizational boundaries via electronic linkages with its trading partners. The electronic linkage is established by a host of information and data communication technologies. Supporting IOS activities requires the following:

- The Internet/extranets/intranets
- Mobile computing/multimedia platforms
- Coordination technologies for coordinating resources, facilities, and projects
  - Workflow management systems
- Monitoring technologies
  - Executive information systems/executive support systems
- Filtering and negotiating technologies
  - Intelligent agents
- Decision-making and knowledge management technologies
  - Groupware

Extranets

Since the invention of the first computer in the mid-1940s, the computing technology has been continuously evolved in response to the changing business and technological environments. There are several forces in the environment to which a business organization must respond (business drivers). A significant force is the globalization of businesses and markets. Global business activities have been intensified by the fundamental economics of comparative advantage and the realization that the large global market share of a firm can eventually increase the firm's profit over the long run. The globalization of business and market, in turn, triggered intensified global competition in all functional areas of business organizations, including price, advertising, quality, manufacturing, etc. To effectively cope with the global level of competition, business organizations have been under constant pressure to produce better products and services, on time, in response to changing customer demands. Consequently, business organizations have to concentrate on the several critical objectives that must be achieved to survive in the new era of global competition. They include increasing productivity, maintaining superior quality, improving responsiveness, and focusing on core business activities. In an effort to further rationalize their operations, some organizations are shifting their strategies from product innovation to scale economies through merger and acquisition, from optimizing the value chain in each firm to optimizing the value chain of the entire organization and industry (Laudon & Laudon, 2004). Furthermore, industrial organizations have begun to realize that information systems are an indispensable means that enable a firm to improve the efficiency and effectiveness of their organizational activities.

To support global business activities, an increasing number of companies built enterprise networks through interconnecting local area networks (LANs) and wide area networks (WANs). This network links the company's headquarters to the branch offices and subsidiaries around the globe and encompasses a range of platforms, operating systems, protocols, and network architectures. Global networking of business organizations and the networked environment are partly attributed to several technology drivers, such as expanded public network infrastructure, development of the Internet and World Wide Web technologies, rapid development of client/server computing technology, and evolution of relational database technology.

Definitions

An extranet is a Web-based private network that interconnects a company's network to the networks of business partners. The extranet is an extended corporate intranet using the Internet technology operating over the Internet for a wide range of applications in the areas of sales, marketing, manufacturing, online publishing, design and development of new product, communications via videoconferencing and real-time voice conversations, business transactions, decision making, etc. The term "business-to-business networks" is often used interchangeably with extranets.

The term "extranet" has been used and defined in many different ways. For example:

An extranet is an intranet that is open to selective access by outside parties. (Baker, 1997, p. xi)

An extranet is an intranet that allows controlled access by authenticated outside parties. Typically an extranet will link the intranets of distributed organizations for the purpose of conducting business. This secure electronic consortium usually consists of an enterprise and its key trading partners, customers, dealers, distributors, supplies, and contractors. (Bayles, 1998, p. 3)

In its basic form, an extranet is the interconnection of the two previously separate LANs or WANs with origins from different business entities. (Maier, 2000, p. 33)

The objective of borderless Internet/intranet networking is to integrate internal corporate networks with the Internet, in a seamless manner, creating a new network facility, known as an extranet. ...many user organizations with mature intranets are connected to the Internet and operated the two networks as if the components were a single network. (Sharp, 1998, p. 31)

The first definition by Baker provides a partial picture of a broad definition of extranets given by Bayles, Sharp, and Maiers. In this chapter, an extranet is defined as a Web-based WAN that links a company's employees, suppliers, customers, and other business partners in a secure, electronic online environment for the purpose of conducting business (see Figures 1 to 3). An extranet is created if more than two companies open parts of their intranets to each other. The extranet is an extended corporate intranet using Internet technology operating over the Internet for a wide rage of applications in the areas of sales, marketing, manufacturing, online publishing, design and development of new product, communications via videoconferencing and real-time voice conversations, business transactions, decision making, etc. Secured extranets allow trading partners to gain limited (controlled) access to companies' intranets, thereby increasing profitability and competitive advantage through managing important organizational activities in the most timely and cost effective manner.

An extranet is created if more than two companies open parts of their intranets to each other and create an inter-intra-net to improve coordination with trading partners in virtually all functional areas of sales, marketing, manufacturing, human resources, information systems, etc. The trading partners include a client that represents a substantial portion of the company's revenue, companies working on a joint development project, distributors, contractors, suppliers of raw materials, vendors, dealers, consultants, etc. A secured extranet is part of a company's intranet. It allows trading partners, including customers, to gain limited (controlled) access or provides a collaborative network linking trading partners to increase profitability and competitive advantages through managing important organizational activities in the most timely and cost-effective manner (Riggins & Rhee, 1998).

Table 1: Two types of extranets

Type	Intronet	Supranet
Sponsorship	Owner sponsored	Consortium sponsored
Gateway access	Proprietary network	Semiopen network
Relationships	One-to-many	Many-to-many
Service offered	Information product	Communication/decision tools
Primary justification	Provide unique resources	Efficiency/timeliness
Primary beneficiary	Initiator with information	All consortium members
Long-term objective	Lock-in partner	Consortium competitiveness
Nature of application	Pull application	Push application
Example	Federal Express' Tracking Systems	Automotive Network eXchange (ANX)

Source: Adapted from Riggins and Rhee (1998, p. 92).

Classification

The extranets can be classified as either intronets or supranets. The widely known examples of each are shown in Table 1. Three automakers (Chrysler, General Motors, and Ford) are cooperating on an industry-wide extranet called the Automotive Network Exchange (ANX) that links them with 100 registered trading partners and more than 3500 sponsored trading partners. The industrial extranet will continue to grow. The ANX network is expected to connect the 1000 Tier 1 suppliers, 9000 Tier 2 and 3 suppliers, and 40,000 others who communicate with automakers in the near future (Liebrecht, 1999). The health-care industry has joined and started to use the ANX. Since the auto industry spends billions of dollars every year to provide health insurance for its employees, it seemed like a logical step for the auto industry to bring insurance companies and hospitals onto the ANX network (Bushaus, 2000).

Extranets in Historical Context

In the late 1980s, many organizations began to link their PCs and other computing devices that were dispersed over a relatively confined area (e.g., a building, a building complex, a university campus, etc.) to create a LAN and the private branch exchange (PBX). The next step of networking is the creation of WANs that connect two or more LANs, which are dispersed over much longer distances (e.g., among many cities, states, and countries). WANs often include enterprise networks, a network of all LANs of a single organization in a country or more than a country (global networks). Multiple computers are being linked to work together over a network to accomplish a common task via sharing processing activities.

Client/Server Computing

The fundamental underlying principle of internetworking computers is sharing computing resources, processing activities, and information. This is also the objective of client/server computing. Client/server computing has often been described as "the perpetual revolution," "a revolution that is forever altering how we think of and build information systems," and "a deep paradigmatic shift in the computer and information system industry." The monolithic mainframe applications that had dominated the 1970s and 1980s are replaced with applications split across client and server lines (Orfali, Harkey, & Edwards, 1996; Renaud, 1996). The essence of the client/server system is that two separate logical entities (clients and servers) work together over a network to accomplish a task. In doing so, it exploits the full computing power of each. Strong economics underlie client/ server computing, including relative computational costs advantages, large capital cost-saving opportunities, reduced system development costs, and improvements in productivity by moving processing power closer to the end user. [Refer to Chapter 5 of Renaud (1996) for further discussion of this topic.] In addition to cost savings, the client/server system increases the productivity of both end-users and system developers; enhances the scalability and flexibility of network and information systems (adding new components and replacing or upgrading existing ones can be done easily); and increases resource utilization, interoperability, and portability of the network and information systems. Most of these benefits are attributable to an open architecture employed by the client/ server architecture, meaning that specifications of the architecture are made public by the designers, and therefore, system enhancements and integration of other software and hardware are relatively easier than with proprietary systems (Harris, 2003).

Intranets

The corporate LANs and WANs have become inseparable parts of the Internet. The emergence of the Internet has transformed the computer and information industry and the way people use computers. Using Internet technology, business organizations have implemented private (closed), proprietary networks for organizational members' use within a corporation to distribute documents (e.g., newsletters, memos, employee handbooks, phone directories, etc.) and software, to provide access to databases, etc. The intranet usually employs applications associated with the Internet, such as Web pages, Web browsers, FTP sites, e-mail, newsgroups, mailing lists, etc. The intranet can also provide functions and services to support collaborative activities of work groups, such as information sharing, group scheduling, computer conferencing, etc. The software that provides those functions and services is known as groupware. The intranet offers an inexpensive way for communicating, disseminating information, and carrying out cooperative activities such as designing products, writing project reports, conducting electronic conferencing, making group decisions, etc., within an organization.

Peer-to-Peer (P2P) computing

P2P computing is different from client/server computing, even though both are considered distributed computing. In client/server computing, clients must inherently rely on their servers to receive services. In P2P computing, nodes can have total autonomy from their servers. Based on the degree of autonomy of clients, P2P computing is divided into two types: pure P2P and hybrid P2P. Nodes under pure P2P architecture (e.g., Limewire) search distributed catalogs in order to locate another client that holds information or files, whereas nodes under hybrid P2P architecture (e.g., Napster) have centralized servers that hold a catalog of IP addresses. Because P2P computing allows end users to directly communicate to each other, companies can utilize the full capacity of desktop computers and thereby reduce the cost of computer systems, including central servers and bandwidth. Intel eliminated the need to buy new mainframes by connecting more than 10,000 computers that are globally distributed to develop its new chip (McDougall, 2000).

The Architecture of Public Network Extranets

There are three different types of extranets: private, public network, and virtual private network (VPN) extranets. Private extranets link the intranets of more than two companies using a private, leased line. The most significant advantage of this type of network is its high security level. On the other hand, the high cost of private phone lines is a significant drawback. Three essential objectives of any information system are communication, information, and decision making. Due to the high cost of private phone lines, public network extranets and VPN extranets seem to be popular choices for many organizations.

The business-to-business network (B2B) is built on the client/server architecture. Understanding the architecture of extranets requires some foundational concepts, including the technology of client/server systems and architectures.

The client/server computing system consists of clients, servers, and networks. The client hardware is a complete, stand-alone personal computer (PC). The user requests services via client software that formulates the user's requests and passes them to the network software, which in turn sends the requests to the server and receives the results from the server and passes the results back to the client software. The server hardware component can be any type of computer (a PC, a minicomputer, a mainframe computer). The server software contains database management software, operating systems, and part of the network management software.

Extranets are designed in many different ways using many different hardware, software, and network technologies. According to Bort and Felix (1997), there are three models of public network extranets that are based on the use of a public network including the Internet to link an organization's intranet to its trading partners:

(1)   The secured intranet access model (Figure 1)
(2)   The specialized application model (Figure 2)
(3)   The electronic commerce model (Figure 3)

The secured intranet access model allows the business partner to log directly onto a company's intranet to access most of it. The highest level of network security planning is necessary to implement this network architecture, as is a high level of trust in the partners. The specialized application model allows the partners to gain limited access to the intranet from the extranet site. A wide

Figure 1: The secured intranet access model

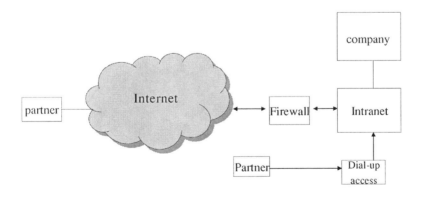

Source: Bort and Felix (1997, p. 10).

Figure 2: The specialized application model

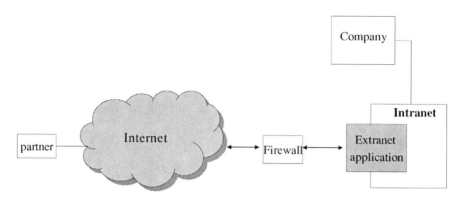

Source: Bort and Felix (1997, p. 11).

Figure 3: The e-commerce model

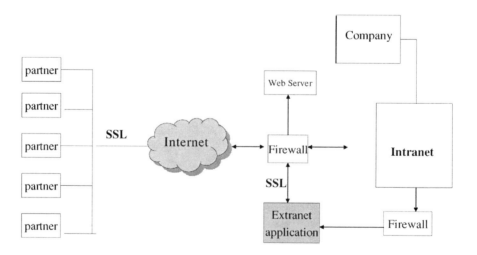

Source: Bort and Felix (1997, p. 11).

variety of extranet applications, both packaged and custom developed, is available over an extranet, including order processing, database access, customer service and support, e-mail, and other communication tools. The electronic commerce model is well-suited to deal with a large number of partners (more than several hundreds of companies) using e-commerce security and transaction-processing techniques.

Architecture/components of virtual private network extranets

A VPN extranet is a type of extranet that overcomes the drawbacks of a private extranet (high costs) and achieves confidentiality of information using encryption technology. This way, messages are safe from being intercepted and understood by unauthorized users, as if the nodes were connected by private lines. According to Brown (Brown, 1999, p. 5), a VPN:

(1)   Is a set of nodes on a public network on a short-term nonpermanent basis among cooperating companies

(2)   Utilizes an encrypted or encapsulated communication process that transfers data from one point to another point securely; the security of that data is assured by robust encryption technology, and the data that flows passes through open, unsecured, routed networks

(3)   Is a technology that simulates a private network

A VPN uses encryption and IP tunneling to provide secure point-to-point network connections across the public Internet. Some VPNs are set up with a network architecture similar to an extranet using a leased line in a DMZ-type arrangement. Generally, there is an addition of a VPN gateway in front of the firewall. A gateway is a device that connects two networks with different protocols. A gateway converts the data from a sending network to a format compatible with the protocols used by a receiving network. A VPN can be built with or without the firewall. This is illustrated in Figure 4 using the PERMIT enterprise product solution of TimeSterp Corporation, a leading provider of secure VPN solutions for corporate intranets, extranets, and Internet remote access. Refer to Chapters 8 and 9 of Brown (1999) for further discussions of different network configurations, architectures, and security for VPNs as well as leading vendors of VPN products.

Applications of VPN technology include (1) secure extranet connectivity with business partners (channel AD), (2) secure intranet connectivity with branch

Figure 4: The architecture of a virtual private network extranet

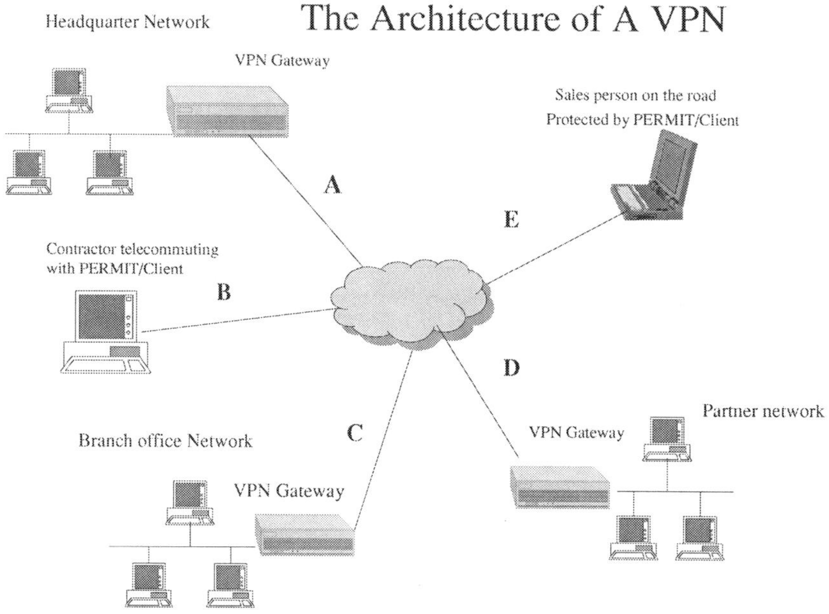

office (channel AC), and (3) secure Internet remote LAN access. A VPN gives telecommuters and mobile workers a way to get back to a corporate network over the Internet or a service provider's backbone. A user dials into a service provider's point of presence, establishes a tunnel (channel AB) back to head-quarters over that provider's network or the Internet, and authenticates him- or herself to gain access to the corporate network.

Groupware/Group Support Systems

The term "GSS" first appeared in 1989 (Nunamaker et al., 1989). Since then, the term GSS has become the umbrella term that includes a wide variety of terms designed to support group activities. Information systems to support group activities have been studied under many different names, such as group decision support systems (GDSS), computer-supported cooperative work (CSCW), electronic meeting systems (EMS), collaboration support systems (CSS), group support systems (GSS), computer-supported collaborative work, computer-mediated communication systems, and group negotiation support systems. The change of the name implies the expanding roles of information technologies and provides a comprehensive set of tools for decision making, communications, meetings, information sharing, etc.

More groupware will be inextricably tied to Internet technology. Many groupware products are integrating more Internet protocols. As of 1999, more than 75 Web groupware products were available (Wheeler, Dennis, & Press, 1999). Many well-known companies such as Lotus, Microsoft, and Novell are developers of Web-based groupware. Furthermore, vendors such as Instinctive Technology Inc., Zap Business Communications Systems Inc., Eastman Software Inc., and even Lotus deliver the thin-client groupware features they need without the expense, complexity, or overhead of fat clients (Gaskin, 2000). Gaskin provided us with several examples of companies that use a new generation of thin-client Web groupware products to communicate with their customers, employees, and virtual team members around the globe. The following cases of Haworth Furniture and True North Communications are condensed versions taken from Gaskin (2000).

Haworth Furniture sells more than $1.5 billion per year worth of furniture products in more than 50 countries with 600 salespeople worldwide. Until they found a solution, they were stuck with e-mail, telephone, voicemail, and faxes. After a comprehensive evaluation of several groupware options, Haworth chose Instinctive's eRoom to support customers, dealers, installers, and even potential customers who needed access to the information suitable to support field sales operations across every time zone, usually from laptops on the road. One of the primary differences between traditional groupware and eRooms is the focus on the team, especially teams from multiple organizations such as suppliers and partners, customers, and vendors.

Haworth hosts eRoom internally, supporting more than 600 worldwide users on a single server. Called the Global Account Information Network, the system uses more than 300 customer "eRooms," or collaborative workspaces, that include documents, issues, tasks, and complete discussion lists. Team leaders add or delete members from their own eRooms, making administration simple.

The company sends product announcements, holds sales meetings, and makes presentations, all through eRooms. Employees inside as well as outside the sales department regularly join eRooms to service particular customer needs, such as engineers helping design installations. Haworth field employees reach their eRooms through the Internet or the corporate VPN.

The case of True North Communications illustrates the use of Groupware using mobile technologies. Widespread availability of Internet-enabled wireless devices creates a new breed of e-business conducted in a wireless environment (mobile business).

True North Communications is an advertising conglomerate with 498 offices around the world and is growing rapidly by acquisition. They used e-mail but had no worldwide collaboration system in place. They were working with a nameless vendor and came close to making a system. That is when True North turned to

Ucone from Zap: Hosted by Linux running on a Cobalt Networks Inc. RaQ3 server, Zap installed their system in less than 2 days and turned it over to the company. True North then customized their needs and started the rollout. Each office creates and manages its own "toolbox" inside the Zap Ucone software. The toolboxes contain the information for everyone to share.

The system is being used by more than 250 people, scattered throughout the nearly 500 offices around the world. New application opportunities popped up immediately. More than a dozen True North employees had brand-new Palm VII's and wanted to use them to access the system. Engineers from Zap translated Ucone's XML output to the brand-new Wireless Access Protocol (WAP). Since Zap uses a standard WAP server for connections, wireless Web telephones and other devices should work when connected. Zap had to write a small Palm Query Application, but nothing changed on the server side. The PQA eliminates the need to type in a specific URL from the organizer.

Workflow Systems

An important information technology for IOSs is a workflow system that needs to be embedded into streamlined, virtual value chains that transcend organizational boundaries. As organizations automate and interconnect their business processes, workflow capabilities are being embedded into most major enterprise application integrations (Margulius, 2002). Workflow systems are business process automation systems that track process-related information and the status of each activity of the business process. They are part of enterprise application integration solutions and business process management, including business activity monitoring and business process automation. The major activity includes job routing and monitoring, document imaging, document managing, supply chain optimization, and control of works. Workflow applications can be classified into collaborative, production, and administrative workflow systems. An IOS focuses on primarily collaborative workflow systems.

Traditional workflow systems were built on departmental server-based architectures. Consequently, they were departmental and forms driven. Now, as workflow engines migrate from departmental server-based architectures to more powerful enterprise application integration (EAI) messaging-based architectures, islands of workflow are starting to get connected throughout the enterprise. Now workflow functionality increasingly becomes part of these broader platforms such as enterprise application integration solutions and business process management.

One obstacle for embedding workflow systems into IOSs is the development of interoperability standards for workflow systems. According to *Margulius* (2002), efforts to develop such interoperability standards as the Workflow

Management Coalition have largely failed, although widely accepted terminology (join, router, tasks, etc.) for workflow components emerged. Several organizations were involved in making efforts toward workflow management standards, such as OMG's jointFlow specification, Simple Workflow Access Protocol (SWAP), and the Workflow Management Coalition (WfMC)'s workflow reference model. Of these efforts, the workflow reference model from the WfMC, even though it only provides an abstract-level architecture, has widely been adopted and used (Yang, 2003). Figure 5 illustrates the workflow reference model from the WfMC (Coalition, 1995). Nevertheless, there has been continuing efforts by big software vendors such as IBM and Microsoft to develop flow interoperability standards including Web Services Flow Language (WSFL) to address the intermingling of machine (straight-through) and human (long-running) processes.

The Kepner-Tregoe Survey (2000) tells us that information for decision making comes from sources such as e-mails, the Internet, and corporate intranets (Kepner-Tregoe, 2000). The coupling of business processes of telecom partners resulted in shared workflow processes through collaborative telecommunication services (van der Aalst, 2000). Likewise, not only does the Internet provide us with vast amounts of information, but it also enables us to link the whole world together in real time. There are many other technologies available to support data

Figure 5: Workflow reference model diagram

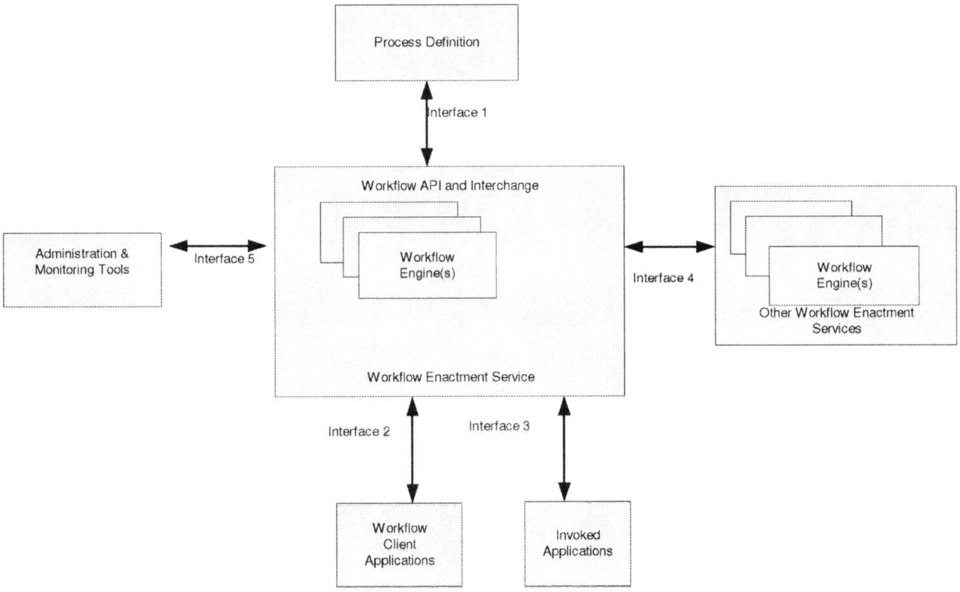

Source: http://www.wfmc.org/standards/model.htm

interchange among different standards of technologies. Van der Aalst and Kumar (2003), for example, showed how eXchangeable Routing Language (XRL) using eXtensible Markup Language (XML) can be used to exchange business data electronically.

In categorizing virtual enterprises utilizing interorganizational workflows, Tagg (2001) took into account business needs and natural patterns of cooperative business activity and provided a number of examples, such as formal joint ventures to share risk and skills, informal supply chain with or without dominant player, and end clients with preferred suppliers.

Managers often use information that they capture on inventory, production, or logistics to help monitor or control those processes. For example, GE has used its procurement marketplace Trading Process Network (TPN) in the process of identifying suppliers, preparing a request for a bid, negotiating prices, and making a contract to a supplier. Electronically linked producers, wholesalers, retailers, and consumers will be able to lower their costs by reducing intermediary transactions and unneeded coordination. Even though information technology is now the preferred technology for conducting business transactions and coordi- nating the business processes, Zhao (2002) pointed out that there are some barriers that have to be overcome by the implementers of inter-organizational workflow management systems:

1. Autonomy of local workflow processing
2. Difference in levels of local workflow automation
3. Variation in workflow control policy
4. Confidentiality preventing complete view of workflow
5. Low interoperability due to heterogeneity in hardware, software, and modeling in multiple organizations
6. Lack of cross-company access to workflow resources (agents, tools, and information)
7. Adaptable workflow processes

The following case of the company AFLAC, taken from Gaskin (2000), shows that Web groupware and workflow systems are being integrated into parts of EAI solutions and business process management.

AFLAC, another company that is using Web groupware, started groupware a decade ago in the guise of electronic filing and document management. The company has been an Eastman Software customer for nearly a decade. The browser gives the company an extra level of flexibility. Employees can work at home, AFLAC associates can enter work items from the field, and even AFLAC payroll accounts can submit work items via the Web. The latest Eastman Software project included placing customer correspondence entered directly on the Web site into the workflow system. Customers wanted information and requested changes, and AFLAC wanted to keep the process paperless while still servicing the customer.

The company's goal is to pull the information straight from the request entered on the Web site and integrate that into the legacy mainframe system, then send the notice to the workflow system. Correspondence is routed to the appropriate person with the skill set to provide the service. All the routing is managed by a browser client, which is new for AFLAC, but welcomed.

Electronic Data Interchange (EDI)

EDI is the computer-to-computer exchange of repetitive, standardized or structured transaction data to trading partners' computers over a telecommunication network. The standard transaction documents include invoices, bills of lading, purchase orders, approval of credit, shipping notices, confirmation sent between business partners, etc. Both parties of the transaction must use the standardized forms of transaction that include the transaction date, transaction amount, sender's name, recipient's name, unit price, total number of products, etc. For EDI to be effective, users must agree on certain standards for formatting and exchanging information according to a set of recommendations for standardizing equipment and protocols used in both public access and private computer networks.

Established companies still rely on EDI to transmit and receive order requests along the supply chain. Traditional EDI uses private networks and value-added networks (VANs). VANs are subscription-fee-based, private, data-only, third-party-managed telecommunication networks. The VANs are usually confined to large trading partners due to expensive fees, including a fixed monthly subscription fee and a variable per-transaction data transmission fee. The VAN provides its subscribers with extra values, including message routing, error checking, resource management, and protocol conversion facilities for computer communicating at different speeds or using different communications protocol. Therefore, traditional EDI has not been a viable option for those companies doing business with small companies that cannot afford to pay the fee. However, the emergence of Internet-based EDI allowed many small businesses to use EDI to conduct electronic business.

Large retailers are pushing their suppliers to adopt the Internet-based EDI. For example, in August 2002, Wal-Mart, the world's biggest retailer, told its suppliers they would have to start sending and receiving electronic data over the Internet. Today, more than 98% of Wal-Mart's EDI exchanges with suppliers are done over the Internet using EDIINT AS2 (Electronic Data Interchange-Internet Integration Applicability Statement 2)(Hayes, Hulme, Kontzer, Whiting, & Colkin, 2002; Zimmerman, 2003). In addition to cost savings, Internet-based EDI provides a cheaper, faster, and more accurate method for trading partners and several functionalities such as collaboration, workflow, and sharing of point-of-sale data among trading partners. Retailers can share point-of-sale data with suppliers over the Internet—something not easily done with the traditional EDI system. Thereby, suppliers can better meet retailers' requirements with more up-to-date demand information (Greenemeier, 2001). Many vendors offer the "value-added network" EDI for sending critical data, while AS2-based Internet EDI can be used for less critical business information (Anonymous, 2003).

Mobile Commerce (m-commerce or m-business)

Mobile commerce is defined as e-commerce done in a wireless environment. Mobile commerce can be applied to both B2B and B2C business activities. While mobile commerce is interested in attracting consumers to use wireless devices to make purchases, mobile business is attracting other business organizations to visit and purchase materials, products, and services. Products and services of mobile commerce range from commodities to complex services, such as stock trading, traffic reports, and wireless games. Whereas, mobile business is also intended to utilize information technologies, including mobile devices, in order to streamline their business processes among corporations and reduce transaction costs.

After interviewing 141 companies, Caldwell and Koch (2000) reported that companies implemented mobile computing to achieve four purposes: (1) improve customer service; (2) reduce cycle time and speed decision making; (3) attract and maintain a high-quality workforce; and (4) manage organizational knowledge and exchange best practices.

Major B2B mobile commerce applications include financial applications (banking, payments, etc.), managing inventory (goods, troops, and people), wireless data management, wireless reengineering, etc. (Barshney & Vetter, 2001). M-commerce is characterized by mobility (portability) using mobile devices, broad reach, convenience, ubiquity, and other attributes. M-commerce is built on the mobile computing infrastructure of mobile networks, software, and hardware. Readers are referred to Chapter 10 of Turban and others (Turban, King, Lee, &

Viehland, 2004) for the introduction to mobile commerce, including the technologies that support m-commerce. See Balasubramanian, Peterson, and Jarvenpaa (2002) for the implications of m-commerce for markets and marketing by means of a formal conceptualization of m-commerce.

M-commerce can be characterized by mobility and broad reach. Customers, anywhere and anytime, do not have to stay in a location to be connected to corporate databases. Mercedes-Benz has utilized mobile computing to control its inventory and manage orders. Mobile computing can also be used to track the status of products and materials on delivery, and financial trading costs among business organizations will be dramatically decreased by removing intermediaries from the value chain. Along with the Internet, new technologies like C/Webtop provide collaborative working platforms that allow users to collaborate efficiently while on the move (Bergenti, Poggi, & Somacher, 2002). To keep its workforce connected, for instance, TRW is implementing the idea that any TRW employee is able to access any information at any time with 250 locations in 35 countries (Sherman, 2002).

Visa International is expanding e-payment technology through mobile phones in Thailand, following its successful debut in South Korea and Japan. More than a third of mobile Net subscribers in Japan have already used their phones to buy goods. A challenge is for telecom operators to integrate wireless network and infrastructure with banks' payment systems in order to link the same protocol and applications (Phoosuphanusorn, 2003).

Mobile devices, such as portable PCs, PDAs, and cellular phones, are among the fastest growing commodities in the world. These wireless machines are also called "thin client," which is a low-cost, centrally managed computer including CD-ROM players, diskette drives, and expansion slots. Because the Internet has the power to connect these thin clients (regardless of time and place) to corporate databases, customers and employees are now able to utilize mobile computing for the purposes of their own businesses. In addition, because these mobile devices need to display colorful information along with sound and motion pictures, multimedia platforms are important supporting tools for mobile computing.

The attributes of m-business are ubiquitous, convenient, and instant. Ubiquity can be achieved by m-business that connects computing devices that are not merely personal computers but are also very tiny devices in the environment. Devices might be invisible so that they are either mobile or embedded in almost any type of object, such as walls, cars, clothing, goods, and the like. These devices are inherently convenient so that customers and employees connected to these devices do not even realize that they are using computers.

Instant connectivity is also provided by the business owners. Personalization and localization are other important attributes of m-business. M-business servers can provide each of their customers with a customized screen, options, and price. Personalization is based on the customer's previous purchases, preferences, and personal records. Localization of products and services can be achieved by m-business using GPS. Customers are allowed to access and update their personal information through mobile devices. For example, a customer might access his or her bank account and make an electronic transfer to someone else's account. When the customer requests a service, the transaction server first checks the customer's identification and password with an authentication server. Once authenticated, bank account databases are accessed. Because the customer might no longer be in the same location that he or she first accessed the transaction server, one or more network paths should dynamically be selected to allow the customer to complete the requests made.

Filtering and Negotiating Technologies (Intelligent Agents)

Intelligent agents are software programs that work in the background to carry out specific, repetitive, and predictable tasks for an individual user or an organization. To accomplish tasks or make decisions on behalf of the user or the organization, the agent uses a built-in or learned knowledge that was obtained from the user or organization. For example, when a person specifies his or her needs, constraints, and preferences, the Internet travel agent would then find some possibilities based upon the travels that have previously been made by the person. We are now seeing many organizations use the intelligent agents as their filtering, negotiating, and coordinating technologies.

As a filtering tool for the digital library, the intelligent agent is used to retrieve information from distributed sources and filter information on contents. As a brokering tool, the intelligent agent finds information not only about products of a specific company but also about prices from another company that provides competing products. By bidding prices based on the competing prices, the intelligent agent helps bidding companies negotiate the prices and specifications of the products. Bui et al. (2002) reported on a Web-enabled hospital that connects its patients to doctors and insurance companies through the Internet. The intelligent agent was used to monitor patients' health conditions in real time, negotiate costs of treatment between different health-care providers, and verify insurance coverage of a particular medical treatment. Agent-based systems can also be used for intelligent automated coordination in managing inter- and intraorganizational business processes, including task scheduling and resource allocation (Deschner, Hofmann, & Bodendorf, 2000).

Many efforts to develop better intelligent agents are underway. For example, Kang and Han (2003) suggested a broker-based synchronous transaction algorithm that can improve the process of transaction between sellers and buyers. The intelligent agents are now being used to realize mass customization. Burgwinkel (2002) also reported on electronic negotiation and contract using XML that allowed business partners to synchronize obligations, rights, and penalties.

Jeff Bezos, the CEO of Amazon.com, mentioned, "If I have 3 million customers on the Web, I should have 3 million stores on the Web." It is possible only because intelligent agents can create a unique store for each of the Amazon customers. Turowski (2002) showed how multiple companies used intelligent agents to interchange business data and coordinate their business activities in providing services and products.

Summary and Conclusions

An IOS is an information and management system that transcends organizational boundaries via electronic linkages with its trading partners. Extranets are the core technology for building IOS. There is a host of other technologies that serve as the infrastructure for managing IOS. They include coordination technologies, monitoring technologies, filtering and negotiating technologies (intelligent agents), and decision-making and knowledge management technologies. This chapter briefly discussed each of these technologies. We examined the architecture and components of both public network extranets and VPN extranets, along with the applications of the extranet. During the late 1990s, an increasing number of companies opened part of their intranets and made information available to their business partners for facilitating business, thereby creating a dynamic wide area network that links suppliers, customers, and other business partners in a secure electronic environment. We are now witnessing the emergence of industrial networks (extended enterprises, integrated industry-wide systems) that link the enterprise systems of multiple firms in the same industry vertically (manufacturers, suppliers, and suppliers' supplier) as well as horizontally (linking competing firms in an industry).

References

Anonymous. (2003, November 13). EDI and As2 "Can live together." *Supply Management, 8,* 13.

Baker, R. H. (1997). *Extranets: The complete sourcebook.* New York: McGraw-Hill.

Balasubramanian, S., Peterson, R. A., & Jarvenpaa, S. L. (2002). Exploring the implications of m-commerce for markets and marketing. *Academy of Marketing Science Journal, 30*(4), 348–361.

Barshney, U., & Vetter, R. (2001). Recent advances in wireless networking. *IEEE Computer, 33*(6), 100–103.

Bayles, D. L. (1998). *Extranets: Building the business to business Web.* Upper Saddle River, NJ: Prentice-Hall PTR.

Bergenti, F., Poggi, A., & Somacher, M. (2002). A collaborative platform for fixed and mobile networks. *Communications of the ACM, 45*(11), 39–44.

Brown, S. (1999). *Implementing virtual private networks.* New York: McGraw-Hill.

Bui, T., Stricker, C., Crettenand, J. -C., & Scilipoti, G. (2002). Mobile computing—Software agents for distributed workflow-based organizational decision making. In F. Adam, P. Brézillon, P. Humphreys, & J. -C. Pomerol (Eds.), *Decision making and decision support in the Internet age: Proceedings of Dsiage 2002 (an IFIP Tc8/WG 8.3 Open Conference)* (pp. 364–365). Cork, Ireland: Oak Tree Press.

Burgwinkel, D. (2002). Decision support in electronic contract negotiation. In F. Adam, P. Brézillon, P. Humphreys, & J. -C. Pomerol (Eds.), *Decision making and decision support in the Internet age: Proceedings of Dsiage 2002 (an IFIP Tc8/WG 8.3 Open Conference)* (pp. 537–546). Cork, Ireland: Oak Tree Press.

Bushaus, D. (2000). Trade the ANX way. *InformationWeek, 776,* 93–97.

Coalition, W. M. (1995). *The workflow reference model, Wfmc-Tc-1003, Version 1.1.* Retrieved January 5, 2004 from the World Wide Web: http://www.aiim.org/wfmc/standards/docs/tc003v11.pdf.

Deschner, D., Hofmann, O., & Bodendorf, F. (2000). Agent-based coordination support for business processes. *INFOR, 38*(3), 283–292.

Gaskin, J. E. (2000, February 21). Enterprise Applications—Groupware gets thin—A new generation of thin-client products proves that Web groupware can scale across an enterprise network. *InternetWeek, 45.*

Greenemeier, L. (2001, November 12). Tile manufacturer turns to Internet-based EDI system. *InformationWeek, 79*.

Harris, M. (2003, May). Client/server systems: Buyer beware! *Bank News, 103,* 34–39.

Hayes, M., Hulme, G. V., Kontzer, T., Whiting, R., & Colkin, E. (2002, October 14). Top of the week: News Scan. *InformationWeek, 32*.

Kang, N., & Han, S. (2003). Agent-based e-marketplace system for more fair and efficient transaction. *Decision Support Systems, 34*(2), 157–165.

Kepner-Tregoe. (2000). *Decision making in the digital age: Challenges and responses.* Princeton, NJ: Kepner-Tregoe, Inc.

Laudon, K. C., & Laudon, J. P. (2004). *Management information systems: Managing the digital firm* (8th ed.). Upper Saddle River, NJ: Prentice Hall.

Liebrecht, D. (1999). A TCP/IP-based network for the automotive industry. *America's Network, 103*(7), 67–69.

Maier, P. Q. (2000). Ensuring extranet security and performance. *Information Systems Management,* 33–40.

Margulius, D. L. (2002, April 22). Workflow meets BPM. *InfoWorld, 24,* 64–65.

McDougall, P. (2000, August 28). The power of peer-to-peer. *InformationWeek,* 22–24.

Nunamaker, J. F., Jr., Vogel, D. R., Heminger, A., Martz, W. B., Jr., Grohowski, R., & McGoff, C. (1989). Experiences at IBM with group support systems: A field study. *Decision Support Systems, 5*(2), 183–196.

Orfali, R., Harkey, D., & Edwards, J. (1996). *The essential client/server survival guide* (2nd ed.). New York, NY: John Wiley & Sons.

Phoosuphanusorn, S. (2003, November 5). Visa to launch mobile commerce; Technology may be introduced in 2005. *Knight Ridder Tribune Business News,* p. 1.

Renaud, P. E. (1996). *Introduction to client/server systems: A practical guide for systems professionals* (2nd ed.). New York: John Wiley & Sons.

Riggins, F. J., & Rhee, H. -S. (1998). Towards a unified view of electronic commerce. *Communications of the ACM, 41*(10), 88–95.

Sharp, D. E. (1998). Extranet: Borderless Internet/intranet networking. *Information Systems Management,* 31–35.

Sherman, E. (2002, March 18). The next step forward. *Newsweek, 139,* 38B.

Tagg, R. (2001). Workflow in different styles of virtual enterprise. *Australian Computer Science Communications, 23*(6), 21–28.

Turban, E., King, D., Lee, J. K., & Viehland, D. (2004). *Electronic commerce 2004: A managerial perspective.* Upper Saddle River, NJ: Pearson Education, Inc.

Turowski, K. (2002). Agent-based e-commerce in case of mass customization. *International Journal of Production Economics, 75*(1-2), 69–81.

van der Aalst, W. (2000). Loosely coupled interorganizational workflows: Modeling and analyzing workflows crossing organizational boundaries. *Information & Management, 37*(2), 67–75.

van der Aalst, W. M. P., & Kumar, A. (2003). XML-based schema definition for support of interorganizational workflow. *Information Systems Research, 14*(1), 23–48.

Wheeler, B. C., Dennis, A. R., & Press, L. I. (1999). Groupware comes to the Internet: Charting a New World. *The DATA Base for Advances in Information Systems, 30*(3–4), 8–21.

Zimmerman, A. (2003, November 21). B-2-B—Internet 2.0: To sell goods to Wal-Mart, Get on the Net. *Wall Street Journal,* p. B.1.

Endnote

[1]   Part of this chapter, extranets, is largely based on the earlier publication, Eom, S. B. (2001). Business-to-business networks. In M. Warner (Ed.), International encyclopedia of business and management (2 ed.; pp. 589–602). London: Thomson Learning. With permission from Thomson Learning.

Chapter V

Application Service Provision:
A Working Tool for Inter-Organization Systems in the Internet Age

Matthew W. Guah
Brunel University, UK

Wendy L. Currie
University of Warwick, UK

Abstract

The Application Service Provision (ASP) business model offers a pragmatic adoption path for inter-organizations in the Internet Age. Given this pragmatic adoption path, academics are beginning to question the following: Where are enterprises adopting ASP technology first? Why are they choosing these areas? Where will they apply the evolving Web services technology next? This chapter's primary purposes are to point out a number of issues that concern management of inter-organizations of the Internet Age and to explore the impact of ASP on such organizations. It will examine the strategies that will enable inter-organizations to better manage ASP resources for competitive advantage. While the phenomenon of ASP is still in an embryonic stage, we draw from seminal works of IS pioneers like Markus, Porter, Checkland, Maslow, and others. Their intellectual contributions, plus findings from research work at Brunel University, provide a framework for discussion. By shedding light on patterns of ASP's trajectory, drivers, benefits, and risks, the chapter will help managers and academics to reflect on determining where ASP—and associated technologies—might be deployed and define a broad implementation program to exploit the potential of the ASP business model. The chapter seeks to find if Web services architectures are distinctively able to enhance the flexible coordination of business processes, which span various enterprises and rely on inter-organization information systems in the Internet Age.

Introduction

This chapter, as its objective, will communicate to its readers an understanding of how a new technology can distinctively solve real business needs. In so doing, the chapter will, at each step along the way, explicitly seek to tie the technology back to the business context. The reader is taken through the process by which Application Service Provision (ASP) affects the business issues and management concerns that arise with information systems (IS) in inter-organizations. It examines the strategies that will enable inter-organizations to better manage ASP resources for competitive advantage (Porter & Millar, 1985). ASP is defined, and the term is used in this chapter to refer to Provision and Providers interchangeably.

To deal with this complex topic, the chapter has been structured into four main sections. The chapter's introduction is immediately followed by detailed definitions of ASP. The second section presents the central theme of the historical shifts from a mainframe to a client-server, and now to an ASP strategy for Innovation Management, thereby empowering the emergence of a new type of organization—inter-organizations—with a new type of IS—an inter-organizational information system (IOIS). Inter-organization here refers to a group of organizations composed of representatives of the participating organizations who coordinate relevant activities. Planning, programming, implementation, and monitoring of activities undertaken jointly or individually by the participating organizations are carried out in consultation with the use of an IOIS. This ensures full consultation among all those involved, with the aim to ensure effective implementation without duplication. The intellectual contributions of IS pioneers (such as Checkland, Markus, Porter, etc.) serve as a framework for discussion of the ASP industry's impacts on the strategic transformation of such organizations—including regional, multinational, and global corporations—in the Internet age.

Next, in the third section, we will dive into the ASP phenomenon and discuss those engines that are driving the ASP industry. Just as the steam, electric, and gasoline engines became the driving forces behind the industrial revolution of the early 1900s, so the Internet and high-speed transmission protocols are making inter-organizations' strategic transformation a reality in the Internet Age. The Internet's ongoing change is a structural feature. The endless evolution of information systems is fueled by new opportunities and ever new technological and commercial vistas. A resulting "information processing" industry is the business sector that is providing the impetus for this revolution in innovative management, with its increasingly improving array of hardware, software, and information products and services (Dussauge, Hart, & Ramanantsoa, 1994). These technologies, in turn, are having and will continue to have profound impacts on an inter-organization's management, competitive advantage, and productivity—all processes that need to be reliably supported by IOIS.

Having set the stage by describing the changing business environment of inter-organizations, we then move to discuss the need for each inter-organization to fundamentally rethink its corporate strategy. Just as the railroad industry in the late 1800s had to change its mindset from one of buying up large land tracts and laying railroad ties to one of moving goods and people from one place to another, so inter-organizations today need to reconsider their traditional lines of business as they begin operating in the Internet Age. For ASP vendors, it is not just a question of selling a product, but of selling a solution to a customer's problem. This is where the lines between delivering the services and between traditional versus emerging markets are blurring and changing. The overwhelming technical and business advantages presented by the ASP business model will have significant repercussions over time on the entire IS ecosystem. Many IS services companies have recognized the opportunities and threats presented by ASP and are beginning to proactively redefine their business strategies. The dilemma for the IS service provider is how to establish the best ASP market position without severely impeding the company's current business progress and developments. The chapter examines the increasing use of acquisitions, mergers, and other forms of joint ventures, but retains its distinctive emphasis on the use of such strategies by inter-organizations operating in an ASP industry. It shows there are few relevant issues and concerns challenging the maturation of the ASP concept. It is probably not coincidental that just as the Internet is beginning to offer a revolution in the free expression and dissemination of ideas, a new mood of creeping commercialization—expressed through the concept of intellectual property rights—is also starting to gain momentum. Is this where danger lies for inter-organizational information systems (IOISs)? The chapter also introduces a human factor into the discussion. It endeavours to point out that there are both risks and opportunities for every organization in the Internet Age.

Finally, the chapter examines the problem of redefining success in the business environment of inter-organizations. Central to this discussion is the idea of adding value at each stage of the IOIS to meet the very high demands for indispensable communication, monitoring, filtering, coordinating, and decision making. Web services are shown to represent a significantly new phase in the evolution of software development which is unsurprisingly attracting a great deal of media and industry hype. The qualitative dimension is as important in an ASP industry as the quantitative dimension. Quality control must be built into the front end of the service delivery cycle, not viewed as a last-minute check to be done just before contracts are reviewed (Guah & Currie, 2003). Much of this discussion implicitly recognizes that doing business in the Internet Age forces suppliers, producers, and consumers into far closer proximity with one another than is the case in an industrial economy.

ASP Definitions

The official body of authority, ASP Industry Consortium, defines ASP as a third-party service firm which deploys, manages, and remotely hosts software applications through centrally located services in a rental or lease agreement (ASP Consortium, 2001). Such application deliveries are done to multiple entities from data centers across a wide area network as a service rather than a product, priced according to a license fee and maintenance contract set by the vendor. This model enables ASPs to serve their customers irrespective of geographical, cultural, organizational, and technical constraints, thereby adding value of location. The apparent complexity of the ASP model led to a taxonomy including Enterprise ASP, Vertical ASP, Pure-play ASP, Horizontal ASP, and ASP Enabler (Currie & Seltsikas, 2001). Evaluation of different ASP business models has resulted into four broad categories of delivery, integration, management and operations, and enablement.

When examined closely, it can be seen that the theory relating to ASP is grounded in theories from other disciplines. This is a view shared by many theories (Chatterjee, Grewal, & Sambamurthy, 2002; Currie & Seltsikas, 2001; Hagel & Brown, 2001). From the definitions of ASP provided below (see Table 1), it is evident that, first, ASP is an IT-enabled change, a different and recent form of organizational change and evidence of the information systems area. Second, it has foundations in the organizational behavior and analysis area (Currie & Willcocks, 1998). Third, evidence of theories regarding project management is also apparent (Dussauge, Hart, & Ramanantsoa, 1994). Fourth,

Table 1: Various definitions of ASP found in the literature

Definitions	Authors
An ASP is a third-party service firm that deploys, manages, and remotely hosts software applications through centrally located services in a rental or lease agreement.	ASP Industry Consortium, 2000
An ASP facilitates a remote, centrally managed "rent-an-application" service for the client.	Cherry Tree & Co., 2000
An ASP is any company that offers specific business applications on a subscription or transaction basis via the Internet or other networked arrangements.	Majority of ITAA Survey respondents; ITAA, 2001
An ASP is any company that delivers and manages applications and computer services to subscribers/clients remotely via the Internet or a private network.	ITAA and ASP Industry Consortium agreed consolidated definition; ITAA, 2001
ASPs represents the first wave to move beyond "the firewall"—key component of existing enterprise architectures—they take traditional enterprise applications like supply-chain management and human resource management and move them outside the firewall in an effort to serve small and medium-size enterprises.	Hagel and Brown, 2001
The concept of delivering business applications as a service, or "apps on tap," used to be called application service provision (ASP).	Kern, Lacity, and Willcocks, 2002
ASP Model (used interchangeably with "software as a service") provides application software via the Internet, through dedicated network or through wireless, through an approach of one-to-many services, usually with standardized offerings, to numerous clients or through customizing offerings to a group of clients in particular markets, such as has already been provided to government and the financial sectors.	Kakabadse and Kakabadse, 2002
An Internet-based company focused on delivering enterprise applications to small and medium-sized enterprises, in a more cost-effective way.	Hagel, 2002
ASPs are firms that manage and deliver application capabilities to multiple entities from data centers across a wide area network.	Currie, 2003

organizational change, which has been identified as rapid change, is also described in the definitions (Kern, Lacity, & Willcocks, 2002).

Table 1 shows a variety of definitions of ASP in common use. When compared, there is a reasonable degree of consistency that generally includes a description of how ASPs are made up from activities and tasks. Discussion about the connectedness of activities and tasks through being logically related, structured, and combined, also features prominently in the literature (Davenport & Short, 1990).

What does this mean? An ASP is really just processing software on the Net. An outside provider in lieu of being on your local network processes an application like a database that stores records of e-mail. A business does not have to worry about maintaining a server full of information. It seems expedient when one considers that an inter-organization has to spend IT resources maintaining servers, not forgetting the agony when the system goes down or an upgrade is needed.

An ASP often charges a fixed fee to manage your network and applications. Considering that the network management takes place at the ASP location, you do not have to operate your own server—saving such costs. Instead, your computers are connected to the ASP's server through an open connection. The hope is that the costs of such connections should really begin to fall soon. If that happens, this way of working will provide an attractive alternative to increasingly expensive network management. Moreover, you will know in advance what your software and management are going to cost, since you are being charged a fixed fee.

A typical ASP has to endure Government audits, provide multiple servers (redundancy), four-way (4-T3) replication, backup power systems, and 24 hour support, 7 days a week. Instead of spending big dollars on licensing and software, small and medium-size firms can afford to be as powerful as their larger competitors by subscribing to an inexpensive monthly ASP service that allows them to be virtually unlimited in their capacities to store information, thereby leveling the playing field.

With big software suppliers—including IBM and Microsoft—beginning to show their commitment to ASP technology and actually proclaiming to their customers that by the year 2004 most software required to perform business will be supported by ASPs, businesses should begin to look into this emotive revolution, driven by the ability to access critical information from any browser location and eventually from any mobile phone or handheld device (Hondo, Nagaratnam, & Nadalin, 2002; Wilkes, 2002). That reflects the type of ASP defined by 15% of IT decision makers below.

Figure 1: Preferred ASP definition

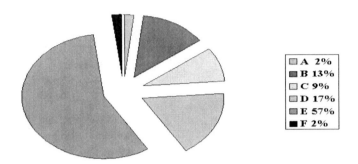

☐ A	2%
■ B	13%
☐ C	9%
☐ D	17%
▨ E	57%
■ F	2%

Source: ITAA.

A recent survey by the ITAA involving mostly IT decision makers within U.S. federal agencies provided the following understanding for what an ASP is (ITAA, 2001).

Please select the answer that best fits your definition of an ASP:

A.   Any company that leases hardware and/or software.

B.   Any company that provides outsourcing/hosting of hardware and/or software.

C.   Any company that provides subscription services and/or content via the Internet.

D.   Any "for-profit" company that provides aggregated information technology resources to subscribers/clients remotely via the Internet or other networked arrangement.

E.   Any company that offers specific business applications on a subscription and/or transaction basis via the Internet or other networked arrangement.

F.   Other, please specify: _____.

Questions

It is hoped that in this chapter, readers will be provided with answers to the following pertinent questions. Based on research work at the Centre for Strategic Information Systems (CSIS), the belief is that the ASP concept is the dawning of a new computing era. The most pronounced change would initially occur among inter-organizations searching for IS alternatives, with a more gradual acceptance among larger enterprises (Guah & Currie, 2003). What would be the most likely features of such brand-new technology? Of course, the assumption is the continuing global spread of inexpensive and reliable infrastructure, as well as the continuing availability of high transmission speeds. Will the emergent archipelago of reliable and immensely useful networked edifices of clarity, logic, and ingenuity, operate side by side with an ever-expanding network of digital slums, that is, systems which will continue to observe the tradition of inexpensive, easy to construct but dump and chaotic technology? Could ASP—driven by the needs of inter-organizations—create the means for automatic recognition and analyses of vast arrays of nuggets of individually addressable, networked data and commentaries? Will IOISs—as an Internet revolution—continue to threaten those who wish, for whatever purpose, to control information?

Research

A research process within large organizations traditionally consists of selecting possible data sources, data collection and data analysis thereby offering the potential for information overload (Roszak, 1994; Shenk, 1997). For the purpose of this research, the choice of which sources to use, which elements to collect, and which elements to analyze was informed by the methodological principles underlying our research. The research takes place within an interpretive tradition (Klein & Myers, 1999), thereby not accepting that there is a single objective reality that all participants are working toward (Walsham, 1993). The research objectives are threefold. First, they consider the prospect of an evolution in the service industry today, which is critical for improving services through the use of IS. Second, it considers how a remote delivery model using ASPs may be applied to horizontal and vertical sectors. Third, it discusses some of the applications that are currently deployed by large ASP vendors, along with others that may be targeted to specific areas, such as health care, airline, and financial industries. The authors took note that organizations pursuing a total outsourcing approach would encounter different problems from those adopting a less ambitious approach. By developing a typology that links scale of IT sourcing with customer interdependency, the results of the extensive fieldwork confirmed that there were distinctive types of IT sourcing decisions pursued by the various inter-organizations.

The overall aim of the research study is to develop a risk assessment framework for evaluating the deployment, hosting, and integration of Web-enabled software applications by ASPs. This framework is intended for businesses that do not adopt formal project selection and management methods and tools for evaluating different vendor offerings. Initial research into the emerging ASP industry was exploratory, and not intended to test or validate a particular theory (Yin, 1994). Field research was conducted in Silicon Valley and Europe to identify key questions for further research (Currie & Seltsikas, 2001). A qualitative research methodology was used, as this would elicit rich data and information on the range of Web-enabled software application from ASPs. At the end of the 1990s, academic and practitioner literature was predicting the following (Bender-Samuel, 1999; Currie & Willcocks, 1998; Subramani & Walden, 1999):

1.   Application outsourcing would become a global phenomenon among businesses, providing new opportunities for the IT industry

2.   The ASP model would utilize a mix of capabilities and skills from telecommunications, Internet Service Vendors, networking, and co-locator firms

3.   Application outsourcing would require new project management methods and tools different from those used in traditional outsourcing.

The researchers considered it important to carry out a scoping study of the emerging ASP market in order to explore the themes above. Key questions, mentioned in the first section of this chapter, were demarcated. To answer these questions, a qualitative methodology was used to elicit rich data from respondents on the supply side and the demand side of application outsourcing. The focus on vendors and customers was deemed essential, particularly as vendor hype was distorting the true picture of how the ASP model was being perceived in the service industry. In this context, field research was appropriate, because it would investigate the experiences and opinions of actors directly involved in defining and adopting the ASP model (Avison & Fitzgerald, 2003; Yin, 1994).

This study explores the business benefits and, to an extent, disincentives, of ASP to the customer in the dynamic and changing IS delivery environment of the Internet Age. Related work has found that, although IT outsourcing is often treated as a panacea to enable organizations to reduce costs and gain access to new staff and skills, many outsourcing deals fail to deliver expected benefits (Currie & Willcocks, 1998).

Prior to conducting the fieldwork, ASP adoption data were collected from various sources, including practitioner conferences (IDC, Gartner group, ASP Industry Consortium, Internet World, and from the trade press and company Web sites). Secondary sources served to build a data bank of market intelligence on a variety of ASP offerings. The use of multiple sources in data collection helps to scope a research study and encourage convergent lines of enquiry. Yet, caution is required in using vendor literature, because it tends to create an overoptimistic picture about the advantages of the ASP model, while underplaying the pitfalls (Currie, 2003). Comparing secondary sources with the results of fieldwork, however, is a useful exercise in assessing the validity of data. The tangible outcome of the research is twofold. First, short case studies were developed from the visits to each firm, which record their different character-istics. Second, the data obtained from field visits and secondary sources are used to develop a knowledge-based risk assessment framework to enable businesses to evaluate the benefits and risks of Web-enabled software applications, from both supply-side and demand-side perspectives.

Historical Shifts in IS

Forty years ago, the world's first computer-controlled communications network used in industry began operations at Westinghouse Electric, serving almost 300 U.S. locations (British Computer Society, 2003). A new Univac 490 computer took over the automatic routing of Teletype messages. The computer read the message destination in certain characters at the beginning. If the lines to a location were already in use, the computer stored the message until a line was free. Ten years later, an organization for Economic Cooperation and Develop-ment report caused some furor in Europe by making a strong case for separating post (mail) from telecommunications (British Computer Society, 2003). The strongest lobbies were on the postal side, while the greatest need for investment and the greatest potential payoff lay in telecommunications. Another 10 years later, data transmission was identified as a major growth area for the future, thus

Figure 2: Four decades of momentous shifts in IS strategy

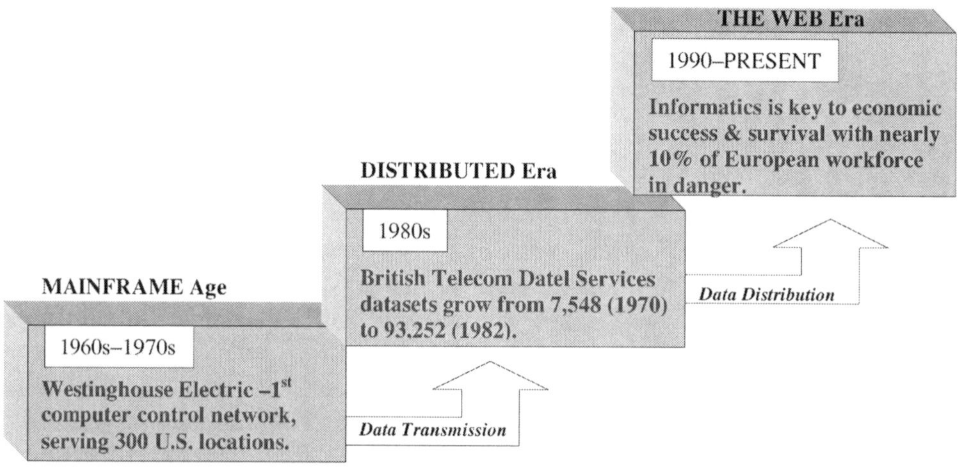

prompting the data communications industry to achieve dramatic growth through the 1970s.

In the 1980s the spread of PCs and networks revolutionized the IT industry. IT managers gained more boardroom influence, but their influence was still limited (Little, 1999). Many IT heads were known as data processing mangers and reported to the finance director. Their role was to provide IT infrastructure and manager systems and suppliers. Even more dramatic changes came 10 years later, when informatics began to prove to be a key factor for economic success and survival. In the early days of business computing, IT was viewed by business executives as an automation tool and a way to cut costs. IT managers, wandering between large mainframe-packed rooms, advised business managers on how to carry out tasks. IT bosses occupied a development and support role with little room for shaping company strategy.

The Web Era: 1990s–Present

During this period, a long era of corporate growth coincided with the longest bull market in history, culminating in the "dot-com" boom and subsequent bust. Throughout this era, computing moved out from the data center with the proliferation of PCs and became part of the infrastructure of almost all organizations (see Figure 2). The central control over IT spending slipped, and a cavalier attitude prevailed.

The whole of the dot-com boom embraced a mania to build Web sites and provide external browser-based interfaces to corporate IT applications, so that corporate software and data could be made available over the Web to customers, partners, and agents (Howcroft, 2001). Among this, there were, of course, many overzealous business initiatives that failed. The demise of many dot-com companies demonstrated that the return on investment was slim or nothing at all—although in many cases it was venture capitalists, investment companies, and private investors that took the hit. Learning from that period, central control of IT spending is being restored, and the IT department may now grow in importance if it can deliver value (Hagel, 2002; Howcroft, 2001; Subramani & Walden, 1999). However, the benefits that wise investment in IT can deliver have not vanished. Technology marches on and continues to create opportunities. Ideas being sought by senior executives, from IT departments, are those that offer quick returns at low risk (see Figure 3). Return on investment (ROI) is the driving dynamic, and the faster it can be delivered the better. At the beginning of the 21st century, the future does not look bright (see Figure 1). Most of the main companies are facing the consequences of unrealistic expectations and feeling the fragility of the field in times of semi or real recession. In some informatics societies in Europe, up to 10% of members have lost their jobs or are in danger of losing them if they do not adapt their skills to the new requirements of the market (Currie & Seltsikas, 2001).

ASP Industry Drivers

What Services Does an ASP Provide?

Currie (2003) reported substantial evidence for the reality of the ASP industry in the recent past and the transitional phase that some organizations have moved through in progressing to the ASP technology. The use of the ASP business model is facilitating the emergence of an intelligent informatics application, which can channel the flood of business information reaching customers and partners in various types of businesses. An ASP offers access to various types of applications—and the infrastructure and hardware to support them—on a subscription basis. An example of an essential service is wherein the ASP pays for the customer's application licenses for you. It then sets up the application at a remote site on its own hardware and offers access to the application via the Internet or through a Wide Area Network (WAN) attached to your company's Local Area Network (LAN), on a pay-as-you-use basis.

Other services an ASP can provide include system integration that facilitates existing legacy systems or new applications to interface with new IOISs and internal networks. Maintenance and support, including disaster recovery, backup, batch routines, and update management are also popular services. These services are usually adjunctive to either Help-Desk and Telephonic-Support or User access and application training. All ASPs promise their customers database security, firewalls, and remote access management as part of standard services.

ASP contracts usually define the minimum standards for the hardware supporting the application, guaranteed service levels, and response time. Fees are typically based on an estimated monthly charge, negotiated at contract inception, and adjusted at preset intervals or at the end of the contract term. The fees are composed of several costs, such as usage (e.g., number of hours or requests for access), license fees (including user and site licenses), services provided, requests for help-desk assistance, database size, backup routines, upgrade frequency, batch processing requests, data conversion frequency, etc.

What follows are a number of categories through which they can be understood:

- Infrastructure ASP: Some ASPs provide only computing power to run applications. They see themselves as successors to ISPs (Internet Server Providers). Rather than simply provide a connection to the Internet, infrastructure ASPs also host application software and make it available through browsers to their subscribers. Infrastructure ASPs do not create the software they host.

- Software ASP: Some software publishers want to give their customers a choice. The customer can license the publisher's software and install and run it on their own machines, or they can rent the software, accessing it through browsers and the Internet. Typically, software ASPs host only their own software, though sometimes they host and integrate third-party software.

- Remote-Windows: Thousands of Windows software applications exist today and are mature and reliable. A straightforward approach to offering software ASP services is to make these Windows programs accessible remotely. As far as the user is concerned, the software is running locally, but, in fact, it is running remotely, with information passing back and forth between local and remote computers via the Internet.

- Native-IP: The remote-Windows approach generally does not take full advantage of the Internet, browsers, and programming languages such as HTML and XML. Therefore, most ASPs want, at least eventually, to host software that is written specifically for the Internet. At present, there are relatively few native-IP applications, and those are sometimes unreliable.

- Single-purpose: Some ASPs offer narrowly focused single-purpose applications. Provided the application solves a real problem, it may not take much effort to research and then choose this type of ASP.

- Comprehensive: Other ASPs provide comprehensive solution sets appropriate for an entire enterprise or major sections of it. These comprehensive solutions can provide more value than single-purpose applications, but they also bring more dependency on the ASP and thus more risk. Today most of the comprehensive solutions come from veteran software publishers who are hosting their Windows applications.

- System-solution: Another type of ASP provides solutions not just to individual entities, like your business, but also to a set of businesses which are elements of a system and interact to complete some cross-entity process.

- Solipsistic: Many ASP offerings do not acknowledge the existence of other software. That means that any data shared between it and other applications must be manually reentered. Over time, one would expect solipsistic ASPs to recognize and interact with other software in the insurance industry using XML standard.

- Background-service: Some ASPs are beginning to realize that their role is as a support function to primary applications. Not all ASPs need to provide a user interface and functionality direct to the user. Some rating engines and report-writing ASPs operate out of sight, feeding policy systems users interact with.

• Integration-platform: Rather than providing much or any real application software, the integration-services ASP provides a platform to link secondary and perhaps primary application services into what appears to be a seamless, broad application.

What Applications Will ASPs Support?

ASPs will support whatever applications can run on a computer, be it mainframe or client server. Systems typically supported include Enterprise Resource Planning (ERP) systems (such as SAP or PeopleSoft), sales, production and distribution applications, human resource applications, HMO billing and utilization review software, college class registration and billing, etc. Essentially, ASPs offer companies the opportunity to stay current with technology and be agile in the marketplace—in whatever line of business they happen to be—without significant outlay for software user licenses, hardware, and infrastructure improvements (see Table 2).

Increased pressures on businesses to improve efficiency and effectiveness today resulted in a significant cash outlay upfront in the Internet Age. Such cost in dollars and internal staff time needed to implement a system internally— including the time initially spent conducting a needs assessment, identifying potential IS partners, and selecting the system—or outside consultant's support during implementation, is in addition to the site and user licenses. An ASP could eliminate some or all of the initial cash outlay for the following.

Table 2: Market drivers for the ASP model

Macroeconomic	Outsourcing	Value-Added
- Increasing global competition - Rapidly changing technology - Level competitive playing field	- Eliminate IT staffing shortage - Minimize up-front cost of ownership - Predict cash flows - Improve internal efficiencies	- Faster time to market - No technology obsolescence - Transfer application ownership - Utilize best-of-breed applications - Obtain technical expertise

- Database, application, middleware, and interfaced applications site and user license fees
- Some implementation fees
- Hardware, network, and infrastructure improvement costs (such as telephony and environment)
- Some training costs

The payment arrangement with the ASP would spread these costs over the term of the agreement. This approach reduces initial funding requirements and potentially offers monthly charges equal to or only somewhat higher than currently experienced monthly costs with an existing IS (for custom report programming, yearly license fees, monthly data conversions, etc.).

Several research works established that management often need to fund an initial capital outlay of $250,000 to $1 million or more (Lauchlan, 2000; Linthicum, 2000; Subramani & Walden, 1999). With the ASP business model, the new IS becomes nothing more than a monthly cash expense, similar to one that is already incurred. Dependability should be improved, considering ASPs provide 24/7 support with service level agreements guaranteeing "uptime" in excess of 99 percent. Most companies cannot guarantee that level of service from internal technology departments. The real value proposition is that IT managers and their departments are left to tend to their own business (business opportunities identification, mitigation, and financing), rather than focusing on technology issues (McGinity, 2003).

Legacy Systems Support

In an ASP-hosted environment, your legacy systems and the database would be resident on the ASP's hardware at their location. Depending on the access approach selected, the IT manager and all remote users would access the application at the ASP's location via the Internet or the WAN. Data would be viewed, analyses conducted, and reports run in the same manner as if the application was resident within your company's technology department. Remote users would have the same type of access as the risk management department, subject to those types of authority restrictions typically in place within your organization.

Monthly data conversions from the ASP site by IT manager/administrators would be set up by the ASP, as would security and firewall protection. Batch files are created, and the reports selected for delayed printing would be run during the night, along with data backup, disaster recovery routines, and other system maintenance. A primary function of the IT manager would be to ensure that these reports are provided and filed at your company location. The ASP also handles updates. The system vendor supplies the update to the ASP. The ASP pays for the license fees, updates the application, and bills you monthly on the same basis as payment is being made for use of the existing application the ASP is maintaining.

What Makes the ASP Business Model Attractive?

Different kinds of ASPs have somewhat different value propositions, but most would claim many of the following potential advantages over local software you manage:

- No need to install software or software upgrades
- No need to do daily backups and store them off site
- A built-in disaster recovery plan (at least in part)
- No need to frequently upgrade hardware to run software upgrades—relief for your capital budget
- Predictable IT expenses based on subscription and fee-for-use arrangements
- Access to applications and solutions not available in a local version, for instance, with cross-entity business system solutions
- Easy provision of Web-based applications to your customers
- Greater flexibility and scalability—expand or contract usage without impacting your technical infrastructure
- Faster time to market with lower capital investment
- Remote work force and telecommuter support

On the other hand, using an ASP poses some potentially new demands and expectations as well. Among them are:

- Need for universal high-speed connection to the Internet
- Access to software and data only when online, which potentially creates problems for travelers on airplanes or employees otherwise disconnected from the Internet
- Potential difficulties with local operations like printing

- Slow Internet response times with sub-ten-second rather than subsecond response times being the norm

ASP Concerns and Risks

The Internet Age is one of highly sophisticated and information-intensive activity involving many interlinked and interdependent business services related transactions. With a move to the ASP model, such transactions are set to grow exponentially, leading to fundamental changes in product and service delivery processes. Changes in technology act as a driving force for subsequent business process change (Davenport, 1993; Davenport & Short, 1990; Orlikowski, & Tyre, 1994; Porter & Millar, 1985; Porter, 1998; Scott, 1991). Considering ASP is a new industry, some providers are old established companies; others are not. The stability of these companies is reflected in the performance of the relevant technology stocks on NASDAQ. However, there are many well-known companies providing ASP services as well, such as IBM and Citrix.

When a company uses one ASP for all applications, integration between mission-critical applications (such as posting payments to accounts payable or to the general ledger) is normally simple. However, if a company has multiple ASPs or only some applications in a hosted environment, the back-end integration of these applications, which allows them to communicate, becomes complicated.

Another issue is that internal technology departments may view surrendering control of the application to an ASP as a vote of no confidence. In addition, there is always some risk in losing control of the application and your data when a third party has sole access (Guah & Currie, 2002; Little, 1999). The relationship between your ASP and the system vendor can also be tenuous, resulting in finger pointing when problems occur.

ASPs also subject subscribers to risks, including:

- Financial failure: ASPs (of all kinds) are subject to financial failure, and many new and promising ASPs have disappeared overnight, sometimes leaving their subscribers in the lurch. One horror story recounts how a business suffered the loss of not one, but two ASPs in succession, an experience that nearly put them out of business. The ASP alternative is new, at least to many trying to be one. They seem to be having a difficult time figuring out how to price their services, so that revenue reasonably matches their capital and operating expenses. It is wise to go into an ASP arrangement assuming that it will not be permanent. That means having an extrication and substitution plan in place.

- Poor performance: Generally speaking, an ASP should be willing to attach a service-level agreement to your contract. The agreement will spell out mutual expectations as well as remedies should the ASP fail to perform. You need to be certain that the ASP is in a position to deliver. If the ASP uses a third party to host its services, you will need to be assured that your ASP takes full responsibility for delivering services to you no matter what the situation is with its infrastructure ASP.

- Software integration problems: If the hosted software lives on a remote server controlled by the ASP, and you retain software locally, and some form of integration is necessary, how will that happen? Sometime in the future, integration may be straightforward, but today the problem can be real and overwhelming. Consider having the ASP explain how the integration will be handled.

- Security breaches: If you use an ASP, you must depend on them. What external and internal security measures do they have in place? It is not a trivial issue, and a legitimate ASP will be able to document and demonstrate their security provisions in some detail. The continued growth in the use of highly distributed networks supporting both Internet and mobile users is creating a continuous problem of making sure that the right person gets the access that is needed to business information, without leaving the systems vulnerable to attack from unauthorized users.

- Doubtful savings: Because ASPs presumably bring economies of scale, at least to smaller businesses, one might expect the ASP alternative to cost less over time compared with locally installed and managed software. But it would be a mistake to expect much, if any, savings. Using an ASP may introduce some additional expenses, for instance, broadband connection to the Internet for all users of the ASP.

Though most ASPs seem to opt for a subscription model, for instance, by identified users, seats, or simultaneous users, that pricing model may not be appropriate for you in cases where your usage is sporadic and clearly transaction based. In that case, you will want some kind of "by-the-slice" pricing. If the ASP pricing algorithm is based strictly on seats, you should be able to predict with some certainty what your monthly charges will be. But if charges are based on storage used, pages printed, bytes transmitted, etc., you may find yourself paying exorbitant fees that you cannot control.

Security

Our research findings highlighted security as a major concern for most of the businesses that took part (Guah & Currie, 2003). What is more, the technology that we are using is becoming increasingly complex, leaving more potential for errors that might just leave our organizations vulnerable to malicious attacks of all kinds.

Security needs to be inherent in all that we do. The first step is usually based around user authentication and control. The major problems are how to make sure that the person at the remote end is who they say they are and how to make sure that they see only the information that they are authorized to see. This simple customization of services provides a positive message for the users—personalization is a good thing—while also ensuring that access to corporate data is available only on a need-to-know basis.

Beyond user authentication, there is a need to protect data as the data passes across networks, and even when it is just sitting on a storage device. Firewalls and antivirus controls should keep our corporate systems fenced off from the dangers of the outside world, but we also need to make sure that the information transmitted to remote users cannot be intercepted. For this, there is encryption and compression that should render the data unreadable if, somehow, it gets misdirected.

Security should not be difficult in theory, but in practice, that can be the most critical aspect of ASP business. This aspect of IT is often neglected, as evidenced by many breaches (Checkland, 1983). More academic research is needed to determine and suggest areas of investigations that will possibly answer the following questions: Where are the potential weak spots, how can we do our best to avoid getting caught out? Furthermore, how can we control all of the

Figure 3: Risk vs. benefit for ASP project

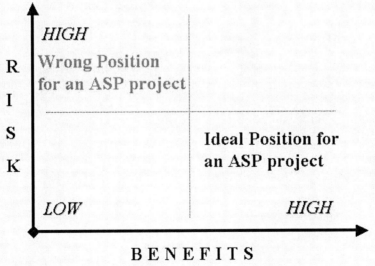

security tasks that we need to keep our IT systems secure without making them too difficult to use for those that need access? These are the challenges the ASP industry has to overcome in the years ahead.

Inter-Organizational Corporate Strategy

Figure 3 shows the vertical axis, representing risk (that runs from low to high), against a horizontal axis representing benefits (also runs from low to high). We indicated that an ideal IT project should occupy the space in the bottom right area, showing low risk with high benefits (Checkland & Scholes, 1990). This is because IT projects that are most likely to attract attention and get approval are those that present low risk and deliver high benefit.

However, risks and benefits are not necessarily well-defined dimensions. Advocates of a given IT project or IT-based business initiative will usually play down the risks and talk up the benefits, often with little more to backup their viewpoints than faith in the vision and a burning desire to proceed. Rather than providing a whole variety of mathematical formulas that depend on what you may or may not want to take into account when calculating risks and benefits, we selected the following to summarize the points to consider when trying to calculate ROI:

1. Benefits that come from reducing cost can be different than those that come from increasing revenues. The latter are often estimated optimistically. Any estimate for them must take into account historical precedent and the capacity of the company to acquire the business.

2. Most IT project costs are real, but most expected benefits are less certain. To be realistic, probability factors need to be applied.

3. A time cutoff should be applied when calculating benefits. A rough rule of thumb is that benefits should only be calculated to apply for 18 months after they appear. The longer the time period used here, the more likely it is that something will change to alter the situation. This is especially so when benefits constitute competitive edge.

4. IT projects are risky, and some types of project have fairly high failure rates. However, this varies from project to project depending on what is being done.

In the current economic climate, the desire to take risks is diminished, and the need to cut costs is paramount. Corporations and IT departments are looking for technology propositions that are low risk and likely to deliver a high return quickly on the money invested (Whelan & McGrath, 2001).

ASP in Business Management

Quite often when companies hit troubled times, they attempt to apply the same solutions as in the past, with the same effect. Some may argue that a completely internal consistent solution could still fail, because it is geared toward earlier market conditions. Most take too long to scale down, which severely impacts profitability. Then, they cut back hard, leaving them unable to take advantage of the u-turn when it arrives. Unfortunately, they end up repeating these up and down cycles rather then planning for, and performing well under, bad conditions, and putting themselves in a position to exploit the good times.

Several authors have argued that the successful companies of the future will be inherently more flexible, more distributed, and more fast moving than in the past. Such efforts must also be undertaken collaboratively with partners (Hagel, 2002; Markus, 1983; Tebboune, 2003). It requires moving from traditional supplier and customer relationships to genuine partnerships based on collaborative goal setting. Partners must be engaged in debates on issues covering the following:

1. How can we coordinate our business processes to work together faster?
2. How can we eliminate the bottlenecks that prevent us from getting our products and services to the customer more quickly?
3. What customer information should we share to our mutual benefits?

Instead of the current attitude toward negotiating, as an art of science, adapting businesses should consider negotiation a part of a successful process. An ASP business model involves alliances that are beginning to come far more naturally and should be faster and easier to consummate, because adaptive business networks mandate that companies adopt standard business processes, enabling them to work together more efficiently. Helping a business to adapt to the new age is not an IT process that should be regarded as some sort of IT project. Rather, it is a business process initiative supported by technology (McLeord, 1993).

People Management in an ASP Environment

In the age that IT is seen as a strategic part of the business, most executives have become familiar with jargon such as ERP and e-business, causing IT to enter the cultural mainstream with the advent of e-mail and Web browsers. Many IT directors are part of their firm's executive team. However, Y2K and the dot-com crash dented the credibility of IT bosses, and budgets were cut back in response to the economic slowdown. The increased focus on business skills means today's IT directors do not necessarily come from technical backgrounds.

In essence, the inter-organization is a distributed network of human talent. Within individual organizations, outmoded human resources management philosophies must be replaced by modern approaches that maximize the brain contribution to the service, not just the brawn contribution. The emphasis is on working smarter, not just harder. The past three decades of Internet existence have been marked by a long series of brilliant software and methodological innovations that have defined, each time afresh, the scope and content of online socializing, entertainment, electronic commerce, business-to-business transactions, directory services, as well as electronic publications and scholarly interaction. An ASP strategy requires inter-organizations to rethink not just the elements of its economic milieu, but also their political and social contexts. This does not suggest some kind of radical shift away from the profit motive to the quality-of-life motive.

As a strategy that emerged from the spread of the Internet, ASP projects require key attributes for people management in the Internet Age. Some of these are leadership, which involves the ability to form and maintain a good team as well as the ability to "steer the ship." Vision involves management having the confidence and skills to deploy required new technology throughout the organization. Managers of ASP vendors must also be able to build relationships by having a cohesive line of communication with people at all levels. A certain degree of political skill is required in managing ASP projects to satisfy the need for collaboration with various directorships in the different organization. More important is the ability to deliver, which is the ultimate aim for any ASP management. This often requires the ability to achieve actual results based on meeting customers' requirements.

Thus, one must agree that these can amount to a tall order for most ASP vendor executives. This is because they are usually from highly technical backgrounds and have very little business management training. They are expected to pick up the relevant skills and succeed in a short period. We must remember that as a programmer trained at university, a prospective manager for an ASP vendor will have been trained to follow rules and has baggage. During the period preceding his or her appointment to management, for example, as a software developer or project manager, he or she would have had very little discretion. Then as manager of an ASP project, one realizes that a manager has lots of discretion and that there are no rules to follow and no right answers. Thus, the ASP executive role has become more focused on business than cutting-edge technology. Some may argue that this has not been a recent change. Other areas such as outsourcing, an IT director's relationship with the board, systems integration, and value for money are other issues just as pressing (Maslow, 1943).

Managing Business Process with ASP

With the ASP business model, inter-organizations are moving from a data-driven view of business and of IT systems, which tend to be hard-wired and inflexible, to a process-driven approach, which is much more fluid and functional and is designed to cross company boundaries. The emerging view is that, sooner rather than later, managers will be able to change their business processes in the same way that they can currently change data—at a high level, with little technical knowledge and little risk. Many refer to this as business process management (BPM) (Information Age Research, 2003).

There is a need for further research to investigate the practice of BPM in an ASP-implemented environment. Questions need to be asked, whether or not customers understand the terms and the technologies. Are customers buying or implementing BPM along with ASP? Who are the major ASP vendors also selling BPM? This would follow up on a less rigorous survey carried out by Internet Age (Information Age Research, 2003).

Table 3 shows that a cautious approach is needed for ASPs selling BPM due to a rather confused marketplace for BPM. While customers appear to have a good understanding of the possible benefits of moving to some form of process-oriented approach, even if most are not ready to buy, only a quarter of companies are actively using BPM, based on their understanding of the term. Encouragingly, more than two-thirds identify better business agility and control over workflow as key benefits.

Recognition of some form of process approach can be seen in almost every product release in the last few years, including business applications from SAP and Microsoft and a Web services orchestration engine from Tibco. However,

Table 3: Benefits of BPM in an ASP environment

Main Benefits of BPM	Main Benefits of ASP
Faster application development 19%	To automate procedures 16%
Better control over workflow 70%	To link together programs 15%
More business agility 64%	As a strategic tool for building business agility 22%
Better integration between application 45%	As an integration backbone 25%
Do not know/no benefits 4%	For managing processes 23%

Figure 4: Leading BPM suppliers

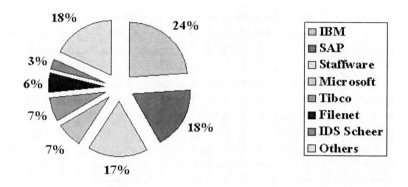

(Source: Internet Age)

this remains a fragmented market, though IBM is the most widely cited supplier, followed by SAP (see Figure 4).

ASP Value Proposition

The value-creating potential of ASP is a critical factor for the success of any ASP business model. In conjunction with the ASP Industry Consortium, a knowledge-based benefits/risks assessment framework was developed that delineates five key performance areas for evaluating the value-creating potential of ASP business models: delivery and enablement, management and operations, integration, business transformation, and client/vendor partnerships (Currie, 2003). In each category, a list of key performance indicators can be evaluated by existing or potential ASP customers. For example, under delivery and enablement, the customer evaluates the importance of receiving an application 24/7 in relation to their own businesses. Customer requirements may vary with this performance indicator, so it is incumbent upon the ASP to evaluate how important this requirement is for an individual customer; 24/7 may be more important to a health-care organization than to a brewery. In another example, management and operations, a customer may adopt an ASP solution because he or she wishes to reduce the total cost of ownership of the IT facility. Using an ASP for collaboration tools may not be done to save money but for reasons of efficiency. Alternatively, a hosted BPR application may reduce the total cost of ownership. The value proposition will, therefore, vary between ASP vendors and their customers. The challenge for ASPs is to understand customer requirements and not assume that all customers want the same things from an ASP solution.

ASP and Business Continuity

While the growth of the ASP market was at its peak by the end of the 20th century, many start-up firms mistakenly described themselves as self-styled ASPs (Currie, 2003). The ASP market quickly became saturated, as ASP became a global phenomenon. Telecommunications firms, with vast IT infrastructure capabilities, needed to partner with SAPs (ISVs and ASPs) to fulfill their aspirations. ISVs and ASPs required the services of data center providers

Table 4: Conceptual framework of the ASP business model

Constructs	Attributes	Description
Strategic positioning	Industry structure Sustainable competitive advantage Market segmentation Customer focus Market differentiation Firm composition	Determines the profitability of the average competitor Allows a firm to outperform the average competitor Type of ASP (enterprise, pure-play, vertical) Target customer market (large, midsize, or small businesses) Geographical reach (international, regional, national, local) Strategic alliances, partnerships, joint ventures
Product and services portfolio	Scale economies Scope of applications Distinctiveness/uniqueness Production/service differentiation	Number of customers needed to make a profit (high volume/low cost or low volume/high cost) Type of products/services offered in relation to degree of standardization/customization (ERP, CRM, e-mail, etc.) Combination of product/services (enterprise, vertical, etc.) Branding, price, bundling, aggregation, switching costs
Value proposition	Applications/services outsourcing Value creation for customer Benefits/risks assessment	Delivery and enablement (24/7 service/data security) Management and operations (reduced total cost of ownership) Integration (EAI across departments/sites/borders, etc.) Business transformation (increased agility/BPO/BPR) Client/vendor partnerships (strength through partnerships)

(telecos) to host their software, unless they invested in this capability (most ASPs did not). No doubt we will see a shakeout of ASPs over the next few years, with mergers, acquisitions, and failures (Bender-Samuel, 1999; Hagel, 2002). You may also notice an implicit battle between entrenched classic technology vendors, who are moving conservatively into the ASP scene, and upstarts, who think they see ways to use Internet technology to encourage substantive industry change in work flow, customer service, and sales. Consider the ASPs you see today as a first wave of a more general transformation. It is not reasonable to expect that all databases supporting the services industry (i.e., insurance, banking, airlines, etc.) will be hosted. It is much more likely that within 5 years we will see hybrid environments with some processing and data storage occurring locally and some on remote servers delivered to the point of use in the background (Sleeper & Robins, 2002).

The above conceptual framework was developed to operationalize the constructs of strategic positioning, produce/services portfolio, and value proposition. The attributes pertaining to these constructs and a description of how they relate to the ASP business model is given in Table 4.

Web Services: The Future for ASP

Like almost all new Internet-related technologies, the immediate opportunities from Web services have been overstated, although the eventual impact could be huge (Hagel, 2002). This can be demonstrated by the immediate and key role of Web services, which is to provide a paradigm shift in the way businesses manage IT infrastructure (Uden, 2002). It provides intelligent enterprises with the capability to overturn the accepted norms of integration and thereby allow all businesses to rapidly and effectively leverage the existing IT and information assets at their disposal. Intelligent enterprises currently running outsourcing services are already seen to be one of the early areas to benefit from the Web service revolution. However, there will be others as enterprises discover the hidden value to their intellectual assets.

Considering most enterprises have until now used the Internet to improve access to existing systems, information, and services, one can envisage the days when Web services promise new and innovative services that are currently impossible or prohibitively expensive to deploy. With such development anticipated to promote the ASP business model, Web service integration is considered to be at the heart of this expectation. Through this process of connecting businesses, ASP will be able to quickly capitalize on new opportunities by combining assets from a variety of disparate systems, creating and exposing them as Web services for the end-game of fulfilling customer expectations (Irani & Love, 2001).

Figure 5: WEB services trajectory

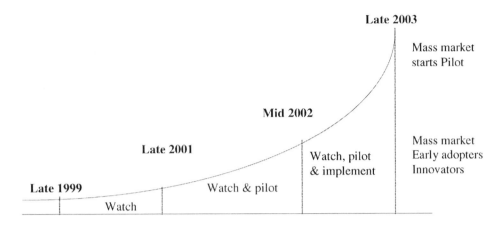

Source: Sandhill Group.

Any inter-organization considering an ASP business model should at least investigate the potential impact of Web service integration, as this will sooner or later become another permanent business necessity and not simply competitive advantage material (Porter & Millar, 1985; Porter, 1998). Those inter-organizations that have adopted our suggested approach will not only gain advantage now in business with lower costs and better returns on assets, but are also expected to develop valuable experience for the first decade of the 21st century. Considering the IS trajectory, as Web services become the standard and the expertise of ASP becomes more established, figures for ASP uptake and vendors' profits should begin to move in one direction only.

Strategic Positioning of Web Services Providers

Observers of business trends can confirm that a major change in the way applications are bought and deployed is already underway. Web services are about to fundamentally change the software industry by introducing a revolution in the way applications are built and deployed. The first generation of the World Wide Web linked users to applications using HTTP and HTML. The second generation, using the XML (Web services) technology, links applications to applications (Uden, 2002). Surprisingly, the enthusiasm for Web services is not confined to the vendor side of the equation, as customers seem to be embracing the technology. In the United Kingdom, a steady stream of organizations has installed Web services technology and services, including UK supermarket giant Tesco. According to a December 2002 survey by IT market research company

Forrester Research, more than a quarter of European financial and investment companies have an ongoing Web services deployment (see Figure 5).

One thing that is just about clear now is that every globally recognized enterprise software supplier has endorsed Web services, and many have already released specific Web services tools, platforms, and services or upgraded their existing products to handle the technology. Could this be because they are competing with traditional foes, as well as new companies (Tebboune, 2003)? The blue chip companies making up the first set to take up the challenge include Microsoft, Oracle, Sun, IBM, BEA Systems, and Novell. They are beginning to successfully provide development tools, application servers, and integration and deployment tools, often around a common set of interfaces and standards. A second set of companies focuses on the enterprise application integration market provided by Web services. These companies are Tibco, Vitria, and Iona, that argue that their products will benefit from standardized interfaces and tools and an expanding market for integration tools. But, these companies are simultaneously fighting a marketing battle against the ones that say that eventually the functions they supply will be commoditized by Web services-based tools.

Another set of companies further down the chain makes up the third grouping, including PeopleSoft, SAP, and JD Edwards. They regard Web services as an approach to provide their own processes and functions using Web services interfaces, and then make these accessible using new Web services brokers, exchanges, and applications servers. This group is closely followed by hundreds of niche suppliers of Web services tools, platforms, and services, many of which are start-ups.

Web Services Market

Figure 5 does not mean that a clear or well-defined market has yet to emerge or that it will ever emerge for Web services. Most researchers not only see Web services as a mere evolutionary step, but also as a disruptive technology. In some sense, the evaluation could be true only if it follows the predicted pattern of rapid take-up, a frenzy of activity, new suppliers, new markets, and then rapid consolidation and ubiquitous take-up.

Web services sceptics could laugh at the current figures being thrown about. While organizations spent $1.7 billion on Web services products and services in 2002, IT research company, Ovum, estimates an increase to $39.8 billion by 2006, though Gartner puts the figure at $21 billion by 2005 for software using Web services standards (Currie & Seltsikas, 2001).

Web services is a major partner in the move to horizontally networked companies. The main players are companies that have many services bought in from outside, which allows them to benefit from Web services' most immediate opportunity of integrating new and existing systems. Considering the biggest contribution of Web services will be integration, it puts the enterprise application integration vendors and their products in the spotlight, thereby explaining why sales of such products have continued to rise, even through the recession and the emergence of Web services.

Some researchers believe integration will not only be easier but also cheaper (Chang, Jackson, & Grover, 2002; Chatterjee, Grewal, & Sambamurthy, 2002). Web services technology can reduce the cost of an integration project by between 9% and 16% the first time an application is integrated and by between 13% to 20% when the integration points are reused, according to San Hill Group, an IT market research company (Chang, Jackson, & Grover, 2002). However, the extent to which customers will share these dividends remains to be seen. Along with this, Web services technology may also have a more profound effect, driving the two or three distinct markets of integration tools, development tools, and applications together, possibly around one platform or a set of interworking tools.

That could put the big suppliers—Microsoft (.NET), IBM (WebSphere), Sun (SunONE), Oracle (Oracle Application Server) and BEA Systems (Web Logic)—in a better position, because they supply middleware tools along with integrated development environments. The fact that IBM and Microsoft have rolled out new Web services tool kits in 2002 and 2003 (closely tied to their new and existing infrastructure products) means one can single them out as the early leaders. However, the ultimate shape of this development and middleware market is unclear, because application development involves managing fine-grained components, while integration involves linking processes together. It is not clear that the two will remain separate indefinitely.

The early, committed involvement of all the big suppliers will definitely leave room for many smaller and specialist companies (Tapscott, 2001). These providers will have an important role to play in the adoption of Web services, although one can be forgiven for being pessimistic about the prospects from other niche Web services platform and tools suppliers. A rather safe bet can be made on infrastructure heavyweights, such as Microsoft, IBM, or Sun, probably acquiring these smaller vendors trying to hold onto a little niche (Tebboune, 2003). Remember that Web services are still in their early days, and there will be new companies and opportunities, especially in managed services.

Web Application Problems

When Web problems occur at high-profile sites, the publicity is embarrassing and often damaging, but it is also typically short-lived. Researchers have found that there is little outside analysis of what went wrong, mainly because of sketchy details and of management's attempts to limit damage. Two of the recent incidents in the United Kingdom involved (MacIver, 2003):

1.   The Inland Revenue: A security flaw breached rules on confidentiality and data protection and forced system downtime, undermining a campaign to win public confidence in filing. In May 2002, the Inland Revenue's self-assessment-only tax returns service suffered a major security breach. As a result of a problem with one Internet service provider, the system regarded two online filers as the same individual, resulting in them sharing a single online session and being able to view each others' submissions. It resulted in 60 known "shared sessions" and 13 where individuals were aware they were viewing others' forms. The revenue admitted there were another 665 cases where it could not be certain a tax return had not been seen.

2.   Argos: A security flaw exposed customer records, triggering large-scale customer inconvenience. In September 1999, Argos found its Web site the center of unwanted attention as a result of a rudimentary programming error that resulted in television sets worth £399 being "rounded up" to the bargain price of £3. Unsurprisingly, the site was swamped with more than £1 million-worth of online orders—including one person asking for 1700 sets.

Conclusions

What makes ASP so promising is its distinctive ability to help organizations operate more flexibly and collaborate more successfully with business partners (Bender-Samuel, 1999). Consumer and technology publications have touted ASPs as the next big technology. Using ASPs, businesses and consumers would plug into software/computer-processing utilities and rent rather than buy applications. No more installation headaches. No more concerns with daily backups. No need to upgrade hardware or software frequently. No more IT departments haggling over budgets. ASPs would allow unlimited, instant scalability. ASPs would provide all the advantages of computer technology without the tears. But this has not happened as predicted, at least not yet. ASPs are going belly-up and threatening the viability of their business customers. Cost savings have not materialized as expected. Problems, such as integrating hosted and legacy applications, prove intractable or more challenging than expected. The rigidity of hosted offerings constrains business flexibility and competitive differentiation.

All the really hard problems (people-related issues) do not disappear with the ASP solution. In fact, sometimes they increase. There are probably as many definitions of "ASP" as there are businesses claiming to be one; though not all ASPs have the same focus (see Figure 2).

There is no disputing that basic Web services can offer value. The concern is they are undoubtedly limited by the multitude of problems—security and reliability being the biggest, followed closely by vendor hype. These issues are further hindered by the reclassification of projects—legacy applications integration, for instance, is nowadays considered a Web services project. Nevertheless, the real value of Web services comes from the ability to deliver software as a service. According to Mark Dearnley, Chief Technical Officer of BOOTS:

Most of the ASP/Web services vision is just pure speculation, with no real consideration of what is achievable and what it will cost to actually build out the vision for full use on the open Internet.

The authors hope this chapter has addressed a few of your questions on ASP management, including how to deal with human resources and how to make the most of the technology. You have also seen that technology is, perhaps, the easiest thing to replace, but people and the IS implementation process are much harder. Offering management a method to obtain newer, faster technology without significant capital outlay can be a powerful tool to eliminate the resistance that IT managers typically experience when trying to implement a new system. With some initial investigation of the ASP vendors available to support inter-organization's chosen project, a new IOIS could be in the future.

References

ASP Industry Consortium. (2000). Industry News. Retrieved December 2001 from the World Wide Web: www.aspindustry.org.

Avison, D. E., & Fitzgerald, G. (2003). Where now for development methodologies? *Communications of the ACM*, January, *46*(1), 79–82.

Bender-Samuel, P. (1999). A fork in the road for ASPs. Retrieved December 2001 from the World Wide Web: www.outsourcing-journal.com/issues/apr2000.

British Computer Society News. (2003). The way we were. *The Computer Bulletin*, May, p. 12.

Chang, K., Jackson, J., & Grover, V. (2002). E-Commerce and corporate strategy: An executive perspective. *Journal of Information & Management*, *20*(23), 1–13.

Chatterjee, D., Grewal, R., & Sambamurthy, V. (2002). Shaping up for e-commerce: Institutional enablers of the organizational assimilation of web technologies. *MIS Quarterly*, *26*(2), 65–89.

Checkland, P. B. (1983). *Systems thinking, systems practice*. New York: John Wiley & Sons.

Checkland, P. B., & Scholes, J. (1990). *Soft systems methodology in action*. New York: John Wiley & Sons.

Currie, W. L. (2003). A knowledge-based risk assessment framework for evaluating web-enabled application outsourcing projects. *International Journal of Project Management*, *21*, 207–217.

Currie, W. L., & Seltsikas, P. (2001). Exploring the supply-side of IT outsourcing: Evaluating the emerging role of application service providers. *European Journal of Information Systems*, *10*, 123–134.

Currie, W., & Willcocks, L. P. (1998). Analysing four types of IT sourcing decisions in the context of size, client/supplier interdependency and risk mitigation. *Information Systems Journal*, *8*, 119–143.

Davenport, T. H. (1993). *Process innovation: Reengineering work through information technology*. Boston, MA: Harvard Business School Press.

Davenport, T. H., & Short, J. E. (1990). The new industrial engineering: Information technology and business process redesign. *Sloan Management Review*, *34*(4), 1–27.

Dussauge, P., Hart, S., & Ramanantsoa, B. (1994). *Strategic technology management: Integrating product technology into global business strategies for the 1990s*. New York: John Wiley & Sons.

Guah, M. W., & Currie, W. L. (2002). Evaluation of NHS information systems strategy: Exploring the ASP model. *Issues of Information Systems Journal*, III, 222–228.

Guah, M. W., & Currie, W. L. (2003). ASP: A technology and working tool for intelligent enterprises of the 21st century. In J. N. D. Gupta, & S. K. Sharma (Eds.), *Intelligent Enterprises of the 21st Century*. Hershey, PA: Idea Group Inc.

Hagel, J., III. (2002). *Out of the box: Strategies for achieving profits today and growth tomorrow through Web services*. Boston, MA: Harvard Business School Press.

Hagel, J. III, & Brown, J. S. (2001). Your next IT strategy. *Harvard Business Review*, *79*(9), 105–113.

Hondo, M., Nagaratnam, N., & Nadalin, A. (2002). Securing Web services. *IBM Systems Journal*, *41*(2).

Howcroft, D. (2001). After the goldrush: Deconstructing the myths of the dot.com market. *Journal of Information Technology*, *16*(4), 195–204.

Information Age Research. (2003). Business process management. *Information Age*, May, p. 75.

Information Technology Association of America (ITAA). (2001). ITAA survey of ASP demand in the U.S. federal market. *GCN Magazine*. June.

Irani, Z. & Love, P. E. D. (2001). The propagation of technology management taxonomies for evaluating investments in information systems. *Journal of Management Information Systems*, *17*(3), 161–177.

Kakabadse, N., & Kakabadse, A. (2002). Software as a service via application service providers (ASPs) model of sourcing: An exploratory study. *Journal of Information Technology Cases and Applications*, *4*(2), 26–44.

Kern, T., Lacity, M., & Willcocks, L. (2002). *Netsourcing: Renting business applications and services over a network*. New York: Prentice Hall.

Klein, H. K., & Myers, M. (1999). A set of principles for conducting and evaluating interpretive field studies in information systems. *MIS Quarterly*, *23*(1), 67–93.

Lauchlan, S. (2000). ASPs: Are you ready to play? *Computing*, *3*, 29.

Linthicum, D. S. (2000). To ASP or not to ASP. April/May. Retrieved May 2002 from the World Wide Web: www.Software Mag.com.

Little, G. R. (1999). Paper 1: Theory of perception. Retrieved June 2002 from the World Wide Web: www.grlphilosophy. co.nz.

MacIver, K. (2003). The UK's 10 worst web application failures... and what could have been done to prevent them. *Information Age*, May, pp. 36–40.

Markus, M. L. (1983). Power, politics and MIS implementation. *Communications of the ACM*, *26*(6), 430–445.

Maslow, A. H. (1943). A theory of human motivation. *Psychological Review*, *50*, 370–396.

McGinity, M. (2003). Getting real, providers have a new boss: The customer. *Communications of the ACM*, *46*(4), 23–26.

McLeord, Jr., R. (1993). *Management information systems: A study of computer-based information systems* (5th ed.). New York: Macmillan Publishing.

Orlikowski, W. J., & Tyre, M. J. (1994). Windows of opportunity: Temporal patterns of technological adaptation in organizations. *Organization Science*, May, pp. 98–118.

Porter, M. E. (1998). Michael E. Porter on competition. Boston, MA: Harvard Business Review.

Porter, M. E., & Millar, V. E. (1985). How information gives you competitive advantage. *Harvard Business Review, 62*(4), 149–160.

Roszak, T. (1994). *The cult of information: A neo-luddite treatise on high-tech, artificial intelligence, and the true art of thinking.* Berkeley, CA: University of California Press.

Scott Morton, M. (1991). *The corporation of the 1990s. Information technology and organizational transformation.* Oxford University Press.

Shenk, D. (1997). *Data smog: Surviving the information glut.* London: Abacus.

Sleeper, B., & Robins, B. (2002). The laws of evolution: A pragmatic analysis of the emerging Web services market. An analysis memo from The Stencil Group. Retrieved April 2002 from the World Wide Web: www.stencilgroup. com.

Subramani, M., & Walden, E. (1999). The dot com effect: The impact of e-commerce announcements on the market value of firms. *International Conference on Information Systems 2000* (pp. 193–207).

Tapscott, D. (2001). Rethinking strategy in a networked world. *Strategy & Business, 24,* 2–8.

Tebboune, D. E. S. (2003). Application service provision: Origins and development. *Business Process Management Journal* (forthcoming).

Uden, L. (2002). Design process for Web applications. *IEEE MultiMedia.* October–December, pp. 47–55.

Walsham, G. (1993). *Interpreting information systems in organizations.* New York: John Wiley & Sons.

Weill, P. (1993). The role and value of IT infrastructure: Some empirical observations. In M. Khosrowpour, & M. Mahmood (Eds.), *Strategic information technology management: Perspectives on organizational growth and competitive advantage* (pp. 547–572). Hershey, PA: Idea Group Publishing.

Whelan, E., & McGrath, F. (2001). A study of the total life cycle costs of an e-commerce investment. A research in progress. *Evaluation and Program Planning, 25*(2), 191–196.

Wilkes, L. (2002). IBM seeks partners to drive adoption of XML Web services. *Interact,* February.

Yin, R. K. (1994). *Case study research: Design and methods.* Thousand Oaks, CA: Sage Publications.

Section III:

Systems Analysis/ Planning

Chapter VI

Business Associations as Hubs of Inter-Organizational Information Systems for SMEs – The 2Cities Portal

Federico Pigni
Universita Cattaneo, Italy

Aurelio Ravarini
Universita Cattaneo, Italy

Donatella Sciuto
Universita Cattaneo, Italy

Carlo Angelo Zanaboni
Universita Cattaneo, Italy

Janice Burn
Edith Cowan University, Western Australia

Abstract

This chapter is a first contribution to the study of the role of a business association (BA) in managing inter-organizational (IO) relationships among its members. The authors describe a model (the Virtual Association Platform, VAP) of an ICT-based platform supporting BA activities and interactions with members. The design of a VAP requires performing a detailed analysis of information flows between the BA and the agents related to its activities. The authors propose a general framework (the IOR4VAP framework) for the design of a VAP, where they identify seven categories of agents, describe the potential information flows exchanged among the parties, and indicate opportunities for the BA to provide innovative services. Finally, the IOR4VAP framework is applied to the case of a VAP established in Western Australia: 2Cities.com.

Introduction

The growing complexity and instability of the worldwide market during the last years forced enterprises in every industry to undertake deep organizational and strategic changes (Tetteh, 1990). Companies had to find new ways to create value and innovate in an environment characterized by the evolving applications of information and communication technologies (ICTs), the development of extended supply chains and global e-markets, and the increasing customer knowledge intensity and sensitivity for time-to-market. Nevertheless, organizational and technological changes often require resources exceeding those available to small and medium enterprises[1] (SMEs) (Buonanno et al., 2002; Fariselli, 1999; Tetteh & Burn, 2001).

It is well documented in literature that, for example, the investments required to meet most of the reorganization cost coming from the adoption of information and communication technologies (ICTs), and the risks involved in these projects, largely exceed the budget and the capabilities of an average SME (Buonanno et al., 2002; Fariselli, 1999; Fink, 1998; Poon, 1999; Tetteh & Burn, 2001). These circumstances suggest the feasibility of a broader approach to the implementation of ICTs in SMEs by examining the potential of inter-organizational (IO) ICT-supported relationships. The risk and the cost sharing coupled with the possibility to better utilize a combined competitive advantage should be able to overcome the typical constraints faced by single SMEs.

However, unless dealing with SMEs participating in supply chains of larger firms or tied in some sort of hubs, it is difficult to gather a sufficient number of enterprises able to leverage on an IO technological solution as a sustainable competitive advantage (Buonanno et al., 2002; Fariselli, 1999).

In this context, the many different forms of aggregation of enterprises—clusters, industrial districts, business associations, business park, etc.—described in the normative literature (Becattini, 1990; Bennett & Robson, 2001; Costa-Campi & Viladecans-Marsal, 1999; Enright & Roberts, 2001; Gordon & McCann, 2000; Markusen, 1996; Marshall, 1922; McDonald & Vertova, 2001; Roelandt &

Hertog, 1998) could play a pivotal role in the development of successful ICT solutions that aim at creating value by improving collaboration, work specialization, information sharing, and responsiveness between SMEs.

Although all the forms of aggregations are interesting and suitable to be the subject matter, this chapter is going to focus only on one of them, namely, the industrial or business associations, as they are undoubtedly relevant forms of industrial aggregation: they provide companies with social activities and collective services and represent the interests of their members within specific domains; they can also take collective action on common problems (Alberti, 1998, 1999; Aldrich & Staber, 1988; Bennett & Robson, 2001). These specificities grant associations a unique competitive position in the market of business service providers (Bennett & Robson, 2001) and a potential key role in driving SMEs through the technological and organizational innovations they need. Associations could leverage on the "critical mass" constituted by associates and on ICT to provide collaborative value-adding solutions (i.e., logistic, procurement, internationalization, and technological innovation). However, the marketed collaborative platforms are specifically designed for large companies, thus making them inadequate to support industrial aggregations of SMEs (Consolati, 2000; Micelli & Di Maria, 2000; Poon, 1999).

Nevertheless, associations cannot expect to achieve any of such positive outcomes without a redefinition of their strategies and an expansion of the services offered, both new and high value and traditional (Alberti, 1998, 1999; Bennett & Robson, 2001).

The next section of this chapter provides an assessment of the main activities of a business association and describes the relevance of relationships management within a business association.

The third section ("Background on IO relationships") will briefly review the main theories and models explaining cooperative behavior and the reasons for IO relationships development. The fourth section ("ICT and IO relationships") will go further and will trace the link between ICT and IO relationships considering the implications deriving from the adoption of Internet technology. The fifth section ("The Virtual Association Platform Model") will propose a framework for the identification of information requirements of a BA, based on the identification of the agents involved in the activities of the BA. Finally, in the last section (2Cities.com), such a framework will be applied to the case of the 2Cities portal, a platform designed to deliver services to BAs in Western Australia.

Business Association Activities

Business associations provide a wide range of key services to members, such as managerial, financial, business, legal, marketing, and technical (Best, 1990). Moreover, they can support members with an equally wide range of complementary functions. Doner and Schenider (2000) identified associational contributions to economic performance into two main categories: market-complementing and market-supporting. Market-supporting functions are instances where associations push underperforming states to provide those public goods that only states can provide, like strong property rights and effective public administration. Associations contribute indirectly through pressure on public officials.

Market-complementing activities involve direct coordination among firms. The authors analyze a wide range of market-complementing activities: macroeconomic stabilization and reform, horizontal coordination, vertical coordination, lowering the costs of information, standards setting, and quality upgrading. Moreover, they identified more productive associations as characterized by high member density, the ability to provide valuable resources to their members and adequate internal mechanisms for mediating member interests. Furthermore, other than economic-related impacts, business associations possess a relevant social dimension (Nadvi, 1999). They can act as a forum, providing members the possibility to meet and interact informally (Bennett, 1996).

Finally, different authors suggest that the functions of local business associations can be categorized in three main types of activities (Alberti, 1999; Nadvi, 1999):

1. Coordination and regulation
2. Representation of association's interests to various levels of government
3. Provision of "real" services

The coordination role of a business association can influence horizontally the local producer, and vertically the supply chain in terms of forward and backward links (Rabellotti, 1999; Rabellotti & Schmitz, 1999). The regulation role is a consequence of the mediating role an association could play in coordinating business conduct between associates. However, any recognition of the regulatory power is totally based on the legitimacy of the association (Nadvi, 1999).

The representation of interest is probably the main aim of the association. It is the result of a three-step process as suggested by Alberti (1999):

1.   Identification of interest: It is the political process that leads to the identification of the association reach versus competitors and potential supporters.

2.   Legitimization: It is the process in which associations gain recognition.

3.   Favorable conditions: Once a business association has identified the interest to protect and is legitimate in representing such interests, it can act on the market, with institutions, local government, or state to obtain the best conditions and benefits for its members.

Thus, other than managing the relationship with its associates, an association lobbies the institutions and brokerages service providers for its members. Among these types of activities, the market-supporting functions discussed above can be comprised. Therefore, even though some studies argue that such conduct results in seeking unproductive rents rather than the common or public interest, it may also provide a range of services that reduce information and coordination costs (Doner & Schneider, 2000).

The provision of real services is the most "visible" part of the traditional business associations' activity. It is represented by all the goods and services the association can provide to its members, including (Alberti, 1999; Nadvi, 1999):

•   General services (technical and managerial advice, information services, accounting and fiscal fulfilments services, personnel training)

•   Technology support (both in terms of product and process)

•   Linkage to local and global trade fairs

•   Benchmarking services

The identification, for each activity, of the relevant organizations involved allows formation of the outline of a relationship framework. Relationships are fundamental, as any business association relays heavily on the relationships among all the different organizations involved in its activities. Thus, the "quality" of the relationships developed by each association is a possible source of its main competitive advantage: the ability to attract members and increase "visibility." Moreover, stable and beneficial relationships with members, service providers, and higher institutions are an essential asset for developing a network of IO relations (Alberti, 1998). Consequently, an improvement in the management of the relations gives to the association the power to satisfy its members' needs, leading to an improvement in the member–association relationship, because members feel more represented. This aspect is even more critical as a plethora of authors has already endorsed the necessity of a rethink in association strategies by focusing on relationship management (Alberti, 1998; Benevolo, 1997; Bubbio, 1997; Zan, 1992).

ICT-based solutions have always proven to be effective means of efficiently managing information flows; thus, the inherited potentials of ICTs to support business association relationships are enormous. The design of a framework of the relationships involved in a business association should then represent the first step to studying the most relevant relations and both impacts and opportunities of ICT support.

Background on IO Relationships

Relationships have been the subject of studies within many research fields. The heterogeneity in contexts and times are reflected into the diversity of such works, which adopted different descriptive models and underlying theoretical perspectives (Haugland, 1999).

In the IS field, Kern and Willcocks (2000) reported that the research on IO relationships approach is still inconclusive. In their attempt to rationalize the existing research work, they first analyzed IS literature and then went further, considering organization and marketing literature. This review highlights four main conceptual models on which those papers are based: the life cycle dynamics, the exchange theory, the resource-dependence theory, the transaction cost theory and organizational learning. Three of the main traditional approaches from organizational and strategic literature are herein analyzed: the resource-dependence model (Pfeffer & Salancik, 1978), the relational exchange theory (Macneil, 1978), and the transaction cost theory (Williamson, 1985). More recent and promising models have been trying to extend organizational theories, such as the resource-based view model (Barney, 1986, 1991; Bharadwaj, 2000; Penrose, 1959) and the dynamic capabilities theory (Teece, Pisano, & Shuen, 1997) by taking into consideration the contribution of IT to company performance.

The Resource-Dependent Model

The resource-dependent model (RDM) aims to describe the multiplicity of relationships that occur between an organization and suppliers and customers as well as banks, shareholding institutions, government, distributors, consultants, associations, etc., namely, organizations expected to interact with their environment in order to acquire resources. According to RDM, organizations would enter into IO relationships to gain access or control over a resource or a perceived resource need. However, the focus is still the single firm and not the network of relationships in which it operates (Easton, 1992).

The Relational Exchange Theory

The relational exchange theory (RET) is based on four main principles of society (Kern & Willcocks, 2000): labor specialization, exchange, choice, and awareness of the future. Labor specialization is the precondition to the exchange as soon as individuals and firms no longer produced everything for their own survival. The exchange is considered the activity emerging between individuals motivated by the returns they can bring from others (Macneil, 1978). The level of choice agents have in terms of exchange represents the extent of their freedom. Finally, awareness of their future is the reason why contracts exist, as those expectations determine the needs for a contract.

In the RET, firms can be seen as complex bundles of contracts as they act by the means of exchanges in order to fulfill their needs and future expectations. Taking into account the uncertainty of the future and the limited awareness of agents, the relational exchange theory, according to Haugland (1999, p. 273), "emphasizes the importance of building personal trust relationships and developing social norms," as each economic action is considered to be related to the context of social relations where trust is a core aspect.

Transaction Costs Theory

Transaction costs theory (TCT), as proposed by Williamson (1985) mainly focuses on governance structures. By postulating the existence of limited rationality and opportunistic behavior of agents, the TCT provides a framework that tries to explain why managers pursuing business objectives should choose to rely on their organization, on the market, or on a mixed relationship (Plunket, Voisin, & Bellon, 2001). The underlying statement is that in a free market, a company would find it cheaper to buy a product from a specialized producer rather than make it on its own. However, market failures limit the management understanding of costs, leading to less then optimal internalization of the production. However, firms still engage in repeated, contract-based transactions when theory suggests hierarchical arrangements. In fact, developments of TCT include interfirm cooperation as a third intermediate choice between the market and the hierarchy (Smith Ring & van de Ven, 1992, 1994; Williamson, 1991). A firm would activate an IO relationship whenever the production and transaction costs related to this choice are lower than hierarchies and markets if considering other variables: trust and risk.

Nevertheless, the application of TCT to inter-organizational issues presents some major drawbacks (Smith Ring & van de Ven, 1992):

1. Motivations other then efficiency such as equitable outcomes (Smith Ring & van de Ven, 1994), learning and legitimacy are understated.

2. The assumption that markets are invariably characterized by opportunistic behavior contradicts observed trusting behavior in designing governance mechanisms (such as cooperation).

3. By essentially being, above all, a "vertical integration theory" (Plunket et al., 2001), it emphasizes the notion of markets and hierarchies, leaving a void in the understanding of alternative forms (such as joint ventures, joint research projects, extractive resources explorations).

Above all, these models provide an insight into the complexity of the research in the field of IO relationships. Despite the lack of a general and accepted framework, the proposed review allows a better understanding of the reasons driving a company to choose a cooperative behavior. A more extensive analysis on this field in IS literature can be found in the work by Kern and Willcocks (2000) or from an organizational standpoint in Barringer and Harrison (2000).

ICT and IO Relationships

A fundamental role in the analysis of implications of ICT adoption on IO relationships should be acknowledged to the work of Venkatraman (1994). In defining the business-transformation levels, he identified four different functions where ICT would have enabled the redesign of the network of relationships of a business: transaction processing, inventory movement, process linkage, and knowledge leverage. The expected redefinition of companies' boundaries through the adoption of ICT should have then produced potential benefits on three main fronts: efficiency, differentiation, and learning.

In a recent extensive review of the literature, Dewett and Jones (2001) investigated the impacts of ICT on organizational characteristics and results by studying the moderating and beneficial effects of information efficiencies and synergies (like higher efficiency, organizational innovation, increased coordination, and collaboration). The study highlighted the effects on IO relations and the resulting benefits in terms of:

•   Cost savings

•   Lower transaction costs, governance costs, and exposure to opportunism

- Smaller firm size
- More efficient suppliers and customers linkage, and customer lock-in
- Divergent value chains linkage
- Support to the building of innovative capabilities
- Collaborative learning process enhancement

Despite this richness of studies suggesting wide IT impacts on IO relationships, a large part of the software industry, as well as a lot of research in the IS field, has been focusing on a more specific matter: the automation of economic and financial transactions.

Well before the advent of the Internet, electronic fund transfer (EFT) and electronic data interchange (EDI) systems had reached a high degree of spread. More recently, the opportunities of Internet technologies have been driving software companies to differentiate their offers, also following the hypes of e commerce, e procurement, e-supply chain management solutions. Such a differentiation makes it difficult to understand the range of applications of each type of system.

On this matter, Pavlou and El Sawy recently summarized several theories on interfirm relations and proposed *the reach of relations* as the most appropriate dimension with which to examine business relationships (Pavlou & El Sawy, 2002). The reach of relations measures the number of potential partners to which a firm has access, i.e., potential trading partners in a B2B exchange. The cross-

Figure 1: The two-dimensional classification scheme of interfirm relations (a) and ICT solutions (b).

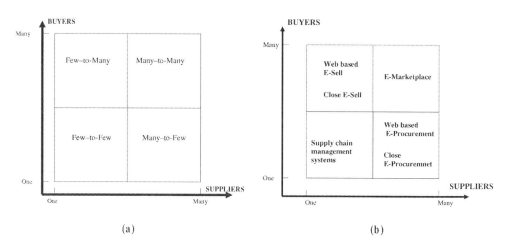

Source: Adapted from Pavlou and El Sawy (2002).

analysis of this dimension for buyers and suppliers results in a two-dimensional classification scheme that allows for the identification of four forms of interfirm relations (Figure 1a).

Within each of the four cells of the scheme, it is possible to map a wide set of ICT solutions for IO relationships (Figure 1b):

- E-marketplaces (many to many): This is defined as a virtual place where multiple buyers and suppliers are able to transact, buying or selling goods or services, asking for cost estimates, offering, and stipulating commercial relationships (Giamminola, 2001). E-marketplaces make it possible to match demand with offer so that buyers can reduce procurement costs and suppliers can improve the visibility of their companies and products (Neef, 2001; Phillips, 2000; Raisch, 2001). On the other hand, the number of firms involved in this type of exchange precludes strong interfirm relations (Pavlou & El Sawy, 2002).

- E-procurement systems (many to few): This is a solution that allows (Pavlou & El Sawy, 2002, p. 13) "traditional powerful buyers [to] capture benefits by leveraging their existing physical power [...] into online B2B exchanges"

- E-sell systems (few to many): This is a virtual sales channel through which few big suppliers put their products and catalogs at many buyers' disposal. It is a mechanism that closely follows the primary model for business-to-consumer e-commerce.

- Supply-chain management systems (few to few): These are solutions that support close and strategic relationships between a small number of firms. They benefit from Web-based technologies to exceed the substantial costs that limited the spread of EDI solutions for this type of relationship.

Although providing a systematic representation of a segment of the software market, this scheme can only partially contribute to the aims of the present study. With respect to such aims, Pavlou's work lacks in completeness, because relationships not dealing with an economic transaction are simply excluded, and in practical relevance, because each of the ICT solutions supports only one type of relationship at a time. It is unrealistic (in terms of costs involved and time needed) that a business association can implement and integrate a set of different solutions supporting each single interfirm relation. The proposed framework should consider a wider range of dimensions, thus including more agents and ICT solutions.

On the other hand, there is evidence that business associations are already making use of Internet technologies to support their members. On this subject,

Table 1: Business associations and Internet services

	Italy (n° / %)	Australia (n° / %)
Informative Portal	85 / 70,8%	58 / 69%
Portal unreachable or Not Checkable	18 / 15,0%	3 / 3,6%
No Presence	17 / 14,2%	23 / 27,4%
Total	103 / 100%	84 / 100%

we collected data (in February 2003) by searching the Internet for the available Internet services offered by the Italian business associations listed by Confindustria (Italian main manufacturers association) (www.confindustria.it) and the Australian business associations listed by Business Entry Point (www.business.gov.au). The outcomes of this research clearly show that most of the Italian and Australian business associations are already present on the Internet, even though they provide members typically with mere information services through Internet portals (Table 1).

The potential improvement of services offered by business associations is thus evidently big, while, it is likewise necessary to overcome a buyer–seller approach in order to develop a solution tailored on business associations' requirements. We name this solution the *Virtual Association Platform* (VAP).

The Virtual Association Platform Model

The Virtual Association Platform (VAP) can be described as a computer-based IO information system supporting what we can refer to as the *association as a whole* (the association as an independent organization and the set of the members of the organization). Such a system should integrate the functionalities typical of a variety of software packages (between the others: the ones cited above) and provide an electronic *front office* easily accessible to all the actors connected to a business association, and mainly the association's members.

Generally speaking, the association as a whole should not involve only intra-associative relationships, i.e., relations between subjects mostly belonging to an environment of a same association (association to members; members to members). In fact, a VAP limited to intra-organizational relations would miss managing the large amount of extra-association relations that could be even more important for the association's members. Therefore, the technological platform of the VAP should be suitable to interact with other ICT solutions both inside and outside the environment of the association, such as:

Figure 2: The VAP and the relationships it should be able to support

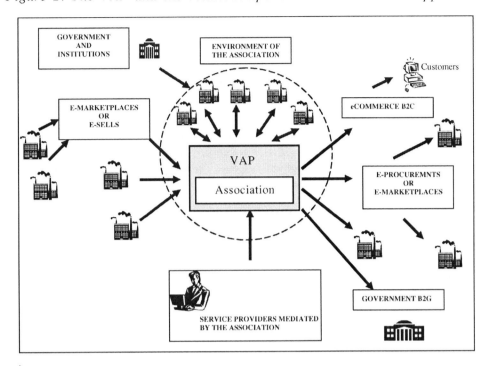

- Other electronic solutions for procurement (e-marketplaces, e-procurements, etc.) to buy or supply strategic or nonstrategic goods and services outside the environment of the association
- B2C e-commerce sites of members of the association and e-malls to which a member may take part
- ERP systems of members and members' partners

The development of a VAP is subject to the definition of a general reference model of a VAP. The VAP model should meet the specific requirements of IO relationships with which a business association has to deal.

Using the business association's functions and activities (described in the section entitled "Business association activities"), it is possible to identify the most relevant actors involved, or, in other words, the actors engaging in relationships with the association's members or directly with the association (Table 2).

Obviously, the fundamental role is played by the association's members, who can be part of different supply chains or of the same one (and, in this case, each member can play at a different level of the supply chain, as supplier or competitor or customer of another member).

Table 2: Activities and actors related to a business association

Activities	Actors involved
Coordination and regulation	Association, Members
Representation of interests	Association, Members, Government (Local and National), Financial Institutions, Suppliers, Customers, Consumers
Provision of services	Association, Members, Government (Local and National), Financial Institutions, Suppliers, Customers, Consumers, Other Associations

Besides them, a number of organizations not belonging to the association interact with it in various ways. Local and national governments impose constraints as well as generate business opportunities for the association's members. Financial institutions are vital for those members whose investment capabilities cannot be sustained only by internal funding.

Moreover, it seems relevant to put into evidence other suppliers and customers (business customers and consumers) who do not belong to the business association. In fact, relationships engaged by members with these actors are not characterized by the same level of trust and sharing of interests of intra-association relationships, but are essentially based on goods and financial transactions.

Finally, a business association can find it efficient or even strategic to sign a partnership agreement with another association, in order to share (or to sell) the services it provides to its own members with the members of the other association.

For the aims of this chapter, it is necessary to analyze the eventual relationships that could occur between each couple of the actors identified. The easiest way to represent such relationships is to draw a table in which these actors represent the headings of both rows and columns and to study if each cell is meaningful, i.e., if the corresponding relationship occurs.

Table 3 shows the framework of such a table—cells shaded gray represent relationships that do not occur in an association's environment; the other cells represent activities involving IO processes, thus an interaction between two different actors, dealing with the activities of a business association. In particular:

- White highlights those cells representing relationships where the association plays an *intermediary* in the relationship between members and other actors.

- Gray highlights those cells representing relationships where the association acts as the *provider* (or the *addressee*) of services and information to (or from) other actors.

The description of the association's functions and activities leads to include in the framework all the interactions between the members and all the actors and vice versa (first row and first column of Table 3) and the interactions between the association and all the actors (second row of Table 3).

The particular role played by the government (third row of Table 3) deserves clarification. In fact, the government engages in relations with the members of an association, playing different roles:

- As a customer of products sold by members
- As a supplier of financial support to members
- As an institution defining rules on transactions

Generally, the government (Administration, Education, Health, etc.) represents a set of actors that influences the characteristics of the environment in which members are located, thus it influences the way members engage in relationships with their customers and suppliers. For instance, Administration laws (at the local as well as the national levels) impose constraints on transactions; likewise, the Education system of the territory where members are located characterizes the overall infrastructure in which the members operate. In this sense, the government has an indirect relation with any actor dealing with the association's members. Once the actual IO relationships are defined, this general framework enables the identification of the most typical IO information flows, and finally allows for the description of the requirements of the VAP model.

As mentioned above, a complete framework should take into account not only buying and selling activities, but also the infrastructural ones (such as company

Table 3: The framework of the relationships occurring between the actors identified

FROM \ TO	members	association	government	financial institutions	NOT-member suppliers	NOT-member customer	members' consumers
members							
association							
government							
financial institutions							
NOT-member suppliers							
NOT-member customers							
members' consumers							

Table 4: The framework of the relationships and the corresponding information exchanged

from \ to	type of information flows	members	association	government	financial institutions	NOT-member suppliers	NOT-member customers (B2B)	members' consumers (B2C)
members	A	procurement and selling information, e.g. stock availabilities and over stocks, product catalogues, financial transaction information	information on production (that the association aggregate to provide information on sector production)	financial/fiscal figures; information on bureaucracy fulfillments (depending on the government laws and procedures; e.g. providing data regarding a newly created		- to suppliers of goods: information about supply chain issues (material flows, material needs) - to suppliers of "real" services: information required by the suppliers to deliver the service (e.g. wages and salaries processing, training)	- updated information on members' activities and products (to promote itself for customer acquisition) - customer support services (e.g. post-sale assistance)	- order management information, - product availability, - delivery and payment terms, - financial transaction, - order status and tracking
	B	know how on specific activities (technical advice), information on ext actors (suppliers and customers) information on members' employees information on ext suppliers information on operative opportunities (e.g. logistics) and strategic business opportunities	request of provision of services information on members' interests and members' instances (to drive association's lobbying)		balance sheet and business plan and other information regarding members' strategy	updated information on members' activities and products (to promote itself for customer acquisition) and extend the reach to new suppliers		- updated information on members' activities and products (to promote itself for customer acquisition) - customer support services (e.g. post-sale assistance)
association	A	information on sector production (allowing price control)	information from one association to another that have signed an agreement and that typically share the same geographical location or the same type of interests (chambers of commerce, local industrial association) or belong the same supply chain; services of 1 association to its members provided to the other association's members, know how and information			aggregated orders from members (group-aggregated acquisition e.g. through auctions) that are clients of the same supplier	aggregated offers from members that are suppliers of the same business customers	
	B	"real" services (info on markets, benchmarking) and vertical diffusion of information on industrial standards (horizontal or vertical coordination)		updated information on members' activities and members' interests in order to perform lobbying, intermediation, negotiation	updated information on members' activities and members' interests in order to perform lobbying, intermediation, negotiation	updated aggregated information on members' activities and products (to promote members and for lobbying)	updated information on members' activities and products (to promote members and for lobbying)	
government	A	- information on call for tenders for member's products and services			information on the legal framework and norms (custom duties, tributes) valid in the geographical area of association	information on the legal framework and norms (custom duties, tributes) valid in the geographical area of the association	information on the legal frameworks and norms (custom duties, tributes) valid in the geographical area of the association	
	B	- information on funding available to members - updated information on government activities (to promote itself and extend the reach to new suppliers) - laws and regulations						
financial institutions	A	- financial reporting on transactions						
	B	- general information on offered products and services						
NOT-member suppliers	A	- from suppliers of goods: information on supply chain management (material flows, material availability, order status and tracking) - from suppliers of "real" services: information constituting the service (that is delivered to the members as customers of the service)						
	B	updated information on suppliers' activities and products (to promote suppliers among the members)						
NOT-member customers (B2B)	A	information necessary to members to perform the transaction (customer's address, terms of the orders, form of payment)						
	B	- request of information on members' activities and products - request of pre- and post-sales support						
members' consumers (B2C)	A	information necessary to members to perform the transaction (customer's address, terms of the orders, form of payment)						
	B	- request of information on members' activities and products - request of pre- and post-sales support						

promotion, human resources management, knowledge management). These activities, even though not directly related to supply-chain management and financial transactions, contribute to the building of and enforcement of IO links. Coherently with this subdivision, information flows pertaining to each relation identified by a valid cell should be specified as follows:

1. Directly related to product/money flows: Those supporting procurement or commerce or supply-chain management activities)
2. Not directly related to product/money flows: Those supporting visibility of a company or cooperation between companies

Remarkably, the scheme does not examine in detail the quality of the service provided through information flows, and therefore, it does not distinguish relationships according, for example, to the timing or the degree of detail or the type (e.g., marketing information rather than technical specification of products) of the information exchanged across the relations. In fact, the VAP model aims at providing a descriptive rather than a prescriptive framework that should be specified according to the characteristics of a business association. Moreover, even though not explicit in the framework, community management activities should be considered to be embedded in the association's role, thus supported by the VAP.

Table 4 shows the framework of the relationships and the corresponding information flows. Association's members exchange the largest part of information that the VAP supports because of their direct relationship with all the actors determined. Members should be provided with all means to interact through the VAP both directly and indirectly on products and money flows, exploiting the potential of being at the same time into an electronic marketplace, a community hub, a communication platform (with financial institutions and governments), and a marketing/support tool (with customer and suppliers). When dealing with transactions of goods and services, the information exchanged would be that of a typical business transaction. The proposed framework adopts a general notion of transaction and related information requirements. Depending on the characteristics and heterogeneity of business association's members, the VAP should support different information flows accordingly.

The following paragraphs describe in detail the content of the framework and provide a general specification and a few examples of the information requirements of each classified IO relationship.

Members to Members

Considering the relationships between members of the association, the VAP should support all the information flows characteristic of an electronic marketplace, thus supporting members in performing procurement and selling activities (i.e., stock availabilities, possible overstocks, and product catalogs). One of the distinctive aspects of interactions in an associative environment is the exchange of general and competitive context-related information (know-how or how to on specific activities, information on external agents, information on foreseeable customers and suppliers or employees of associates' firms). Other interactions could concern information for the coordination of joint competitive strategies or business opportunities.

Members to Association

The association operates at a higher level than the other actors, providing intermediation services (thus, in this context, "infomediation") other than being an aggregator of members' instances. If members would provide the association with timely information on range and availability of their products, then the association could propose an aggregated offer by composing the offers of different members.

A second category of information exchanged between members and the association relates to requests of services provisioning. Differently, the association could act as a hub and thus aggregate possible instances from members. The collected information could then be used by the association in order to drive its actions for the creation of new supporting services. Moreover, the collected instances could require associations to leverage on their representative power and pursue lobby activities on specified institutions.

Members to Government

The interaction between members and government is not direct but is mediated by the association (and the VAP). In this context, it is possible for the association to provide support to members replying to government's calls for bid.

A simpler approach would consist of using the VAP to enhance government procurement activities. Finally, the VAP could be used to support, in the interaction between business and government, the information exchanges required to fulfill fiscal or "bureaucratic" obligations.

Members to Financial institutions

Generally speaking, financial institutions act as service providers for business associations supporting members' transactions. At the same time, it is common for business associations to have strong relationships with selected financial institutions and banks. These preferred partners could grant members better terms and conditions in force of an agreement with the business association.

Members could use the VAP to support the information exchange with the financial institutions and share or transfer, for example, financial figures, balance sheets, or business plans.

Members to Not-Members Suppliers

The typical information flows between members and not-member suppliers involve procurement activities: because such suppliers are not-members, their transactions should take place outside the boundaries of the association. Even in this case, the VAP could come to aid by allowing nonmembers to have restricted access to specific types of information related to members. Through the VAP, members could provide:

- To their supplier of goods, information useful for effective supply-chain management (data on material flows, material needs and availability, etc.)

- To their supplier of services, information required for the service provision, such as names of the employee for wages and salaries processing, or the mailing list for a mailing campaign; it should be noted that whenever in the presence of a well-established relationship, the association and the not-member supplier could find it helpful to agree on a common data interchange standard, e.g., making use of XML templates

Members to Not-Members Customers (B2B)

The application domain is similar to the one described above for not-members suppliers. Specifically, the VAP can act as a portal, offering all the services needed to engage a prospective customer. It is typical for a portal to require registration before starting the true transaction, and thus, the VAP should provide just an informative service or those services that the association decided to make publicly available.

Members to Member's Consumer (B2C)

The only difference with the case of the B2B transaction with not-members is the subject interacting with the VAP: an individual or consumer instead of a business. The implications on the VAP deal with the services offered that should be tailored to suit consumer's needs. In fact, B2B versus B2C sales management activities can differ substantially. The association should consider carefully the market or markets in which it intends to operate and design the VAP accordingly.

Association to Members

The interaction between the association and its members is fundamental to strengthen the relationships among them and to improve commitment and trust. The typical coordination role of business associations could be played to enhance the transfer of information to members via the VAP. In particular, the VAP could keep companies updated with aggregated figures regarding cumulative production and prices of a sector or local area. This information could allow companies to pursue price control strategies.

The most typical communication from the association to its members is related to the provision of general information services. However, many associations have recognized the strategic relevance of the provision of educational services, through which they can improve the average competitiveness of their members by developing their competences as well as by propagating information on an industrial standard that could possibly influence industry efficiency. As a consequence, training activities sponsored and managed by associations are becoming increasingly popular. In this case, the VAP might be employed as a platform supporting e-learning activities.

Association to Association

Very often, business associations interact continuously with other institutions that aggregate companies (such as other associations geographically localized, associations in the same value chain or synergic interests, chambers of commerce, etc.). These relationships can sometimes be formalized and enforced by a signed agreement based on the reciprocal provision of services to members. The VAP could facilitate the coordination and the reach of such services to the entire set of members of the associations involved.

Association to Government

The information exchanged from the association to government concerns member's activities and interests. This case is similar to the one discussed above (association to association), in fact, associations compose their members' interests and deal with governmental institutions, such as local governments or public administrations. In such a position, associations can act as brokers of members' requests and lobby government. The VAP could help with these tasks by simplifying the collecting and aggregating of members' instances.

Associations to Financial Institutions

It is well known how SMEs, which represent by far the majority of members of a BA, experience obstacles in gaining access to funding from financial institutions. One of the reasons is the lack of information (and subsequently, lack of trust) about firms' activities and expected results, which are essential to determine the risk level of any investment. In its role of members' representative, the BA is in the position to act as an intermediary and negotiator by providing and granting financial institutions the necessary exchange of information concerning members' activities, and finally, negotiating credit facilities for its members. In this sense, the VAP could prove another effective application.

Whenever banks or insurance companies belong to the BA, as the financial system is double tied with the interests of the local community, this information exchange is obviously made even more effective.

Association to not-members suppliers

When dealing with not-members suppliers, the BA plays the typical role of a broker. VAP can collect orders from members, aggregate them, and act as a purchasing group in order to achieve better conditions from the not-members suppliers.

Moreover, in this case, BA could play an informative role by promoting and informing suppliers on members' activities and products.

Association to not-members customers (B2B relationship)

The relationship occurring between the association and the not-members' customers is symmetrical to the one with not-members. Associations can aggregate members' offers for prospecting suppliers, increasing the reach of the single company or raising their contractual powers. This aggregation allows the acquisition of new customers by enhancing the ability to enter new markets or to generate larger orders of supplies.

Eventually, the association might pursue promotion and lobbying also among these actors.

Association to Not-members Consumers (B2C Relationship)

In this type of relationship, the BA can help members through the VAP by promoting on the Web their brand or even their specific products. In some context, the VAP could also feature order management features and could be used as a direct distribution channel.

Government to Members

The relationship between government and members is characterized by size. First, the VAP could propagate updated information on the legal framework, on activities, and eventually on the services offered. Moreover, assuming that local laws would admit it, governmental institutions could place and manage directly through the VAP their tenders and the possibly following procurement activities.

Government to other actors

Through the VAP, government can promote its activities among citizens and companies and propagate information on the legal framework and on local laws.

If a government institution subscribes to the VAP, it would gain access to the same set of functionalities of BA members, and therefore, it could use the VAP as a channel through which to distribute information related to its activities.

Financial Institutions to Members

We assume that financial institutions are involved in two main information flows. The first concerns information on transactions completed by members; the second flow concerns the possible promotional communications on products and services offered.

The first flow contains Internet banking and the information that originates from the management of online payments made by customers on members' sites.

The second flow could be seen as an alternative form of unsolicited advertisement, so the association should carefully consider the option to support this activity.

Not-Members Suppliers to Members

In order to support these information flows, the VAP should allow suppliers to provide members with updated information on the supply chain. Remarkably, this function could operate only under two conditions: first, the absence of a generally accepted standard for information exchange on the supply chain; second, before exchanging supply chain information, the BA should require the not-member to subscribe or associate.

Besides, the VAP could be used as a distribution channel of information, news, and software by not-members companies characterized by information intensive services (e.g., consulting companies).

Finally, as above, the VAP could allow not-members suppliers to advertise their products, after having taken into consideration the possible outcomes.

Not-members customers and consumers to members

The information exchange between not-members customers and members is generally part of a transaction: customers provide information to members when requesting the pricing or information on terms and conditions of the sale or when filling in all the forms for completing a transaction. Information flows not directly related to products and services are generally linked to pre- and post-sales support.

The next section provides a case example of a VAP from design to deployment.

2Cities.com

The Background

As early as 1999, a small group of interested parties came together to discuss whether the Internet could be used to facilitate a community portal for a regional community area north of Perth in Western Australia. The region was Joondalup, a rapidly developing suburban "new town" area. Founders realized that funding support would be needed and that they could substantially increase their bargaining power by extending the concept to their neighboring region, Wanneroo (only recently established as a separate council splitting out of the Joondalup council region). The stakeholders group thus included:

1.   The two councils (Joondalup and Wanneroo)

2.   The Joondalup Business Enterprise Centre

3.   The two local Business Associations (Joondalup and Wanneroo)

4.   Edith Cowan University (ECU) and two local colleges in the same education precinct

Table 5: E-commerce usage in Joondalup and Wanneroo

Internet usage	Joondalup %	Wanneroo %	Australian Average	
			Small %	Medium %
Internet Connection	58	60	60	89
Web Page	44	40	25	56
Purchase on Line	31	27	17	28
Sell on Line	31	N/A		
Business needs Web Page	23	20		

The stakeholders were approximately 220,000 residents, 7000 small businesses (2002 estimate carried out by local Business Associations), and three tertiary education facilities.

A survey of 1000 local businesses conducted in association with Edith Cowan University, comprising 600 businesses in Joondalup and 400 businesses in Wanneroo, indicated that current e-commerce usage was fairly high, as shown in Table 5.

This indicated that businesses in the region were at least as well advanced as average Australian businesses, and possibly more advanced in the areas of online transactions and Internet technology business applications in general.

The project was given the go-ahead by the North Metro Community On-Line Association (NMCOA) in conjunction with business, for the benefit of businesses in the region and to develop the Northern Suburbs as an attractive location in which new businesses can develop and grow.

Table 6: Milestones and key players in 2Cities platform development

.Year	Stage	Project Manager	Situation	Income
1999	Joondalup Stakeholders Group	PM-A	Small group gathering	N/A
2000	Waneroo/Joondalup Regional Online Steering Committee +ECU	PM-A	Creating the basic group of stakeholders, the "demonstration site" is put online by Joondalup Business Association	20.000 AU$ from the State Government
March 2001	NMCOA	PM-A	The NMCOA is created to be a separate financial and political body from stakeholders that can receive and manage founds	90,660 AU$ from Federal Government (RAP) 108.000 AU$ from the 2 cities and ECU
Feb 2002	IBC win contract	PM-A becomes part time consultant	Development of the Portal	70.000 AU$ for contract
May 2002		PM-B	PM-A resigns PM-B appointed TM (Team Manager) appointed	92,000 AU$ SBDC (Small Business Development Corporation) grant for TM
August 2002	Portal in test phase	PM-C	PM-B appointment withdrawn PM-C appointed TM resigns	
Dec 2002	Portal completed (6 months overdue) 60 users	PM-C	Soft launch of 2Cities.com	A$190 each
Feb 2003	Intended launch	PM-C	Delayed – new business plan developed	$50,000 additional revenue sought from 2 councils
April	Official Launch	PM-C		

The stakeholder group together sought seed funding of AU$20,000 from State Government, and in 2000 developed a demonstration site to sell the concept.

Specifications were developed and budgets proposed, and when the extent of funding and commitment required was fully understood, the NMCOA was formed in March 2001. At this time, the three main players, the two councils and the university, were asked to make a substantial investment in the concept and provided funding of AU$190,000. In addition, the State Government was asked to contribute AU$100,000. NMCOA would act as an independent body to manage finances and control the development of the platform. Table 6 shows the development timetable, some of the key players, and the major milestones impacting the implementation of 2Cities.

2Cities Supported Relationships

The general objective of the project was to develop a VAP within the community of stakeholders mentioned above.

2Cities.com is meant to permit Joondalup and Wanneroo region-based businesses to sell, supporting basically a local "member to member" relationship, but theoretically anyone worldwide, once registered, can buy through the VAP. In fact, 2Cities.com can be accessed by anyone, but in order to sell through the VAP, businesses must be registered as members of the portal (AU$199). This means that tenders from buyers are accessed only by members.

This policy is intended to give to business settled inside this region an infrastructure that can be a competitive advantage, and it could also encourage relocation of business. This choice limits the potentials of the VAP, as it reduces dramatically the interaction opportunities between members and not-members, leaving only the ability to exchange basic information on products and services. On the other hand, requiring the registration before a transaction automatically changes the relationship into one of member to member.

Organizations seeking to purchase goods or services can use the VAP to send requests for quotations (RFQs), lodge orders, and segment members by locality. Seller members can be notified of RFQs by e-mail, fax, or SMS (Short Message Service), and orders can be placed in a similar manner.

In order to sustain the market, large corporate buyers have to commit to the market and to the support agreed from the cities of Joondalup and Wanneroo, Mindarie Regional Council, and the university. The VAP provides member buyers with easy access to a large range of suppliers and choice of goods, and increases their ability to obtain competitive pricing. In addition, it is anticipated that suppliers operating within the VAP will use the process to purchase their own requirements, thus increasing the level of trade within the region.

In addition, 2Cities is meant to develop the communities of Joondalup and Wanneroo and to offer a marketing service for promoting the area, through directories like environment, sport, tourism, and education.

Finally, the 2Cities.com project plans to foster local job recruitment as another way to improve the attractiveness of the region.

A possible future expansion of the system, allowing the domestic consumers to purchase online, has the potential to result in rapid growth in transaction levels. Furthermore, once familiar with e-trading and having benefited from increased regional sales, businesses will be in a position to expand outside the region, to state, interstate, and overseas markets.

NMCOA and the business associations will be well placed to assist companies in this type of expansion and, where required, arrange introductions to local companies already operating in these marketplaces. Such a mentoring process can lead to efficient entry into new markets. Training is an additional requirement, and the Small Business Development Corporation provided 92,000AU$ to recruit a training officer for the platform.

The conservative estimate used in the business model is that some 1200 companies will be operating within the VAP within 5 years. Indications from the business associations and seminars held by NMCOA are that uptake will be significantly higher than that allowed for in the business model. An example of this is that the Joondalup Business Association has recently approached NMCOA to incorporate 1100 companies onto the business listing section of the site.

The business model adopted by 2Cities.com is totally dependent on a critical mass of large corporate buyers. The platform, however, does not necessarily offer any advantages to these groups, because the sellers, typically SMEs, are unlikely able to offer discounted prices for large orders. Moreover, as indicated above, even though promotion is essential to build the success of the VAP, 2Cities.com has no marketing budget.

Table 7: Application of the IOR4VAP framework to 2Cities.com

From \ To	type of information flows	members	Association	government	Financial institutions	NOT-member suppliers	NOT-member customers (B2B)	consumers (B2C)
members	A							
members	B					Membership required	Membership required	Membership required
association	A							
association	B							
government	A							
government	B							
financial institutions	A							
financial institutions	B							
NOT-member suppliers	A	Membership required						
NOT-member suppliers	B							
NOT-member customers (B2B)	A	Membership required						
NOT-member customers (B2B)	B							
members' consumers (B2C)	A	Membership required						
members' consumers (B2C)	B							

Table 7 presents the application of the IOR4VAP (inter-organizational relationship for virtual association platform) framework to the case of 2Cities.com: white cells represent supported relationships, while black corresponds to relationships not supported.

Even though 2Cities supports nearly all the information flows relevant for a VAP, it does not offer support to four types of relationships:

1. From association to external suppliers and customers (A-directly related to product/money flows): The aggregation of both members' supply and procurement activities is not supported. Each member is offering its products and is managing the procurement by itself.

2. From association to members (A-directly related to product/money flows): The information on aggregate production is not collected, and coordination does not exist. Thus, it is not possible to provide price control services.

3. From members to government (B-not directly related to product/money flows): 2Cities supports only a buyer and seller relationship with government.

4. From members to financial institutions (B-not directly related to product/ money flows): Only payments and transactions are provided by the platform.

The first two relationships are unsupported, mainly because they require a certain critical mass before being set up. The other two depend more on design choices made in the development phase.

Because the 2Cities project is still taking its first steps, its support to relationships is still basic. Available services are generally informative, and only commerce relations have received good support. Once the portal is well established, the set of supported relationships will be broadened.

Problems Faced

Given its high degree of innovation, the development of 2Cities.com encountered a number of critical issues and obstacles, impacting several aspects of the project:

*   Poor business plan
*   Low capitalization
*   Project overrun

- Poor project management—three separate project managers
- Mistiming of training requirements
- No marketing and training budgets

The initial business plan was almost wholly dependent on grant income that did not materialize and with unrealistic costs for platform users ($500 per annum as compared to a final fee of $199). The founding members did not realize the extent to which additional funding would be required or the full extent of technical expertise that would be required to implement the portal. Project managers came and went (three over 1 year: PM—A, B, and C in Table 6), and a training manager was appointed over 6 months before the implementation of the portal and resigned prior to the test period. The 2Cities budget had no provision for marketing or training costs, and while the revised business plan now includes a provision for marketing, additional funds (through government grants or through voluntary contributions from the partners) must be obtained.

2Cities.com began operating in December 2002, although the "official" launch did not take place until March 2003. To date, 60 businesses and 39 community groups are registered in the portal, and communities need critical mass to remain active.

Furthermore, online community management is still poor, mainly because of the following:

1. The VAP stakeholders and customer communities are very different.
2. The differences in VAP-supported relations involve very different players but all are required to adopt some basic standards.

Both of these issues impact content creation and value generation from the online communities, thus reducing the ability of VAP to provide support to players' interactions.

Development Process and Practical Implications

2Cities.com was developed without explicitly adopting a formal methodology, because ECU was not involved in the earliest stages of the project. The initiators' group did not perform any real requirements analysis and no real business plan was drawn up. Instead, a semistructured deployment model was adopted that centered on three activities essential to the success of every online community (Williams & Cothrel, 2000): member development, asset management, and community relations. The following paragraphs discuss these activities and the related issues that arose within 2Cities.com.

Member Development

Communities need critical mass to remain active.The2Cities business model adopted is one that is totally dependent on a critical mass of large corporate buyers. The portal, however, does not necessarily offer any advantages to these groups, because the sellers, typically SMEs, are unlikely to be able to offer discounted prices for large orders. Promotion is essential to build the community, but, in fact, 2Cities.com has no marketing budget.

Asset Management

Assets in an online community range from content, to alliances with other groups, to the knowledge and experience of experts, to the community infrastructure. The community coordinator needs to capture the information members need, but 2Cities has two customer communities as a focus—the regional marketplace community and the social community. These two groups have very different needs from an online community, require different support, and need different training. Content generation is required for each of the five types of e-commerce supported in the portal, each involving very different players but all required to adopt some basic standards. An ongoing project manager is essential.

Community Relations

Interaction with other people is essential for successful creation of an active online community but requires online moderation and facilitation. The desired "village community" of 2Cities.com will require constant moderation, yet has to stimulate member-generated content that will be seen to be of value to a very diverse community. There is an additional political dimension here, because the two communities are, in fact, quite competitive and do not normally view themselves as a single group.

Ownership

A further factor identified in this review of 2Cities.com revolves around ownership. The portal is "owned" by a consortium, all with different motives, varying degrees of investment, and often conflicting aspirations for the outcomes. Inevitably, other factors such as politics intrude on the funding and operation of the portal. A recent proposal that may well be a longer-term solution is to sell ownership to the stakeholders.

Conclusions and Discussion

This chapter is a first contribution to the study of ICT application to improve BA environment.

The IOR4VAP model herein presented is a comprehensive framework for the analysis of the information requirements of BA activities. The roles and the descending relationships identified could be used by BAs to design ICT-supported applications.

Previous studies on BA came from organizational and institutional research, and little or no literature was found on ICT adoption within this context. Only recently has the research on the role of institutions in economic growth begun to highlight the activities of a BA and recognize its contributions. More attention to BAs has been given by organizational and industrial network studies, where IS research has been focusing on industrial districts (Micelli & Di Maria, 2000).

Despite the fact that ICT impacts on IO relationships are not questioned, the nature of these impacts is still not clear for two main reasons. On one hand, the IS literature has not yet come to a generally accepted understanding of ICT effects on relationships, and the literature is mainly based on the typical arguments of automation. On the other hand, even when considering the literature on "organizational models," the main stress seems to be on efficiency and costs.

According to these approaches, a BA should adopt a VAP because of the deriving selective benefits of information in terms of decrease in information and transaction costs and locking of the members to the specific platform (a sort of lock-in as the exit from the VAP becomes costly).

Another issue that arises from the study is whether such benefits are sufficient to generate a real and sustainable competitive advantage. This question is even more difficult to answer: it is not clear if BAs can truly contribute to economic growth (Doner & Schneider, 2000) and if ICT can be a source of competitive advantage (Powell & Dent-Micallef, 1997). The monitoring of the 2Cities.com initiative and the study of other BAs could, in future works, fill these gaps.

Governance issues are not explicitly covered in this chapter despite the centrality in the literature regarding BAs and industrial districts. However, the VAP model is an extremely flexible approach, and it is sufficiently general to be applicable in heterogeneous BA environments or in situations characterized by the interaction of different agents.

Finally, authors acknowledge that another issue needs further investigation: the review of the technology used or usable to support the identified relationships. In fact, the chapter is focused on the analysis of information requirements, which is the step just before the identification or development of ICT applications supporting IO relationships.

Yet, considering these limitations, authors believe this study has a major implication for practitioners working in the BA environment. The proposed IOR4VAP framework is a global model for the definition of the information requirements for the design of a technological platform supporting its activities. In this perspective, it is a valid tool that allows a BA to better understand which relationships support and which information will be exchanged.

The significance of this model comes also from the fact that it meets two main requirements for a successful implementation. In fact, a VAP could be, at the same time, *secure* and *trusted*—like every service supplied by an association is generally considered (Bennett & Robson, 2001)—and *effective*, being developed on the specific requirements of the associate enterprises that should use it. Equally, the *Virtual Association Platform* complies with the current opinion that business associations have to redefine their strategies and expand their services. Associations should facilitate SMEs in those activities that cannot be accomplished by single organizations (i.e., logistic, procurement, internationalization, and technological innovation) and that, therefore, require IO relationships and a certain "critical mass."

In this sense, the main achievement of the developed archetype is to be able to manage not only a specific type of IO relationship (many to many, many to few, etc.), like the solutions that have been found out in the market. Through the VAP, each member of the association and the association can relate at the same time with different organizations and for different aims—information exchange, request for quotations, supply-chain management, etc.—using just one simple interface.

However, as shown by the case example, it should not be taken for granted that a BA is willing to have a comprehensive platform supporting all information flows. Associations first try to support the more value-generating ones (informative and buyer/seller relationships) and then try to exploit community services, often not taking into account the inherent potential of a broader approach.

With respect to the software systems on the market, no "all in one" solution is available, yet. Supporting so many and different relations requires going beyond the current specialization level of commercial applications. Even the 2Cities VAP was custom designed and developed. Therefore, on the technological side, the success of this archetype will be measured by the ability of a VAP to integrate the existing applications or to develop an open platform integrating or exchanging information with the members' current information systems.

References

Alberti, F. (1998). L'evoluzione delle associazioni di piccoli imprenditori: il caso Confartigianato Alto Milanese/The evolution of small entrepreneurs' business associations: The case of Confartigianato Alto Milanese, *LIUC papers* (Vol. 49, pp. 1–35). Castellanza: LIUC.

Alberti, F. (1999). *The transformation of business associations services for SMEs. Theory and empirical evidence.* Paper presented at the International Council for Small Business, Naples.

Aldrich, H., & Staber, U. (1988). Organizing business interests: Patterns of trade associations foundings, transformations and deaths. In G. R. Carrol (Ed.), *Ecological models of organisations.* Cambrige, MA: Ballinger Publishing Company.

Barney, J. (1986). Organizational culture: Can it be a source of sustained competitive advantage? *Academy of Management Review, 11*(3), 656–665.

Barney, J. (1991). Firm resources and sustained competitive advantage. *Journal of Management, 17*(1), 99–120.

Barringer, B. R., & Harrison, J. S. (2000). Walking a tightrope: Creating value through interorganizational relationships. *Journal of Management, 26*(3), 367–403.

Becattini, G. (1990). The Marshallian Industrial District as a socio-economic notion. In *Industrial district and inter-firm cooperation in Italy*: International Institute for Labor Studies.

Benevolo, F. (1997). *Crisi e Prospettive dell'Associazionismo Imprenditoriale*: Fondazione CENSIS.

Bennett, R. J. (1996). The logic of local business associations: An analysis of voluntary Chambers of Commerce. *Journal of Public Policy, 15*(3), 251–279.

Bennett, R. J., & Robson, P. J. A. (2001). Exploring the market potential and bundling of business association services. *Journal of Services Marketing, 15*(3), 222–239.

Best, M. H. (1990). *The new competition: Institutions of industrial restructuring*. Boston, MA: Harvard University Press.

Bharadwaj, A. S. (2000). A resource-based perspective on information technology capability and firm performance: An empirical investigation. *MIS Quarterly, 24*(1), 169–196.

Bubbio, A. (1997, 27 September). *La Gestione dell'Impresa Artigiana in un Ambiente Ipercompetitivo*. Paper presented at the Lo Sviluppo delle Imprese Artigiane nel Nuovo Mercato. Come Cambiano gli Scenari., Castellanza (Va).

Buonanno, G., Faverio, P., Ravarini, A., Sciuto, D., Tagliavini, M., & Zanaboni, C. (2002). *E-Marketplace nei Distretti Industrilai: Analisi e Modelli Applicativi/E-Marketplace in industrial districts: Analysis and models*. Paper presented at the AICA 2002 ICT, Globalizzazione e Localismi, Conversano (Ba).

Consolati, L. (2000). *Innovazione e Trasferimento Tecnologico nei Distretti Industriali/Innovation and technological transfer within industrial districts*. Retrieved from the World Wide Web: http://www.clubdistretti.it/Newsletter/z-innovazione/consolati_convegno.html.

Costa-Campi, M. T., & Viladecans-Marsal, E. (1999). The district effect and the competitiveness of manufacturing companies in local productive systems. *Urban Studies, 36*(12), 2085–2098.

Doner, R. F., & Schneider, B. R. (2000). Business associations and economic development: Why some associations contribute more than others. *Business and Politics, 2*(3), 261–288.

Easton, G. (1992). Industrial networks: A review. In B. Axelsson & G. Easton (Eds.), *Industrial networks* (pp. 3–27). New York: Routledge.

Enright, M. J., & Roberts, B. H. (2001). Regional clustering in Australia. *Australian Journal of Management, 26*.

European Commission. (1996). Commission Recommendation of 3 April 1996 concerning the definition of small and medium-sized enterprises. *Official Journal L 107*, 0004-0009.

Fariselli, P. (1999). *Small enterprises in the digital economy: New and old challenges*. Paper presented at the Micro, Small, and Medium Enterprises Challenges for Competitiveness, Rio De Janeiro, Brazil.

Fink, D. (1998). Guidelines for the successful adoption of information technology in small and medium-sized enterprises. *International Journal of Information Management*, (18), 243–253.

Giamminola, G. (2001). *E-Marketplace*. ISEDI.

Gordon, I. R., & McCann, P. (2000). Industrial clusters: Complexes, agglomeration and/or social networks. *Urban Studies, 37*(3), 513–532.

Haugland, S. A. (1999). Factors influencing the duration of international buyer-seller relationships. *Journal of Business Research, 46*(3), 273–280.

Kern, T., & Willcocks, L. (2000). Exploring information technology outsourcing relationships: Theory and practice. *Strategic Information Systems, 9*(4), 321–350.

Macneil, I. R. (1978). Contracts: Adjustment of long-term economic relations under classical, neoclassical and relational contract law. *Northwestern University Law Review*, (72), 854–905.

Markusen, A. (1996). Sticky places in slippery spaces: A typology of industrial districts. *Economic Geography, 72*, 293–313.

Marshall, A. (1922). *Principle of economics*. New York: MacMillan Publishing Company.

McDonald, F., & Vertova, G. (2001). Geographical concentration and competitiveness in the European Community. *European Business Review, 13*(3), 157–165.

Micelli, S., & Di Maria, E. (2000). *Distretti Industriali e Tecnologie di Rete: Progettare la Convergenza/Industrial districts and network technologies: Planning the convergence*: Franco Angeli.

Nadvi, K. (1999). *Facing the new competition: Business associations in developing country industrial clusters*. Geneva: ILO International Institute for Labor Studies.

Neef, D. (2001). *E-Procurement. From strategy to implementation*. New York: Financial Times, Prentice-Hall.

Pavlou, P. A., & El Sawy, O. A. (2002). A classification scheme for B2B exchanges and implications for interorganizational eCommerce. In M. Warkentin (Ed.), *Business-to-business electronic commerce: Challenges and solutions*. Hershey, PA: Idea Group Publishing.

Penrose, E. P. (1959). *The theory of the growth of the firm*. New York: John Wiley & Sons.

Pfeffer, J., & Salancik, G. R. (1978). *The external control of organizations*. New York: Harper & Row.

Phillips, C. M. (2000). *The B2B Internet Report*. Morgan Stanley Dean Witter.

Plunket, A., Voisin, C., & Bellon, B. (2001). Introduction: Research on inter-firm collaboration, evolution and perspective. In A. Plunket, C. Voisin, & B. Bellon (Eds.), *The dynamics of industrial collaboration* (pp. 1–13). Cheltenham, UK: Edward Elgar Publishing Limited.

Poon, S. (1999). Small business and Internet commerce: What are the lessons learned? In F. Sudaweeks (Ed.), *Doing business on the Internet: Opportunities and pitfalls*. Heidelberg: Springer-Verlag.

Powell, T. C., & Dent-Micallef, A. (1997). Information technology as competitive advantage: The role of human, business, and technology resources. *Strategic Management Journal, 18*(5), 375–405.

Rabellotti, R. (1999). Recovery of a Mexican cluster: Devaluation bonanza or collective efficiency? *World Development, 27*(9), 1571–1585.

Rabellotti, R., & Schmitz, H. (1999). The internal heterogeneity of industrial districts in Italy, Brazil and Mexico. *Regional Studies, 33*(2), 97–108.

Raisch, W. D. (2001). *The e-marketplace strategies for success in B2B eCommerce*. New York: McGraw-Hill.

Roelandt, T. J. A., & Hertog, P. D. (1998). *Cluster analysis & cluster-based policy in OECD-countries: Various approaches, early results & policy implication*. Hague/Utrecht: OECD.

Smith Ring, P., & van de Ven, A. H. (1992). Structuring cooperative relationships between organizations. *Strategic Management Journal, 13*(7), 483–498.

Smith Ring, P., & van de Ven, A. H. (1994). Developmental processes for cooperative interorganizational relationships. *The Academy of Management Review, 19*(1), 90–118.

Teece, D. J., Pisano, G., & Shuen, A. (1997). Dynamic capabilities and strategic management. *Strategic Management Journal, 18*(7), 509–533.

Tetteh, E. O. (1990). *From business networks to virtual organisation: A strategic approach to business environment transformation in online small and medium-sized enterprises*. Paper presented at the 10th Australasian Conference on Information Systems (ACIS), Wellington, New Zealand.

Tetteh, E. O., & Burn, J. M. (2001). Global strategies for SME-business: Applying the SMALL framework. *Logistics Information Management, 14*(1/2), 171–180.

Venkatraman, N. (1994). IT-Enabled business transformation: From automation to business scope redefinition. *Sloan Management Review, 35*(2), 73–87.

Williams, R. L., & Cothrel, J. (2000). Four smart ways to run online communities. *Sloan Management Review, 14*(4), 81–91.

Williamson, O. E. (1985). *The economic institutions of capitalism*. New York: The Free Press.

Williamson, O. E. (1991). Comparative economic organization: The analysis of discrete structural alternatives. *Administrative Science Quarterly, 36*(2), 269–296.

Zan, S. (1992). *Organizzazione e Rappresentanza/Organization and Delegation*. Rome: La nuova Italia scientifica.

Endnote

[1]   The Commission of European Community indicates that SMEs have less than 250 employees, an annual turnover not exceeding Euro 40 million, or an annual balance-sheet total not exceeding Euro 27 million and which are owned for less than 25% by non-SMEs, except banks or venture capital companies(European Commission, 1996).

Section IV:

Systems Management

Chapter VII

IOIS and Interfirm Networks –
Interdependencies and Managerial Challenges

Stefan Klein
University College Dublin, Ireland

Angeliki Poulymenakou
Athens University of Economics
and Business, Greece

Kai Riemer
University of Muenster, Germany

Dimitris Papakiriakopoulos
Athens University of Economics
and Business, Greece

Marcel Gogolin
University of Muenster, Germany

Athanasios Nikas
Athens University of Economics
and Business, Greece

Abstract

Inter-organizational information systems (IOIS) are information systems (ISs) embedded or deployed in inter-organizational relations. Predominantly, these inter-organizational relations can be qualified as interfirm networks. In order to understand the specific challenges of designing and running ISs in an inter-organizational setting, we will use and expand the notion of information management, which focuses on the information and systems dimensions of IOIS, and we will use a framework which structures and classifies network management issues. While network information management (NIM) primarily addresses managerial issues of IOISs, it does so in the broader context of network management.

Introduction

Although networks are traditional (but until recently neglected) forms of organizing commercial activities, they have become more prominent throughout the 1990s (e.g., Little, 2001). Even though various strategic drivers of network formation can be identified, the development of information and communication technologies (ICT) and of innovative forms of information flows across companies' boundaries (Konsynski, 1993) has significantly contributed to the fast and vast proliferation of networks. Inter-organizational information systems (IOISs) have been developed in various industries like airlines, automotive, banking, health care, etc. Global, standardized communication infrastructures have lowered the cost and facilitated new forms of cross-company collaboration (Bender, 2002). The diffusion of the World Wide Web has led to the emergence of numerous network business models (e.g., Franke, 2002; Häcki & Lighton, 2001), in which companies quickly try to exploit windows of technologically facilitated, commercial opportunities. IOISs aim to reorganize the interfirm value creation by supporting or replacing processes and by enabling new value creation structures and new flexible arrangements such as virtual organization networks.

Technological and organizational developments have become increasingly intertwined. Organizational changes call for new ICTs that give birth to a range of new IOISs, while these IOISs enable new organizational forms at the same time.

Acceptance and adoption are frequently far below the sponsors' expectations, and, even if they have been launched successfully, their stabilization in a dynamic business environment is quite challenging. Most critical issues and challenges that are well known from the IS field also apply- often in an exacerbated manner- to IOISs. Thus, in order to understand fully the impact of IOISs and to address the resulting management challenges, we looked at the nature of network management in general and network information management (NIM) in particular.

The notion of strategic alignment (Henderson & Venkatraman, 1993) highlights the need to coordinate along two dimensions: first between IT and the business sphere and second between strategic and operational issues. Applied to IOISs, strategic alignment addresses the issue of coordination between NIM and network management in general and between IOISs and the underlying network structures and processes. Our findings show that the managerial challenges of establishing and running IOISs successfully extend beyond NIM. The IOIS is seen as embedded in an interfirm network and facilitating interfirm processes, in particular, inter-organizational collaboration and coordination, which will eventually determine the outcome of the network. The underlying assumption is that systematic network (information) management practices are needed in order to facilitate the overall outcome and performance of the network. In order to address these challenges, such as the IOIS-enabled transformation of business processes or the stabilization of IOISs through the development of social capital and trust, NIM will be embedded into a network management model. Network management in a broad sense comprehends information management issues. However, it addresses, in particular, the network business and organizational environment within which the IOIS is functioning, it specifies support needs, and provides an institutional support structure for the IOIS.

Ouchi (1980) suggested that cooperation between operational units implies that a certain level of interdependence exists between these units. Extending this concept across organizational boundaries, we suggest that collaboration of firms in new organizational forms reshapes traditional managerial practices and creates new requirements for coordination, collaboration, and joint action. IOISs are essentially precarious systems: they have to accommodate the interests of various independent actors, they are difficult to design, and they have to adhere to existing standards or establish standards (or conventions) themselves.

The next section will present a brief taxonomy and three cases that illustrate the linkage between IOISs and inter-organizational networks. The third section will expand the notion of NIM, which will then be embedded in the broader notion of network management in the following section.

IOIS Taxonomy and Examples: ICT Support for Inter-Organizational Cooperation

A widely used approach to providing a taxonomy of collaborative systems is to distinguish them by when and where the interaction takes place (space/time taxonomy, see DeSanctis & Gallupe, 1987; Ellis, Gibbs, & Rein, 1991; Johansen,

1988). Apart from the space/time taxonomy, Ellis et al. (1991) described a taxonomy based on application functionality, and Coleman (1995) provided 12 categories of collaborative systems in the same domain. Kumar and van Dissel (1996) provided an alternative IOS typology based on the evolution of interdependencies between inter-organizational units, which is more relevant to this study. To examine such interdependencies, we take Thompson's "interdependence" view of the organization. Thomson (1967) distinguished between three different ways in which the work of organizational subunits may be dependent on each other. *Pooled dependency* comes first, where the subunits may share and use common resources but are otherwise independent. In *sequential dependency*, various subunits work in series, where the output from one unit becomes input to another unit. Finally, in *reciprocal dependency*, subunits receive inputs from and provide output to others, usually interactively.

Kumar and van Dissel (1996) built upon Thomson's notion of the association between technology and interdependence. In correspondence to the three types of inter-organizational interdependence, they suggested a three-part classification for IOISs: *pooled information resource IOIS; value/supply-chain IOIS; and networked IOIS* (see Figure 1). The first type, *pooled information resource IOIS* is an inter-organizational sharing of common IS/IT resources, as exemplified by Konsynski and McFarlan (1990). The basic ingredients of typical IS/IT resources shared in a pooled fashion include common databases, common communication networks, and common applications such as airline reservation systems (Copeland & McKenny, 1988). The high levels of structure in these systems come from commonly agreed-upon transaction standards. To this end, there is necessary demand for a high level of standardization and specification of the shared or pooled resources.

The second type of IOIS, *value/supply-chain IOIS*, enables customer–supplier relationships and occurs as a consequence of these relationships along the value chain. Mannheim (1993) defined these systems as pipeline management systems. Furthermore, he noted that these systems are becoming strategic necessities rather than strategic advantages. Kumar and van Dissel (1996) added that structured sequential interactions could range from formal EDI-based orders and order tracking to database lookup of adjacent partners in the chain to anticipate customer needs. The most important motives behind these collaborations are the reduction of the uncertainties in the supply chain, e.g., cost and quality control, and cycle time.

The third type of IOIS, *networked IOIS*, operationalizes and implements reciprocal interdependencies among organizations participating in a network environment. In the network form, organizations are collaborating usually for a finite duration, and collaboration involves the development of specific target

Figure 1: A typology of inter-organizational information systems

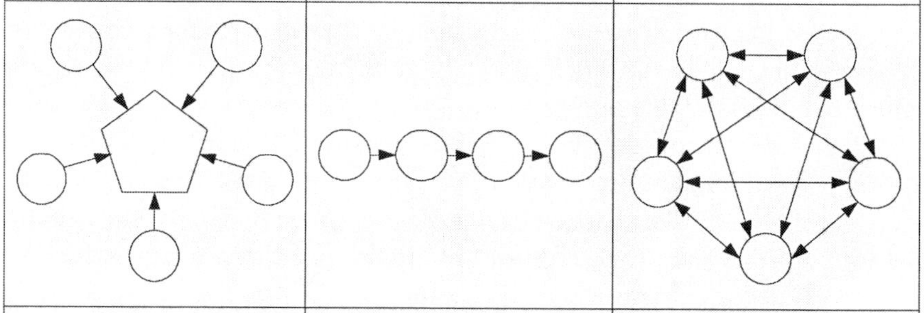

Pooled Information Resource IOIS	Value/Supply Chain IOIS	Networked IOIS
• Shared databases • Shared applications • Electronic markets	• EDI applications • Order, order-tracking, invoice and payment systems	• CAD/CASE systems • Video conferencing • Integrated health networks

Source: Adapted from Kumar and van Dissel (1996).

products or services. Networked IOISs include the use of e-mail, fax, and voice communication, and, at a more advanced level, shared screens, CAD/CASE data interchange, knowledge repositories, and computer-based systems for supporting collaborative work to co-ordinate inter-organizational partnerships. Information entities exchanged within the network arrangement are much less structured than in other IOIS types.

There are two dominant motives for the development of IOISs:

- IOISs as enablers or core building blocks of innovative, networked business models (Riemer, Klein, & Gogolin, 2002). This reflects the earlier discourse about business network (re-)design (Kambil & Short, 1994), i.e., IOISs are used in new or transformed networks with new players or new roles (network management).

- IOISs as enablers for the transformation of existing inter-organizational relations, earlier discussed as inter-organizational business process redesign (Klein & Schad, 1997) (inter-organizational network and processes).

Even more than ISs, IOISs are precarious arrangements that require careful management. Various scholars of the field have recognized specific management issues of IOIS:

- Strategic underpinnings of IOIS: Strategic rationale (Johnston & Vitale, 1988)
- Organizational drivers of IOIS development: ioBPR, BNR (Clark & Stoddard, 1996)
- Understanding the economics of IOISs (e.g., Clemons, Reddi, & Row, 1994; Whinston, Stahl, & Choi, 1997)
- Requirements engineering and systems design in an inter-organizational environment (Cavaye, 1995b)
- Designing inter-organizational information flows and workflows (Österle, Fleisch, & Alt, 2000)
- Standardization or the use of de facto (semantic) standards or conventions (Buxmann, 1996)
- IOIS adoption and acceptance (e.g., Iacovou & Benbasat, 1995; Eistert, 1996)
- Reconfiguration of existing business relationships (Holland, 1995)

Faced with a plethora of different IOISs, we will present three cases, which are set in different industries and business environments and exhibit different strategic intentions, functional scopes, and properties. The common theme among these cases is ICT support for inter-organizational cooperation or collaboration. ICT is utilized as an infrastructure to facilitate information flows among the network partners, i.e., to share or exchange information, to provide access to information, and hence, to increase transparency throughout the network (across the chain).

DIMER: Web-based Project Collaboration in Construction Industry Consortia

DIMER, a construction company, is the prime contractor in a construction consortium. Dimer has adopted a Web-based collaboration platform in order to improve coordination of project work (in this case, the network's mission concerns the construction of a new hospital wing), monitoring and reporting the progress of the construction project. A significant amount of information is exchanged between various parties in a construction project, such as drawings, ordering forms, progress reports, etc. Furthermore, multiple coordination and communication activities have to take place between project participants. The construction industry is divisive and fragmented. Poor communication and coordination often result in misunderstandings, misinterpretation, and ignorance of information that seriously affects the performance of a construction project in terms of quality, time, cost, and value, which may result in serious delays regarding project completion.

The construction consortium examined in the Greek construction industry is a temporary, project-driven organizational network. It consists of five geographically dispersed partners bound by contractual agreements (Technical and Financial Annexes). This case concerns collaborative technology mediation of complex processes (task allocation, time scheduling, coordination of the building process), of coordination among the multiple organizations (prime contractor, contractors, and their various subcontractors) participating in the consortium, and the creation of an emergent network information infrastructure.

The particular project work practices supported by the platform refer to the construction phase of a particular project. The construction phase typically is planned in more detail than any other construction project stage (design stage, bidding, etc.), but it often ends up being the most troublesome, particularly for the prime contractor. This is due, in part, to the high complexity and coordination difficulties that the prime contractor confronts with both contractors and subcontractors. It is very difficult from the prime contractor's view, to monitor all the processes and the coordination activities that evolve during the construction process. Decision making and resolving conflicts demand a highly structured information environment, where the prime contractor can easily retrieve the information needed in order for critical and objective decisions to be made. Otherwise, an unstructured information environment might lead to false decisions due to an incomplete representation of the situation.

The complex nature of the construction phase requires extensive communication and collaboration among the various subcontractors. For example, the construction site manager communicates on a daily basis with the construction workflow supervisor and on a regular basis with the raw material supplier. Specific pieces of information such as shop drawings, approvals, change orders, inspection reports, and reviews augment the actual construction work. Management, in this case project management in a network setting, is required to meet tangible goals related directly to project performance (such as monitoring costs, assuring quality, meeting time schedules) as well as intangible goals such as establishing mutual trust and sharing a common vision. During the construction phase, efficient and effective collaboration among the network participants is crucial.

A Web-based Project Management Platform

In this context, the prime contractor decided to adopt a Web-based platform tailored to support the following project management tasks:

- Project progress monitoring
- Coordination of project activities
- Project record keeping
- Information sharing and exchange within the construction consortium

The system is comprised of a management platform available through the Internet, addressing the specific needs of the construction industry. It offers users instant information access via the Internet. It is an integrated management information system, while it also supports daily project operations and administration by providing a construction site diary and communication logs (create/ update project plan, timesheets), collaboration and communication (online meetings, videoconferencing, chatting, redlining), document workflow in real time for requests for information (RFIs), and task assignments to project members (permissions, authoring, logs, redlining). DIMER can be qualified as a pooled information resource IOIS. The introduction of the new information system posits new management challenges to be addressed concerning the handling and diffusion of information resources among the network nodes. A prerequisite for efficient and effective collaboration is the accurate and timely handling and monitoring of the exchanged information among the construction consortium and the management of the emerging information lattice. Internet-based systems provide the capabilities of sharing, diffusing, and managing information across time and space.

Causes of Failure

Nevertheless, the actual use of the system lasted only 8 months until its permanent abandonment. An analysis of causes of failure indicated that an information classification scheme was missing. The project manager could not find the information needed when needed (RFIs, progress reports, invoices, etc.). This problem occurred because the set of action plans describing the daily progress of work in the construction site corresponding to the planned level of resource usage for each task, work package, and work unit in the projects, was not embedded in the document management function. The collected information had been identified; it consisted of periodic progress reports, specification changes, and similar information. However, it had not been determined precisely which data should be collected and allocated to specific contractors. This fact caused an information overload, due to the ineffective organization of project documents, and led to situations where users received irrelevant information. Furthermore, the degree of detail that the exchanged reports entailed, both in the reports and in the input being solicited from the contractors, was unstructured. Consequently, the prime contractor claimed that the technology destabilized the current network strategy and created imbalances by failing to accomplish current needs. The introduction of the system also created new ambiguities in the existing work practices. Furthermore, frequent misunderstandings occurred among contractors and created distrust in the new technology. Hence, many preferred to use traditional media, e.g., fax instead of e-mail.

Lessons Learned

A dominant trend in inter-organizational collaboration is to increase the ease of accessing information resources resident in collaborating organizational nodes. Consequently, the need to create common information resources arises across network organizations. A common "vocabulary" presupposes that substantial data modeling has been carried out and that commonalities have been established by enforcing common information handling processes across the organizational network. Thus, this leads to the reorganization of work practices in a manner that exploits emergent, shared information infrastructures as a knowledge resource on a network level. To this end, a crucial dilemma emerges regarding the information infrastructure design and deployment: "Is one of the key goals of a shared or common ICT infrastructure in interfirm business networks to achieve common definitions and meanings of key information entities across the network, or rather flexibility needed in order to improve existing work practices?"

ONIA NET: Mediation Platform for Grocery Supply Chains

The improvement of operational efficiency through collaboration has been a motive for the formation (or reconfiguration) of inter-organizational relationships (Oliver, 1990). Nowadays, grocery supply chains contain numerous inefficiencies that exist in the collaboration with trading partners (e.g., high inventory levels, rush orders, unstable production plans, frequent changeovers of promotional plans, running out of stock, lack of accurate forecasts, inaccurate order plans, etc.). The common root of these problems is the limited availability of information resources on the supplier side or on the retailer side, often causing problems in the forecast and order-replenishment processes (Holland, 1995).

The ONIA NET Platform

ONIA NET is a business venture to develop and implement business solutions in the grocery retail industry. ONIA NET has formed an inter-organizational platform with a network mission to reduce the out-of-shelf problem, which is considered a major problem in the industry. In doing so, ONIA NET aggregates all the network-relevant information resources from the suppliers and the retail stores within the network. The chosen information infrastructure, a collaboration platform, is based on the essential information requirements of the trading partners and supports the specific network roles (salesman and store manager). In more detail, the collaboration platform offers tools (e.g., product assortment, product mix management for the store, order status tracking, management of the POS data, etc.) both to salesmen (supplier side) and to store managers (retailer side) in order to effectively collaborate throughout the order-replenishment process. Thus, the network linkage between the members of the network is mainly supported by a centralized system. However, the managers realized that the social ties between salesmen and store managers are very important (Anderson, 1985).

Suppliers and retail chains collaborate in the ONIA NET network at an inter-organizational level and share network-relevant information resources (e.g., catalog data, assortment data, daily point-of-sale data, order proposals, final orders sent by the buyer, information on order fulfillment, product out-of-shelf alerts, promotion and production plans) in order to achieve more efficient replenishment at the store level and thus to increase efficiency and effectiveness. ONIA NET can be qualified primarily as a supply-chain IOIS, however, as it spans across several supply chains, it also incorporates characteristics of pooled information resource IOISs.

ONIA NET has been initiated by three major suppliers (offering about 65,000 products/product codes) and one large retail chain (with 200 stores in South Eastern Europe). The business development plan of ONIA NET is to become the major transaction hub between suppliers and retailers in the region.

Empirical data gathered during trials of the ONIA NET operating model shows that the market mediation of ONIA NET has increased the effectiveness and efficiency of operations both for the supplier and for the retailer (e.g., decreased out-of-shelf and out-of-stock situations, more efficient inventory levels, etc.), and in this sense, the network mission has been achieved (Steinfield, 1986). During the successful operation, the value proposition of the network business model shifted and became broader:

- To support all suppliers and retailers in the region, and
- To expand collaboration along the supply chain.

Management Issues

The network business model of ONIA NET, however, raised a broad range of management issues at different networking levels (Huber, 1990). At the NIM level, the relation of information sharing to joint decision making between suppliers and retailers was examined. Moreover, the exploitation of the POS data forced the managers of ONIA NET to develop sales reports for nonparticipating suppliers of the network, which provided an updated and detailed view of the demand forces (the trading partners were also recipients of these reports). At a network organization level, the existence of commitment and mutual trust between the suppliers and retailers facilitated the adoption of the new working system. Nowadays, salesmen are working together in the office and they have the ability to exchange ideas, monitor market trends, and make recommendations to the store managers through the collaboration platform. However, the threat of the technological "substitution" of the existing social relationship between salesman and store manager forced the managers to maintain physical contact by asking the salesman to periodically visit the stores. The management idea was to sustain the social relationship and safeguard mutual trust. Finally, at the network strategy level, the existence of a new order-replenishment model did not affect the individual strategic missions of the organizations. However, managers expect that in the near future, competition will shift from a single firm to the network level, through the development of large collaborative supply chains.

Examining in more detail the NIM level of the ONIA NET setting, we argue that the efficient management of information resources reduces information asymmetries in the negotiation process, thus establishing a basis of trust for effective joint decision making in the order-replenishment process (Korezynski, 1994). The provision of timely and accurate information and the partners' commitment to the ONIA NET network increased the efficiency of planning and decision making in the following categories:

- Production plan decisions: The manufacturer's production plan, i.e., the statement of its production rates, workforce levels and inventory holdings, is based on estimates of customer requirements and capacity limitations. The process of preparing production plans is dynamic in the ONIA NET setting, as aspects of the plan are updated when new information becomes available.

- Resource planning decisions: The need for production resources depends on forecasts of retailer's requests for products that the suppliers provide. The existence of daily up-to-date information resources improves the accuracy of the forecasting methods.

- Forecasting demand management decisions: Sales forecasts are inputs for production plans, logistics plans, and budgets. Thus, it is legitimate to say that the forecasting process is the touchstone for the rest of the operating decisions. Therefore, it would be extremely valuable for retailers and suppliers to have information utilizing the existing forecasting models (or developing new models).

- Marketing decisions: Measurement of the product's profitability, regional clusters, customer groups, and order sizes is essential for all the participants in the network. This information helps management to determine whether any products and marketing activities should be expanded, reduced, or eliminated. In this respect, retailers and suppliers are interested in improving marketing efficiency regarding various marketing directions (e.g., target market, product assortment and procurement, promotion place, sales promotion efficiency).

Another important issue had been the provision of information resources to the managers and the determination of the required detail level (Garbe, 1998; Ives, Olson, & Baroudi, 1983). In the ONIA NET case, the network-relevant information resources were exploited in two ways:

- Through the development and delivery of reports to managers, including all the required data on a weekly basis. These reports included information on sales by category, the daily ratio of sales for each product, sales of each retail store, etc. Moreover, the participants of the IOIS agreed to sell on-demand reports to nonmembers of the network.

- The information resources will be the basis for the development of a management control system to monitor the efficiency and effectiveness of the IOIS setting.

In summary, the infrastructure of the IOIS facilitated the exchange of information resources, which helped to constitute and stabilize the network. However, the technical setup was supported by trust-building measures. The trust level was achieved through the nurturing of social relationships and the pooling and sharing of information resources.

TELCO: Customer Relations and E-Collaboration

As a major European vendor of PBXs (private branch exchanges), TELCO is facing a difficult market. While the complexity of PBX has increased in recent years, and all suppliers of PBX have to maintain extensive service networks, the customers tend to prefer arms-length relationships. At the same time, major innovations have initiated a transformation of the product market toward IP-based telecommunication solutions, which are becoming a core building block of customers' e-business solutions. Hence, their existing core product base will change profoundly, and the systems integration and consulting segments of TELCO's business are expected to grow.

Against this backdrop, TELCO's sales organization is attempting to transform its market-like customer relations into collaborative relations. A cornerstone of this transformation process is the setting up of a collaboration platform in order to intensify the collaboration with key customers and to create more stable relationships. By introducing the platform, TELCO is pursuing three goals:

- To improve the efficiency of service processes and to lower service costs,
- To improve buyer–supplier coordination, and
- To intensify the relationship with key customers through electronic communication and collaboration.

Hence, TELCO's e-collaboration project is embedded in and instrumental for a broader customer-oriented strategy. In effect, TELCO is trying to transform existing practices of collaboration into new, computer-supported practices. The practices refer to inter-organizational processes, information flows, and media of collaboration between the TELCO sales and services organization and its customers. It is foreseen that for customer service requests or orders, an electronic service ticket will be created, which will be accessible to the customer and will document the status of the service delivery. It is expected that this transformation will yield higher efficiency and simultaneously closer customer relationships (performance). Like ONIA NET, the TELCO combines characteristics of a supply-chain IOIS with a pooled information resource IOIS.

The challenge for TELCO is to properly design the collaboration platform, the related services, and processes in order to make the new model of collaboration beneficial for customers and economically viable. A broad acceptance of the platform is a precondition for achieving TELCO's internal efficiency goals. The following items were identified as major issues:

- Requirements analysis and identification of value proposition (and incentives) for customers
- Channel management and relationship impact of computer-mediated communication
- Customization needs of services and architecture and integration options

Requirements Analysis and Value Propositions

The envisaged e-collaboration platform is an information and communication infrastructure to support (eventually) a wide range of collaboration partners, processes, instruments, and applications. The notion of infrastructure (or platform) encompasses a portfolio of applications. TELCO is facing the question of service design and the related selection of applications: which processes should be supported by the platform, what is the expected level of online support, which services will be available online only, is there a need for new services? Participatory requirements engineering, which in theory is expected to contribute to a higher level of acceptance (Cavaye, 1995b), is a politically sensitive process. While TELCO has to understand their customers' needs and expectations, it must be careful not to raise expectations—especially with core customers—it later cannot or does not want to meet.

In order to facilitate the collaboration, more information (e.g., technical specifications) will be made available electronically which will enable the customers to take a more informed and active role in specifying service requests. It is foreseen that features like the service ticket will provide more transparency over the interorganizational processes and will at the same time lower the administrative burden on both sides.

Efficiency gains (i.e., net benefits after considering the costs of setting up and maintaining the linkage) as a result of integration with TELCO are definitely incentives for the customers. Nevertheless, TELCO is facing an asymmetry of incentives: while for them the collaboration platform is core, for most of their customers it will only be of peripheral importance (Cox & Ghoneim, 1994). Hence, TELCO has to provide incentives for their customers in order to overcome the sponsor–adopter gap (Cavaye, 1995a).

Channel Management and Relationship Impact of Computer-mediated Communication

The e-collaboration platform will be embedded into an existing set of organizational rules and routines (practices). These practices will be complemented, transformed, and, to a limited degree, substituted. From the customer's point of view, TELCO is adding a new communication and collaboration channel. Hence, the role and range of the new channel in relation to the existing channels (call center, service personnel) needs to be clearly positioned and communicated. It is necessary to get the right mix of online and offline activities (Gulati & Garino, 2000) and to coordinate and integrate offline and online activities carefully.

The introduction of the collaboration platform is expected to affect the division of labor among the participating companies as well as related roles and linkages. The initial focus is on improving or redesigning inter-organizational business processes (Clark & Stoddard, 1996). However, eventually, the network structure might be affected, e.g., if industry solutions can be developed or intermediaries are introduced or bypassed.

While TELCO is trying to transform existing arm's length customer–buyer relationships into closer, more stable, collaborative relations, those closer relationships are, at the same time, a precondition for the successful implementation of an e-collaboration platform. Only if customers value the relationship and expect it to last will they be prepared to invest in this relationship and the accompanying technology, process transformation, and training (Clemons & Reddi, 1993).

Customization Needs Regarding Services, Architecture, and Integration Options

As the usage patterns and the internal organizational models for communication services vary a lot among different companies (e.g., in some cases there is a combined information and communication services unit, in others there is a clear distinction between the two), so do the needs for support. TELCO has to decide about technical (functional service portfolio, levels of standardization, platform concepts, etc.) and organizational aspects (organizational structures, responsibilities, work routines, etc.). A standardized set of applications has to be designed, from which customized portfolios of services and information will be derived. Furthermore, on an architecture level, TELCO's clients are using different administrative systems and have different requirements for integration solutions. Some clients may want an interface to an ERP system, while others would go for a Web interface or Web services. Given the peripheral role of the collaboration platform for the customer's business, they will expect TELCO to set or appropriate industry standards for service support and e-collaboration, in order to avoid a situation where the customers end up with a plethora of different, albeit useful, e-collaboration systems for different ICT vendors.

Because the organizational and technical perspectives are interdependent, it is advisable to design and specify both aspects simultaneously.

Lessons Learned

The TELCO example, which is in the configuration stage, shows the range and interdependence of design issues. The political dynamics at TELCO and in relation to their customers add to the complexity of the decision-making process. The case highlights the interdependence of IOISs and relationship issues. As technology is transforming existing practices and business relationships, the project needs to be strategically embedded, and the transformation of relationships has to be actively managed.

Summary of Case Descriptions

The three cases illustrating different development stages of an IOIS—configuration, operation/stabilization, transformation—are embedded in network settings. The introduction of IOISs in the three cases was meant to stabilize and intensify existing business relationships (TELCO), to improve the efficiency of collaboration and coordination (all cases), or to change the network structure by introducing a new intermediary (ONIA NET).

In order to discuss the identified challenges of managing an IOIS in a more systematic way, we will introduce the notion of NIM. However, the examples (and the understanding of IOISs we are elaborating) go beyond information management and require embedding into a broader network management framework.

Network Information Management and IOISs

Information management (IM) was established as a discipline during the 1970s and 1980s (paperwork reduction act) in order to facilitate the informatization of organizations (Zuboff, 1988). The terms "enabler" and "facilitator" are widely used in the literature to characterize ICT as the platform of inter-organizational networks. However, the introduction of new technological artifacts reshapes the firm's business practices and raises an explanatory discussion in various research fields. The development and deployment of information and communication infrastructures and systems need to be professionally managed in order to ensure their contribution to the companies' goals and, more specifically, to foster information utilization and processing capabilities (Teubner, 2003). Little research has been done to address the specifics of inter-organizational or NIM

Figure 2: Information management framework

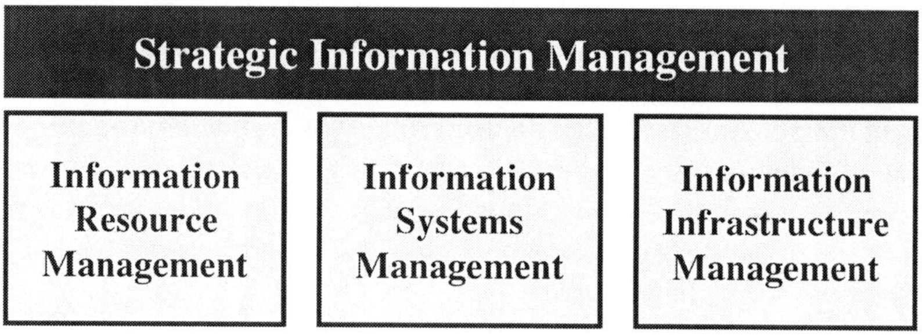

Strategic Information Management		
Information Resource Management	**Information Systems Management**	**Information Infrastructure Management**

Source: Adapted from Wollnik (1988).

(e.g., Buxmann, 2001; Homburg, 1999), which is, in its focus on the functional domain that has been selected for the IOIS, more specific than IM. On the other hand, managing information systems and infrastructures in an inter-organizational environment or managing information flows across companies' boundaries poses huge challenges. Peppard (1999) posits that network organizations strive to manage the interdependencies among geographically dispersed units, for example, in construction consortia, distribution centers, and sales offices at different locations. Information exchange is the key mechanism through which this integration is achieved, and ICT is increasingly being conscripted to facilitate efficient combinations of centralized and decentralized decision making (Wyner & Malone, 1996) and to integrate and manage distributed, yet interdependent operations.

Wollnik (1988) introduced a framework for information management that analytically distinguishes three domains of management tasks (Figure 2): (1) information deployment or information resource management, (2) information and communication systems management, and (3) information infrastructure management. While the managerial tasks of planning, organization, and control are part of each domain, we added a layer of strategic information management in order to highlight the need to integrate the three pillars of IM and to align them to the network strategy. We will use Wollnik's classification schema to describe the different NIM domains and their interdependencies.

NIM comprises the information and ICT issues and extends the notion of information management to IOISs and related interfirm networks. From a systemic point of view, the focus is to improve the management of information flows (Klein, 1993). From a strategic and relational point of view, the focus is on information partnerships (Konsynski & McFarlan, 1990). The goal of NIM is to make sure—by managing information infrastructures, systems, and resources—that information can be deployed throughout the network efficiently and effectively. Hence, NIM addresses the network's (structural, institutional, and human) capabilities to process information (cf., the goal of IM; Teubner, 2003; Wigand, Picot, & Reichwald, 1997). However, this is not a goal in itself but has to contribute to the performance of the network.

Strategic Network Information Management

The development of information partnerships and alignment between network strategy and IOIS strategy are preeminent tasks of strategic network information management (SNIM).

Information Partnerships

In 1990, Konsynski and McFarlan introduced the notion of information partnerships (which later led to the development of the concept of IOISs): by sharing information resources (foremost) and information infrastructures, companies would be able to join forces and achieve efficiency gains as well as unique value propositions. Shared vision at the top and coordination on business policy are among the success factors they identified.

As the relationship between information partners or network members is typically cooperative and competitive at the same time, SNIM has to make sure that the often delicate and dynamic balance of strategic goals and incentives among network members is reflected in the information flows. ONIA NET is a good example of an information partnership between suppliers and retail stores facilitated by an intermediary. ONIA NET as the intermediary has convinced competing suppliers and competing retail stores to join the system and share a wide range of information resources along the supply chain in order to achieve overall efficiency improvements. Hamel (1991) introduced the notion of a learning competition to describe the dialectics of information sharing and appropriation of information within networks. While information sharing can foster the development of trust, network participants do not want to lose control of critical information resources (Badaracco, 1991). Hence, it is a critical issue for TELCO how much information they are prepared to share with their customers, as some of that information might leak to their competitors. In the case of DIMER, the fact that the different contractors are working in various changing consortia might have restrained the exchange of information.

Network Business Models and Strategic Alignment

Concepts such as partner relationship management (PRM), supply chain management (SCM), customer relationship management (CRM), or e-collaboration represent organizational and strategic visions that have guided the development of numerous IOISs. The implementation of those concepts can be elaborated by using the notion of a business model, which describes architectures for the product, service, and information flows, including the various business actors and their roles; and an account of the potential benefits for the various business actors; and an explanation of the sources of revenues (Timmers, 1998).

Business models for IOISs combine the organizational vision, such as SCM in the ONIA NET case or e-collaboration in the DIMER and TELCO cases, with a description of the network model (roles of the participants) and the information systems, infrastructures, and resources. In many cases, ICT-based communication and coordination among the business partners is the precondition for viable business models. Information management practices are thus focused on facilitating organizational performance. As illustrated in the ONIA NET case, the use of POS data enabled the development of a Web-based platform for the grocery retail sector, which interconnected the entire retail chain. The notion of a business model thus incorporates the idea of strategic alignment: linking strategic and organizational as well as technical and business perspectives (Henderson & Venkatraman, 1993).

Network Information Resource Management

By default, IOIS settings are information-rich environments, where accurate and relevant information is crucial for the stability of the whole arrangement. IOISs are characterized by information flows, which have been agreed between the organizations. The goal of network information resource management (NIRM) is to secure the provision of information to the network in an economic manner. NIRM therefore aims to identify information requirements, to design network information and communication flows, to facilitate the deployment of information, and to assess the value of information. It has to facilitate the distribution of information as well as its integration based on common semantic references (e.g., ontologies) and collaborative processes of sense making, e.g., in the area of forecasting or trend analysis.

Purposes of Information Deployment

The information value and payoff depend on the purpose of information deployment (Wollnik, 1988). Information may be a product or service or an increasingly important part of products and services. The latter aspect has been addressed by Porter and Millar's notion of information intensity of products and services (1985).

In most cases, information has a facilitating function; it is deployed for:

- Transaction support (e.g., DIMER)
- Coordination
- Collaboration support (e.g., TELCO)
- Problem solving (Dawes, 1996) and decision support (Mennecke & Valacich, 1998; see also ONIA NET)
- Relationship support, i.e., developing shared understanding and common themes (Craig, 1995)
- Learning support

Information sharing increases transparency across the network, stimulates the inter-organizational cooperation and collaboration, and facilitates partnerships and trust among the network members. It thus potentially improves the overall success of the participating organization (Dawes, 1996; Kumar & van Dissel, 1996). NIRM has to identify the range of purposes that are addressed in a given network and has to cater for the related needs.

Instruments of Network Information Resource Management

Based on the understanding that the use of information is embedded in routines and work practices, we are suggesting a systematic analysis of information requirements, information flows, and practices of information deployment. However, the role that an institutionalized information management can play vis-à-vis the users has to be carefully reviewed, as most of the functions we describe are integral parts of managerial work.

Information Requirements Analysis

Based on the purpose of the information deployment, information management can identify basic or obvious information requirements and related information sources. As information needs cannot be fully anticipated, not even by the information users themselves, the requirements analysis can only be a first step.

As the meaning and representation of information is highly context dependent, NIRM has to raise the awareness for differing information needs within networks. For example, the information TELCO provides for its customers is targeted at different groups, such as system planners, service engineers, or users. TELCO is not fully aware of the information requirements these various groups have. Different contractors in the DIMER case may have different information needs and even different conventions and standards for the same objects.

Within a network, NIRM has to monitor information behavior, as asymmetric behavior can quickly impair the network relations.

Managing Information Flows

The metaphor of information logistics (Klein, 1993) describes quite well the goal of NIRM: to provide the right type, quantity, and quality of information to the right people at the right time. The resulting information flows reflect existing sources of information and (centralized or decentralized) decision structures (Hanseth & Braa, 1998; Wyner & Malone, 1996). The establishment of new or changed information flows will have an immediate impact on existing decision structures. For example, as ONIA NET provides more transparency, more decisions can be made centrally. As TELCO provides more information to their customers, they will be able to make more informed choices and will probably be able to solve minor technical problems themselves.

Managing Information Deployment

Davenport, Harris De Long, and Jacobson (2000) argued that one of the most important traits of the information age is that organizations have focused too much on mastering transaction data and not enough on turning it into valuable information and knowledge that can lead to business results. One reason for neglecting obviously valuable purposes of information may be that most of the organizations are still struggling to develop the appropriate capabilities to aggregate and analyze rather than use information for decision making and to generate real business value in a network environment. In other words, many organizations are still focusing on the early stages of the information life cycle, i.e., collecting, retrieving, verifying, or rearranging information (Levitan, 1982). In later stages, information sources are turned into information resources, which are made accessible within (and beyond) the network or are actively sent to information users according to predefined rules or thresholds (Wigand et al., 1997).

Network Information Systems Management

The objective of network information systems management (NISM) is to support NIRM and specifically to ensure the appropriate usage of information and communication technology (ICT) for the completion of inter-organizational tasks and, in particular, the inter-organizational information flows (Riggins, Kriebel, & Mukhopadhyay, 1994). This implies the selection (with a particular emphasis on the relevant functional scope), implementation, and maintenance of inter-organizational applications.

Typically, IOISs permit information access to other organizations and enable new forms of cooperation (Garbe, 1998). As a result, the organizational boundary of a single firm may be redefined and extended toward a network level. Moreover, an IOIS comprises organizational and technological perspectives. From an organizational perspective, IOISs enable and drive new forms of organization (e.g., the fulfillment of tasks in an interfirm context) (Webster, 1995). From a technical perspective, IOISs have an integrative function. The primary focus of NISM is the technical perspective of IOISs.

Depending on the information requirements and the strategic intent of the IOIS, managers have to design the functionality of the IOIS. Because various organizations exist in the context of IOISs, the offered functionality depends on the individual needs of each organization. TELCO, for example, intends to carry out a requirements analysis in order to determine an appropriate service design for its e-collaboration platform. The DIMER example indicates that implementing an IOIS into an existing network is a challenging task threatened by various pitfalls and obstacles. The project management platform did not really meet the expectations, because it was not well integrated into the existing network structures and work practices. In the end, the platform caused dissatisfaction and even a destabilization of the whole network and was abandoned.

Each organization, and consequently the managers, normally views an IOIS as an enabling/facilitating context to increase employee awareness through new sources of information, to establish closer links with other companies, to exchange product characteristics between buyers and suppliers, to monitor the supply chain, etc. Generic functions that IOISs support are:

- Information: The IOIS is the carrier of information sources, which enables new methods of decision making, increases the transparency in a supply network, smoothes the production processes, etc. Examples are electronic catalogs or FAQs.

- Communication: The IOIS brings together geographically dispersed units that allow the formal communication and the establishment of standards. A whole portfolio of communication applications such as e-mail, structured message exchange (EDI), or videoconferencing and virtual meeting rooms is available.

- Transaction: The exchange of valuable data is also carried through the IOIS. These data support the inter-organizational business processes of the organizations.

- Collaboration: The IOIS may be a context of long-term collaboration, where the trading partners develop a platform in order to fulfill exact strategic demands and increase participants' commitment. In this case, the potential to expand the network arrangement is high, because it is a stable IOIS. Examples include CSCW, knowledge management, etc.

- Coordination: In the case where scarce resources exist in a network setting, managers view the IOIS as the coordination mechanism with which to efficiently manage the resources. Examples include WFMS, SCM, group decision support, or negotiation support systems.

Potentials and benefits of IOISs can only be attained completely if the IOIS design is well integrated into existing systems and co-evolves with the inter-organizational processes (Ives & Jarvenpaa, 1991). Thus, the NISM is not an isolated issue, but it interacts with the information resources and the dynamic nature of the information infrastructure. In particular, the existing information infrastructure has a great impact on the design of the technical architecture of an IOIS.

Network Information Infrastructure Management

The notion of infrastructure or platform addresses those elements or aspects of ICT that do not have a single, dedicated functional scope but rather provide a broad range of support for network information systems, i.e., numerous applications and users. The information infrastructure provides the basis for a system's development, transformation, and adaptation to future needs. However, the development and maintenance of a collaborative platform incorporates issues that the manager needs to address. For example, misfits between the platform's functionality and the actual user requirements might cause network members to abandon the platform. Immature technology can become a barrier of acceptance; it can result in delays and cost overruns.

Strader, Lin, & Shaw (1998) argued that a network information infrastructure provides at least the following services:

1. An information network that supports electronic brokerage, electronic meeting and collaboration, electronic payments and banking, business transaction processing, and online information services.

2. Electronic access to external environment data, such as customer data, external firm data, market research data, and economic data.

3. Electronic connections among the network participant organizations to support business processes, system integration, and process coordination.

4. Electronic access to operational data, such as design data, marketing data, transaction data, manufacturing data, legal data, etc.

5. Intra-organizational information system support for software development, process support, decision support, database support, telecommunications, local area networks, and a network interface.

6. Electronic connections to customers that support activities such as order fulfillment and customer service.

All three case examples use a platform as a basic inter-organizational information infrastructure. Although the functional design and specifications differ, they all provide information and communication services, electronic connections among the network participants, and access to operational data.

NIIM highlights two issues. First, network infrastructures have to be open and standardized in order to support interoperability. This is more important in a network than in a firm context, because a proprietary infrastructure may require specific investments (asset specificity) by participating members that may lead to a lock-in situation or dependency regarding the network. Second, infrastructures have to facilitate the integration of distinct components.

Information Infrastructure Standards

Corporate infrastructure emphasizes the standardization of systems, data, and processes throughout the corporation as a way to reconcile the centralized IS department and resources on the one hand, and the distribution of systems and applications on the other. To this end, standardization refers to:

•   A wide range of and ever-expanding range of hardware equipment,

•   Communication standards: The information itself, referring to the forms being diffused among the network nodes (video programming, scientific databases, sounds, images, library archives, documents),

•   Applications and software that allow access, manipulate, organize, and digest the proliferating mass of information,

- The network standards and transmission codes,
- The people who create information, develop applications and services, construct the facilities, and train employees.

The standardization issue is a central challenge in the TELCO example. TELCO's customers have different requirements for integration solutions. Due to the peripheral role of the platform, the customers expect TELCO to use or appropriate industry standards rather than to develop a proprietary solution.

Alignment and Integration of Independent Components

Hanseth (2000) pointed out that information infrastructures are large and complex systems involving significant numbers of independent actors as developers as well as users. Further, information infrastructures grow and develop over a long period of time, new parts are added to what is already available, and extant parts are replaced by improved ones. An information infrastructure is built through extensions and improvements to what exists, as well as through the integration and alignment of the independent components to make them interdependent. Thus, integration and alignment can be demonstrated by qualities such as connectivity, compatibility, and modularity.

- Connectivity refers to the ability of any technological component to attach to any of the others inside a single firm and outside in the organizational network.
- Compatibility is the ability to share any type of information across the technological component. For example, at one extreme, only simple e-mail messages can be shared, while at the other extreme, any document, process, service, video, image, audio, or a combination of these can be used by any other system.
- Modularity relates to the degree to which IT software, hardware, and data can be seamlessly or effortlessly diffused into the infrastructure or even supported.

More recent developments in networking focus on the aspects of infrastructure that deal with more fundamental changes to management control brought about by the intrinsic properties of information resources. Ciborra (2000) stated that corporate information infrastructures are embedded in larger, contextual puzzles and collages. Interdependence, intricacy, and interweaving of people, systems, and processes are the culture bed of infrastructure. To this respect, the standardization of the information infrastructure refers to the interpersonal and management skills needed to operate within an organizational network.

Network (Information) Management Issues Illustrated by Case Examples

The range of network management issues is illustrated by the selected cases (Table 1). The cases also highlight issues of embedding NIM into a broader network management structure.

Table 1: Case synopsis: Managerial challenges

Scope	Managerial challenges			Management Area
	DIMER	ONIA NET	TELCO	
Alignment model: drivers and requirements, information partnership	Efficiency of collaboration in construction consortia. DIMER as a hub of an information partnership.	Information exchange in order to improve the coordination along supply chains.	Introduction of e-collaboration and customer relationship management.	Strategic Network Information Management
Information exchange, sharing	Common vocabulary (and interpretation) [semantics], monitoring and handling of information within and across the participating organizations [pragmatics]	Improving the information flow among the trading partners. Application of the information sharing practice to increase the trading partners' visibility along the supply chain.	Customer information requirements analysis. Plan for sharing technical information via a portal and providing customized information (service ticket, status info …).	Network Information Resource Management
Solution design: shared applications, services …	Web based collaboration platform for improving project monitoring and coordination.	Transaction support (order-replenishment) and management information support.	Service design and related application and infrastructure development.	Network Information Systems Management
Infrastructure, standards vs. competitive edge	Distributed information infrastructure.	Institutional and technical platform for the information exchange.	Proprietary vs. standardized solution elements. Customized integration solutions.	Network Information Infrastructure Management
Managerial integration, process integration	Building relationships, establishing organizational routines, lowering asset specificity of ICT infrastructure as preconditions for acceptance.	Establishing collaboration and information partnerships among the trading partners	Aligning technology and business relationship. Multi channel management.	Network Management

Embedding Network Information Management into Network Management

NIM is considered to be a very powerful tool for the analysis and deployment of management practices in the field of IOISs. NIM has various perspectives to examine network phenomena as presented earlier. However, NIM (and consequently, the perspectives) is not able to address all the management challenges and issues, because it, in principal, focuses on information requirements of the IOIS setting and does not examine organizational or strategic issues of the network (English, 1996). In more detail, management issues like the motives of developing an IOIS, the development of a revenue model for the network business model, the contractual agreements between the trading partners, the collaborative behavior, or the social ties between people are not originated from the NIM. Thus, NIM is seen as an integral part of a broader, more comprehensive network management.

Network management deals with the coordination of activities and sharing of resources between the network participants (Konsynski, 1993). Normally, network management addresses organizational and strategic concerns. Nevertheless, the role of the ICT as an enabler of inter-organizational relationships creates a link between information management and network management (English, 1996). Regional and international organizations across different sectors utilize the ICT capabilities to organize their supply chains more efficiently (observed in the grocery retail industry) (Holland, 1995). Some settings where network management is applicable are as follows: knowledge and learning networks exploit mediation platforms for disseminating knowledge and announcing research results (observed in the biotechnology industry) (Barley, Freeman, & Hybels, 1992). Organizations operating with many suppliers introduced collaborating platforms to monitor activities and restructure the existing relationships (observed in the construction and automotive industries) (Korezynski, 1994). In all these instances, NIM acquires different roles and provides manifold contributions to network management.

On the one hand, the adoption and the acceptance of the IOIS, the preconditions for information partnership, and the relationships between the trading partners are usually factors of network management that affect the function of the NIM (Hagedoorn, 1993). On the other hand, the technical capabilities, the coverage of the information requirements, and the end-user acceptance and engagement are factors coming from NIM and influencing the network management level.

NIM has been highlighted as a distinct and focused part of management with an emphasis on managing information, systems, and infrastructures. However, as Figure 2 illustrates, NIM is seen as closely linked to network management.

Network management introduces the requisite concepts, views, and distinctions for NIM.

Network Management

Generally, network management can be seen as the coordination of activities between companies (Konsynski, 1993). The managerial actions that are necessary from a network perspective are more selective and focused than general management of single firms, because a network usually serves a specific purpose for its member organizations (Castells, 1996; Riggins et al., 1994). Consequently, networks rarely demand the coverage of a whole range of issues that a single firm has to address. Nevertheless, network management is not simpler or easier. It has to deal with the collection, combination, and allocation of labor and tasks, knowledge and resources, as well as benefits and profits among network members.

Network management aims to establish structures and mechanisms that are needed to sustain ongoing coordination efforts among network members (Johnston & Vitale, 1988). Hence, management within a network environment faces a series of complexities: coordinating different actors with different knowledge and backgrounds, creating an environment where collaborative action can evolve and take place, and aligning different strategic, organizational, and technological perspectives and systems.

A Multiperspective Framework for Network Management

Figure 3 depicts an integrative framework for network management covering several managerial issues, dimensions, and structural relationships among various management areas. With ICT, and in particular with the management of IOISs at its core, the framework can be understood as a landscape of typical management areas in an interfirm context. In order to understand the network interplay of players in the adoption process of IOISs and to manage the resulting organizational structure, it is paramount to take into consideration strategic and organizational aspects complementing the technological perspective that is related to IOISs.

The network management framework distinguishes three views: the context, the firm, and the network view. The context view is related to industrial and

Figure 3: The network management framework

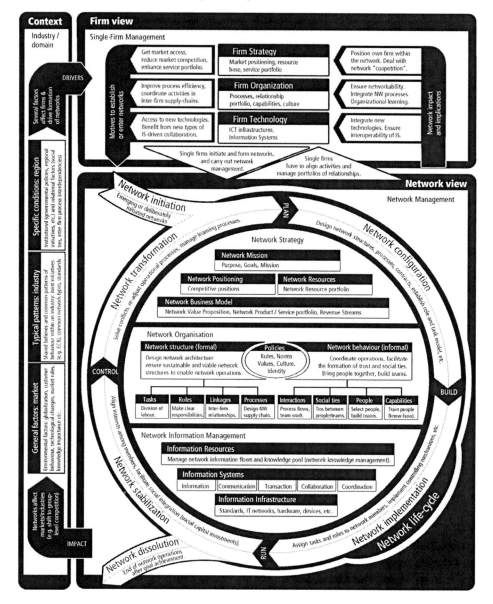

environmental factors and contingencies that influence the way firms and networks interact with each other.

Firms are the central actors within networks. They establish or participate in networks pursing certain goals and are simultaneously influenced by the participation in networks. Hence, the firm view addresses the perspectives of individual firms and their objectives and strategies as well as their roles within the network, such as network members, network managers, or network initiators. Network achievements have to be internally exploited, and intrafirm structures have to be aligned to external network requirements.

Management at the single-firm level can be divided into the three basic pillars: strategy, organization, and technology:

1. A firm has to position itself strategically in the market in a way that ensures an advantageous competitive position. It must gain access to a superior resource base in order to be able to set up a unique service portfolio (Hagedoorn, 1993; Johnston & Vitale, 1988). The establishment of an IOIS and, hence, the formation of organizational network arrangements might be a suitable approach.

2. The firm has to design appropriate organizational structures that ensure efficiency, flexibility, and sustainability (Zuboff, 1996). IOISs and networks in general often promise efficiency improvements and access to new (external) organizational capabilities (learning, benchmarking).

3. The technology (or information management) perspective highlights the increasing relevance of ICT infrastructures and information systems for conducting business (Ives & Jarvenpaa, 1991; Hanseth, 1998). Consequently, IOIS adoption often means network participation.

The DIMER network, for example, implemented an IOIS in order to improve the coordination of project work, especially in terms of monitoring and reporting practices. From the DIMER perspective, a new technology was used to achieve organizational benefits. Thus, the reasons for establishing the IOIS and changing the network custom of project coordination are of an organizational nature. The effect of adopting the IOIS, however, caused significant problems that affected the strategic level and threatened the stability of the network setup. The IOIS has thus been abandoned.

In the ONIA NET example, we have to distinguish between the ONIA NET and the participant perspective. ONIA NET's motive for setting up the IOIS and the corresponding network is clearly strategic, because it aims to transform the industry structure and become the major transaction hub between retailers and suppliers in its region. The benefits for participants are organizational, because ONIA NET is offering a new business solution for interfirm process improvements. The adoption of the ONIA NET IOIS provides the business partners with an efficient solution to tackle inefficiencies such as out-of-shelf problems.

Finally TELCO aims to transform its relationships with key customers by providing new collaborative services using a new IOIS. The motive is partly of strategic and partly of organizational significance. By locking in key customers via new specific IOISs, TELCO wants to stabilize its customer base. Additionally, new organizational practices aim to improve key customer processes in terms of service quality and efficiency.

Network View: Building Blocks of Network Management

The network view as the core of the network management framework distinguishes a static and a dynamic life cycle perspective. The static perspective differentiates, corresponding to the firm-level view, between network strategy, network organization, and NIM. The life cycle perspective visualizes the dynamics of network management. Starting with the initiation of a network, it covers the management tasks throughout the lifetime of the network, including configuration, implementation, stabilization, transformation, and finally dissolution. The dynamic perspective emphasizes particular management tasks depending on the maturity and the importance of the network.

Network Strategy

The strategy level comprises network mission, network resources, network market positioning, and the network business model. Particularly because new Internet-based IOISs have dramatically impacted the way firms are able to operate, scholars and practitioners have paid a great deal of attention to the discussion of new business models (e.g., Timmers, 1998; Riemer et al., 2002). The proliferation of networks is supposed to impact entire industries by shifting competition from a firm level to a group or network level (Gomes-Casseres, 1994). In this scenario, entire supply chains or networks of firms compete with each other. ONIA NET, for instance, is aware of these industry changes and takes into account the prospect of becoming the nucleus of one of these networks in the grocery industry.

Network Organization

Following Mitchel's definition of a social network (Sydow & Windeler, 2000), a network comprises a structural dimension with linkages among actors and a behavioral dimension with interactions that take place between the people within the structure of the network. That implies not only a structural but also a behavioral understanding of a network, defining an interfirm network by the relations between a set of independent organizations (the network structure) and their interactions within that structure (the network behavior). To be more specific, network management is concerned with the following:

- Network structure: In order to design sustainable and viable network structures to enable the intended network operations, network tasks have to be identified and assigned to appropriate roles fulfilled by the participating firms. The linkages (dyads) between the partners have to be designed, and network-wide (interfirm) processes have to be specified and agreed upon. While ONIA NET has successfully established its network structures, TELCO faces the challenge of segmenting its customers in order to identify the key customers and to assign appropriate roles to the potential network participants that are supposed to adopt a future IOIS solution.

- Network behavior: Managing network behavior means taking care of people, team building, and establishing social ties among the people working within the formal relationships between firms. This means coordinating, often informally, interactions that take place within the formal organizational structure of the network. Besides, managers have to deal with the capabilities of the cooperating people. The ONIA NET case showed how important it is to take into account the roles and behaviors of people in IOIS-mediated network arrangements.

- Network governance comprises formal rules and norms as well as informal aspects, such as culture and identity. Network culture and identity sustain the network as a whole (the network will be perceived as an organizational entity by network participants). Appropriate network policies encourage network participants to work together without any reason to distrust each other. In order to enable the coordinating effect of network policies, content and interpretation of rules and values have to be communicated clearly. Network managers have to consider in which way norms, values, etc., can be communicated to all network participants and how to ensure the internalization of these values.

A Life Cycle Perspective of Network Management

As already noted, organizational networks, like single-firm businesses, are dynamic arrangements that are subject to evolutionary changes. Although the network life cycle, as shown in Figure 3, is a conceptual or an idealistic rather than an empirical approach, it has proven useful to structure management thinking. Management challenges vary considerably in the different life cycle phases and depend on the maturity of the network.

The initiation phase is concerned with activities related to the formation of organizational networks in the formation process of IOISs. The goals of the initiation phase are (from an initiator's perspective) to find the right partners, to determine a basic network structure, and to define a network mission and strategy. "Fit" can be distinguished in different dimensions as being strategic, cultural, or technical. It is closely related to the concept of networkability. In other words, initiators should look for potential partners that fit into the network and show significant networkability in the relevant dimensions. Sometimes it is most important that the "fit" be strongest on the cultural side and at other times on the technical side. From a single-firm perspective, it is important to make sure that the necessary internal support is available. This includes creating a positive vision for middle management and employees working in the network. Finally, it includes everybody being aware of the reasons why the single firms are working in networks.

In our case example, TELCO is aiming to transform the arms-length relationships of key customers into cooperative ones by implementing collaborative IOIS services. Therefore, TELCO specifies a strategic direction for its IOIS and the resulting organizational network, and it segments its customer base in order to identify the key customers that will be addressed. This is part of the strategic network information management (SNIM).

The configuration phase comprises the specification of the IOIS and its services as well as the business model of the network. Starting from strategic decisions, the organizational configuration of the network follows. The latter aspect covers roles and linkages among the participating partner firms, the assignment of roles to the players involved, and the design of contracts. On an IOIS level, the issues of network information resource and systems management (NIRM and NISM) have to be addressed.

During this phase, the members of the network should succeed in designing useful processes and structures. Various sources for conflicts are avoidable in the later stages of the network life cycle, when misunderstandings and conflicting expectations can be eliminated in this early stage. The structures and processes determine the interactions in networks and are affected by the overall atmosphere and quality of the relationship. Atmosphere is a product of organizational behavior and derives from the power and dependence structure between the participating firms, the absence or presence of cooperative behavior, and the mutual expectations of the firms and the individuals. In this phase, the network roles, responsibilities, and positions related to each participant within the single firm are unknown to its partners and need to be specified and communicated. It always takes some time before these traditional group processes are in line. Moreover, the selection of people for working in the network might have a significant influence on the process. The design of the network can incorporate procedures that reward collaborative behavior, and thereby motivate the participants in succeeding with networking. Top management plays a crucial role inasmuch as they can set a good, and visible, example in collaborative behavior.

In the TELCO example, the imminent service specification and design is part of the configuration phase.

The implementation phase is concerned with the realization of the results of the configuration phase. The structures and processes developed have to be put into practice, and IOISs have to be implemented, which often goes along with the challenge to "make things work" as they are intended. The issues emerging in the implementation phase furthermore comprise the implementation of a controlling mechanism and the starting of network operations. The network information infrastructure management (NIIM) has to take care of an effective alignment and integration of network IOISs with the network participants' infrastructures. The processes and structures are key implementation elements in this phase of the network life cycle. The major challenge is to align the daily business operations with the network strategy. Thus, it is very important to be distinct about the division of tasks and roles, enabling members to have a clear understanding of the governance structure of the network.

However, the implementation of structures and processes does not automatically lead to efficient operations. Consequently, the implementation phase is complemented by a stabilization phase. A functioning collaboration within the network can only be assured by aligning the different interests of the network partners and by facilitating the social integration among the people involved. The emergence of social ties among people ensures a frictionless flow of information, facilitates the emergence of trust, and helps to avoid misunderstandings and conflicts. Thus, besides configuring the organizational structure of the network, the social structure has to be dealt with to foster collaboration among the partners and to ensure smooth network operations. The ONIA NET network (and IOIS) is in its postimplementation stage, where the organizational network is subject to an ongoing stabilization process in which the relevance of trust and the face-to-face nature of the sales business have been successfully identified and addressed. The ONIA NET network initiated the development of a management control system in order to monitor the effectiveness of the operations. The application of the management control system in this specific case, will force the whole arrangement to the next stage of the network life cycle.

However, situations do not remain stable, and thus, network transformation is required in order to adjust a network to changing environments. Network controlling mechanisms help to monitor performances and processes within the network and to discover opportunities and needs for changes and rearrangements. An important issue is the observance of the IOIS adoption processes and the initiation of appropriate support measures. Monitoring and controlling in this sense does not only mean to collect and analyze formal (e.g., financial) data. It

Figure 4: IOIS cases in different life cycle stages

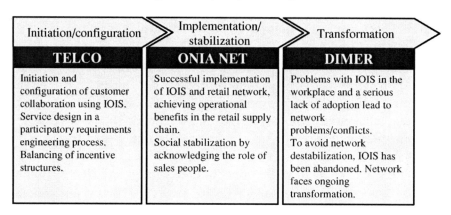

Initiation/configuration	Implementation/stabilization	Transformation
TELCO	**ONIA NET**	**DIMER**
Initiation and configuration of customer collaboration using IOIS. Service design in a participatory requirements engineering process. Balancing of incentive structures.	Successful implementation of IOIS and retail network, achieving operational benefits in the retail supply chain. Social stabilization by acknowledging the role of sales people.	Problems with IOIS in the workplace and a serious lack of adoption lead to network problems/conflicts. To avoid network destabilization, IOIS has been abandoned. Network faces ongoing transformation.

is also concerned with observing and assessing interpersonal collaboration, the social performance of teams, as well as the impact of IOISs on work practices. In doing so, potential conflicts and inefficiencies can be discovered, teams can be rebuilt, processes can be adjusted, and IOIS issues can be addressed. Moreover, learning processes can be nurtured. Ideally, the organizational network is able to continuously learn from past experiences and to adapt to changing needs and requirements coming from network partners and the surrounding network environment. The DIMER case is a good example of a network in its transformation stage, where an ongoing observance of work practices leads to the discovery of serious problems in the adoption of the IOIS solution that destabilized the network setup. Due to an immediate need for reaction, the IOIS was abandoned, and the network operations were adjusted. The DIMER network now faces the decision to reenter the network management cycle concerned with the redevelopment of a new IOIS. Figure 4 summarizes the case interpretation using the network management life cycle perspective.

Conclusions

How can we explain the different outcomes of IOISs? In order to summarize our conceptually based answer, underscored with evidence from three cases, we will refer to the elements of the IOIS management framework (Figure 5) and their interrelations.

The network management framework has introduced different perspectives. Throughout this chapter, we argued from the firm's perspective, primarily from a network initiator or operator's perspective, which focuses on network issues.

Figure 5: IOIS management framework

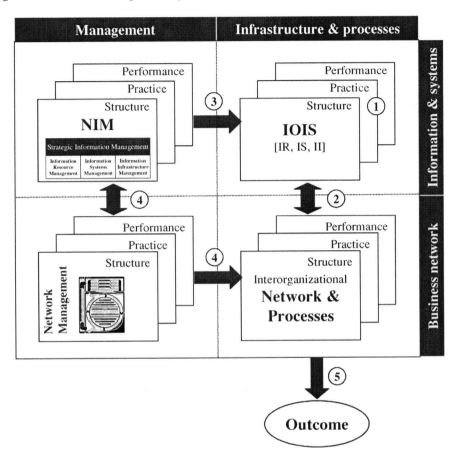

(1) Perspective on IOISs

IOISs can be characterized by their structural properties, i.e., information resources, systems and infrastructures, established practices and procedures for coordination, and collaboration and information exchange and their performances. Practices have to match the structural properties.

The three cases show the different outcomes or levels of success of IOISs: open in the TELCO case, initially negative in the DIMER case, and positive in the ONIA NET example. The underlying systems structure has been carefully planned in all cases, and the practices, e.g., for systems maintenance or security, do not provide evidence to explain the different outcomes.

(2) IOISs and Networks

IOISs are facilitating network business models by extending the ranges of services and innovative value propositions and by network processes and practices, e.g., by improving the efficiency of distributed work. In return, network relations provide the strategic and organizational setting within which IOISs are run and which they are supposed to support.

While in the ONIA NET case the strategic rationale was supported by the participants and translated into the IOIS structure and practices, the contractors in the DIMER case did not buy into the new practices of collaboration.

(3)   Managing IOISs

IOISs are at the same time strategically promising and organizationally precarious arrangements that call for systematic and professional manage- ment, i.e., planning, organization, and control.

The domains of management tasks address the structural properties (and the related practices) of the IOIS. The value propositions of the three IOIS examples are based on improved availability and exchange of information throughout the network, which need to be supported by requisite systems and infrastructures. The three cases illustrate the interdependencies of managing information resources, systems, and infrastructures.

(4)   The network management framework

Even meticulous NIM alone cannot secure the outcome of IOISs. IOISs need to be strategically aligned with the purpose of the network and the strategic goals of its members. Furthermore, they need to be organization- ally embedded so that they can support network relations and processes.

The cases have highlighted the need to develop shared visions and incentives for the IOIS—successfully in the ONIA NET case, unsuccess- fully in the DIMER example—and to build relationships and inter-organi- zational practices that provide initial support for the IOIS. Once in place, we observe a reciprocal relationship between the technically mediated and the social relationships: initial trust is essential for the setup of the IOIS, which then has to confirm and reinforce trust, e.g., through extended transparency among the network members.

(5)   Network processes lead to outcomes

Improved network (business) performance can hardly be directly linked to IOISs. The effects of IOISs are typically moderated by the network and processes.

The IOIS examples exhibit a high degree of versatility and a broad range of supporting or enabling properties. Again, it comes back to a management challenge to leverage the support potential into improved processes and outcomes and to do this in an efficient manner.

References

Anderson, E. (1985). The salesperson as outside agent or employee: A transaction cost analysis. *Marketing Science, 4*(1), 234–254.

Avgerou, C., & Cornford, T. (1998). *Developing information systems: Concepts, issues and practise*. London: MacMillan Press.

Badaracco, J. L. (1991). *The knowledge link—How firms compete through strategic alliances*. Boston, MA: Harvard Business School Press.

Barley, S. R., Freeman J., & Hybels, R. C. (1992). Strategic alliances in commercial biotechnology. In N. Nohria, & R. G. Eccles (Eds.), *Networks and organizations: Structure, form and action* (pp. 311–347). Boston, MA: Harvard Business School Press.

Bender, C. (2002). The theory of the firm revisited: Changing firm boundaries in a new information & communication environment. *Proceedings of the 6th Annual Conference of ISNIE.*

Buxmann, P. (1996). *Standardisierung betrieblicher Informationssysteme*. Wiesbaden: Gabler.

Buxmann, P. (2001). *Informationsmanagement in vernetzten Unternehmen: Wirtschaftlichkeit, Organisationsänderungen und der Erfolgsfaktor Zeit*. Wiesbaden: Deutscher Universitäts-Verlag.

Castells, M. (1996). *The rise of the network society*. Oxford: Blackwell Publishers.

Cavaye, A. L. M. (1995a). The sponsor-adopter gap—differences between promoters and potential users of information systems that link organisations. *International Journal of Information Management, 15*(2), 85–96.

Cavaye, A. L. M. (1995b). Participation in the development of IOS involving users from outside the organization. *Journal of Information Technology, 10*, 135–147.

Ciborra, C. U. (2000). *From control to drift*. New York: Oxford University Press.

Clark, T. H., & Stoddard, D. B. (1996). Inter-organizational business process redesign: Merging technological and process innovation. In J. F. Nunamaker, & R. H. Sprague (Eds.), *Proceedings of the 29th HICSS*, Vol. IV: Information Systems, Organizational Systems and Technology. Los Alamitos, CA: IEEE Computer Society Press.

Clemons, E. K., & Reddi, S. P. (1994). The impact of I.T. on the degree of outsourcing, the number of suppliers, and the duration of contracts. In J. F. Nunamaker, & R. H. Sprague (Eds.), *Proceedings of the 27th HICSS*,

Vol. IV: Collaboration Technology, Organizational Systems and Technology (pp. 855–864). Los Alamitos, CA: IEEE Computer Society Press.

Clemons, E. K., Reddi, S. P., & Row, M. C. (1993). The impact of information technology on the organization of economic activity: The "move to the middle" hypothesis. *Journal of Management Information Systems, 10*(2), 9–36.

Coleman, D. (1995). Groupware technology and applications: An overview of groupware. In D. Coleman, & R. Khanna (Eds.), *Groupware: Technology and applications* (pp. 3-41). Englewood Cliffs, NJ: Prentice Hall.

Copeland, D. G., & McKenny, J. L. (1988). Airlines reservations systems: Lessons from history. *MIS Quarterly 12*(3), 353–370.

Cox, B., & Ghoneim, S. (1994). Benefits and barriers to adopting EDI in the UK—A sector survey of British industries. In W. R. J. Baets (Ed.), *Proceedings of the Second European Conference on Information Systems* (pp. 643–653), Nijenrode.

Craig, W. (1995). Why we can't share data: Institutional inertia. In J. Harlan, & G. Rushton (Eds.), *Sharing geographic information* (pp. 107–118). New Jersey: Center for Urban Policy Research.

Davenport, T., Harris J., De Long, D. W., & Jacobson, A. L. (2001). Data to knowledge results: Building an analytic capability. *California Management Review, 43*(2), 117–138.

Dawes, S. (1996). Interagency information sharing: Expected benefits, manageable risks. *Journal of Policy Analysis and Management, 15*, 377–394.

DeSanctis, G., & Gallupe, R. B. (1987). A foundation for the study of group decision support systems. *Management Science, 33*(5), 589–609.

Ebers, M. (Ed.) (2001). *The formation of inter-organizational networks.* New York: Oxford University Press.

Eistert, T. (1996). *EDI adoption and diffusion.* Wiesbaden: Gabler.

Ellis, L. (2000). *An evaluation framework for collaborative systems.* Colorado University Technical Report CU-CS- 901-00.

Ellis, L., Gibbs, S. J., & Rein, G. L. (1991). Groupware: Some issues and experiences. *Communications of the ACM, 34*(1), 38–58.

English, L. (1996). Redefining information management: IM as an effective business enabler. *Information Systems Management, 13*, 65–67.

Franke, U. (Ed.) (2002). *Managing virtual web organizations in the 21st century: Issues and challenges.* Hershey, PA: Idea Group Publishing.

Garbe, M. (1998). The impact of information technology on the boundaries of the firm. *Proceedings of the International Telecommunications Society,* Twelfth Biennial Conference, Stockholm, Sweden (June 21–24).

Gomes-Casseres, B. (1994). Group versus group: How alliance networks compete. *Harvard Business Review, July–August*, 62–74.

Gulati, R. (1999). Network location and learning: The influence of network resources and firm capabilities on alliance formation. *Strategic Management Journal, 20*(5), 397–420.

Gulati, R., & Garino, J. (2000). Get the right mix of bricks & clicks. *Harvard Business Review, May–June*, 107–114.

Häcki, R., & Lighton, J. (2001). The future of the networked company. *The McKinsey Quarterly*, 2001(3), 26–39.

Hagedoorn, J. (1993). Understanding the rationale of strategic technology partnering: Interorganizational modes of cooperation and sectoral differences. *Strategic Management Journal, 14*(2), 371–385.

Hamel, G. (1991). Competition for competence and inter-partner learning within international strategic alliances. *Strategic Management Journal, 12*(4), 83–103.

Hanseth, O. (2000). The economics of standards. In C. U. Ciborra (Ed.), *From control to drift* (pp. 56–70). New York: Oxford University Press.

Hanseth, O., & Braa, K. (1998). Technology as traitor: Emergent SAP infrastructure in a global organization. In E. Hirscheim et al. (Eds.), *Proceedings of the 19th International Conference on Information Systems* (pp. 188–196), Helsinki, Finland (December 13–16).

Henderson, J. C., & Venkatraman, N. (1993). Strategic alignment: Leveraging information technology for transforming organizations. *IBM Systems Journal, 32*(1), 4–16.

Holland, C. (1995). Cooperative supply chain management: The impact of interorganizational systems. *Journal of Strategic Information Systems, 4*(2), 117–133.

Homburg, V. M. F. (1999). The political economy of information management: A theoretical and empirical analysis of decision making regarding interorganizational information systems (Doctoral dissertation, University of Groningen, 1999). Retrieved July 7, 2003 from the World Wide Web: http://www.ub.rug.nl/eldoc/dis/management/v.m.f.homburg/.

Huber, G. (1990). A theory of the effects of advanced information technology on organizational design, intelligence, and decision making. *Academy of Management Review, 15*(1), 47–71.

Iacovou, C. L., & Benbasat, I. (1995). Electronic data interchange and small organizations: Adoption and impact of technology. *MIS Quarterly, 19*(4), 465–485.

Ives, B., & Jarvenpaa, S. (1991). Applications of global information technology: Key issues for management. *MIS Quarterly, 15*(1), 33–47.

Ives, B., Olson, M. H., & Baroudi, J. J. (1983). The measurement of user information satisfaction. *Communications of the ACM, 26*(10), 785–793.

Johansen, R. (1988). *Groupware. Computer-support for business teams.* New York: The Free Press.

Johnston, H., & Vitale, M. (1988). Creating competitive advantage with interorganizational information systems. *MIS Quarterly, 12*(2), 153–165.

Kambil, A., & Short, J. E. (1994). Electronic integration and business network redesign: A roles-linkage perspective. *Journal of Management Information Systems, 10*(4), 59–84.

Klein, S. (1993). Information logistics. *Electronic Markets, 3*(3), 11–12.

Klein, S., & Schad, H. (1997). The introduction of EDI systems in healthcare supply chains: A framework for business transformation. *International Journal of Electronic Commerce, 2*(1), 25–44.

Konsynski, B. (1993). Strategic control in the extended enterprise. *IBM Systems Journal, 32*(1), 111–142.

Konsynski, B. R., & McFarlan, W. E. (1990). Information partnerships—Shared data, shared scale. *Harvard Business Review, September–October,* 114–120.

Korezynski, M. (1994). Low trust and opportunism in action: Evidence on inter-firm relations from the British engineering construction industry. *Journal of Industrial Studies, 1*(2), 43–63.

Kumar, K., & van Dissel, H. G. (1996). Sustainable collaboration: Managing conflict and cooperation in interorganizational systems. *MIS Quarterly, 20*(3), 279–300.

Levitan, K. B. (1982). Information resource as "goods" in the life cycle of information production. *Journal of the American Society for Information Science, 33*, 44–54.

Little, A.D. (2001). *Partnering. Challenges for the old and new economy. Facts—Assessments—Recommendations based on a global Arthur D. Little survey* (September 2001). Retrieved from the World Wide Web: http://www.adlittle.de/asp/orderpublications.asp?ID=28.

Manheim, M. (1993). Integrating global organisations through task/team support systems. In L. M. Harasim (Ed.), *Global networks; computers and international communication.* Cambridge, MA: MIT Press.

Mennecke, B., & Valacich, J. (1998). Information is what you make of it: The influence of group history and computer support on information sharing, decision quality, and member perceptions. *Journal of Management Information Systems, 15*(2), 173–197.

Oliver, C. (1990): Determinants of interorganizational relationships: Integration and future directions. *Academy of Management Review, 15*(2), 241–265.

Österle, H., Fleisch, E., & Alt, R. (Eds.). (2000). *Business networking— Shaping enterprise relationships on the Internet.* Berlin: Springer.

Ouchi, W. (1980). Markets, bureaucracies, and clans. *Administrative Sciences Quarterly,* 25, 129–141.

Peppard, J. (1999). Information management in the global enterprise: An organising framework. *European Journal of Information Systems, 8*(2), 77–94.

Porter, M. E., & Millar, V. E. (1985). How information gives you competitive advantage. *Harvard Business Review, July/August,* 149–160.

Riemer, K., Klein, S., & Gogolin, M. (2002). Network business model configuration—New roles for dynamic network arrangements. In B. Stanford-Smith, E. Chiozza, & M. Edin (Eds.), *Challenges and achievements in e-business and e-work—Proceedings of e2002 Conference* (pp. 892–899), Amsterdam: IOS Press.

Riggins, F. J., Kriebel, C. H., & Mukhopadhyay, T. (1994). The growth on inter-organisational systems in the presence of network externalities. *Management Science, 40*(8), 984–998.

Selz, D., & Klein, S. (2002). Value webs: Cases, features and success factors. In U. Franke (Ed.), *Managing virtual web organizations in the 21st century: Issues and challenges.* Hershey, PA: Idea Group Publishing.

Steinfield, C. W. (1986). Computer-mediated communication in an organizational setting: Explaining task-related and socioemotional uses. In M. I. McLaughlin (Ed.), *Communication Yearbook,* 9 (pp. 777–804). Newbury Park, CA: Sage.

Strader T. J., Lin, F. R., & Shaw, M. J. (1998). Information infrastructure for electronic virtual organization management. *Decision Support Systems, 23*(1), 75–94.

Sydow, J., & Windeler, A. (2000). Steuerung von und in Netzwerken - Perspektiven, Konzepte, vor allem offene Fragen. In J. Sydow, & A. Windeler (Eds.), *Steuerung von Netzwerken* (pp. 1–24). Opladen: Westdeutscher Verlag und Gabler.

Teubner, A., Rentmeister, J., & Klein, S. (2000). IT-Fitness für das 21 Jahrundert - Konzeption eines Evaluationsinstruments. In L. J. Heinrich, & I. Häntschel (Eds.), *Evaluation und Evaluationsforschung in der Wirtschaftsinformatik* (pp. 75–92). München: Oldenbourg.

Teubner, R. A. (2003, February). Grundlegung Informationsmanagement. *Working Paper Series of the Department of Information Systems, Working Paper No. 91*. Münster: University of Münster.

Thompson, J. (1967). *Organisations in action*. New York: McGraw-Hill.

Timmers, P. (1998). Business models for electronic markets. *Electronic Markets, 8*(2), 3–8.

Webster, J. (1995). Networks of collaboration or conflict? Electronic data interchange and power in the supply chain. *Journal of Strategic Information Systems, 4*(1), 31–42.

Whinston, A. B., Stahl, D. O., & Choi, S. Y. (1997). *The economics of electronic commerce*. Indianapolis, IN: Macmillan.

Wigand, R. T., Picot, A., & Reichwald, R. (1997). *Information, organization and management: Expanding markets and corporate boundaries*. New York: John Wiley & Sons.

Wollnik, M. (1988). Ein Referenzmodell des Informations-Managements. *Information Management, 3*(3), 34–43.

Wyner, G. M., & Malone, T. W. (1996). Cowboys and commanders: Does information technology lead to decentralization. In J. I. DeGross, S. Jarvenpaa, & A. Srinivasan (Eds.), *Proceedings of the 17th ICIS* (pp. 63–80), Cleveland, OH, December 16–18.

Zuboff, S. (1988). *In the age of the smart machine: The future of work and power*. New York: Basic Books.

Zuboff, S. (1996). Foreword. In C. U. Ciborra (Ed.), *Groupware and teamwork: Invisible aid or technical hindrance?* Chichester: Wiley.

Section V:

Implementation and Applications

Chapter VIII

Inter-Organizational Information System Adoption and Diffusion:

A Review and Analysis of Empirical Research

Hope Koch
Baylor University, USA

Abstract

New technology, fueled by the Internet's commercialization, has led to new types of business partner connectivity. However, statistics show business-to-business (B2B) electronic commerce (EC) and electronic market growth are slower than anticipated (Bartlett, 2001). Realizing the full potential of this emerging inter-organizational connectivity requires understanding what facilitates its adoption and diffusion. Given the need for research in this area, this chapter reviews the existing inter-organizational information systems (IOISs) adoption and diffusion research. The chapter analyzes twenty-five empirical inter-organizational information system adoption and diffusion studies. This study identifies several IOIS types and lists and categorizes variables found to significantly influence adoption and diffusion of each IOIS type. This study has two main contributions. The study finds that variables found to significantly influence IOIS adoption and diffusion fall into three categories: inter-organizational, organizational and technical. The study also brings the IOIS adoption and diffusion literature together. As such, this study provides a starting point for conducting research on emerging IOISs.

Introduction

Before inter-organizational information systems (IOISs), particularly electronic commerce (EC) and electronic markets, can change society or work practices, they must be adopted and diffused. However, statistics show business-to-business (B2B) electronic commerce (EC) and electronic market growth are slower than anticipated (Bartlett, 2001). What facilitates IOIS adoption and diffusion?

A history of IOISs adoption research exists in electronic data interchange (EDI). In a synthesizing empirical study, Chwelos, Benbasat and Dexter (2001) brought significant variables from 11 previous EDI studies into one model. Using this model, the authors tested the significance of these variables with a survey of purchasing managers with significant EDI experience. The authors found that readiness, perceived benefits and external pressure significantly predict EDI adoption intentions. Their model's constructs include technological, organizational and inter-organizational categories. Based on their findings, Chwelos et al. hypothesized that technological, inter-organizational and organizational levels determine emerging IOIS adoption.

This chapter evaluates and extends Chwelos et al.'s hypothesis by reviewing significant adoption and diffusion facilitators for an array of IOIS types. This review includes 25 empirical IOIS adoption and diffusion studies published between 1985 and 2001. This chapter categorizes variables found to significantly influence adoption and diffusion of various IOIS forms. The categorization supports and extends Chwelos et al.'s hypothesis. Variables in both adoption and diffusion stages for an array of IOISs fall into Chwelos et al.'s technical, organizational and inter-organizational categories. However, some variables fall into multiple categories. Given this, we propose variables found to significantly influence IOIS adoption and diffusion also facilitate adoption and diffusion of emerging IOIS forms.

This chapter is organized into five sections. The second section describes IOIS types. The third section summarizes IOIS adoption and diffusion research. Section four shows the frequency of significant independent variables in IOISs research, by IOIS type (EDI, B2B EC and other) and category (technological, organizational, inter-organizational). Section five provides concluding remarks.

Inter-organizational Information System (IOIS)

Cash and Konsynski (1985) defined an IOIS as an infrastructure made up of computers and communication that crosses company boundaries and permits information sharing. The literature mentions several IOIS types, including B2B EC, customer-oriented strategic systems, EDI and electronic markets. Zwass (1996, p. 3) defined B2B EC as sharing business information, maintaining business relationships and conducting business transactions via telecommunication networks. Reich and Benbasat (1990) defined a customer-oriented strategic system as "an information system linking a company to its customers used to support or shape the company's competitive strategy" (p. 326). Premkumar et al. (1997) defined EDI as "the direct computer-to-computer communication between an organization and its trading partners of business documents and information in a machine-readable, structured format that permits data to be processed by the receiver without rekeying" (p. 108). Bakos (1997, p. 1679) defined an electronic market as an IOIS that allows participating buyers and sellers in a market to exchange information about prices and product offerings and execute transactions.

The literature does not offer a typology or distinction between the different IOIS types. The author definitions offer a few distinctions. Electronic markets require a critical mass of buyers and sellers, whereas EDI, B2B EC and customer-oriented strategic systems do not. Customer-oriented strategic systems primarily focus on linking a company with its customers and EDI includes other business

Table 1: Summary of 25 studies on facilitators of IOIS adoption and diffusion

TYPE OF IOIS	STUDY		
	ADOPTION	DIFFUSION	TOTAL
B2B EC	1	4	5
EDI	10	6	16
Electronic Markets	0	1	1
Other	4	1	5
Total	15	12	27

partners. There is not a clear distinction between B2B EC and the other IOIS types. One could argue that B2B EC encompasses the other IOIS types.

Table 1 shows 25 reviewed studies categorized by IOIS type and whether they concentrate on adoption or diffusion. The IOIS type categorization is based on the IOIS name used in each study. Table 1 shows 27 studies, because two studies (Hart & Saunders, 1997; Premkumar & Ramamurthy, 1995) concentrate on both EDI adoption and diffusion. The "other" category includes variations of customer-oriented strategic systems.

Table 1 indicates that 15 of the 27 IOIS studies focus on EDI. Only one empirical study discusses electronic market diffusion facilitators.

IOIS Adoption and Diffusion Research

Most researchers (Cavaye & Cragg, 1995; Reich & Benbasat, 1990; Rogers, 1995) agree that technology adoption occurs in stages. A number of stages have been proposed, with adoption and diffusion the most common (Rogers, 1995).

Technology adoption is characterized by actions related to learning about an innovation. These include collecting information, building knowledge, examining relevance and evaluating appropriateness. Technology adoption culminates in an innovation adoption decision. Rogers (1995) distinguished between technology adoption and diffusion stating that it is possible for an organization to adopt an innovation and not use it.

Technology diffusion involves an innovation's implementation and use spreading over time. Technology diffusion studies focus on why and how an innovation's use spreads and innovation characteristics lead to widespread acceptance. Many diffusion studies have use as the dependent variable. As such, in the review of these studies, we specifically cite "use" as the dependent variable rather than diffusion.

Table 2 categorizes IOIS research focusing on technology adoption and technology diffusion. We organize the table alphabetically by adoption/diffusion phenomenon. Studies focusing on B2B EC appear first, followed by EDI and then other IOISs. We include the power of the independent variables in parentheses in the significant independent variables column. Only Grover's work in 1993 reported this information.

Table 2 indicates that a number of theories underpin IOIS research, with *innovation diffusion theory* the most common. Rogers' (1995) innovation diffusion theory applies to the study of adoption (decision to use) and diffusion (extent of implementation) of innovations within organizations by identifying

Table 2: Facilitators of IOIS technology adoption and diffusion

Authors	Facilitators of Adoption and Diffusion (Significant Independent Variables)	Adoption/ Diffusion Phenomenon (Dependent Variable)	Research Method	Data Source	Theoretical Base
Deeter-Schmelz, Bizzari, Graham, & Howdyshell (2001)	Supplier support and communication convenience	B2B EC adoption	Survey	222 members of the National Association of Purchasing Managers	Innovation diffusion theory
Ranganathan, Teo, Dhaliwal, Ang, & Hyde (2001)	Top management support, organizational change, strategy-related, project management, valuation, internal information technology, external information technology, collaboration, and external business environment	B2B EC deployment	Survey	100 firms in Singapore	Innovation diffusion theory
			Case study	Information technology executives	
Hope, Hermanek, Schlemmer, & Huff (2001)	Clear e-business vision, customer readiness and technological awareness, top management support, creative managerial thinking, information sharing and open communication, system marketing and promotion, staff skilled in technical and business issues, appropriate timing of project startup, clear and certain legislative and policy environment, current technology, and external expertise	B2B EC diffusion	Case study	5 medium-sized companies in the transportation and logistics industry of New Zealand	None
Han & Noh (1999–2000)	System stability and data security	B2B EC use	Survey	325 people with EC experience	None
Tabor (2001)	Customer-focused approach, easy-to-use technology, leadership, consistent goals and strategy, culture supporting innovation, relative advantage, product equity/trust, innovative characteristics, management commitment, team composition, core competence, project management, and technology performance	B2B EC use	Case study	A major U.S. airline	None
Premkumar, Ramamurthy, & Nilakanta (1994)	Relative advantage, technical compatibility, cost, and duration	EDI adaptation, internal diffusion, and external diffusion	Survey	Information systems and sales/ purchasing executives from 201 firms	Innovation diffusion theory
Bouchard (1993)	Key business partner implementation and key business partner mandating organization's implementation	EDI adoption	Survey	75 retail suppliers	Innovation diffusion theory and critical mass theory
			Case study	2 retail suppliers	
			Computer-supported interviews	10 retail suppliers	
Hart & Saunders (1997)	Power	EDI adoption	Theoretical framework and case study	1 retail firm	Power
Premkumar et al. (1997)	Firm size, top management support, competitive pressure, and customer support	EDI adoption	Survey	181 firms in the trucking industry	Innovation diffusion theory and resource dependency theory
Saunders & Clark (1992)	Cost	EDI adoption	Survey	192 vendors	Power
Williams (1994)	Demand uncertainty, power, and relative advantage	EDI adoption	Interviews	Firms with and without channel power, consultants, EDI third-party providers	Organizational theory and power theory
			Survey	156 from customers, suppliers, shippers, and carriers, who are members of the Council of Logistics Management	

Table 2: Facilitators of IOIS technology adoption and diffusion (continued)

Authors	Facilitators of Adoption and Diffusion (Significant Independent Variables)	Adoption/ Diffusion Phenomenon (Dependent Variable)	Research Method	Data Source	Theoretical Base
Premkumar & Ramamurthy (1995)	Internal need, top management support, competitive pressure, and exercised power	EDI adoption decision modes (proactive vs. reactive)	Survey	Information systems and sales/ purchasing executives from 201 firms	Power and social exchange theory
Teo, Tan, & Wei (1995)	Complexity, operational risk, strategic risk, and observability	EDI adoption intention	Survey	112 senior managers of firms listed in the Singapore stock exchange	Innovation diffusion theory
Chwelos et al. (2001)	External pressure, perceived benefits, and readiness	EDI adoption intentions	Survey	268 small to medium organizations in the Purchasing Managers Association of Canada	Critical mass theory, innovation diffusion theory, and power
Iacovou, Benbasat, & Dexter (1995)	Perceived benefits and external pressure	EDI adoption of small organizations	Case study	7 managers of small organizations	Innovation diffusion theory and resource dependency theory
O'Callaghan, Kaufmann, & Konsynski (1992)	Perceived relative advantage	EDI computer-based interface offerings, adoption decision	Field interviews	10 members of the Independent Insurance Agents of America	Innovation diffusion theory
			Focus group	1 member of the Independent Insurance Agents of America	
			Surveys	1242 members of the Independent Insurance Agents of America	
Damsgaard & Lyytinen (1998)	Inter-organizational collaboration, herd effect, environment favoring cooperation, trade organization support, and infrastructure	EDI diffusion	Field study	9 organizations from 3 industries in Finland	Institutional theory and innovation diffusion theory
Cox & Ghoneim (1996)	Coherent strategy, top management support, meeting needs, review and continuous improvement, and integration into core business activities	EDI implementation and EDI integration benefits and barriers	Survey	85 organizations from a variety of industries	None
			Case study	1	
Premkumar & Ramamurthy (1995)	Proactive adoption	EDI implementation outcomes and effect of decision modes (proactive vs. reactive)	Survey	Information systems and sales/ purchasing executives from 201 firms	Power and social exchange theory
Crook & Kumar (1998)	Organizational context (organizational size, information technology capability, senior management commitment), environmental context (industry experience with EDI, nature of suppliers, nature of customers), external pressure, system benefits, and implementation support	EDI use	Case study using grounded theory	4 organizations in four different industries	None
Hart & Saunders (1997)	Trust	EDI use	Theoretical framework and case study	1 retail firm	Power
Grewal, Corner, & Mehta (2001)	Emphasizing efficiency motivations, deemphasizing legitimacy motivations, and information technology capabilities	Electronic market use	Survey	306 participants in the Polygon marketplace	Institutional theory, transaction cost theory, and motivation-ability framework

Table 2: Facilitators of IOIS technology adoption and diffusion (continued)

Authors	Facilitators of Adoption and Diffusion (Significant Independent Variables)	Adoption/ Diffusion Phenomenon (Dependent Variable)	Research Method	Data Source	Theoretical Base
Cavaye & Cragg (1995)	Champion existence, extension of existing systems, experienced information systems staff, perceived customer need, user participation, low system cost, good marketing programs, and user technological awareness	Customer-oriented IOIS adoption	Case study	9 profit-oriented firms selling a product/service	None
Reich & Benbasat (1990)	Product champion, top management support, proactive information systems function, external pressure, customer involvement, marketing the system, and perceived need	Customer-oriented strategic system adoption	Case study	11 customer-oriented strategic systems, interviews with line and information systems management	None
Grover (1993)	Top management support (0.91), champion existence (0.69), compatibility (0.92), complexity (less)(-0.56), proactive role of information technology group (0.84), large size (0.67), existing information technology infrastructure (0.63), strategic information systems planning (0.47), and management risk-taking propensity (0.45)	Customer-based IOIS adoption	Survey	226 senior executives	None
Runge (1985, 1988)	Product champion, customer involvement in development process, marketing efforts, extension of existing information systems, and ignoring or circumventing normal information system planning and approval processes	Telecommunication-based information system adoption	Case study	35 systems in Britain	None
Sabherwal & Vijayasarathy (1994)	Product information intensity, value chain information intensity, and environmental uncertainty	Telecommunication use between customers and suppliers	Survey	86 senior executives from medium-sized companies	None

innovation attributes influencing adoption. Innovation diffusion theory posits a user's technology adoption decision as a rational choice based on perceived technological characteristics such as relative advantage, compatibility, trialability, observability and complexity.

Power theories also underpin IOIS studies. There are several notions on power. Emerson (1962) did some of the first work in power with social exchange theory. According to Emerson (1962), social exchange theory notes that "the dependence of actor X on actor Y is (a) directly proportional to X's motivational investment in goals mediated by Y, and (b) inversely proportional to the availability of those goals to X outside the Y–X relationship" (p. 32). Thompson (1967) has a similar observation on power. Thompson (1967, p. 31) noted that an organization is dependent on some element of its task environment (a) in proportion to the organization's need for resources or performances which that element can provide, and (b) in inverse proportion to the ability of other elements to provide the same resource or performance" (p. 31).

Another notion on power is *resource dependency theory* (Pfeffer, 1987; Pfeffer & Salancik, 1978). Resource dependency theory posits that an organization's environment is unstable and organizations try to reduce vulnerabilities and increase power relative to their constituents in order to survive. The degree to which an organization is dependent upon external resources is determined by the resource's importance, the organization's discretion over it and whether alternatives exist. In applying this theory to technology adoption, resource dependency theory explains that inter-organizational relationships may not be based on efficiency. Rather, inter-organizational relationships may be formed to reduce environmental uncertainty and may be the result of having power and influence over dependent organizations.

Many IOIS studies cite the importance of achieving critical mass. *Critical mass theory* (Dybvig & Spatt, 1983; Granovetter, 1978, 1985; Markus, 1990; Oliver, Marwell, & Teixeira, 1985; Rohlfs, 1974) posits that some innovations require collaboration among potential adopters for any adopter to benefit. It further posits that if a network cannot obtain an installed base equal to the largest equilibrium network size, it will have to exit from the market if it cannot surpass critical mass and become self-sustaining. Critical mass theorists believe collective action participation is based on perceptions of what the group is doing. Participation decisions are influenced by who has participated, how many have participated and how much others have contributed.

A few IOIS studies mention *institutional and organizational behavior theories*. *Institutional theory* suggests that in efforts to survive, organizations strive to satisfy external stakeholders by adopting rules and practices that may not necessarily increase technical efficiency but increase legitimacy in external stakeholders' eyes (DiMaggio & Powell, 1983; Meyer & Rowan, 1977). *Organizational behavior theory* (Thompson, 1967) suggests that organizational variables, such as size, influence technological innovation adoption. IOIS research studies find that a large firm size facilitates EDI adoption (Premkumar et al., 1997), EDI use (Crook & Kumar, 1998) and customer-based IOIS adoption (Grover, 1993).

Analysis

In testing their EDI adoption model, Chwelos et al. (2001) observed that their model's constructs fall into technological, organizational and inter-organizational categories. Based on this, Chwelos et al. hypothesized that these categories of influence will be adoption determinants for other IOIS forms. We test and extend this hypothesis in Table 3 by taking the 25 IOIS studies reported in Table 2 and trying to place the variables found to significantly influence IOIS adoption and diffusion into Chwelos et al.'s proposed categories.

In this test, we categorize each variable by comparing the common variable definition in the existing research to Chwelos et al.'s category definitions. Chwelos et al. defined the inter-organizational level as focusing on how environments and or other firms' actions influence technology adoption and diffusion. The authors defined organizational-level research as research focusing on internal attributes influencing technology adoption and diffusion. The authors explained that technological level research focuses on adoption and

Table 3: Categorization and frequency of significant independent variables by study type and technology type

Significant Independent Variable	Category	Number of Studies Focusing on		Number of Studies Focusing on		
		Adoption	Diffusion	B2B EC	EDI	Other IOISs
Customer involvement	Inter-organizational	2	3	2	1	2
Environmental uncertainty	Inter-organizational	1	1		1	1
External expertise utilization	Inter-organizational		1	1		
External pressure (includes implementation of key business partners, implementation being required by key business partners, and power)	Inter-organizational	8	2		9	1
Implementation support	Inter-organizational	2	1	1	2	
Information intensity (value chain)	Inter-organizational		1			1
Legislative and policy environment (clear and certain)	Inter-organizational		2	2		
Timing of project startup	Inter-organizational		1	1		
Trade organization support	Inter-organizational		1		1	
Trust	Inter-organizational	1	1	1	1	
Inter-organizational Total		**14**	**14**	**8**	**15**	**5**
Environment favoring cooperation (includes information sharing)	Inter-organizational		3	2	1	
	Organizational					
Need (perceived)	Inter-organizational	3			1	2
	Organizational					
Readiness	Inter-organizational	1	2	1	2	
	Organizational					
Technology (awareness)	Inter-organizational	1	1	1		1
	Organizational					
Inter-organizational/Organizational Total		**5**	**6**	**4**	**4**	**3**
Adoption decision (proactive)	Organizational		1		1	
Champion existence	Organizational	4				4
Culture supporting innovation	Organizational		1	1		
Duration of project (longer)	Organizational		1		1	

Table 3: Categorization and frequency of significant independent variables by study type and technology type (continued)

Significant Independent Variable	Category	Number of Studies Focusing on		Number of Studies Focusing on		
		Adoption	Diffusion	B2B EC	EDI	Other IOISs
Evaluation procedures	Organizational		2	1	1	
Firm size (large)	Organizational	2	1		2	1
Goals, strategy, and vision (consistent and clear)	Organizational	1	4	3	1	1
Information intensity (product)	Organizational		1			1
Information system function (proactive)	Organizational	2				2
Information system staff experience	Organizational	1				1
Information system staff skill	Organizational		2	2		
Innovativeness	Organizational		1	1		
Integration into core business activities	Organizational		1		1	
Leadership	Organizational		1	1		
Management of project	Organizational		2	2		
Managerial thinking (creative)	Organizational		1	1		
Marketing and promotion	Organizational	3	1	1		3
Organizational change	Organizational		1	1		
Planning and approval processes (ignoring existing)	Organizational	1				1
Risk (operational)	Organizational	1			1	
Risk (strategic)	Organizational	1			1	
Risk-taking propensity of top management	Organizational	1				1
Team composition	Organizational		1	1		
Top management support	Organizational	4	5	3	4	2
Organizational Total		**21**	**27**	**18**	**13**	**17**
Compatible technology	Technological	1	2	1	1	1
Complexity of technology (less)	Technological	2			1	1
Data security	Technological		1	1		

Table 3: Categorization and frequency of significant independent variables by study type and technology type (continued)

Significant Independent Variable	Category	Number of Studies Focusing on		Number of Studies Focusing on		
		Adoption	Diffusion	B2B EC	EDI	Other IOISs
Observability	Technological	1			1	
Relative advantage (perceived) (also includes perceived benefits)	Technological	5	5	2	7	1
Stability (system)	Technological		1	1		
Technology (adaptability)	Technological	1				1
Technology (cost)	Technological	2	1		2	1
Technology (current)	Technological	3	2	1	1	3
Technology (ease of use)	Technological		1	1		
Technology performance	Technological		1	1		
Technological Total		**15**	**14**	**8**	**13**	**8**
	Grand Total	**55**	**61**	**38**	**45**	**33**

diffusion influenced by perceived innovation characteristics and often uses innovation diffusion theory.

Table 3 also shows independent variables having significant relationships with dependent variables related to technology adoption and diffusion. Table 3 further shows types of IOISs (B2B EC, EDI, other) investigated by independent variables. For example, customer involvement significantly influences IOIS adoption in two studies and IOIS diffusion in three studies. Of the studies finding customer adoption a significant facilitator of adoption or diffusion, one focused on EDI, two focused on B2B EC and two dealt with other types of IOISs.

Our categorization supports Chwelos et al.'s hypothesis and finds IOIS adoption and diffusion research also addresses technological, organizational and inter-organizational levels. The categorization extends Chwelos et al.'s hypothesis, as this study's scope includes an array of IOIS types, whereas Chwelos et al.'s study focuses on EDI. This review included diffusion studies, whereas Chwelos et al.'s study focuses on adoption studies only.

Chwelos et al.'s (2001) hypothesis did not mention that the same variable may have multiple categorizations. In categorizing independent variables reported in the IOIS literature, four variables (perceived need, environment favoring cooperation, readiness and technology awareness) belong to both organizational and inter-organizational categories. Perceived need in IOISs relates to the organization's perception of their business partners' needs. Perceived customer needs falls into the inter-organizational category. In recognizing customers' needs, these needs become organizational needs. As such, perceived need belongs to both organizational and inter-organizational categories. In IOISs, both the organization's environment and the organization's relationship with other organizations involved in implementing the IOIS must be cooperative. Therefore, an environment favoring cooperation falls into both organizational and inter-organizational categories. Readiness as a facilitator of adoption and diffusion also falls into organizational and inter-organizational categories. Because IOISs span organizational boundaries, the organization and its partners must be ready to adopt the IOIS. Technology awareness also falls into organizational and inter-organizational categories. The organization and its business partners must be aware of new technology for it to be adopted and diffused.

Several authors (Grover, 1993; Premkumar et al., 1997) used "environmental" for what Chwelos et al. called "inter-organizational." Grover's environmental variables include four industry variables (maturity, competition, information intensity and adaptable innovations) and two customer variables (power and vertical coordination). Premkumar et al.'s environmental category includes climate, net-dependence, competitive pressure and customer support. Future IOIS research would benefit by breaking Chwelos' inter-organizational category into two categories: environmental and inter-organizational. The inter-organizational category would include how business partner relationships influence technology adoption and diffusion. The environmental category would focus on how other surroundings influence technology adoption and diffusion.

The analysis brings up several shortcomings in the existing research. First, based on the type of IOIS identified in each study, the analysis categorizes significant independent variables by IOIS type (B2B EC, EDI and other IOIS). While every study provides a definition of the study's IOIS type, existing research has not addressed the distinction between these different IOIS types. This is a weakness of this categorization and the existing research. Based on previous definitions, one may argue that EDI, customer-oriented strategic systems, and B2B electronic markets are all types of B2B EC. Future research will benefit from providing a clear definition, categorization and distinguishing characteristics of the different types of IOIS.

Most of the studies and the significant independent variables focus on EDI. Given the heavy weight placed on EDI, determining whether some variables are significant for EDI and not for other types of IOISs requires future research. This review provides a starting point for empirical research on other types of IOIS. Revisiting the review when there is a greater body of research on adoption and diffusion of other IOIS types will help researchers determine if significant variables differ for EDI compared to other IOIS types.

Except for the EDI studies, most of the studies of the other types of IOIS systems use a qualitative approach. Greater understanding of emerging IOIS adoption and diffusion will occur with more rigorous investigations of the significant variables found in these qualitative studies. The EDI research stream consists of both qualitative and quantitative investigations.

Conclusion

In their 2002 *MIS Quarterly* article, Webster and Watson (2002) stated, "the progress of information systems as a field is impeded because there are few published review articles" (p.13). This chapter contributes to the field by bringing together IOIS research and providing a starting point for work on emerging IOISs. This chapter summarizes significant independent variables, dependent variables, study focuses, research methods and theoretical approaches of 25 IOIS studies. (See Table 2.) We further analyzed significant independent variables found in IOIS research. (See Table 3.)

Chwelos et al.'s (2001) synthesis of EDI research and EDI adoption model test provide the hypothesis framing this research. Chwelos et al. hypothesized that constructs at organizational, technological, and inter-organizational levels facilitate IOIS adoption. This paper evaluates Chwelos et al.'s hypothesis by reviewing independent variables, from 25 empirical IOIS studies, found to significantly influence IOIS adoption and diffusion. This paper supports and extends Chwelos et al.'s hypothesis by applying it to an array of IOISs and to both adoption and diffusion.

In this review, significant independent variables fell into Chwelos et al.'s categories, however, a few variables fell into multiple categories (organizational and inter-organizational). As such, we extend Chwelos et al.'s hypothesis and propose that variables found to significantly influence IOIS adoption and diffusion also facilitate adoption and diffusion of emerging IOIS forms, such as varying forms of B2B electronic marketplaces.

Table 3 shows occurrences of independent variables influencing adoption and diffusion to be about equal. Fifty-five independent variable occurrences facilitate adoption, and 61 independent variable occurrences influence diffusion. Most variables with significant IOIS adoption and diffusion relationships are in the organizational category. The technological and inter-organizational categories have nearly equal occurrences of significant independent variables. External pressure, top management support, and relative advantage have been frequently proven to significantly influence IOIS adoption and diffusion.

The main limitation of this paper is the process by which we categorized the many significant independent variables in Table 3. We categorized the variables based on a comparison of Chwelos et al.'s category definitions to each variable's definition from the studies. Enhancing this approach with Q-sort would have added more rigor to the categorization. Q-sort uses statistics to measure the areas of concurrence between experts.

Table 1 indicates that 59% of the reviewed work focuses on EDI. This is because EDI is more widespread and has been in existence longer than B2B EC, customer-oriented strategic systems and electronic markets. The field will benefit from further empirical investigations into the adoption and diffusion of the emerging types of IOISs. For example, Table 1 indicated one investigation of electronic market adoption and diffusion facilitators. This review provides a starting point for such investigations. This chapter guided a dissertation investigating electronic market adoption and diffusion facilitators (see Koch, 2003).

References

Bakos, J. Y. (1997). Reducing buyer search costs—Implications for electronic marketplaces. *Management Science, 43*(12), 1676–1692.

Bartlett, M. (2001). B2B exchanges still working out kinks—Study. *Newsbytes.* Retrieved November 20 from the World Wide Web: http://www.newsbytes. com.

Bouchard, L. (1993). Decision criteria in the adoption of EDI. Paper presented at the *13th International Conference on Information Systems,* Orlando, FL.

Cash, J. I. J., & Konsynski, B. R. (1985). IS redraws competitive boundaries. *Harvard Business Review, 63*(2), 134–142.

Cavaye, A. L. M., & Cragg, P. B. (1995). Factors contributing to the success of customer oriented interorganizational systems. *Journal of Strategic Information Systems, 4*(1), 13–30.

Chwelos, P., Benbasat, I., & Dexter, A. S. (2001). Research report: Empirical test of an EDI adoption model. *Information Systems Research, 12*(3), 304–321.

Cox, B., & Ghoneim, S. (1996). Drivers and barriers to adopting EDI: A sector analysis of UK industry. *European Journal of Information Systems, 5*(1), 24–33.

Crook, C. W., & Kumar, R. L. (1998). Electronic data interchange: A multi-industry investigation using grounded theory. *Information & Management, 34*(2), 75–89.

Damsgaard, J., & Lyytinen, K. (1998). Contours of diffusion of electronic data interchange in Finland: Overcoming technological barriers and collaborating to make it happen. *Journal of Strategic Information Systems*, 7(1998), 275–297.

Deeter-Schmelz, D. R., Bizzari, A., Graham, R., & Howdyshell, C. (2001). Business-to-business online purchasing: Suppliers' impact on buyers' adoption and usage intent. *Journal of Supply Chain Management*, 37(1), 4–10.

DiMaggio, P., & Powell, W. (1983). The iron cage revisited: Institutional isomorphism and collective rationality in organizational fields. *American Sociological Review*, 48(2), 147–160.

Dybvig, P. H., & Spatt, C. (1983). Adoption externalities as public goods. *Journal of Public Economics*, 20(2), 231–247.

Emerson, R. M. (1962). Power-dependency relations. *American Sociological Review*, 27(1), 31–41.

Granovetter, M. (1978). Threshold models of collective behavior. *American Journal of Sociology*, 83(6), 1420–1443.

Granovetter, M. (1985). Economic action and social structure: The problem of embeddedness. *American Journal of Sociology*, 91(3), 481–510.

Grewal, R., Corner, J. M., & Mehta, R. (2001). An investigation into the antecedents of organizational participation in business-to-business electronic markets. *Journal of Marketing*, 65(July), 17–33.

Grover, V. (1993). An empirically derived model for the adoption of customer-based interorganizational systems. *Decision Sciences*, 24(3), 603–640.

Han, K. S., & Noh, M. H. (1999–2000). Critical failure factors that discourage the growth of electronic commerce. *International Journal of Electronic Commerce*, 4(2), 25–43.

Hart, P., & Saunders, C. (1997). Power and trust: Critical factors in the adoption and use of electronic date interchange. *Organization Science*, 8(1), 23–42.

Hope, B. G., Hermanek, M., Schlemmer, C., & Huff, S. L. (2001). Critical success factors in the development of business-to-business electronic commerce. *JITCA: Journal of Information Technology Cases and Applications*, 3(3), 7–34.

Iacovou, C. L., Benbasat, I., & Dexter, A. S. (1995). Electronic data interchange and small organizations—Adoption and impact of technology. *MIS Quarterly*, 19(4), 465–485.

Koch, H. (2003). Business-to-business electronic marketplaces: Membership and use drivers. Unpublished Ph.D. dissertation, Texas A&M University, College Station, TX.

Markus, M. L. (1990). Toward a "critical mass" theory of interactive media. In J. Fulk, & C. Steinfield (Eds.), *Organizations and communication technology* (pp. 194–218). Newbury Park, CA: Sage Publications.

Meyer, J. W., & Rowan, B. (1977). Institutionalized organizations: Formal structure as myth and ceremony. *American Journal of Sociology, 83*(2), 340–363.

O'Callaghan, R., Kaufmann, P. J., & Konsynski, B. R. (1992). Adoption correlates and share effects of electronic data interchange systems in marketing channels. *Journal of Marketing, 56*(2), 45–56.

Oliver, P., Marwell, G., & Teixeira, R. (1985). A theory of the critical mass I. Interdependence, group heterogeneity, and the production of collective action. *American Journal of Sociology, 91*(3), 522–556.

Pfeffer, J. (1987). A resource dependence perspective on intercorporate relations. In M. Mizruchi, & M. Schwartz (Eds.), *Intercorporate relations* (pp. 25–55). Cambridge, MA: Cambridge University Press.

Pfeffer, J., & Salancik, G. (1978). *The external control of organizations: A resource dependence perspective.* New York, NY: Harper & Row.

Premkumar, G., & Ramamurthy, K. (1995). The role of interorganizational and organizational factors on the decision mode for adoption of interorganizational systems. *Decision Sciences, 26*(3), 303–336.

Premkumar, G., Ramamurthy, K., & Crum, M. R. (1997). Determinants of EDI adoption in the transportation industry. *European Journal of Information Systems, 6*(2), 107–121.

Premkumar, G., Ramamurthy, K., & Nilakanta, S. (1994). Implementation of electronic data interchange: An innovation diffusion perspective. *Journal of Management Information Systems, 11*(2), 157–186.

Ranganathan, C., Teo, T. S. H., Dhaliwal, J., S., Ang, J. S. K., & Hyde, M. (2001, December 16–19). Facilitators and inhibitors for deploying business-to-business e-commerce applications: A multi-method, cross-cultural study. Paper presented at the *22nd Annual International Conference on Information Systems*, New Orleans, LA.

Reich, B. H., & Benbasat, I. (1990). An empirical investigation of factors influencing the success of customer-oriented strategic systems. *Information Systems Research, 1*(3), 325–347.

Rogers, E. M. (1995). *Diffusion of innovations.* New York, NY: The Free Press.

Rohlfs, J. (1974). A theory of interdependent demand for a communication service. *Bell Journal of Economics and Management Science, 5*(1), 16–37.

Runge, D. A. (1985). Using telecommunications for competitive advantage. Unpublished Ph.D. dissertation, Oxford University, England, United Kingdom.

Runge, D. A. (1988). *Winning with telecommunications.* Washington, DC: International Center for Information Technologies Press.

Sabherwal, R., & Vijayasarathy, L. R. (1994). An empirical investigation of the antecedents of telecommunication-based interorganizational systems. *European Journal of Information Systems, 3*(4), 268–285.

Saunders, C., & Clark, S. (1992). EDI adoption and implementation: A focus on interorganizational linkages. *Information Resources Management Journal, 5*(1), 9–19.

Tabor, S. W. (2001). Success factors in e-commerce adoption: An analysis of an early adopter airline. *JITCA (Journal of Information Technology Cases and Applications), 3*(3), 57–75.

Teo, H. H., Tan, B. C. Y., & Wei, K. K. (1995). Innovation diffusion theory as a predictor of adoption intention for financial EDI. Paper presented at the *International Conference on Information Systems,* Amsterdam, The Netherlands.

Thompson, J. D. (1967). *Organizations in action.* New York: McGraw-Hill.

Webster, J., & Watson, R. T. (2002). Analyzing the past to prepare for the future: Writing a literature review. *MIS Quarterly, 26*(2), 8–23.

Williams, L. R. (1994). Understanding distribution channels: An interorganizational study of EDI adoption. *Journal of Business Logistics, 15*(2), 173–203.

Zwass, V. (1996). Electronic commerce: Structures and issues. *International Journal of Electronic Commerce, 1*(1), 3–23.

Chapter IX

Evolution of DSS from Single User DSS to Inter-Organizational DSS

Sean B. Eom
Southeast Missouri State University, USA

Abstract

Extranets are triggering a revolution in the structure and operations of many organizations in the new Internet-driven global economy. Extranets along with other technologies and business drivers are changing the way we view the firm from discrete firm-based to industry-based perspectives of cooperation. This paper discusses the evolution of decision support systems (DSSs) from single-user decision support systems to inter-organizational decision support systems (IODSSs). To better understand the IODSS, we briefly discuss two predecessors, organizational DSS and global DSS, followed by presenting the IODSS definition, architecture, and applications.

Introduction

Since the U.S. Department of Defense initiated the development of networked computers in 1969, Internet technologies have rapidly advanced and revolution-ized the way we communicate and conduct business. They have narrowed geographical and temporal boundaries rapidly. The second wave of the techno-logical revolution came with intranet technology in the mid-1990s. With the intranet, organizations have strengthened the powers and speeds of data gathering/sharing, communication, collaboration, and decision making within a firewall-protected organizational boundary. The third wave of this technological evolution, extranets, began in the second half of the 1990s.

Many believe that it is the key technology enabler that is triggering a revolution in the structure and operations of many organizations in the new Internet-driven global economy (Goldmann, 1997). In addition to maturing Internet technologies, several technology drivers, as well as business drivers, further pushed the emergence of industrial networks and trans-enterprise systems. The technology drivers include expanded public network infrastructure, the development of Internet and World Wide Web technologies, a rapid development of client/server computing technology, the evolution of relational database technology, and the development of crossware applications. Globalization, information and knowl-edge-driven economies, business process reengineering, and changes in man-agement process thinking (viewing the firm from discrete firm-based to industry-based perspectives of cooperation) have been strong driving forces of the development of industrial networks (Laudon & Laudon, 2000). With the third wave of the Internet technologies (extranets), we are witnessing the growing importance of new types of organizations—virtual corporations, virtual organi-zations, extended enterprises, and trans-enterprise systems. All of these orga-nizations are built on Internet technologies, including intranets and extranets.

This paper discusses the evolution of DSSs from single-user DSSs to IODSSs to support inter-organizational decision-making activities. The concepts of extranets and inter-organizational systems are inseparable parts. We will review the concept of extranets, including intronets and supranets. The following section describes and contrasts organizational DSSs, global DSSs, and IODSSs, along with a discussion of the differences between Web-based DSSs and IODSSs. The subsystems of IODSSs will be described in the next section. The last section discusses the applications of IODSSs.

Emergence of Extranets as the Key Technology Enabler

An extranet is defined as an *ex*tended or *ex*panded corporate in*tranet,* using Internet technology, operating over the Internet for a wide range of applications by building bridges between the public Internet and private intranets. The Internet-based wide area network (WAN) links an organization and its trading partners in a secure, electronic online environment (Baker, 1997; Bayles, 1998; Bort & Felix, 1997). An extranet is created if more than two companies open parts of their intranets to each other and thereby create an inter-intra-net in order to improve coordination with trading partners in virtually all functional areas. The trading partners include a client that represents a substantial portion of the company's revenue, companies working on a joint development project, distributors, contractors, suppliers of raw materials, vendors, dealers, consultants, etc. A secured extranet allows trading partners to gain limited (controlled) access to a collaborative network to increase profitability and competitive advantages through managing important organizational activities in the most timely and cost-effective manner (Riggins & Rhee, 1998).

The extranets can be classified as either intronets or supranets (see Table 1 of Chapter 1 in this book). Three automakers (DaimlerChrysler, General Motors, and Ford) are cooperating on an industry-wide extranet called the Automotive Network Exchange (ANX). The industrial extranet will continue to grow. The ANX network is expected to connect the 1000 Tier 1 suppliers, 9000 Tier 2 and 3 suppliers, and 40,000 others who communicate with automakers in the near future (Liebrecht, 1999). The health-care industry has joined and started to use the ANX. Because the auto industry spends billions of dollars every year to provide health insurance for its employees, it seemed like a logical step for the auto industry to bring insurance companies and hospitals onto the ANX network (Bushaus, 2000).

Organizational DSS

As shown in Figure 1, an inter-organizational DSS has evolved from two predecessors, organizational DSS and global DSS. As we progress to IODSSs, the focuses, tools, and functional capabilities have been shifted, added, and strengthened, while the core concepts of DSSs suggested by many (Dennis, George, Jessup, Nunamaker, & Vogel, 1988; DeSanctis & Gallupe, 1987; Jessup & Valacich, 1993; Keen & Scott Morton, 1978) have remained unchanged.

Table 1: Applications of extranets

Data/Information/Knowledge	Communication	Decision Making
Gather transaction data from trading partners and share it with them; the data includes purchase orders/payment instructions, product catalogs, and product shipments	Private newsgroups among the members of cooperating organizations sharing ideas	Collaborative decision making using groupware via brainstorming, voting, outlining, and writing virtual teams through synchronous as well as asynchronous communication (e.g., new product developments)
Training/education program materials	Advanced videoconferencing systems	Joint project management and control through application sharing
Knowledge management by creating an inter-organizational repository of data, information, and knowledge (CAD/CAM/CAE files, design specifications, etc.)	Text-based chatting and white board	Collaborative/interactive computer-aided design/computer-aided manufacturing/computer-aided engineering using multiple workstations
	E-mails and electronic bulletin board systems	Operational planning based on trading partners' monthly forecasts for sales
	Real-time voice communication	High-speed prototyping with fastest communication links
	Workflow management	Supply chain management

Research on computer-based information systems to support group activities was conducted under the titles of group decision support systems (GDSSs) (DeSanctis & Gallupe, 1985), computer-supported cooperative work (Greif, 1988), group support systems (Jessup & Valacich, 1993), electronic meeting systems (Dennis et al., 1988), and collaboration support systems. GDSSs have focused on decision making/problem solving, while computer-supported cooperative works are driven more by the communication needs of a group. There seems to be a consensus that GSS is a broad umbrella term referring to the collection of computer-assisted technologies used to aid group efforts directed at identifying and addressing problems, opportunities, and issues (Jessup & Valacich, 1993).

Since the first notable concept of organizational DSSs appeared in the late 1980s (Lee, McCosh, & Migliarese, 1988), the topic of organizational DSSs has been continuously researched. Readers are referred to George (1991–1992) for a comprehensive review of organizational DSS (ODSS) literature up to 1990. Based on the review, George synthesized the different ODSS concepts and presented three common features (p. 114):

- The focus of an ODSS is an organizational task, activity, or decision that affects several organizational units or corporate issues.
- An ODSS cuts across organizational functions or hierarchical layers.
- An ODSS almost necessarily involves computer-based technologies and may also involve communication technologies.

An organizational DSS is defined as a DSS that is used by individuals or groups at several workstations in more than one organizational unit which makes varied (interrelated but autonomous) decisions using a common set of tools (Carter, Murray, Walker, & Walker, 1992). According to the same source, an important goal of organizational DSSs is to provide "the glue that holds a large organization together and keeps its part marching to the beat of the same drummer toward common goals."

Key components of ODSS technologies include (1) communication technologies; (2) coordination technologies for coordinating resources, facilities, and projects; (3) filtering technologies for filtering and summarizing information using intelligent agents; (4) decision-making technologies such as GSSs; and (5) monitoring technologies such as executive information systems/executive support systems (George, Nunamaker, & Valacich, 1992). The organizational DSS is often built on intranet technology (Ba, Lang, & Whinston, 1997).

Global DSS

The essential role of the global DSS is to support global decision making, which must deal with multidimensional complexity. This stems from the multiplicity of the global environments in which multinational corporations (MNCs) operate. The global environment consists of legal (patent and trademark laws, laws affecting multinational operations, etc.), cultural (languages, customs, value systems, religious beliefs, etc.), economic (currency, tax, inflation, interest rates, monetary and fiscal policy, etc.), and political (form and stability of government, governmental policy toward MNCs, etc.) forces.

A global management support system is defined as a management support system to support managers of multinational corporations in their decision-making processes and deal with one or more variables that constitute the multidimensional complexities of global decision making that stem from the global environments. Global DSSs consist of a network of DSSs that links parent companies with foreign subsidiaries via telecommunication networks (Eom, 1996).

The global DSS must have several unique functional requirements, such as:

- Global consolidated reporting
- Effective means of communication between the MNC headquarters and its subsidiaries
- Global risk (foreign exchange, political, and tax) management support
- Global joint decision support between headquarters and overseas subsidiaries

Inter-Organizational DSS

Definition of Inter-Organizational DSS

An IODSS is a DSS built on the extranets which can be executed over the Web to provide information, communication, and decision support tools in order to create and sustain the competitive advantages of all consortium members of industrial networks. Industrial networks (extended enterprise or integrated industry-wide system) electronically link multiple organizations in the same industry vertically (manufacturers, suppliers, and suppliers' supplier) as well as horizontally (linking competing firms in an industry). Industrial networks enable the coordination of business processes across an industry vertically as well as horizontally.

The competitive advantages stem from cost leadership and product/service differentiation. To gain competitive advantage, the firm must cope with five competitive forces that determine industry profitability (Porter, 1985). The forces are the bargaining powers of buyers and suppliers, the threat of new entrants, and the threat of substitute of products or services. The extranets interlock trading partners so that the value chain can be created within and outside the organization. According to Porter (1985), "competitive advantage in one industry can be strongly enhanced by interrelationship with business units competing in related industries, if these interrelationships can actually be achieved" (p. 3). The electronic link created by extranets is a strong force that can most likely overcome the organizational impediment to creating those interrelationships.

Web-Based DSS and Inter-Organizational DSS

"Web-based DSS" is a loosely defined term that refers to any DSS that can be executed over the Web, as shown in Figure 1. Web-based DSSs have reduced technological barriers and made it easier and less costly to make timely decisions on a global scale within geographically dispersed companies. The World Wide Web has become the client–server platform of many business organizations due to its network and platform independence and very low software/installation/maintenance costs. Consequently, many organizations are using this global computer network-based DSS to overcome temporal, geographical, and technological barriers. According to Power (1998), the Web-based DSS has become a synonym for "organizational DSS" or "enterprise-wide DSS." More groupware products are inextricably tied to Internet technology. Many groupware products are integrating more Internet protocols. As of 1999, more than 75 Web groupware products were available (Wheeler, Dennis, & Press, 1999).

Figure 1: Evolution of decision support systems

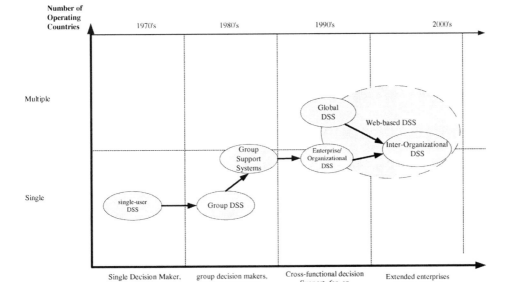

The Architecture of Inter-Organizational Decision Support Systems

Traditional (non-Web-based) single-user DSSs include every component on the user's computer hard disks without communication components. IODSSs are based on the client-server architecture consisting of the client, server, and communication middleware. The server contains most of the DSS components, such as data, models, algorithms, etc. Using their Web browsers, users can access IODSSs deployed on the Web server. The data components and the model components do not have to be in the same physical locations. Web-based data warehousing has also become an important data management tool. Web-based DSSs are usually equipped with the tools to access the data residing on the data warehouses located on a Web server. They may be distributed anywhere on the company's or trading partners' network. Components of IODSSs include communication subsystems (extranets), hardware, software, people, and procedures.

The Communication Network

There are three different types of extranets: private, public network, and virtual private network (VPN). Private extranets link the intranets of more than two organizations using private, leased lines. The most significant advantage of this type of network is its high security level. On the other hand, the high cost of private phone lines is a significant drawback. An alternative approach to using private extranets is to subscribe to commercial network services, which are completely private networks that are isolated from the public Internet solely for the use of network subscriber traffic. Public network extranets allow outside parties to selectively access the information resources of the sponsoring organization through the Internet, not through private, leased lines. The purpose of an IODSS is to increase consortium competitiveness of all consortium members. To achieve this goal, supranets can be used for building IODSSs using public network extranets, using virtual private networks, or subscribing to commercial service networks.

IODSSs can use commercial network services such as the ANX network. The ANX network was originally designed for use for the automotive industry. Now its technology is being extended and applied to many different industries to facilitate information exchange, communications, and decision making among trading partners. In the case of subscribing to the commercial service network, the organization's networks must be configured to be connected to the commercial network via a system integrator. By subscribing to the commercial network services, many cumbersome tasks in managing the security of a network, such as detecting intrusion, maintaining confidentiality and integrity of data, etc., will be managed by the network service providers.

There are three models of public network extranets based on the use of a public network (including the Internet) to link/open an organization's intranet to its trading partners. The *secured intranet access model* allows the business partner to log directly onto a company's intranet to access most of it. The highest level of network security planning, as well as a high level of trust in the partners, is necessary to implement this network architecture. The *specialized application model* allows the partners to gain limited access to the intranet from the extranet site. A wide variety of extranet applications, both packaged and custom developed, are available over an extranet. These include order processing, database access, customer service and support, e-mail, and other communication tools. The *electronic commerce model* is well suited to deal with a large number of partners (more than several hundred companies) using e-commerce security and transaction processing techniques. For more information on the three models of public network extranets, see Bort and Felix (1997).

The External Connection

An extranet links the intranets of distributed organizations (trading partners) for the purpose of conducting business. The link can be made through a direct lease line from intranet to intranet or through a secure line over the Internet. A dedicated Internet connection is necessary to connect the corporate headquarters to the Internet, while a remote salesperson may use a dial-up local Internet service provider to access a sales database at headquarters.

Software

The Web technology used in an extranet includes the following built-in technologies: electronic mail, group collaborations, business partner extensions, real-time audio and video communication, information publishing and sharing, network navigation, full-text indexing and searching, and directories (Baker, 1997). In addition, IODSS software needs to install Web-based groupware (Web groupware) to facilitate diverse communication and decision-making functions under different scenarios: same time and same place (brainstorming, voting, outlining, writing), same time and different place (text-based chatting, video-/audioconferencing, whiteboard/application sharing), and different time and different place (e-mail, listserve, and threaded discussions, organizing workflow).

Depending on the network configuration of the organization, when an organization becomes a subscriber of network service companies such as ANXeBusiness Corporation, they will have access to a multitude of applications that are hosted in subscriber data centers, including applications that support engineering, product design, purchasing, logistics, materials handling, financial transactions, supply chain management, and many other mission-critical time-sensitive business processes. Readers are referred to http://www.anx.com/ for more information on the services.

An essential element of IODSS software is the management science (MS)/ operations research (OR) model software. A recent trend in this area is that many MS/OR software developers are using Web technologies for the design of user interface. Another noteworthy trend is the use of application service providers (ASPs) for delivery of DSS models. Rather than purchasing and installing the software on the server of their organizations, it can be rented on a per-use basis from an ASP who hosts MS/OR applications and provides secure access over the Internet (Shim et al., 2002).

Several researchers have successfully developed Web-based optimization tools and deployed them on the Web. Some examples include WWW-NIMBUS systems (nondifferentiable interactive multiobjective bundle-based optimization system). This is the first interactive multiobjective optimization system on the Internet, solving nonlinear problems involving nondifferentiable and nonconvex functions (Miettinen & Mäkelä, 2000). The second example is Web-HIPRE (hierarchical preference analysis on the Web) system. This is a Java Applet for multiple criteria decision analysis for individual/group decision making with diverse weighing methods including analytic hierarchy process, value function, multi-attribute value theory, etc. (Mustajoki & Hämäläinen, 2000). There are other group and negotiation support systems such as joint gains (Kettunen & Hämäläinen, 1999) and INSPIRES for negotiation support (Kersten, 1996).

People and Procedures

Inter-organizational DSSs permit the largest number of participants to share data and information, support communication and decision-making activities from participating organizations anywhere over the global networks of intranets, extranets, and the Internet. The procedure component includes procedures for effective use of all hardware, software, and communication systems (extranets), as well as rules for conducting threaded discussions using electronic bulletin board systems and procedures for organizing workflow, etc.

Inter-Organizational DSS Applications

Coordinated Decision-Making Support Among Business Partners

Extranet-based IODSSs provide retailers and their suppliers with the necessary tools for coordinated decision making between the two groups. Retailers often experience difficulties with the demand forecast for each product, which is a key for inventory management and delivery scheduling. The forecast could sometimes show a significant difference between the one made by the retailer and the other one made by the supplier. Such good examples are the cases of Heineken U.S.A., and Wal-Mart and Warner-Lambert (a manufacturer of consumer products). Heineken Operational Planning System (HOPS) is an extranet that links its network of regional suppliers and resellers. The HOPS extranet allows resellers to place their monthly forecasts for sales and product orders. The extranet significantly reduced the time needed to move beers from the brewery in Europe to the U.S. retail channel in just about the same time it takes Anheuser-Busch to ship from its domestic breweries (Merkow, 1997). Wal-Mart created an extranet that links its network to the network of Warner-Lambert to be used to collaborate on short-term product demand forecasts. Wal-Mart buying agents use a spreadsheet to make a preliminary forecast from the data stored in their CFAR (Collaborative Forecasting and Replenishment) server. A copy of this forecast is sent to Warner-Lambert's CFAR server so that Warner-Lambert's planners can revise the forecast until an agreed-upon forecast is made for each product. Refer to Darling and Semich (1996) for further details of the process and other DSS components.

A stream of recent research portends that sharing MS/OR models and data among many organizations on the Internet will become much easier. Consequently, seamless exchange or integration of MS/OR models on the Web facilitates the inter-organizational decision-making activities among trading partners (Kim, 2001).

Decision Support for Virtual Enterprises and Virtual Teams

Virtual enterprise (also known as virtual integration) is a temporary consortium of independent member companies interconnected via private and public networks to quickly exploit fast-changing worldwide manufacturing, marketing, and R&D opportunities. Virtual enterprise companies share costs and skills, and they focus on core competencies that collectively enable them to access global markets with world-class solutions that members could not deliver individually (Hardwick & Bolton, 1997). A virtual enterprise such as Cisco Systems concentrates on core competencies (the superior abilities in producing goods and services that are difficult for competitors to replicate) in which it can be world-class and relies on someone else to perform the rest (Hammer, 2000).

A frequent type of decision-making style in virtual corporations is using virtual teams. A virtual team is an electronically linked group of people who collaborate closely, even though they are separated by space (including national boundaries), time, and organizational barriers, to effectively deal with a specific task that cannot be done as efficiently or as effectively through traditional organizational structures and policies. Virtual teams have been applied to the completion of joint projects such as remote application development, new product design and development, project management, and so forth. See Lipnack and Stamps (1997) and Vest (2002) for successful examples of virtual team applications.

The development of ubiquitous computing based on secure wireless devices such as Web-enabled digital phones and digital assistants ensures greater connectivity and robust communication and decision support for virtual teams and virtual organizations (Shim et al., 2002). Some groupware such as the "decision organizer" run very well on pocket PCs connected to the Internet (i.e., iPAQ) or a pocket communicator (i.e., Nokia 9210). A virtual team member with a wireless mobile support platform can use groupware to initiate a session, organize, rate, and rank the ideas of virtual team members. The virtual support platform can also interact with personal computers with the Internet (Shakun, Pomerol, Bui, & Carlsson, 2002).

Global Supply Chain Management

The supply chain is a series of physical entities associated in the process beginning with procurement of raw materials through several multiple-tier suppliers (upstream supply chain), and internal manufacturing processes used by an organization (internal supply chain), and ending with the delivery of the finished goods to the customers, distributors of finished products, and retail outlets (downward stream supply chain). Management of the supply chain is concerned with cooperation among an organization, its multitier suppliers, distributors, and customers in the area of inventory management, order fulfillment, shipment, just-in-time manufacturing, financial settlement, transportation and logistics, and sales support to compress the time between each stage of the chain and to minimize costs associated with the chain through sharing/exchanging data, information, and knowledge.

The key to orchestrating a wide range of activities in the management of the global supply chain is to streamline business processes in a seamless manner. In doing so, the key ingredient is the seamless flow of structured/unstructured information among the organizations in the supply chains through the Internet, intranets, and extranets. For example, customer demand forecasts by retailers often need an adjustment based on the viewpoints of retailers and manufacturers. Extranets facilitate the process of the adjustments by allowing smooth and secured exchange of data/information as shown in the case of Warner-Lambert's Collaborative Forecasting and Replenishment system. Extranets-based IODSSs can also be used to keep track of inventory flow information available at all points of the supply chain. Furthermore, IODSSs can be used to proactively feed forward the actual/forecasted customer demand to all suppliers and manufacturers in the chain to minimize the inventory costs (e.g., the Heineken Operational Planning System).

The development of extranets has allowed many organizations to effectively manage the industry's supply chain by forming industry business to business (B2B) intermediaries. The B2B intermediary is an intermediate agency between suppliers and customers to streamline business processes, enhance productivity, and reduce costs. It offers (1) a comprehensive, one-stop e-marketplace of hundreds of thousands of products; (2) personalized access to the e-marketplace to find and order products from the most trusted suppliers through powerful search engines; (3) analysis and comparison of product and pricing information, and purchase from the trusted suppliers; (5) electronic procurement to support business workflow, and controls through the easy-to-use interface.

Conclusions

Inter-organizational DSSs are emerging as a new frontier in DSSs. The focus of DSSs has been shifting from teams, work groups, and intranet-based organizational DSSs to extranet-based inter-organizational DSSs. The extranets' built-in technologies are sufficient to make the extranets as rudimentary IODSSs. With the addition of many readily available Web groupware to extranets, IODSSs are an indispensable communication/decision support tool for enhancing inter-organizational competitiveness to achieve system-wide global objectives. In doing so, costs must be minimized, and products must be differentiated. The cost minimization can be achieved by a series of decisions in the value chains, such as inbound logistics, operations, outbound logistics, marketing, services, etc. Over the past three decades, numerous DSSs have been developed to manage each stage of the value chain (Eom & Lee, 1990; Eom, Lee, Kim, & Somarajan,

1998). The goal of future research is to develop integrated models to optimize the extended enterprise as a whole. To do so, a change in management process thinking from a discrete firm-based view to an industry-based perspective of cooperation is necessary.

Furthermore, several ongoing technological developments in the DSSs area can make IODSSs an effective management support tool. They include cross-organizational workflow integration (Kuechler, Vaishnavi, & Kuelchler, 2001; Weigand & van den Heuvel, 2002); an XML (eXtensible Markup Language)-based modeling language for the open interchange of decision models (Kim, 2001); intelligent negotiation agents to interact and negotiate with users or with other agents (Wang, Liao, & Liao, 2002; Wu & Sun, 2002); and an architectural integration of knowledge management, decision support, artificial intelligence, and data warehousing (Bolloju, Khalifa, & Turban, 2002; Nemati, Steiger, Iyer, & Herschel, 2002).

References

Ba, S., Lang, K. R., & Whinston, A. B. (1997). Enterprise decision support using intranet technology. *Decision Support Systems, 20*(2), 99–134.

Baker, R. H. (1997). *Extranets: The complete sourcebook*. New York: McGraw-Hill.

Bayles, D. L. (1998). *Extranets: Building the business to business Web*. Upper Saddle River, NJ: Prentice Hall PTR.

Bolloju, N., Khalifa, M., & Turban, E. (2002). Integrating knowledge management into enterprise environments for the next generation decision support. *Decision Support Systems, 33*(2), 163–176.

Bort, J., & Felix, B. (1997). *Building an extranet: Connect your intranet with vendors and customers*. New York: John Wiley & Sons.

Bushaus, D. (2000). Trade the ANX way. *InformationWeek, 776*, 93–97.

Carter, G. M., Murray, M. P., Walker, R. G., & Walker, W. E. (1992). *Building organizational decision support systems*. Boston, MA: Academic Press.

Darling, C. B., & Semich, J. W. (1996). Extreme integration. *Datamation*, 140.

Dennis, A. R., George, J. F., Jessup, L. M., Nunamaker, J. F., Jr., & Vogel, D. R. (1988). Information technology to support electronic meetings. *MIS Quarterly, 12*(4), 591–624.

DeSanctis, G., & Gallupe, B. (1987). A foundation for the study of group decision support systems. *Management Science, 33*(5), 589–609.

DeSanctis, G., & Gallupe, B. R. (1985). Group decision support systems: A new frontier. *Data Base, 16*(2), 3–10.

Eom, H. B., & Lee, S. M. (1990). A survey of decision support system applications (1971–April 1988). *Interfaces, 20*(3), 65–79.

Eom, S. B. (1996). Global management support systems: The new frontiers in MIS. In P. C. Palvia, S. C. Palvia, & E. C. Roche (Eds.), *Global information technology and systems management: Key issues and trends* (pp. 441–460). Nashua, NH: Ivy League Publishing.

Eom, S. B., Lee, S. M., Kim, E. B., & Somarajan, C. (1998). A survey of decision support system applications (1988–1994). *Journal of The Operational Research Society, 49*(2), 109–120.

George, J. F. (1991–1992). The conceptualization and development of organizational decision support systems. *Journal of Management Information Systems, 8*(3), 109–125.

George, J. F., Nunamaker, J. F., Jr., & Valacich, J. S. (1992). ODSS: Information technology for organizational change. *Decision Support Systems, 8*(4), 307–315.

Goldmann, N. (1997). *Extranet: The "third wave" in the Internet electronic commerce* [WWW]. ARRAY Development. Retrieved November 23, 2001, from the World Wide Web: http://www.arraydev.com/commerce/jibc/9701-18.htm.

Greif, I. (Ed.). (1988). *Computer-supported cooperative work: A book of readings.* San Mateo, CA: Morgan Kaufmann Publishers, Inc.

Hammer, M. (2000). The rise of virtual enterprise. *InformationWeek, 778,* 152–153.

Hardwick, M., & Bolton, R. (1997). The industrial virtual enterprise. *Communications of the ACM, 40*(9), 59–60.

Jessup, L. M., & Valacich, J. S. (Eds.). (1993). *Group support systems: New perspectives.* New York: Macmillan Publishing Company.

Keen, P. G. W., & Scott Morton, M. S. (1978). *Decision support systems: An organizational perspective.* Reading, MA: Addison-Wesley.

Kersten, G. (1996). *Inspire—Internet Support Program for Intercultural Research,* Center for Computer Assisted Management, Carleton University.

Kettunen, E., & Hämäläinen, R. P. (1999). *Joint gains—Negotiation support in the Internet.* Helsinki: Systems Analysis Laboratory, Helsinki University of Technology.

Kim, H. -D. (2001). An XML-based modeling language for the open interchange of decision models. *Decision Support Systems, 31*(4), 429–441.

Kuechler, W., Jr., Vaishnavi, V. K., & Kuelchler, D. (2001). Supporting optimization of business-to-business e-commerce relationships. *Decision Support Systems, 31*(3), 363–377.

Laudon, K. C., & Laudon, J. P. (2000). *Management information systems: Organization and technology in the networked enterprise* (6th ed.). Upper Saddle River, NJ: Prentice Hall.

Lee, R. M., McCosh, A., & Migliarese, P. (Eds.). (1988). *Organizational decision support systems.* Amsterdam: North-Holland.

Liebrecht, D. (1999). A TCP/IP-based network for the automotive industry. *America's Network, 103*(7), 67–69.

Lipnack, J., & Stamps, J. (1997). *Virtual teams: Reaching across space, time, and organization with technology.* New York: John Wiley & Sons.

Merkow, M. S. (1997, August 27). *Extraordinary extranets* [WWW]. Retrieved November 29, 2001, from the World Wide Web: http://webreference.com/content/extranet/Examples.html.

Miettinen, K. M., & Mäkelä, M. M. (2000). Interactive multiobjective optimization system WWW-Nimbus on the Internet. *Computers & Operations Research, 27*(7/8), 709–723.

Mustajoki, J., & Hämäläinen, R. P. (2000). Web-Hipre: Global decision support by value tree and AHP analysis. *INFOR, 38*(3), 208–220.

Nemati, H. R., Steiger, D. M., Iyer, L. S., & Herschel, R. T. (2002). Knowledge warehouse: An architectural integration of knowledge management, decision support, artificial intelligence and data warehousing. *Decision Support Systems, 33*(2), 143–161.

Porter, M. E. (1985). *Competitive advantage: Creating and sustaining superior performance.* New York: The Free Press.

Power, D. J. (1998). Web-based decision support systems. *The On-Line Executive Journal for Data-Intensive Decision Support, 2*(33).

Riggins, F. J., & Rhee, H. -S. (1998). Towards a unified view of electronic commerce. *Communications of the ACM, 41*(10), 88–95.

Shakun, M., Pomerol, J. C., Bui, T., & Carlsson, C. (2002). Panel: Frontiers of decision and negotiation support in the Internet Age. In F. Adam, P. Brèzilion, P. Humphreys, & J. -C. Pomerol (Eds.), *Decision making and decision support in the Internet Age: Proceedings of Dsiage2002, an IFIP Tc8/WG 8.3 Open Conference, University College Cork, Cork, Ireland, 4–7 July 2002* (pp. 786–787). Cork, Ireland: Oak Tree Press.

Shim, J. P., Warkentin, M., Courney, J. F., Power, D. J., Sharda, R., & Carlsson, C. (2002). Past, present, and future of decision support technology. *Decision Support Systems, 33*(2), 111–126.

Vest, K. F. (2002). *Virtual teamwork: Collaborative computing at British Petroleum*. Science Applications International Corporation. Retrieved July 27, 2002, from the World Wide Web: http://publications.saic.com/satt.nsf/externalbyaut2.

Wang, H., Liao, S., & Liao, L. (2002). Modeling constraint-based negotiating agents. *Decision Support Systems, 33*, 201–217.

Weigand, H., & van den Heuvel, W. -J. (2002). Cross-organizational workflow integration using contracts. *Decision Support Systems, 33*(3), 247–265.

Wheeler, B. C., Dennis, A. R., & Press, L. I. (1999). Groupware comes to the Internet: Charting a New World. *The DATA Base for Advances in Information Systems, 30*(3–4), 8–21.

Wu, D. J., & Sun, Y. (2002). Cooperation in multi-agent bidding. *Decision Support Systems, 33*(3), 335–347.

Chapter X

An Examination of Inter-Organizational Decision Support Systems

Daniel J. Power
University of Northern Iowa and DSSResources.COM, USA

Shashidhar Kaparthi
University of Northern Iowa, USA

Abstract

A broad range of Inter-Organizational Decision Support Systems (IODSSs) can be built to support external stakeholders of an organization. This article examines recent developments associated with building and deploying such systems. The IODSS concept is defined, and an information technology architecture for such a system is explored. Examples of current implementations are categorized as communication, data, document, knowledge, and model-driven IODSSs. Further, implementations of IODSSs are categorized as customer- and supplier-focused. Advantages, disadvantages, and current issues associated with IODSSs conclude the discussion.

Introduction

According to Microsoft Chairman Bill Gates (1996, p. 158), the Internet "will carry us into a new world of low-friction, low-overhead capitalism, in which market information will be plentiful and transaction costs low." To help managers and companies exploit this radically different business environment, more innovative decision support capabilities must be developed. It is especially important that more decision support capabilities be made available by organizations to external stakeholders. Organization stakeholders make many interdependent decisions that can be supported and potentially enhanced using information technologies. Decision interdependencies impact the success of the organizations making them.

For many reasons, the logical technologies to use for building IODSSs are the global Internet infrastructure and Web development and server technologies. The dominant information technology platform in companies is changing from mainframes and LAN-based, client-server systems to Web and Internet technologies. This technology change is expanding the possibilities for computerized decision support. The target users for DSSs can expand significantly to serve a large group of external stakeholders. The variety of decision support applications that can be developed, delivered, and shared is also becoming much larger.

Today, innovative inter-organizational examples of all five generic DSS types (cf., Power, 2002) can be found in organizations, including communications-driven, data-driven, document-driven, knowledge-driven, and model-driven DSSs. These five types of DSSs are the foundation of an expanded decision support framework (cf., Power, 2000, 2002). In the context of IODSSs, communications-driven DSSs can enhance communication in inter-organizational work systems, including supply chains and distribution networks; data-driven DSSs can provide stakeholders with access to historical data warehouses and other relevant data; document-driven DSSs encourage knowledge sharing; knowledge-driven DSSs help distribute expertise more widely to those who could benefit; and finally, model-driven DSSs can provide assistance to any stakeholder who needs access to the "what if?" analyses made possible by the model. The expanded DSS framework also identifies three secondary issues that must be understood and specified when planning and examining specific DSSs. These issues are the enabling technology used in building the DSS, the purpose of the specific DSS, and the targeted users, including external stakeholders.

If the primary targeted users of a DSS are external stakeholders, it is best described as an IODSS. What is the need for IODSSs? IODSSs can help create an extended enterprise, improve stakeholder satisfaction, reduce inventories, speed response to stakeholder requests, reduce decision cycle time, and improve cooperation among partner organizations. To realize these benefits, managers need to know more about how to build and evaluate specific IODSSs that support customers, suppliers, and other stakeholders. Finally, managers and MIS personnel need to try a wide variety of examples of IODSSs to experience the potential benefit and grasp the need that might be met.

This article expands upon materials in Power (2000, 2002) about recent developments associated with building and deploying IODSSs. The next section defines key concepts. The following section discusses design and development of IODSSs. Then, managing IODSSs is discussed. The fourth section summarizes examples of IODSSs. Then, the advantages and disadvantages of deploying IODSSs are discussed. The final section draws some conclusions related to building IODSSs.

Defining the IODSS Concept

IODSSs really only became practical in the late 1990s. Prior to the widespread diffusion of the Internet and Web-based technologies, it was very expensive and tedious to use dial-up connections or value added networks (VAN) for data

Figure 1: Potential inter-organizational DSS target users

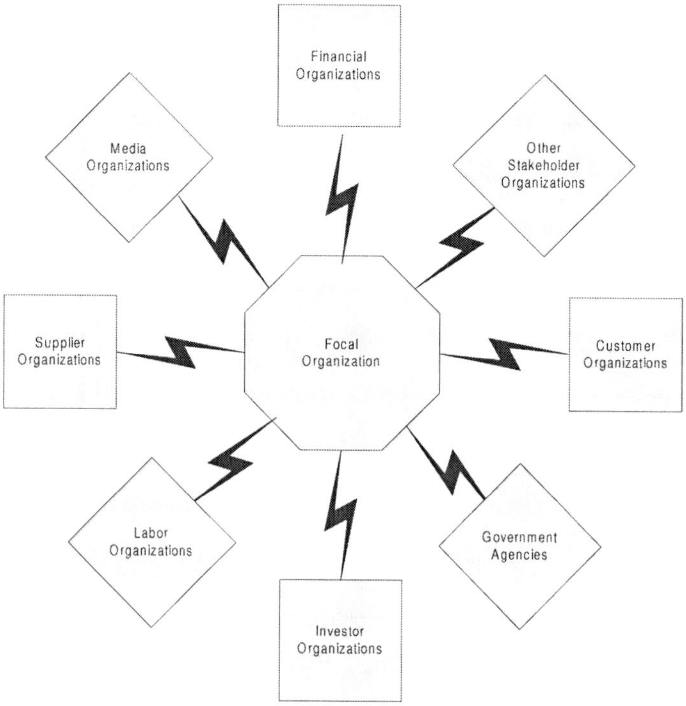

interchange and inter-organizational decision support. Until recently, it was almost impossible to provide any stakeholders with access to knowledge-driven DSSs. Some model-driven DSSs were accessed using time-sharing systems when and if that was practical. Communications-driven and document-driven DSSs were confined to intracompany LANs. Extranets, collaboration and coordination mechanisms, and improved information-sharing practices and processes are helping companies streamline their supply chains.

As noted, IODSSs serve a focal organization's stakeholders, including investor organizations (stockholders, mutual funds), financial organizations (banks), government agencies, and customer, supplier, media, and labor organizations (see Figure 1). An IODSS usually provides selected stakeholders with access to a company's extranet and authority or privileges to use specific decision support capabilities. Companies are creating Web-based, IODSSs that customers can use to evaluate products or that suppliers can use to control costs or reduce inventories. The target users are managers and knowledge workers in a customer, supplier, or partner organization and in some cases retail customers of the organization deploying the specific DSS. IODSSs should provide benefits beyond the elimination of paperwork and the reduction in human processing errors that occur as a result of inter-organizational transaction processing systems.

Creating inter-organizational, communications-driven, data-driven, and docu-ment-driven DSSs is closely linked to improving supply chain management (SCM). DSSs in a supply chain can enhance value for participants by helping integrate the management of the flows of goods/services and associated information, from initial sourcing of raw materials to final delivery to consumers. An organization's competitors are aware of such an IODSS, and they may have easy access and can imitate or even improve upon the system. Because IODSSs are externally facing systems, it is especially hard to maintain a competitive advantage. Realistically, competitive benefits will usually be transitory, but any other benefits from IODSSs should be lasting.

Designing and Developing IODSSs

IODSSs should be built using a decision-oriented diagnosis approach (cf., Stabell, 1983). Simply making an existing DSS accessible using a Web browser or accessible to customers or other external stakeholders will usually lead to unsatisfactory results. Once a diagnosis of decision support needs is complete, a feasibility analysis is definitely required for building such a potentially large-scale DSS. A systematic development approach must then be explicitly chosen, and managers must be involved in the development process.

Developing the user interface, models, and data store for IODSSs remain major tasks. A user interface is important in a Web development environment, and it probably becomes more important because so many stakeholders of various levels of sophistication can potentially access some or all IODSS capabilities. The charting, "what if?", drill-down, and other decision support capabilities available to designers of Web-based IODSSs are comparable to those for stand-alone, PC-based DSSs, but the number of available decision support operations expands enormously with the additions of hyperlinks and the availability of external data and document sources.

Figure 2: Web-based IODSS architecture

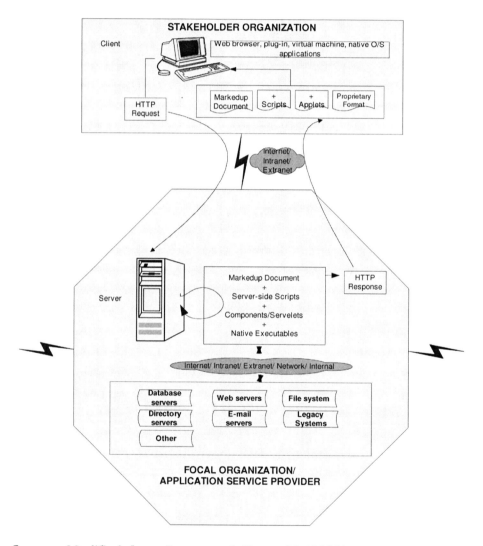

Source: Modified from Power and Kaparthi (2002).

The actual architecture implemented for IODSSs is usually simple. Most Web-based IODSSs are built using a three- or four-tier architecture and are designed to allow any authorized user, with a Web browser and an Internet connection, to interact with them. The application code usually resides on a remote server, and the user interface is presented at the client's Web browser. A person in a stakeholder organization, using a Web browser, sends a hypertext transfer protocol (HTTP request) to a Web server provided by a focal organization or its subcontractor (application service provider, ASP) (see Figure 2). The Web server processes the request. This typically includes server-side scripts like VBScript, JavaScript, or ColdFusion Markup Language (Kaparthi & Kaparthi, 2001). In addition, the server-side processing may include execution of Java Servlets or other native executables. The script may implement or link to a model, process a database request, or format a document. The server may access other database servers, Web servers, or directory servers in a multitier architecture. The results are returned to the user's Web browser for display as an HTTP response. The client receives the response that is formatted using the hypertext markup language (HTML) or other markup languages like the extensible markup language (XML). In addition, client-side processing may include scripting using JavaScript or VBScript, Java applets, ActiveX components, or other proprietary formats like Macromedia flash or Adobe Portable Document Format (PDF).

When a company embarks on building Web-based IODSSs, some problems can be anticipated and minimized. First, Web-based DSS applications will probably encounter some peak load problems. During the business day, many managers will want to access the corporate intranet, and so a "high-performance" hardware architecture that can expand to serve a large number of concurrent users is needed. This load problem is associated with the "scalability" of the hardware and software and the planning of the developers. Quality of service (QoS) will be a major issue when using the Web for IODSSs. Virus and denial of service attacks can further impact IODSS reliability.

Second, the Web is a "stateless" environment that does not automatically keep track of configuration settings, transaction information, or any other data for the next page request. To avoid requiring users to reenter information such as user name and password, Web-based DSS applications must keep state information from one Web page to another. This creates new security issues for companies wishing to make sensitive, internal data accessible to users. User authorization and authentication are challenging in the Web environment because of the large number of potential users.

Third, Web technologies continue to evolve and mature. The technology uncertainty forces organizations and managers to monitor the changes and fund frequent upgrades. The cost of deploying IODSSs is decreasing, and there is a continuing danger that competitors will implement systems that "leapfrog" existing IODSSs. Despite these problems and challenges, the Web is and should be the platform of choice for new IODSSs.

Managing IODSSs

Companies are using Web-based extranet technologies to build "trading communities." These inter-organizational systems can support transaction processing and cooperative and shared decision making. Despite the many possibilities, creating IODSSs involves resolving a number of real-world issues, including how to adapt or change business processes and how to provide incentives for stakeholders to use IODSSs. Managers in interdependent organizations need to cooperate to build IODSSs, and managers in focal organizations need to consider what types of DSSs can assist their stakeholders. Also, managers in focal organizations must confront a variety of business, technical, and legal issues and impediments if they want to build effective IODSSs. Generally, the "focal organization" owns the IODSS.

The first major business issue that must be confronted is who will use the system—customers, suppliers, or others? Then focal organization managers need to ask a number of more specific questions: What is the cost of the proposed IODSS, and who will pay the cost? Then managers need to ask: Do we need to reengineer or redesign our processes? Does the Internet increase the speed of decisions and transactions and create efficiencies for our business? Will the use of networks, Web-based DSSs, and the Internet create new value for customers? Too many "No" answers to such questions and proposed IODSS projects will certainly fail.

In terms of technical issues, managers need to ask if the initiating company has the staff and technology in place to build the proposed IODSS. Someone needs to determine what hardware and software the partners and participants will need to acquire. Technical issues can be overcome if potential problems and needs are identified early in the development process.

Finally, from a legal perspective, managers need to determine what material can be made available to external users, especially customers and suppliers, to support their decision making. And, focal organization managers should ask: Do we have privacy or liability issues or copyright issues associated with the proposed IODSS project?

Implementation can be especially difficult, because an IODSS Project Team needs the support of at least two sets of senior executives. Also, the team needs to address all of the above issues in terms of two or more different business and information technology cultures.

Table 1: Examples of inter-organizational decision support systems

Type of IODSS	Focal Organization and Purpose	Target Users
Communication-driven	NEC Leasing Services (03/22/01): Credit decisioning and workflow management	Dealers
	Deltek Systems (02/27/01): Web-based interactive client support for diagnosis and problem solving	Clients
Data-driven	Anderson Clayton Corp. (Vollmer, 2002): Provides real-time access to all relevant data and reports to support decision making	Cotton growers
	H-E-B Grocery Company (11/11/2002): Provides Collaborative Planning, Forecasting and Replenishment (CPFR)	Suppliers
Document-driven	Florida Hospital (02/11/03): Provides documents and images for medical decision making	Physicians
	BF Goodrich (Documentum Staff, 2003): AirFLOW system supports nonroutine aircraft maintenance	Internal and customers
Knowledge-driven	Canon U.S.A (05/20/02): Deploys technical service and operating details of its electronic products	Licensed dealers
	DRUGFACTS.com (03/23/01): Assists in identification of causes of abnormal lab results	Medical professionals
Model-driven	Artesyn Technologies (Power, 2000): Virtual design tools provide customers its power supply products with technical decision support	Customers
	Ironmax, Inc. (03/01/01): Selling subscriptions to its Custom Cost Evaluator (CCE) tool to the construction equipment industry	Equipment managers

The most advanced IODSSs use the public Internet to create communication links. The systems may involve any stakeholder with access to the Internet and authority or privileges to use specific capabilities. These advanced systems are associated with collaboration and decision support. The increasing use of the Internet/Web is significantly decreasing the costs of building IODSS networks between suppliers, customers, and manufacturers/retailers. The Web facilitates cooperative processes and can include buyers, suppliers, and partners in redesigned business processes. With IODSSs supporting value chains, the supply-chain management system and the customer support system can be integrated. Integration can provide sharing of manufacturing, inventory, sales, and other data. Such a data-driven IODSS helps suppliers build to order and stock inventory based on more accurate projections.

Some Examples of IODSSs

Communication-driven IODSSs

This type of IODSS includes communication, collaboration, and decision support technologies that span two or more organizations. It is an interactive computer-based system intended to facilitate the solution of problems by decision makers working together as a group. Such systems support electronic communication, scheduling, document sharing, and other group productivity and decision support enhancing activities. For example NEC Leasing Services (03/22/01) provides credit decisioning and workflow management tools to NEC and its dealers for streamlining the financing workflow process. Deltek Systems (02/27/01) provides Web-based interactive client support for diagnosis and problem solving. Deltek uses its system to conduct interactive client support. Deltek support staff can view, troubleshoot, diagnose, and fix client problems over the Web in real-time. The Web-based meeting services enhance communications in areas such as sales, design, marketing, training, support, and partner management.

Data-driven IODSSs

These systems include management reporting systems, data warehousing and analysis systems, executive information systems (EISs) and spatial DSS shared by two or more organizations. Data-driven IODSSs emphasize access to and manipulation of large databases of structured data. Simple file systems accessed by query and retrieval tools provide the most elementary level of functionality. Data warehouse systems that allow the manipulation of data by computerized tools tailored to a specific task and setting or by more general tools and operators provide additional functionality. Data-driven IODSSs with online analytical processing (OLAP) provide the highest level of functionality and decision support that is linked to analysis of large collections of historical data. For example, Anderson Clayton Corp. (ACC) (Vollmer, 2002) provides real-time access to all relevant data and reports to support decision making. ACC is using arcplan's dynaSight as a reporting interface to company and industry data stored in several Microsoft SQL servers and data warehouses. ACC can now track bales from ginning to warehousing and marketing with one reporting system. ACC's customers (growers) can access predefined reports on ACC's Web site.

H-E-B Grocery Company (11/11/2002) uses collaborative planning, forecasting, and replenishment (CPFR). The company plans to use the Manugistics' CPFR Solution, in multiple supply chain deployments, to better manage the 50,000 to 60,000 products available at more than 280 H-E-B Stores. With this system, H-E-B and its suppliers can more effectively anticipate demand, update inventory, identify market changes, and respond accordingly.

Document-driven IODSSs

Document-driven IODSSs are evolving to help users from multiple organizations retrieve and manage unstructured documents and Web pages. A document-driven IODSS integrates a variety of storage and processing technologies to provide complete document retrieval and analysis. The Web provides access to large document databases, including databases of hypertext documents, images, sounds, and video. A search engine is a powerful decision-aiding tool associated with a document-driven IODSS. For example, Florida Hospital (02/11/03) provides documents and images for medical decision making to over 2000 physicians. The system allows the hospital to merge reports and capture images, such as pathology slides, and forward them to referring physicians. BF Goodrich (05/17/03) implemented a system (AirFLOW) that supports nonroutine aircraft maintenance. AirFLOW supports the process that begins when mechanics submit an engineering support request (ESR) and supporting information to the engineering group, which responds with an engineering repair (ER) procedure. Before the repair can be scheduled, the customer must approve the ER. Engineering may consult with the manufacturer before issuing the ER, and, in some cases, FAA approval is required. When relying on paper and manual workflow, it could take several weeks to complete these processes.

Knowledge-driven IODSSs

These IODSSs contain specialized problem-solving expertise that can be shared across organizational borders. The "expertise" consists of knowledge about a particular domain, understanding of problems within that domain, and "skill" at solving some of these problems. For example, Canon U.S.A (05/20/02) deploys technical service and operating details of its electronic products in a system accessible by its licensed dealers. Canon's customer service representatives and licensed dealers can access a knowledge base that is always up-to-date with new information for all the company's products. Canon also uses this system to provide a "download center" where service representatives and dealers will be able to find and download software drivers for its entire line of hardware devices.

DRUGFACTS.com (03/23/01) has a system that assists in identification of causes of abnormal lab results by physicians, pharmacists, and nurses. The online tool identifies diseases, situations, and drugs that can increase or decrease the normal range of a tested value. Users can verify normal ranges; view key points and clinical reminders; and review diseases, conditions, situations, and drugs that can alter specific lab values.

Model-driven IODSSs

Model-driven IODSSs include systems that use accounting and financial models, representational models, and optimization models. Model-driven IODSSs emphasize access to and manipulation of a model by users in two or more organizations. Simple analytical tools provide the most elementary level of functionality. Some systems that allow complex analysis of data may be classified as model-driven DSS systems providing modeling, data retrieval, and data summarization functionality. Model-driven IODSSs use data and parameters provided by decision makers to aid them in analyzing a situation, but they are not usually data intensive. For example, Artesyn Technologies (Power, 2000) provides virtual design tools that are used by customers of its power supply products with technical decision support. Ironmax, Inc. (03/01/01) sells subscriptions to its Custom Cost Evaluator (CCE) tool to the construction equipment industry.

Examples of IODSSs Categorized on Target Users

Another useful way to study IODSSs is by examining the relationship of target users with the focal organization. In this section, we look at some additional examples of IODSSs that focus primarily on customers or suppliers.

Customer-focused IODSSs

Many of the examples of IODSSs in Table 1 are customer focused. For example NEC Leasing is targeting its dealer customers. Deltek, Artesyn Technologies, and BF Goodrich are targeting clients. Additionally, many Web sites have decision support for customers. Microsoft Carpoint at URL http://carpoint.msn.com demonstrates both data-driven and model-driven DSSs. Users can use a "Compare" feature to make pair-wise comparisons of car models across prespecified attributes.

Retirement and investment planning is facilitated at a number of Web sites. Also, many 401(k) plans are supported by Web sites. Plan participants and sponsors do the work of entering data, transferring investments, and researching investments. Model-driven DSSs can show how an investment may grow over time; and knowledge-driven DSSs provide advice. Some sites with DSSs include that of Fidelity Investment (http://www.401k.com), Principal Financial group (http://www.principal.com), and American Express (http://www.americanexpress.com). The Fidelity "Retirement Planning Calculator" is a model-driven DSS that helps a person decide how much to invest for retirement each month. Principal Financial has an "Investor Profile Quiz" that is a knowledge-driven DSS.

Netscape Decision Guides are good examples of model-driven and knowledge-driven IODSSs. One can find more than 25 Decision Guides at Netscape's site (http://home.netscape.com/decisionguides). Topics of guides include choosing pets, bikes, and business schools.

Stockfinder (http://www.stockpoint.com) has a data-driven DSS that helps investors identify stocks based on criteria like price, earnings, and type of industry. Stockpoint also has an investment profile knowledge-driven DSS. A user answers a short questionnaire about income constraints, personal financial goals, and risk tolerance. The DSS processes the responses and provides a list of possible investments that match the person's personal goals and budget constraints. A number of investment Web sites provide their users with DSS capabilities. Document-driven DSSs provide company information from many sources; charting software lets users manipulate financial comparisons of large time series databases; and search and agent software alerts users to news, stock prices, and changes in stock prices.

Supplier-focused IODSSs

Table 2 also identifies supplier-focused examples including Anderson Clayton and H-E-B Grocery. CPFR (2003) is a concept that allows collaborative processes across the supply chain, using a set of process and technology models that are open, secure, flexible, extensible, and support a broad set of requirements. CPFR is not widely adopted throughout the industry, but there are many pilot implementations in progress, and they have been very encouraging. For more information on CPFR, please visit www.cpfr.org. These pilots have shown an increase in sales, reduced inventories, and improved production forecasting accuracy (Heineken USA, 1995; Nabisco, 1998). CPFR allows retailers like Wal-Mart and vendors (e.g., Lucent or Sara Lee) to share information regarding events (i.e., promotions, store openings, etc.) impacting forecasts and communicate/resolve variances within item level forecasts. According to JD Edwards (2003, p. 1):

An effective CPFR program is a win–win option. Because supply chain partner trading relations are placed at the center of the decision-making process, CPFR provides numerous competitive advantages. Manufacturers who have invested in CPFR quickly realize increased product availability, reduced inventory, and strengthened business partnerships. In addition, CPFR can often be accomplished with minimum change to existing business processes using Internet-based technologies.

Advantages and Disadvantages of Inter-Organizational DSSs

Web-based DSSs have reduced technological barriers and make it easier and less costly to make decision-relevant information available to managers and staff users in geographically distributed locations. Because of the World Wide Web infrastructure, enterprise-wide DSSs can now be implemented at a relatively low cost in geographically dispersed companies to dispersed stakeholders including suppliers and customers. Using Web-based DSSs, organizations can provide DSS capability to managers over an intranet, to customers and suppliers over an extranet, or to any stakeholder over the global Internet.

The Web has increased access to DSSs, and it should increase the use of a well-designed DSS in a company. Using a Web infrastructure for building DSSs improves the rapid dissemination of "best practices" analysis and decision-making frameworks, and it should promote more consistent decision making on repetitive decision tasks across a geographically distributed organization. The Web also provides a way to manage a company's knowledge repository and to bring knowledge resources into the decision-making process. One can hope that Web-based delivery of DSS capabilities will promote and encourage ongoing improvements in decision-making processes.

Also, the Web can reduce some of the problems associated with the competing "thick client" enterprise-wide DSS design, where special software needs to be installed on a manager's computer. Web-based DSSs should reduce IT management and support costs as well as end user training costs.

With IODSSs, managers in stakeholder organizations with a browser can have access to the same Web-based DSSs used by managers in the primary organization. Web technology is and will continue to change the way organizations deliver all types of documents and data.

What are the potential problems with IODSSs? First, stakeholder user expectations may be unrealistic, especially in terms of how much information the user wants to be able to access from the Web. Second, there may be technical implementation problems, especially in terms of peak demand and load problems. Third, it is costly to train decision support content providers and to provide them with the necessary tools and technical assistance. Fourth, Web-based IODSSs create additional security concerns. Finally, using the Web for decision support may result in the accumulation of obsolete materials, especially management reports and documents, or alternatively, require hiring someone to monitor the currency of decision information.

Conclusions about IODSSs

The Internet and World Wide Web have created a major opportunity to deliver more quantitative and qualitative information to a firm's external stakeholders to support their decision makers. Web architectures and networks permit information systems professionals to centralize and control information and yet easily distribute it in a timely manner to managers who need it. The Web has not resolved all problems associated with building, developing, and delivering IODSSs, and many questions about such systems remain controversial. The following questions are still being debated, but at this point, the associated responses seem like reasonable answers. Can an IODSS provide a company with a competitive advantage? Sometimes, especially in knowledge-oriented businesses, an IODSS can provide a competitive advantage. If knowledge sharing reduces costs, improves customer loyalty, or increases sales in the focal organization, then an advantage may result. A major concern is that any advantage is temporary due to technology changes. Does an IODSS have significant cost advantages for all parties, including the focal organization and stakeholders? Usually it does, especially in large-scale implementations where companies have multiple, geographically dispersed sites.

Will an IODSS improve decision making? Perhaps it will—the optimists think so. Will IODSSs provide a broader knowledge base for decision making? Yes, in most cases, once the "knowledge" is on-line. Does a Web-based, IODSS provide timely, user-friendly, and secure distribution of business information? Yes, if a good development product is selected and if the implementation is successful. Can a Web-based, IODSS be managed and maintained? Yes, the tools for managing the Web server and Web content are maturing. Does a Web-based

IODSS help customers and suppliers? Yes, customers and suppliers can make better choices.

Will Web-based, IODSSs facilitate corporate growth? Will they improve productivity and improve profitability? Yes, appropriately designed IODSSs can impact the corporate bottom line. Profits can improve in the focal organization and its stakeholder organizations. Communication-driven, document-driven IODSSs can improve productivity and, consequently, impact the bottom line.

Along with the Web-based opportunities for building innovative IODSSs come new challenges. Managers must choose which stakeholders need what information and support and decide how to deploy these capabilities. Also, managers must learn how to use Web and Internet technologies to really gain a competitive advantage. This means that to implement IODSSs, it is essential to develop appropriate strategies and organizational structures, redesign business processes, integrate the technologies and associated information into decision-making processes, evaluate costs and benefits, and manage new types of business relationships.

The Web is the platform of choice and the new frontier for innovative DSSs. All of the Web DSS development environments have strengths and weaknesses, but the capabilities are increasing rapidly, and the Web DSS user interfaces are impressive compared to those of only a few years ago. DSSs built using Web technologies will take on a new importance as accessible and useful tools for improving business decisions (cf., Power, 2000, 2002).

References

Canon U.S.A. (05/20/02). *AT&T Wireless, Canon & Sharp select KnowledgeBase Solutions for Web-based customer support.* Retrieved August 29, 2003 the World Wide Web: http://dssresources.com/subscriber/password/news/news2002/mayjun2002/knowledgebasesolutions05202002.

Collaborative Planning, Forecasting, and Replenishment. (2003). Retrieved August 29, 2003 from the World Wide Web: http://www.jdedwards.com/content/enUS/Product-SupplyChainExecution/AdvPln_CollabPln.pdf.

Deltek Systems. (02/27/01). *Deltek improves customer support, increases productivity with WebEx real-time meetings.* Retrieved August 29, 2003 from the World Wide Web: http://dssresources.com/subscriber/password/news/news2001/feb2001/webex02272001.html.

Documentum Staff. (2003). *Optimizing aircraft maintenance operations using a document-driven DSS.* Documentum, Inc., 2001, posted at DSSResources.COM May 17, 2003.

DRUGFACTS.com. (03/23/01). *DRUGFACTS.com adds free Lab Values Analyzer to assist medical professionals in interpreting abnormal lab results.* Retrieved August 29, 2003 from the World Wide Web: http://dssresources.com/subscriber/password/news/news2001/mar2001/drugfacts03232001.htm.

Florida Hospital. (02/11/03). *Florida hospital selects Cypress to power information access and delivery.* Retrieved August 29, 2003 from the World Wide Web: http://dssresources.com/subscriber/password/news/news2003/february/cypress02112003.html.

Gates, W., Myhrvold, N., & Rinearson, P. (1996). The road ahead. New York: Penguin USA.

H-E-B Grocery Company. (11/11/2002). *H-E-B Grocery Company selects Manugistics' Collaborative Forecasting and Replenishment solutions.* Retrieved August 29, 2003 from the World Wide Web: http://dssresources.com/subscriber/password/news/news2002/november/manugistics11112002.html.

Ironmax, Inc. (03/01/01). *New online decision-support tool from Ironmax automates equipment cost evaluations.* Retrieved August 29, 2003 from the World Wide Web: http://dssresources.com/subscriber/password/news/news2001/mar2001/ironmax03012001.html.

Kaparthi, S., & Kaparthi, R. (2001). Macromedia ColdFusion, MA: Course Technology.

NEC Leasing Services. (03/22/01). *NEC Industries chose eFinance software for Online Credit decision support and transaction finance processing.* Retrieved August 29, 2003 from the World Wide Web: http://dssresources.com/subscriber/password/news/news2001/mar2001/efinance03222001.htm.

Power, D. J. (2000). DSS Hyperbook. URL http://dssresources.com/dssbook/contents.html.

Power, D. J. (2002). *Decision Support Systems: Concepts and resources for managers.* Westport, CT: Greenwood/Quorum Books.

Power, D. J., & Kaparthi, S. (2002). Building Web-based Decision Support Systems. *Studies in Informatics and Control, 11,* (4/ December).

Stabell, C. B. (1983). A decision oriented approach to building Decision Support Systems. Chapter 10 in J. L. Bennett (Ed.), *Building Decision Support Systems.* Reading, MA: Addison-Wesley.

Vollmer, E. (2002). *Anderson Clayton Corp. delivers real-time business intelligence to U.S. cotton growers.* arcplan, May 2002, posted at DSSResources.COM July 12, 2002.

Endnote

[1]   The authors wish to acknowledge Professor Sean Eom of Southeast Missouri State University and Professor Karthik Iyer of University of Northern Iowa for their valuable comments and feedback.

Section VI:

Evaluation

Chapter XI

Evaluating Inter-Organizational Information Systems

Jill Drury
The MITRE Corporation, USA

Jean Scholtz
National Institute for Standards and Technology (NIST), USA

Abstract

This chapter describes different means of evaluating the usability and suitability of computer-based inter-organizational information systems (IOISs). It begins with describing why doing so is important yet difficult, and provides an assessment of the advantages and disadvantages of the major types of evaluation. It continues with a case study focusing on determining whether an application provides the necessary insight into other collaborators' identities, presence, and activities while keeping sensitive information private from a subset of the collaborators. The goal of this chapter is to provide practical guidance to organizations seeking IOISs to help them choose (or develop) an IOIS that best meets their needs.

Introduction

Information technology can be used to support collaborations and partnerships among organizations for competitive purposes. Organizations have developed the notion of inter-organizational systems (IOSs), also known as inter-organizational information systems (IOISs), to support these collaborations and partnerships. An IOIS is defined as an automated information system shared by two or more organizations (Cash & Konsynski, 1985) in a collaborative fashion.

Compare the definition of an IOIS with the definition of computer-supported collaborative work (CSCW) applications: applications that support coordinated activity carried out by groups of collaborating individuals (Greif, 1988). CSCW applications are also known as multiuser, groupware, or collaborative applications.

Collaborative applications normally provide capabilities beyond simple information access to facilitate communication and collaboration among partners. Depending upon the collaborative application, both synchronous and asynchronous communications may be supported, and documents can be shared. Some collaborative applications incorporate video to support communications and negotiations. These coordination mechanisms are essential to efficient collaboration among cooperating organizations. In fact, because IOISs are computer-based systems used to collaborate across organizations, they are a subset of collaborative applications.

Hong and Kim (1998) built on Cash and Konsynski's (1985) work by developing a framework for classifying the various types of IOISs. Their classification scheme is based on three categories: vertical linkage, horizontal linkage, and cross linkage. Vertical systems connect suppliers with sellers with the goal of more efficient marketing. This type of system gives sellers, for example, the capability to place orders quickly and gives suppliers sales data to help them plan production. Horizontal systems link homogeneous groups of businesses. Partnerships within an industry, often consisting of smaller businesses, benefit from improved access to information. Cross systems are an attempt to integrate horizontal and vertical links into one complete system.

It is necessary to understand the roles of the participants or collaborators in IOISs in order to provide the necessary system capabilities to support a variety of tasks. For example, consider a vertical IOIS that links a manufacturer with a number of suppliers. A subset of those suppliers may be competitors who are negotiating terms with the manufacturer. Suppliers may want to use this system to share contractual information with the manufacturer but not with each other. Vertical and cross IOISs will need to support the most diverse set of users (e.g., suppliers, manufacturers, and retailers), though horizontal IOISs might also need to support differing groups of collaborators (e.g., manufacturers from the

Eastern United States versus manufacturers from the Western United States). The roles of participants and their different information sharing needs should be taken into account when evaluating which IOIS is appropriate for a set of cooperating organizations.

To help organizations evaluate which IOIS they should adopt, and provide guidance for developing an IOIS, this chapter includes an assessment of the advantages and disadvantages of using different types of evaluation methods for determining the suitability of IOIS applications. The other contributions of this chapter are as follows:

- An explanation of why IOISs are difficult, yet important, to evaluate

- A description of how the Synchronous Collaborative Awareness and Privacy (SCAPE) awareness framework could be used to evaluate an IOIS application

- A case study of evaluating the Groove™¹ application's suitability for use by a collaborating team that includes members from organizations with different goals

Outline

The rest of this section discusses the importance of evaluating IOISs, the difficulties of doing so, and the critical distinctions between evaluating single-user computing applications versus multiuser applications, such as IOISs. The second section describes evaluation methods for multiuser applications in general, and one method in particular, SCAPE, will be described in the third section. The fourth section presents a case study of using SCAPE to evaluate Groove, a popular tool that aids inter-organizational information sharing. Finally, a discussion of what can be learned by evaluating IOISs completes the chapter.

The Importance of Evaluating IOISs

Much research has centered on evaluating the usability of collaborative applications, because it is extremely important to ensure that these applications can be effectively and efficiently used by their intended audiences. The success of a collaborative application normally depends on a "critical mass" of users accepting and making proper use of the application. For example, picture:

- An inventory control system so cumbersome to use that some of the staff receiving inventory neglect to log the inventory into the system or log it incorrectly

- An instant messaging application that users did not find easy and rewarding to use, so very few of a user's business or social contacts bother to remain accessible via instant messaging

- An automated calendar management application that takes a lot of work to enter activities into, so many people within a workgroup do not make an effort to keep their calendars up-to-date

Clearly, each of these situations constitutes a recipe for failure. These cases illustrate the fact that a collaborative application is likely to fail if the work people need to put into the application exceeds the perceived value of their benefits from using the application (Grudin, 1988).

Besides an imbalance in work versus benefits, there are other reasons why adoption of an IOIS may fail. For example, we have seen adoption of a collaborative application fail when:

- *Users did not perceive a need to collaborate*: Such a finding is consistent with Rogers' (1995) work on diffusion of innovations, which notes that the rate of adoption of innovations is related to the extent to which the innovation (e.g., a new collaborative application) satisfies users' needs.

- *The application did not provide functionality that users felt was relevant*: Relevant functionality is dependent on the tasks the users need to perform and the conditions under which they normally perform those tasks. For example, an IOIS intended for use by personnel driving delivery trucks that requires a substantial amount of typing (instead of, say, using a bar code reader) would be likely be unsuccessful.

- *Users were not available to log in frequently*: Users who often attend meetings or engage in other activities that preclude access to the IOIS, for example, would be unlikely to embrace use of the IOIS.

- *Users did not develop a well-articulated communications strategy*: An example of an incomplete communications strategy is one that does not define situations in which to use the collaborative application versus e-mail.

- *The application was not easy to learn or use*: Rogers (1995) noted that adoption of innovations is related to the complexity or ease with which an innovation can be understood.

There is normally a large financial difference to a collaborating group of organizations between failure to adopt an IOIS and adopting—and making good use of—an IOIS that is well-suited to those organizations. When adoption failure occurs, the organizations must count as a loss the purchase price of the IOIS plus the loss in productivity represented by the hours spent installing, training, and experimenting with the IOIS. Collectively, these costs could be substantial, especially for large organizations that may have asked hundreds of people to try the IOIS. In addition, there is an intangible cost: members of the organizations may be less open to use of IOISs in the future once they have had a negative experience with an IOIS.

Contrast this failure situation with the case in which organizations choose an IOIS that meets their needs and streamlines their business processes. Depending on how an IOIS is used, an effective IOIS may result in a decreased need to travel (because IOIS technology can often mitigate the need for face-to-face meetings), shorter document production review cycles, decreased time-to-market, increased sales, and better customer support.

The difference between adoption failure and success hinges on defining collaboration requirements that take into account the work characteristics of users, the likely benefits to users, as well as ease of use from the point of view of the intended set of users. A further prerequisite for success is an evaluation program that examines how well an IOIS is likely to meet those requirements.

Evaluation goals differ depending on whether an IOIS is being chosen from among a set of existing products, or a custom (bespoke) IOIS product is being developed. If an IOIS is being chosen, the candidate applications are each examined against a tailored set of requirements, using one or more evaluation methods such as those discussed later in this chapter. Because the commercial IOISs cannot normally be modified substantially, the one that comes closest to meeting the requirements is chosen. If a custom IOIS is being developed, the goal of evaluation is to find problems that can be corrected as early as possible in the product design and development life cycle. The later in the development process that interface problems are found, the more costly they are to correct. Mantei and Teorey (1988) found that changes made to the interface designs of systems after production coding had begun cost four times as much as changes to the designs made during prototyping phases.

The Challenges of Evaluating IOIS Applications

There are several reasons why evaluating collaborative applications is more difficult than evaluating single-user computing applications. Malone (1985) cited the difficulties in assembling a group of people in a lab that reflect the social, motivational, economic, and political characteristics of typical users—yet these characteristics are likely to affect performance when using the collaborative system. If evaluation is attempted in the users' normal work environments ("in the field"), Grudin (1988) observed that it is extremely difficult to disperse evaluators to the various locations of the collaborators as well as take into account the wide variation in user group composition and work environments. Regardless of whether they occur in a lab or in the field, Grudin (1988) noted that evaluations of collaborative applications take much more time than evaluations of single user applications, because the relevant group interactions "typically unfold over weeks."

Adding to the difficulty of collaborative application evaluation is the fact that sophisticated applications allow users to take on a number of different roles. Users' expectations of an applications' behavior may change depending upon the roles users are playing at the time and the specific tasks they are performing. More generally, collaborative applications are challenging to evaluate due to the need to take into account how the application mediates users' interactions with each other.

Although difficult to perform, evaluations of collaborative applications are extremely important due to the cost implications described above. The purpose of this chapter is to provide insight into the state-of-the-art in evaluating collaborative applications in general, and into one evaluation method in particular (which will form the basis for the case study presented later in this chapter).

The Critical Difference Between Evaluating Single-User and Multiuser (e.g., IOISs) Computer Applications

The preceding subsection touched upon the crucial distinction between evaluations of single-user systems, such as word processors, and multiuser systems, such as IOIS applications. An evaluation of multiuser (collaborative) systems needs to investigate whether the application adequately supports collaborators' awareness of each others' presence, identities, and activities. Awareness is important in collaborative applications because it aids coordination of tasks and resources, and it assists in transitions between individual and shared activities (Dourish & Bellotti, 1992). Dourish and Bellotti (1992, p. 107) defined awareness as "an understanding of the activities of others, which provides a context for your own activities." "Workspace awareness" was defined by Gutwin et al. (1995) as the up-to-the-minute knowledge of other participants' interactions with the shared workspace, such as where other participants are working, what they are doing, and what they have already done in the workspace.

To understand the importance of awareness, picture trying to use a chat application without being able to read the contributions of the other participants; clearly, the application is useless without an understanding of the other participants' activities. Chat is an example of a synchronous collaborative application (those that are used by collaborators at the same time, although not necessarily at the same place). An "up to the moment" awareness of others' activities is especially pertinent to the class of synchronous (as opposed to asynchronous) collaborative applications. An example of an asynchronous collaborative application is e-mail.

Awareness and privacy are in tension with one another, as are awareness and information overload. Hudson and Smith (1996) expressed the trade-offs very well:

This dual tradeoff is between privacy and awareness, and between awareness and disturbance. Simply stated, the more information about oneself that leaves your work area, the more potential for awareness of you exists for your colleagues. Unfortunately, this also represents the greatest potential for intrusion on your privacy. Similarly, the more information that is received about the activities of colleagues, the more potential awareness we have of them. However, at the same time, the more information we receive, the greater the chance that the information will become a disturbance to our normal work. This dual tradeoff seems to be a fundamental one. (p. 247)

Any evaluation method that pertains to collaborative applications should be sensitive to issues of privacy and awareness. For example, a student using a distance-learning application may want to make the instructor aware of all of his or her online activities, while the instructor would want to keep grading activity private (except to the student directly affected).

It is difficult to apply evaluation techniques developed for single-user applications to multiuser applications, because they do not address the issues of awareness and privacy. Only recently has there been a push toward developing evaluation methods specifically for collaborative applications.

Usability/Suitability Evaluation Methods for IOIS Applications

An important prerequisite for applying usability and suitability evaluation methods is a thorough understanding of the users' requirements and desires. Thus, the first part of this section provides a brief discussion of how to acquire such an understanding.

The remainder of this section provides an overview of the three broad categories of evaluation methods: formal methods (analytic methods such as dialogue and task modeling techniques), empirical methods (experiments and user studies involving human test subjects), and inspection methods (expert examination of user interfaces). Despite the difficulties enumerated above, some usability evaluation methods have been developed for collaborative systems.

Understanding Users' Needs

There are many techniques for learning about users' collaboration needs. Some of them are as follows:

- Task analysis: A family of different techniques that involve breaking apart users' tasks, from the standpoints of either cognitive or physical activities, at a high level of abstraction or in great detail, depending upon the particular task analysis technique chosen. For practical advice on performing task analyses, we recommend Mayhew (1999).

- Ethnographic observation: A broad-based approach originating in anthropology in which users are observed while they pursue their normal activities; observers become participants by immersing themselves in the users' environment. For examples of ethnographic observation applied to adoption of collaborative applications, see the work of Bonnie Nardi (e.g., Nardi & O'Day, 1999).

- Contextual inquiry: An ethnographic-based technique in which the observer becomes an apprentice of the person being observed; besides observation, contextual inquiry involves focused interviews, discussion, and reconstruction of past events (Holtzblatt & Jones, 1993).

- Critical incident interviews: A method in which users are interviewed about the events and activities surrounding an unusual or high-impact event. Klein (2000) described the use of critical incident interviews for collaborating teams.

Without understanding users' characteristics and work environments, it is impossible to determine whether an IOIS would be "natural" or "intuitive" for those users, or whether the IOIS would be compatible with the users' normal work practices. Consider an application targeted at scientists and mathematicians, such as Mathematica™. Mathematicians expect to see terminology in the interface such as "factorial" and "cosine"; they do not need definitions of these terms. Factorial and cosine functions also exist in Excel™, which was designed for a general audience. In Excel, mathematical terms are defined, and the definitions are readily visible (they are not buried in a "help" file, for example).

Formal Methods

An example of a formal method that can be used to evaluate collaborative systems is Critical-Path-Method (CPM)-Goals, Operators, Methods, Selection rules (GOMS) (John & Kieras, 1994). CPM-GOMS is also known as Cognitive-Perceptual-Motor-GOMS because of its purpose to model the parallel, multi-stage processor nature of human information processing. CPM-GOMS is a task modeling technique that allows the analyst to break down a task at a very fine level of granularity, such as individual eye and hand movements. The method does not assume that each subtask happens serially; it takes into account the parallel nature of performing activities (e.g., both hands can be moving at the same time while eye movement is also occurring). The end results are predictions for task execution times. While CPM-GOMS was originally envisioned as a method for analyzing a task performed by an individual, its assumption of parallelism enables its use in analyzing a task performed by a team of individuals.

An advantage of using a formal method such as CPM-GOMS is the fact that little to no user participation is required, which simplifies the problem of trying to recruit and schedule users and either replicate a realistic work environment in the lab or capture all facets of the users' environment in the field. A disadvantage of using a formal method is that evaluators normally require extensive training in the method, because the methods are usually complex and can require grounding in specific theories. CPM-GOMS is useful for obtaining a detailed understanding of how quickly a particular task can be done using an interface but cannot be used to answer broader questions such as, "how satisfied will the users be with this interface?"

Empirical Methods

We are not aware of any empirical methods that have been tailored or created specifically for collaborative systems. Some researchers have applied empirical methods developed for single-user systems to small-scale collaborative systems with success. For example, Gutwin and Greenberg (1998) performed usability testing to compare two different interface approaches for a collaborative computer-assisted welding application. In general, usability tests consist of typical users performing typical tasks under controlled, but realistic, conditions, either in a laboratory or in the field. In Gutwin and Greenberg's test, the subjects worked in pairs in two different locations and performed their tasks over the course of a few hours. The study goals were focused enough to involve only two people at a time performing a few tasks with minimal training. As a result, the study conductors could obtain a rich amount of data and insights within a manageable time period.

Usability tests are often considered to be the "gold standard" in terms of the amount of data and the subtlety of problems that may be uncovered; thus, they are advantageous to perform whenever it is not too difficult to do so. The difficulties normally arise when duplicating a realistic environment of use, recruiting appropriate users, and scheduling them in groups. The challenges only increase when "typical" user group sizes rise; testing with two to five people at a time is much more tractable than 50, for example.

Although it is highly desirable to perform realistic usability tests, such tests have proven to be too difficult and expensive to perform on collaborative applications in many cases. Baker, Greenberg, and Gutwin (2001, p. 123) stated, "we have not yet developed techniques to make groupware [collaborative] evaluation cost-effective within typical software project constraints." Thus, collaborative applications are often developed or chosen without any evaluation whatsoever. Recent work in tailoring inspection methods for collaborative applications has taken place in an attempt to provide a reasonable means for collaborative application evaluation to take place.

Inspection Methods

Inspection methods are promising, because they can often be performed more quickly and inexpensively than the other usability evaluation methods. Savings accrue because they do not involve scheduling users (as do empirical methods) or extensively training evaluators (often needed for formal methods). They are often used when there is insufficient time or budget to perform usability testing or to analyze an interface using a formal method. Further, they are often used early in the development process on low-fidelity prototypes to gain early insight into whether the proposed design is consistent with general principles of human–computer interaction (even if empirical evaluations are scheduled for later versions of the application). The disadvantage with inspection methods is that they do not always result in finding the subtle problems that occur due to mismatches between the application design and the user's mental model of how the application is working.

The classic inspection method is heuristic evaluation (Molich & Nielsen, 1990). It is useful to describe it, because several methods have been developed for evaluating multiuser systems that are adaptations of heuristic evaluation. When performing an heuristic evaluation, inspectors (often, but not necessarily, usability specialists) judge whether each user interface element conforms to established usability principles known as heuristics. Examples of heuristics are,

"The interface should be consistent," and "The interface should provide clearly marked exits." To apply the heuristics, individual evaluators independently step through all parts of a user interface, noting cases where the interface violates the heuristics. After looking at the interface, each evaluator may assign a score to how well the interface meets each heuristic in general. Once each individual assessment is complete, evaluators normally discuss their findings and agree upon a joint set of problems and scores. The power of this method comes from combining the observations of several inspectors, because people normally find somewhat different subsets of the problems. Heuristic evaluation is straightforward enough that people other than human–computer interaction experts or human factors engineers can successfully perform an heuristic evaluation with as little as an hour's training.

Other inspection methods compare an application against a set of guidelines (either general or application-specific) or a "capabilities" (function) checklist tailored to the users' needs. An example of a tailorable function checklist for collaborative applications can be found in Drury et al. (Drury, Damianos, Fanderclai, Hirschmann, Kurtz, & Linton, 1999).

Three inspection methods developed for collaborative systems employ heuristics-based inspection: benchmarks for workspace awareness (Villegas & Williams, 1997), the Locales Framework heuristics (Greenberg, Fitzpatrick, Gutwin, & Kaplan, 2000), and the "Mechanics of Collaboration" (Baker, Greenberg, & Gutwin, 2001). An additional inspection method, Synchronous Collaborative Awareness and Privacy Evaluation (SCAPE) (Drury, 2001) provides both a means of specifying awareness and privacy requirements and evaluating whether the application satisfies the requirements via an heuristic approach. We describe two methods in more detail, the Mechanics of Collaboration and SCAPE, because they are more recent and more mature than the others.

Gutwin and Greenberg (2000) maintained that there are some basic collaboration activities that should be supported by any collaborative application:

These activities, which we call the mechanics of collaboration, are the small scale actions and interactions that group members must carry out in order to get a shared task done. Examples include communicating information, coordinating manipulations, or monitoring one another. (p. 98)

Gutwin and Greenberg proposed that the mechanics of collaboration framework can be used to construct heuristics. They formed eight heuristics (Baker, Greenberg, & Gutwin, 2001, p. 125):

•   Provide the means for intentional and appropriate verbal communication

•   Provide the means for intentional and appropriate gestural communication

- Provide consequential communication of an individual's embodiment
- Provide consequential communication of shared artifacts
- Provide protection
- Provide management of tightly and loosely coupled collaboration
- Allow people to coordinate their actions
- Facilitate finding collaborators and establishing contact

The idea behind the Mechanics of Collaboration method is that evaluators inspect the interface using the heuristics from Baker, Greenberg, and Gutwin (2001) instead of the ones developed by Molich and Nielsen (1990) or, more recently, Nielsen (1994). Otherwise, the method is essentially the same as that developed by Molich and Nielsen (1990).

Note that the heuristics of Baker, Greenberg, and Gutwin (2001) are broad and make the assumption that the role of the user is not a factor in the evaluation. The SCAPE method was developed to provide a finer-grained evaluation technique, acknowledging that users of an application may have different awareness and privacy needs.

The SCAPE Method

Later in this chapter, we will give an example of how SCAPE was used to evaluate the awareness and privacy support of a particular application being considered for use by a retailer and supplier. Because we will give examples of developing SCAPE analysis materials that were culled from our case study, we introduce the case study scenario in the next subsection. The fine-grained awareness framework and awareness relationships that underpin SCAPE are introduced in the following subsections, ending this section with a by a step-by-step description of the SCAPE method.

Case Study Scenario

We developed a scenario based on recent events in the popular business press (e.g., (Bianco & Zellner, 2003)). The scenario centers on the partnership between a fictitious major retailer ("Wal-Store") and an equally fictitious nationwide distributor of juice drinks ("Sea Spray").

Joy Brown is a beverages buyer at Wal-Store, and Jenn Smith is a manufacturer's representative from Sea Spray. Jenn works with two product managers, Rod

Leeds and Sally Steele. Joy wants to get the Sea Spray juice drink products on the shelves at Wal-Store at the lowest possible price by probing Sea Spray's manufacturing, inventorying, and distribution processes and suggesting ways to streamline these processes. Jenn would like to get as many different Sea Spray products on Wal-Store's shelves as possible and so is willing to work with Joy— up to a point. She does not want to give Joy information about the recipes for the newest juice drinks because Wal-Store has a history of using "inside" product information to manufacture similar products under the "Sal's Choice" in-house label, thus eating into the market share of national brands.

Jenn would like to use the same IOIS with Joy as well as Rod and Sally, her product managers for the two new juice drinks. She would like to keep the proprietary information private from Joy, however.

By highlighting the natural tension between competitors, this Wal-Store scenario includes the notion of *adversarial collaboration* (Cohen, Cash, & Muller, 2000): situations in which collaborators have widely divergent goals yet must work together to perform specific tasks. Other situations that involve adversarial collaboration are merger/acquisition negotiations and document sharing among opposing legal teams. We expect that, as technology becomes more widely used to facilitate communications between organizations with divergent goals, computer-based adversarial collaboration support will become increasingly more important.

Both Cohen et al.'s study and the Wal-Store scenario illustrate a need for IOISs to support detailed awareness and privacy requirements and to ensure that everything that is visible to others is revealed intentionally instead of being revealed accidentally or by default.

Awareness Framework

Before describing the SCAPE method, we first need to refine the definitions of awareness cited earlier into a more fine-grained analysis framework. Although there are many definitions of awareness (a few of which were cited above), there is no standard definition. We define awareness as follows (Drury, 2001):

> Awareness - Given two participants p_1 and p_2 who are collaborating via a synchronous collaborative application, awareness is the understanding that p_1 has of the identity and activities of p_2.

To support p_1's understanding of p_2, an application provides p_1 with information about the identity and activities of p_2 *without* p_1 *having to request the information or* p_2 *having to explicitly transmit it*. Awareness information is intended to emulate the kinds of nonverbal cues that people get about each other when they work face to face in the same physical environment.

The awareness information that p_1 might have access to regarding p_2 includes (but is not necessarily limited to) p_2's presence in the shared workspace, p_2's identity, the task that p_2 is performing, the tools and artifacts that p_2 is using, the changes p_2 is making, the area of the workspace viewable by p_2, and p_2's focus within that viewable area. We refer to the aggregation of all of the awareness information that all of the participants may have about each other as the *awareness information space*.

Although the awareness literature largely assumes that the more awareness information available, the better, there are times when awareness information should be withheld. For our purposes, we define *privacy* as follows:

> Privacy - The intentional withholding of awareness information.

Evaluation of awareness support has two underlying principles: (1) ensure that awareness information that should be provided is provided; and (2) ensure that awareness information that should not be provided is kept private. A different type of awareness-related error is associated with each of these principles (Drury & Williams, 2002):

> Type 1 - Awareness violation. Awareness information that should be provided is not (a violation of the first principle).
>
> Type 2 - Privacy violation. Awareness information that should be kept private is revealed (a violation of the second principle).

A method for evaluating awareness support must provide for the identification of awareness violations and privacy violations.

There is currently no theory *per se* of awareness support. We constructed a general-case default specification for the kinds of awareness information after examining eight theories and frameworks for collaborative work [see Drury & Williams (2002)]. We developed a general, application-independent awareness specification, expressed as heuristics (see Figure 1). These *awareness heuristics* are of two types: *activity heuristics* pertaining to activities only, regardless of who is performing them; and *identity heuristics* pertaining to participants.

The general awareness specification has two assumptions built into it: (1) all participants using a collaborative application have the same awareness needs, and (2) participants require access to all possible awareness information about each other. The general specification may be tailored for specific applications where these assumptions do not hold.

Figure 1: General awareness specification, expressed as activity heuristics and identity heuristics. This specification is application-independent.

Type	Heuristic
Activity	Show the tasks being performed
	Show the tools being used
	Show the changes being made
	Show the historical changes made
	Show the time of each historical change
Identity	Show participants' identities
	Show the immediate intentions of each participant
	Show the focus of each participant
	Show area viewable by each participant
	Show the participant(s) performing each task
	Show the participant(s) using each tool
	Show the participant(s) making changes
	Show the participant(s) who made each historical change

We refer to the situation where a participant has access to all possible awareness about another participant as *complete awareness*:

> Complete awareness - Given two participants p_1 and p_2 who are collaborating via a synchronous collaborative application, if all information regarding p_2 in the awareness information space is available to p_1, we say that p_1 has complete awareness with respect to p_2.

It is common for a participant to need (or to be permitted) only limited, rather than complete information about another participant, so that *partial awareness* should be provided:

> Partial awareness - If some, but not all, information regarding p_2 in the awareness information space is available to p_1, we say that p_1 has partial awareness with respect to p_2.

Whether a participant p_1 needs complete or partial awareness of another participant p_2 depends on the *roles* played by p_1 and p_2. For example, in the application supporting the retail scenario, p_1 may be a buyer and p_2 may be a sales representative. We define a *role* to be a participant's activities and responsibilities with respect to the other participants in a collaborative session.

Participants using a collaborative application can be partitioned into role-based equivalence classes (e.g., buyer, sales representative). All participants in the same role have the same awareness and privacy needs.

Awareness Relationships

Each role is related to every other role by an *awareness relationship* that characterizes the awareness information participants in one role may have about participants in another.

An awareness relationship may be either complete or partial, depending whether participants have complete or partial awareness of each other. It is also possible for participants in one role to have no awareness information about participants in another role, in which case we describe the awareness relationship as *no awareness*.

Awareness relationships are unidirectional. Given two roles r_1 and r_2, there is an awareness relationship for r_1 with respect to r_2, characterizing the information available to participants in r_1 about participants in r_2. The relationship may be complete, partial, or no awareness. Similarly, there is an awareness relationship for r_2 with respect to r_1. It also may be complete, partial, or no awareness, independent of the type of the relationship for r_1 with respect to r_2.

Figure 2 shows a matrix of awareness relationships for evaluating a hypothetical collaboration application used by buyers and sales representatives, assuming use by one participant in the buyer role, one in the sales representative role, and two

Figure 2: Awareness relationship matrix for the hypothetical application used by retailers and suppliers. (Numbers indicate the number of participants in each role.)

What these roles...	...can know about the roles below		
	Buyer	Sales representative	Product manager
Buyer (1)	—	Partial	No awareness
Sales representative (1)	Partial	—	Partial
Product manager (2)	No awareness	Partial	Complete

in the product managers' roles. Some roles (e.g., product managers) have awareness relationships with themselves, which characterize what participants in the same role may know about each other (what one product manager may know about another). Because there is only one buyer (and one sales representative), there is no buyer–buyer (or sales representative–sales representative) awareness relationship.

Steps for Performing a SCAPE Evaluation

SCAPE is based on the awareness framework and awareness relationships. It can be used to determine whether users' awareness and privacy needs would be met by an application. In particular, SCAPE is especially useful for evaluating a synchronous collaborative application, because such systems require an up-to-the-moment awareness of fellow participants' identities and activities. Figure 3 illustrates the difference in awareness needs for synchronous versus asynchronous applications. A "yes" under the "Sync." column means the heuristic is applicable to synchronous applications; similarly, a "yes" in the "Async." column implies that the heuristic pertains to an asynchronous application. A "no" in either column means the heuristic is not relevant for that type of collaborative application.

Figure 3: Awareness needs in synchronous versus asynchronous applications. ("Yes" means the heuristic is applicable; "No" means the heuristic is not applicable.)

Heuristic	Sync.	Async.
Show the tasks being performed	Yes	No
Show the tools being used	Yes	No
Show the changes being made	Yes	No
Show the historical changes made	Yes	Yes
Show the time of each historical change	Yes	Yes
Show participants' identities	Yes	Yes
Show the immediate intentions of each participant	Yes	No
Show the focus of each participant	Yes	No
Show area viewable by each participant	Yes	No
Show the participant(s) performing each task	Yes	No
Show the participant(s) using each tool	Yes	No
Show the participant(s) making changes	Yes	No
Show the participant(s) who made each historical change	Yes	Yes

SCAPE is an inspection method performed by evaluators, and it is based on the awareness framework described earlier in this section. It is designed to help evaluators find both awareness violations and privacy violations. SCAPE takes into account the roles that participants play and the awareness relationships between the roles.

The SCAPE method has two parts: (1) development of a detailed, application-specific specification of awareness and privacy requirements; and (2) evaluation of the application for compliance with the specification. The SCAPE Handbook (Drury, 2001) contains more detailed explanations than can be included here, as well as examples, advice, and worksheets.

There are three steps to developing an awareness specification for a collaborative application: define the awareness relationships, develop role-based awareness policies, and identify activity-based exceptions to the policies.

Step 1 - Define awareness relationships. The goal of this step is to identify roles and the high-level awareness relationships between them. Knowledge of the application domain is needed to perform this step. Roles are identified, and an awareness relationship matrix, such as the one shown in Figure 2, is created. The output of this step is the matrix.

Step 2 - Develop role-based awareness policies. The goal of this step is to develop a set of awareness policies, based on the relationships between roles. The approach is to modify the general awareness specification from Figure 1 according to the awareness relationships identified in Step 1. While awareness policies can be created for each role pair, in practice, usually only one awareness policy is needed; it indicates the superset of what participants can know about other participants. Exceptions to this policy are identified in the next step. The awareness policy for the case study is shown in Figure 4.

For each awareness relationship, the evaluator begins with the general awareness specification and deletes any portions of the specification that are not applicable. (For example, if the application requires anonymity, then all identity heuristics are deleted.)

We also leave open the possibility that the evaluator may need to add to the specification. The evaluator performs this step as many times as necessary:

- Once for all of the complete awareness relationships, because they all have the same requirements
- Once for each partial awareness relationship, because they may all have different requirements

Figure 4: Awareness policy for the case study. (None of the awareness heuristics are deleted in this example, and no extra heuristics have been added. Notations to the worksheet are indicated by the Comic Sans MS font.)

Awareness Policy:
What Participants CAN Know About Other Participants
Worksheet for Step 2

Date: **13 May 2003**

Evaluator: **J. L. Drury**

Application: **Groove**

Instructions:
1. Add missing heuristics.
2. Cross out heuristics that are not applicable to participants in any role.

Identity awareness heuristics:
Show the identity of each participant.
Show the immediate intentions of each participant.
Show area viewable by each participant.
Show the focus of each participant.
Show the participant(s) performing each task.
Show the participant(s) using each tool.
Show the participant(s) making changes.
Show the participant(s) who made each historical change.

Other heuristics for identity awareness information:
None.

Activity awareness heuristics:
Show the task(s) being performed.
Show the tool(s) being used.
Show the change(s) being made.
Show the historical change(s) made.
Show the time of each historical change.

Other heuristics for activity awareness information:
None.

The output of this step is a set of role-based awareness policies expressed as heuristics.

Step 3 - Identify activity-based exceptions. The goal of this step is to tailor the role-based awareness policies developed in Step 2 so that they include any activity-related exceptions that are necessary to ensure privacy. All of the policies for partial awareness relationships must be tailored in this way. (There is no need to tailor the policies for complete and "no awareness" relationships.)

The evaluator begins with the awareness relationship matrix from Step 1 and the set of awareness policies from Step 2, and uses domain knowledge about tasks that participants will perform. The evaluator identifies the activities during which parts of an awareness policy should be suspended. (For example, it may be OK for a product manager to be aware of what a buyer is doing, *except* when the buyer is working on another purchase in which the product manager is not involved.)

The result can be seen in Figure 5, which is a portion of a privacy policy for the case study. The set of tailored awareness and privacy policies constitutes an application-specific awareness requirements specification.

There are three steps to evaluating an application for compliance with an awareness specification: assess the level of effort a complete evaluation would entail, develop scenarios to use during evaluation, and perform the evaluation.

Figure 5: Sample privacy policy for the case study, showing what the buyer cannot know about the sales representative's activities.

**Privacy Policy: What Participants
CANNOT Know About Other Participants
Worksheet for Step 3**

Date: 13 May 2003

Evaluator: J. L. Drury

Application: Groove

Role pairs analyzed: What <u>Buyer</u> CANNOT know about <u>Sales rep.</u>

Instructions:
- List privacy needs as exceptions to applying the heuristics.
- Note impacts to violating the privacy needs.

Privacy Needs Table

Apply the *identity* awareness heuristics except for information related to the following activities:	Impact of privacy violation (low, medium, or high)
Sales rep's bottom-line price (unless he or she chooses to reveal it deliberately)	High
Manufacturer's recipes for juice drinks	High

Apply the *activity* awareness heuristics except for information related to the following activities:	Impact of privacy violation (low, medium, or high)
Same as above	

Step 4 - Assess level of effort. The goal of this step is to assess the level of effort that a full-fledged evaluation would entail. A SCAPE evaluation involves a series of mini-evaluations, because each awareness relationship needs to be evaluated. The level of effort can be substantial, because the worst-case number of awareness relationships can be roughly estimated as the square of the number of roles. Thus, it is prudent to calculate the level of effort needed for a complete SCAPE evaluation, compare the result to the resources available, and select the highest-priority awareness relationships to evaluate.

The evaluator begins with the role relationship matrix from Step 1, the specification from Step 3, and an understanding of resources (time, money, etc.) available. If the evaluator expects that evaluating one awareness relationship will take e effort (measured in evaluators' time, money, etc.), and if there are a awareness relationships, then the level of effort for a complete evaluation is proportional to e multiplied by a.

To identify the awareness relationships that are the highest priorities for evaluation, the evaluator annotates the awareness policies, indicating whether violations would have high, medium, or low impact. The output is a list of prioritized awareness relationships.

Step 5 - Develop scenarios. The goal of Step 5 is to specify activities that will cause SCAPE evaluators to perform sequences of actions that will exercise the application's awareness support capabilities. Scenarios are a well-established technique for evaluation; Nielsen pointed out the advantages of using scenarios for heuristic evaluation when it is important to examine participants' interactions (Nielsen, 1995). The evaluator uses the awareness specification from Step 3 and the prioritized list of awareness relationships from Step 4 to develop a master scenario and scenario worksheets to use during the evaluation. The master scenario worksheet from the case study can be seen as an example in Figure 6.

Step 6 - Perform the evaluation. The goal of this step is to identify awareness violations and privacy violations. Teams of evaluators perform the scenarios developed in Step 5 and examine the application for compliance with the specification from Steps 2 and 3. The output of this step is a set of problem reports.

Before performing a SCAPE evaluation, it is critical that the evaluators understand the users' tasks and roles and the applications' functionality. Without a good understanding of the users, the evaluation results may not predict how well the application will meet users' needs (that is, the

Figure 6: Example portion of master scenario worksheet developed for the case study.

Master Scenario
Worksheet for Step 5

Date: 26 May 2003
Evaluator(s):   Jill Drury, Jean Scholtz
Application: Groove

Instructions:
1. Determine who will participate in what roles. Not everyone who participates needs to be an evaluator.
2. List sequences of actions or subtasks that cover all evaluated role relationships and include both typical situations and situations where violating the awareness and privacy policy would have a high impact.

Participants

Name	Role	Evaluator?
Rod	Product Manager (PM)	No
Jill	Buyer (B)	Yes
Jean	Sales Rep (SR)	Yes

Master Scenario

Time	Activity	Roles	Verify privacy/awareness needs
8:00	Discuss the new juice flavors	PM, B, SR	B cannot see juice recipes
8:20	Share manufacturing process info	PM, B, SR	B cannot see juice recipes
8:40	Discuss pricing strategies	B, SR	B cannot see SR's bottom price; SR cannot see B's top price

evaluation may point out issues that the users would not consider problems or may miss problems entirely). To understand the users, we performed a task analysis and critical incident analysis based on structured interviews with a buyer for a large Eastern-U.S. retailer. One of the evaluators already had significant prior experience with using the collaborative application and helped train the other (supplementing training provided by the developer's tutorial information).

An explanation of the evaluation performed for the case study can be found below, after a description of the application evaluated.

Case Study: Evaluating Groove Using Scape

We evaluated Groove™ to understand how well it can support the awareness and privacy needs of a retail buyer/supplier team. Groove was chosen because there is currently a lot of interest in using Groove (Groove's customer list, as published on its Web site, shows approximately 100 organizations, including large and small businesses, nonprofits, educational, and government entities). Also, Groove's functionality is similar to that of several others in its class; it is a general-purpose collaboration application intended to be used by a wide variety of organizations.

After the Groove overview, we discuss how we performed the case study and summarize its results.

Overview of Groove Functionality

Groove peer-to-peer collaboration software provides users with synchronous as well as asynchronous collaboration. Groove uses the metaphor of shared spaces to create collaboration environments. Templates are provided for spaces, and a number of different functionalities can be incorporated into a space. Functions provided by Groove include file storage, calendar facilities, discussion spaces, sketch pads, project planning, and meeting spaces with support for agendas, minutes, and action items. A built-in browser lets participants pull up Web pages within Groove and browse the pages together.

Many of the tools available in Groove are compatible for use with Microsoft Office; these functions provide asynchronous collaboration. In addition, Groove provides text chat and audio chat for synchronous collaboration. Microsoft NetMeeting can be launched from within Groove as well.

Figure 7 shows a Groove shared space with the files tool open. The participant bar is to the left, and the audio chat tool is at the bottom left. A portion of a text chat message is shown at the bottom of the window.

Groove provides role-based access for three predefined, standardized roles. A manager sets up the shared space and can invite people as participants or guests. The privileges that one has in a shared space are based upon these roles. In general, guests are allowed read-only privileges, while participants are able to post and edit as well as read.

Groove has two models of working. In tools such as the sketchpad, multiple users can work together at the same time and they see each other's contributions in real time (as they are made). However, in tools such as the file space, participants open a file that creates a local copy on the user's machine. Groove

Figure 7: A shared Groove space

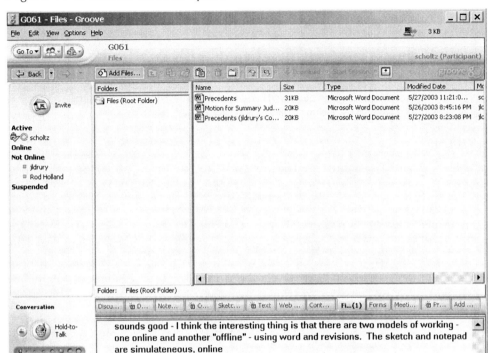

contains synchronization detection that updates the document when a user stores a modified file back to the file manager.

Document creation and revision is supported via a document revision tool and an outliner. Document revision automatically creates a folder for the participants who have edited a document, separate from the folder for the original document. Documents in Groove are marked as to whether they have been read or not; this feature enables users to keep track of work they have done.

Groove also provides a "navigate together" feature. All participants who selected the "navigate together" feature will be taken from one tool in the space to another when one of the participants changes location within the space. This feature can be used during a meeting to make sure that everyone is working in the same location.

Groove provides some mechanisms for being aware of the presence, identities, and activities of fellow Groove space users. For example, there is a persistent part of the display showing the participants who are logged in, those who are active, and those who belong to the space but are currently logged off or have been inactive for some time (suspended). The toolbar shows the number of participants viewing any particular tool space. A notice is shown when someone enters a tool space. When users are engaged in text chat, Groove shows when one of the participants is typing.

Evaluating Groove Using the SCAPE Method

Prior to evaluation, we became familiar with Groove functionality and the users' tasks/roles and prepared the SCAPE materials described earlier in this chapter. We (the two evaluators) decided upon the roles we would play and recruited a third person to assist us. While not an evaluator, this third person agreed to play a role and answer specific questions relating to the levels of privacy and awareness that he observed in the Groove shared spaces during the session.

During the evaluation session, the three of us logged into a shared Groove space from three different geographic locations. We assumed the roles of a buyer, sales representative, and product manager. The buyer created the space and thus was considered the Groove Manager. The other two people were given Groove Participant privileges at first. Over the course of the session, the manager changed their Groove roles to Guest and back to Participant to see how these changes affected their awareness and privacy.

We followed the Master Scenario excerpted in Figure 6, beginning with a discussion of the new juice flavors. After performing the actions indicated in the Master Scenario worksheet, we checked to see if the privacy and awareness requirements highlighted in the worksheet were supported by Groove. We made note of the situations and conditions under which the requirements were not supported.

We communicated with each other nearly continuously during the evaluation session using the Groove chat tool. This tool provides a persistent transcript of all messages; we noted our evaluation observations in chat messages to each other and saved the chat file for post-session analysis. During the main evaluation session, we used Groove for approximately 4 hours.

Results of Evaluating Groove

We combed through the chat file notes and compared our observations to the Awareness and Privacy Policies and the specific requirements noted in the Master Scenario worksheet. Highlights of the results are presented below.

Groove does a reasonably good job of providing awareness but does not support many of the privacy needs for the case in which proprietary information needs to be seen by some collaborators but not by others. For example, Groove provides at least read-only privileges to all users for all documents. It is impossible to mark documents as being readable by only a subset of Groove users. This means that the Sea Spray team members cannot work on a document in a shared Groove space and keep that document private from members of Wal-Store's team. This situation violates the privacy need specified as, "it is OK to be able to read some documents but not others."

Of course, the problem of keeping some documents private from some collaborators can be resolved by creating new Groove "spaces" for subgroups of collaborators, such as the Sea Spray team members. This approach has the drawback of requiring collaborators to remember what documents and other information were stored in what spaces, and manage version control of documents that are stored in both spaces for the convenience of avoiding moving back and forth between spaces.

Similar to the document privacy issue, chat messages in Groove cannot be addressed to a subset of the shared space users; the messages are displayed to all users. Thus, team members from the manufacturer cannot caucus privately among themselves using the shared chat tool. This means that the privacy need specified as "The buyer cannot see the sales representative's bottom price; the sales representative cannot see the buyer's top price" cannot be satisfied if the relevant pricing material is included in the Groove space.

Groove does not provide the means for two people to have management privileges in a shared space; thus, either the buyer or sales representative would be the manager, and the other could be a participant, at best. While not violating an awareness or privacy requirement, such a situation would not be palatable to two people who are trying to achieve a status in which they are equals in their collaborations.

By default, Groove participants are allowed to invite others into the shared space. Unless the manager revokes this "invitation" privilege for everyone, it is possible for a participant to invite another to be a participant, who invites someone else, etc. Thus, it may not be known to everyone who has been invited and may subsequently join a session. Once someone has joined, their user name will be visible to everyone in the space unless that person restricts what group can see their online identity; but by that time, the damage may have been done if they were not supposed to have had any access to the materials in the shared Groove space. Imagine the consequences of the relatively uncontrolled invitation mechanism for a sensitive shared space containing pricing or budget documents.

While Groove provides awareness of who has revised documents, it does not provide notification of who has revised other shared artifacts. For example, a meeting agenda can be erased or revised by anyone—even a guest—and there is no indication that such a revision has taken place. In fact, most people would be likely to assume that the agenda was authored by the person who scheduled the meeting; this may not be true. Also, the original author does not have any notification that their work was changed. This situation violates the heuristics in the awareness policy: "Show the participant(s) making changes" and "Show the participant(s) who made each historical change."

Discussion

Based on our knowledge of other collaborative applications, we do not believe that Groove is unique in its lack of privacy support. Privacy is enhanced in applications that provide access control on a document-by-document basis and that provide the capability to address chat messages to subsets of participants (e.g., a private, "whispered" chat message). In general, however, most collaborative applications are akin to Groove in that they aim to provide support to participants who wish to share everything, all the time. Such an approach is not consistent with the move toward greater computer-aided collaboration across organizations with somewhat divergent goals.

Of all the evaluation methods discussed, SCAPE is the only method to specifically focus on whether an application supports the awareness and privacy needs of a particular group of users. SCAPE does not address basic usability issues such as whether the interface was designed to be consistent or to have clearly marked exits. Inspection techniques developed for single-user applications can provide this type of insight, even for multiuser systems, and should generally be used. Thus, SCAPE should be used in conjunction with techniques such as Nielsen's heuristic evaluation and function checklists. If an IOIS will be used in situations where awareness and privacy are important concerns, however, a SCAPE analysis would be appropriate and beneficial.

SCAPE does not involve users as evaluation subjects; this is both a strength and a weakness. Usability testing (structured testing with users) can be very expensive and time-consuming but yields rich data. Rather than forgoing evaluation completely, however, an inspection evaluation method constitutes a less expensive and less time-consuming approach. We recommend that usability testing be conducted if doing so involves small numbers of users, the users' environment can be easily recreated or accessed, and the user population is readily available. Even if usability testing is performed and a full SCAPE evaluation or other inspection evaluation is not attempted, we recommend performing the first three steps of SCAPE to understand the roles that users play and the need to provide information to, or conceal information from, each other. Once SCAPE Awareness and Privacy Policies have been developed, they can act as a specification against which the application's performance can be compared during a usability test. Awareness and Privacy Policies can also provide guidance in determining which tasks the users should be asked to perform to ensure that sensitive or critical information is revealed or concealed in certain situations.

If the buyer and sales representative in the case study scenario were truly looking for an IOIS to manage information sharing in an adversarial collaboration environment, they would be well advised to perform SCAPE evaluations on several systems as part of a comparative analysis. At a minimum, the most sensitive situations should be included in scenarios developed for the SCAPE evaluation. For example, SCAPE quickly highlighted the fact that Groove does not provide for documents to be read by only a subset of the application's users; this fact alone means that Groove may not be a suitable choice for this particular group of users.

References

Baker, K, Greenberg, S., & Gutwin, C. (2001). Heuristic evaluation of groupware based on the mechanics of collaboration. In M. R. Little, & L. Nigay (Eds.), *Engineering for human–computer interaction* (8th IFIP International Conference, EHCI 2001, Toronto, Canada, May 2001), Lecture Notes in Computer Science, Vol. 2254 (pp. 123–139). Heidelberg: Springer-Verlag.

Bianco, A., & Zellner, W. (2003). Is Wal-Mart too powerful? *Business Week,* 6 October 2003, 100–110.

Cash, J. I., Jr., & Konsynski, B. R. (1985). IS redraws competitive boundaries. *Harvard Business Review, 63*(2), 134–142.

Cohen, A. L., Cash, D., & Muller, M. J. (2000). Designing to support adversarial collaboration. *ACM: Proceedings of the Computer Supported Cooperative Work (CSCW) 2000 conference* (pp. 31–39), Philadelphia, PA.

Dourish, P., & Bellotti, V. (1992). Awareness and coordination in shared workspaces. *ACM: Proceedings of the Computer Supported Cooperative Work (CSCW) '92 conference* (pp. 107–114), Toronto, Canada.

Drury, J. (2001). Extending usability inspection evaluation techniques for synchronous collaborative computing applications. Sc.D. thesis, Department of Computer Science, University of Massachusetts Lowell.

Drury, J., & Williams, M. G. (2002). A framework for role-based specification and evaluation of awareness support in synchronous collaborative applications. *IEEE: Workshops on Enabling Technologies, Infrastructure for Collaborative Enterprises (WETICE)* (pp. 12–17), Pittsburgh, PA.

Drury, J., Damianos, L., Fanderclai, T., Hirschmann, L., Kurtz, J., & Linton, F. (1999). *Methodology for evaluation of collaborative systems, v. 4.0.*

DARPA Intelligent Collaboration and Visualization Project: published at http://zing.ncsl.nist.gov/nist-icv/documents/methodv4.htm.

Greenberg, S., Fitzpatrick, G., Gutwin, C., & Kaplan, S. (2000). Adapting the Locales Framework for heuristic evaluation of groupware. *Australian Journal of Information Systems (AJIS)*, 7(2), 102–108.

Greif, I. (1988). *Computer-supported cooperative work: A book of readings*. San Mateo, CA: Morgan Kaufmann.

Groove™ (2003). Groove Networks: www.groove.net.

Grudin, J. (1988). Why CSCW applications fail. *ACM: Proceedings of the Computer Supported Cooperative Work (CSCW) '88 conference* (pp. 85–93), Portland, OR.

Gutwin, C., & Greenberg, S. (1998). Effects of awareness support on groupware usability. *ACM: Proceedings of the CHI 98 Conference on Human Factors in Computing Systems* (pp. 511–518), Los Angeles, CA.

Gutwin, C., & Greenberg, S. (2000). The mechanics of collaboration: Developing low cost usability evaluation methods for shared workspaces. *IEEE: WETICE Workshop on Collaborative Enterprises* (pp. 98–103), Gaithersburg, MD.

Gutwin, C., Stark, G., & Greenberg, S. (1995). Support for workspace awareness in educational groupware. *Proceedings of the First CSCL Conference on Computer Supported Collaborative Learning* (pp. 147–156), Bloomington, Indiana. Hillsdale, NJ: Lawrence Erlbaum Associates.

Holtzblatt, K., & Jones, S. (1993). Contextual inquiry: A participatory technique for systems design. In D. Schuler, & A. Namioka (Eds.), *Participatory design: Principles and practice* (pp. 177–210). Hillsdale, NJ: Lawrence Erlbaum Associates.

Hong, I. B., & Kim, C. (1998). Toward a new framework for interorganizational systems: A network configuration perspective. *IEEE: Proceedings of the Thirty-First Hawaii International Conference on Systems Science*, Vol. 4 (pp. 92–101).

Hudson, S., & Smith, I. (1996). Techniques for addressing fundamental privacy and disruption tradeoffs in awareness support systems. *ACM: Proceedings of the CSCW 96 Conference on Computer Supported Cooperative Work* (pp. 248–257).

John, B. E., & Kieras, D. E. (1994). The GOMS Family of analysis techniques: Tools for design and evaluation. Pittsburgh, PA: Carnegie Mellon University.

Klein, G. (2000). Cognitive task analysis of teams. In J. M. Schraagen, S. F. Chipman, & V. L. Shalin (Eds.), *Cognitive task analysis* (pp. 417–429). Mahwah, NJ: Lawrence Erlbaum Associates.

Malone, T. W. (1985). Designing organizational interfaces. *ACM: Proceedings of the CHI 85 Conference on Human Factors in Computing Systems* (pp. 66–71), San Francisco, CA.

Mantei, M. M., & Teorey, T. J. (1988). Cost/benefit analysis for incorporating human factors in the software lifecycle. *Communications of the ACM, 31*(4), 428–439.

Mayhew, D. (1999). *The usability engineering lifecycle: A practitioner's handbook for user interface design.* San Francisco, CA: Morgan Kaufmann.

Molich, R., & Nielsen, J. (1990). Improving a human–computer dialog. *Communications of the ACM, 33*(3), 338–348.

Nardi, B. A., & O'Day, V. L. (1999). *Information ecologies: Using technology with heart.* Cambridge, MA: MIT Press.

Nielsen, J. (1994). Enhancing the explanatory power of usability heuristics. *ACM: Proceedings of the CHI 94 Conference on Human Factors in Computing Systems* (pp. 152–158), Boston, MA.

Nielsen, J. (1995). Scenarios in discount usability. In J. M. Carroll (Ed.), *Scenario-based design: Envisioning work and technology in system development* (pp. 59–83). New York: John Wiley & Sons.

Rogers, E. M. (1995). *Diffusion of innovations* (4th ed.). New York: Free Press.

Villegas, H., & Williams, M. G. (1997). Benchmarks for workspace awareness in collaborative environments. *International Institute of Informatics and Systemics: Proceedings of the 1997 World Multiconference on Systemics, Cybernetics and Informatics* (pp. 480–486), Caracas, Venezuela.

Endnote

[1]   The identification of any commercial product or trade name does not imply endorsement or recommendation. Groove is a trademark of Groove Networks.

Section VII:

Research Method and Empirical Study

Chapter XII

Comparative Pairs Analysis for Inter-Organizational Information Systems (IOIS) Research

Christine E. Storer
Curtin University of Technology, Australia

Geoffrey N. Soutar
University of Western Australia, Australia

Mohammed Quaddus
Curtin University of Technology, Australia

Abstract

This chapter suggests the use of comparative pairs analysis as a method of collecting data for inter-organizational information system and chain research. It is argued that chains of organizations can be analyzed by collecting data from a focal firm about upstream suppliers and downstream customers. By comparing pairs of respondents within the focal firm, the differences between customers and suppliers can be analyzed. In addition, it is suggested that by asking each respondent to discuss two third-party organizations, differences in responses can be highlighted and explained during the data collection process. This can provide a rich source of data to explain results obtained.

Introduction

When conducting inter-organizational information systems (IOIS) research, a decision needs to be made about which third-party organizations to analyze and how to collect the data. When analyzing buyer/seller relationships, many researchers ask one of the parties in the dyad to rate their perceptions of the relationship with a buyer/seller (e.g., Anderson & Narus, 1990; Batt & Rexha, 1999; Doney & Cannon, 1997; Gundlach, Achrol, & Mentzer, 1995; Heather, 2001; Kumar, Stern, & Achrol, 1992; Leuthesser & Kohli, 1995; Morgan & Hunt, 1994). Similarly, when studying information systems interactions between buyers and sellers, many researchers ask one party in the dyad to rate their perceptions of communication flows and how the information system operates (e.g., Bensaou, 1997, 1999; Bensaou & Venkatraman, 1995; Mohr, Fisher, & Nevin, 1996; Mohr & Sohi, 1995). Yet when looking at data collected from both parties in the dyad (Figure 1, "matched dyadic pairs"), it was found that buyers and sellers have significant differences in perceptions about the relationship and what information is shared (Spekman, Kamauff, & Myhr, 1998; Storer et al., 2002). From this, it may be concluded that it would be more valid to collect data from matched dyadic pairs or at least from samples of pools of buyers and pools of sellers (Figure 1, "pooled dyadic pairs"). However, it is proposed that an alternative may be to collect data from the one focal organization but to ask questions about two third-party organizations so that comparisons of responses can be made (Figure 1, "comparative pairs").

Figure 1: Alternative units of data collection for IOIS chain research

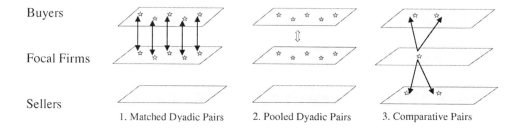

A chain is normally defined as three or more linked organizations (Hines, 1998), such as the focal firm, a supplier, and a customer, e.g., a food processor, a primary produce supplier, and retailer customer. However, many quantitative chain studies only evaluate dyadic relationships such as a manufacturer and their suppliers (e.g., Ellinger, Daugherty, & Plair, 1999; Holland, 1995). Other than research done by Spekman et al. (1998), the main exception is when case studies of the chains or networks of a focal firm are examined (e.g., Gifford, Hall, & Ryan, 1998; Samuel & Hines, 1998; Trienekens, 1999; Van der Vorst, 2000). To gain a full chain perspective, some researchers start by studying cases and follow up with surveys of focal firms (e.g., Kanflo, 1998). This two-phase research process extends the time taken to conduct the research.

The concern in relying on quantitative chain research based on focal firm or dyadic studies is that only part of the chain is being studied. The differences in responses of sales and purchasing staff found by Spekman et al. (1998) and Storer et al. (2002) may have more to do with the greater bargaining power of customers compared to the lesser power of suppliers. Responses may be affected by the position of the organization in the chain.

As an alternative to multiple case studies, dyadic studies, or focal firm surveys, it is proposed that data can be collected from a focal firm about both customers and suppliers (Figure 1, "comparative pairs"). For example, data could be collected from a food processor about their customers (retailers, wholesalers, or other food processors) and their suppliers (primary producers, packaging suppliers, and other food processors).

Comparative Pairs Analysis

In the comparative pairs analysis method, data can be collected from the focal firm about both buyers and sellers (customers and suppliers) so that a chain of three organizations is analyzed. Sales staff can be asked questions about customers, and mirrored questions can be asked of purchasing staff about suppliers. It may be possible to get one respondent to answer questions about both customers and suppliers in smaller organizations, where the respondent is sufficiently knowledgeable about both organizations (e.g., chief executive officer or owner). For many organizations, it may be more appropriate to have sales staff discuss customers and purchasing staff discuss suppliers. This would be highly recommended for larger organizations, where a marketing/customer service department has more contact with customers and a purchasing/logistics department has more contact with suppliers. A similar approach could be taken for any third-party organization of interest. While the unit of analysis is the focal firm's perception about the other organizations, a chain perspective is provided by collecting data about organizations both upstream (suppliers) and downstream (customers) in the chain. Comparisons can be made "within the organization" to see if those dealing with customers and suppliers have different responses.

Another key element of the comparative pairs analysis method is the suggestion that respondents be asked to answer each question about two organizations (pair). By simultaneously looking at two organizations, the differences in responses are highlighted during the data collection process. Each respondent can be asked to explain why he or she perceives that the differences arise and can provide details to explain answers given. The explanations provide a test of validity of responses given as well as provide rich qualitative data that can be used to suggest reasons for differences in variables that can later be tested in the data analysis. While it is assumed that respondents can make meaningful differences about pairs of third parties (customers, suppliers, etc.), this can be tested. A "within respondent comparison" can be made by analyzing the consistency of each respondent's answers with the unit of analysis being the individual respondent.

To examine the usefulness of comparative pairs analysis for IOIS research in chains of organizations, this chapter addresses the following questions:

1. Does each respondent perceive there are significant differences between pairs of third-party organizations evaluated? (within respondent comparison)

2. Do supplier-oriented boundary spanning staff (purchasing staff) have significantly different responses to customer-oriented boundary spanning staff (sales staff)? (within organization comparison)

Research Method

The research was conducted in two phases using a linked "sequential mixed methods" approach, with the first phase based on the "interpretivist" paradigm (qualitative approach) that was linked to the second phase based on the "positivist" paradigm (quantitative approach) (Tashakkori & Teddlie, 1998). The first phase involved a literature review, informal in-depth interviews with experts internationally, and a case study of an Australian food processor centered netchain. A theoretical framework (Figure 2) was developed in the first phase using a grounded research method, with literature used to support the description of what was observed in the case study. [For a more detailed description, see Storer (2001).] In the model, it was suggested that expected future outcomes from the relationship were related to the nature of the inter-organizational information feedback system adopted in the chain, which, in turn, was related to current perceived outcomes of the chain (as suggested by Benedict & Margeridis, 1999; Bowersox & Closs, 1996; Stank, Emmelhainz, & Daugherty, 1996; Vijayasarathy & Robey, 1997). Further, the model argued that the results would be moderated by factors such as product and market uncertainty, relationship dependency and power, experience in the relationship and in the industry, as well as personal characteristics (as suggested by Ancona & Caldwell, 1992; Bensaou, 1999; Spekman, Kamauff, & Myhr, 1998).

The aim of the second phase was to evaluate, test, and refine the theoretical framework based on a survey of food processors and a further perishable product chain case study. Support for the second phase of the research was received from a large Australian retail chain that provided introductions to four of their significant suppliers for each major food product category. All suppliers

Figure 2: Theoretical framework – Inter-organizational information feedback system in a chain context

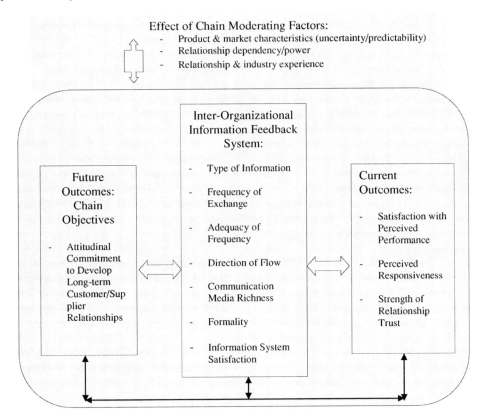

Source: Adapted from Storer (2001).

were significant to the retail chain in terms of volume, value, or strategic significance. A total of 45 food categories were covered and included dry, fresh, chilled, and frozen food products based on meat, dairy, fruit, vegetable, and cereals in the form of ingredients as well as snacks, meals, and drinks. Food processors varied from large multinational and national organizations to smaller regional suppliers.

Data Collection

In-depth interviews of 111 Australian food processor purchasing managers (30%), sales/marketing mangers (47%), and general managers/owners (23%) were conducted during April to December 2002. Where possible, interviews were conducted face to face, with phone interviews and self-completion used as a last resort. Relationships with 176 suppliers and 297 customers were discussed in the interviews. Interviewees were asked to discuss two suppliers or two customers that were significant in terms of volume, value, or strategic intent. Some interviewees answered questions for several different product categories, e.g., milk, cheese, and small goods.

A structured questionnaire (Appendix 1) was developed based on the framework developed in the food processor netchain case study (Storer, 2001). The aim was to get a description of the IOIS used to manage relationships with customers and suppliers. Of interest were the formal systems, such as biannual product and pricing reviews, as well as informal ad hoc systems used occasionally to resolve problems or discuss an opportunity.

To operationalize the model, the inter-organizational information system (IOIS) was examined by asking participants about the *types of information exchanged* to manage the relationship (Mohr & Nevin, 1990). Specifically, participants were asked whether they exchanged information for problem resolution, new product development, forecast supply and demand, and opportunities and threats (Anderson, Lodish, & Weitz, 1987; Andraski, 1998; Bowersox & Closs, 1996; Christopher, 1997; Cunningham & Tynan, 1993; Hines, Rich, & Hittmeyer, 1998; Van Hoek, 1998; Womack, Jones, & Roos, 1990). Based on the netchain case study, performance feedback was expanded to cover product quality, on-time delivery, completeness of orders, flexibility to change orders, invoicing accuracy, profitability, costs, and prices.

For each type of information shared, details were sought of: *communication media* used; *formality* of the process; the *frequency* it was shared on average in a year (absolute frequency); *frequency adequacy*, i.e., was information exchanged as often as necessary (relative frequency); and the *direction* the information flowed (upstream, downstream or both directions) (Anderson,

Lodish, & Weitz, 1987; Bensaou & Venkatraman, 1995; Borgen & Ohren, 1999; Choo, 1996; Daft & Lengel, 1986; Daft & Lengel, 1996; Dansereau & Markham, 1987; Ellinger, Daugherty, & Plair, 1999; Farace, Monge, & Russell, 1977; Huber & Daft, 1987; Mohr & Nevin, 1990). Perceived *satisfaction with the information system* was measured in terms of accuracy, reliability, and completeness; usefulness and relevancy; depth and range of content; and being timely and up to date (O'Brien, 1999).

Expected future outcomes from the relationship were measured as attitudinal *commitment* to develop long-term customer–supplier relationships (Ganesan, 1994; Gundlach, Achrol, & Mentzer, 1995; Sharma, Young, & Wilkinson, 2001).

Current outcomes from the relationship were measured by comparing perceptions of the buyer/seller's *performance, responsiveness and willingness to change,* and *trustworthiness* compared to others in the industry (Anderson, Lodish, & Weitz, 1987; Anderson, Håkansson, & Johanson, 1994; Bensaou & Venkatraman, 1995; Doney & Cannon, 1997; Ganesan, 1994; Gassenheimer & Scandura, 1993; Gundlach, Achrol, & Mentzer, 1995; Kohli, Jaworski, & Kumar, 1993; Kumar, Stern, & Achrol, 1992; Womack, Jones, & Roos, 1990).

Moderating variables included uncertainty, dependency/power, and experience. *Uncertainty* was measured as predictability of demand, production yield, and quality and quantity of supply; market competition; and changing consumer preferences (Ganesan, 1994; Kumar, Stern, & Achrol, 1992). The relationships *dependency and power* were measured as follows: availability of alternative customers and suppliers; importance to each other; influence; and ease of replacement (Ganesan, 1994; Kumar, Stern, & Achrol, 1992). *Experience* was measured in terms of the number of years working in the industry and with the organization (Doney & Cannon, 1997; Ganesan, 1994) as well as how well the industry and the other organization's business were understood.

To explore the dynamics of the interaction over time, the information satisfaction and relationship outcome variables were measured in terms of the current situation and how it had changed over the last 5 years. Comments were recorded about respondents' perceptions about the reasons for change. As a result of explanations about reasons for change, two additional questions were added about perceptions of customers/suppliers initiating new ideas to improve the category/business or to improve the organization's knowledge of the industry.

Data Analysis

A *within respondent comparison* was made between the pairs of third-party organizations, discussed by each respondent to determine if they were perceived to be significantly different. However, some respondents provided answers about a customer or supplier for more than one food product category (maximum five). Therefore, the following question arose: Were answers given generically about the customer/supplier organization as a whole, or did answers depend on which food category was being discussed? The first test was to determine whether each respondent was able to give different views across multiple product categories for one organization ("*within respondent comparison of one organization*"). Euclidean distances were calculated across the metric scale questions so that each respondent could get a measure of the similarity of the responses given for organizations dealing with different food product categories. A low or zero Euclidean distance meant that all the responses were similar (Hair et al., 1998). A high Euclidean distance meant that responses were different (Hair et al., 1998). As the Euclidean distance was calculated based on all questions simultaneously, no comparison could be made between categories of variables or constructs. Euclidean distances were calculated for each pair of food categories. For example, if the third party dealt with milk, cheese, and ice cream, then Euclidean distances were calculated between responses about milk and cheese, milk and ice cream, and cheese and ice cream. The average Euclidean distance score for each respondent was calculated where three or more food product categories were discussed for a customer or supplier organization ("average Euclidean distance for one organization'"). One-sample t-tests were run on average Euclidean distances for one organization. The null hypothesis was that respondents' average Euclidean distance for one organization was equal to zero, i.e., responses were the same for a third-party organization no matter what product category was discussed. If the null hypothesis was accepted, each respondent's answers about different food categories would be essentially the same. Therefore, these responses could be averaged together and treated as one case or unit of analysis in subsequent analysis.

The next test was to determine if respondents provided different answers about each pair of third-party organization ("*within respondent comparison of organizational pairs*"). Each respondent's average Euclidean distance score for one organization was averaged for all organizations discussed to give an "average Euclidean distance of organizational pairs." A one-sample t-test was run on respondent average Euclidean distances of organizational pairs. The null hypothesis was that respondents' average Euclidean distances of organizational pairs were equal to zero, i.e., responses were the same for every pair of third-party organizations.

The final series of tests were to determine if supplier-oriented boundary spanning staff (purchasing staff) had significantly different responses to customer-oriented boundary spanning staff (sales staff). For each focal firm where data was collected about both customers and suppliers, a "*within organizational comparison*" was made of pairs of respondents. Initially bivariate analyses were conducted. The t-tests were run for metric scale variables, and chi-square tests were run for nominal and ordinal scale variables (Hair et al., 1998). When significant differences resulted across multiple variables, a discriminant analysis was run to determine which variables better explained the differences, as the dependent variable (customer or supplier) was nominally scaled (Klecka, 1980).

Within Respondent Comparisons

The first test was to determine if respondents discussing multiple food products for one organization give different answers for each product category ("*within respondent comparison of one organization*"). There were 124 responses about multiple food categories. Overall, the mean of the "average Euclidean distance for one organization" was 1.4 with a standard deviation of 1.8. A one-sample t-test was run to test the hypothesis that the average Euclidean distances for one organization were zero. Based on a t-score of 8.7 significant at 99% confidence, this hypothesis was rejected. It was concluded that the nature of the food product category discussed affected responses provided about the relationship with a customer or suppliers; the business environment; the satisfaction with the information system, and if it was perceived that information was exchanged as often as necessary. As a result, each respondent's answers about each food product category were treated as a separate case for the remainder of the analysis.

The second test was to determine whether each respondent could make meaningful comparisons between each pair of customer/supplier organizations discussed ("*within respondent comparison of organizational pairs*"). There were 90 responses about pairs of customers/suppliers. Overall, the average between organization Euclidean distance was 5.8 with a standard deviation of 3.7. After removing one extreme outlier, a one-sample t-test was run to test the hypothesis that the average between organization Euclidean distances was zero. Based on a t-score of 14.9 significant at 99% confidence, this hypothesis was rejected. It was concluded that respondents made different responses about pairs of organizations.

There was a possibility that the differences between organizations were due to perceived differences within organizations for each product category. Therefore, a further one-sample t-test was run to test the hypothesis that the average "between organization Euclidean distances" was significantly different than the mean of the average "within respondent Euclidean distance" (1.4). Based on a t-score of 11.37 significant at 99% confidence, this hypothesis was rejected. It was concluded that respondents can make meaningful comparisons between pairs of customer/supplier organizations. In addition, responses vary depending on what food product category is being discussed.

The next research question addressed was whether staff in different departments within an organization had different perceptions about customers and suppliers. A comparison was made within the organization between sales and purchasing staff.

Within Organization Comparison of Sales and Purchasing Staff Results

Comparisons of the responses given by sales and purchasing staff were made about their experience and understanding, the nature of the inter-organizational information system (IOIS), satisfaction with the IOIS, and perceptions about the relationship and the nature of the business environment. There were many significant differences across each category for many variables in that category.

Experience and Understanding

The t-tests were undertaken to compare purchasing and sales staff experience and understanding of the customer/supplier (Table 1). Overall, while both sales and purchasing staff had similar number of years experience working in the industry, purchasing staff had more experience working for the current organization, and the organization had been in a relationship longer with the customers for longer than with the suppliers. Both groups of staff had a similar rating of their understanding of the other organization being discussed.

Table 1: Sales and purchasing staff comparison of experience and understanding

	Sales		Purchasing		Difference	
	Mean	Std Dev	Mean	Std Dev	in Means	Sig
Experience in organization (years)	9.9	8.2	12.9	10.2	-3.0	a
Experience in industry (years)	18.5	9.3	19.0	10.2	-0.5	c
Organizational experience in relationship (years)	23.6	13.5	18.9	20.0	4.7	a
Understanding of other organization*	6.2	0.9	6.1	0.8	0.1	c
Understanding of industry*	6.0	0.8	5.8	0.8	0.2	b
Significance: a = 99% confidence; b = 95% confidence; and c = no significant difference.						
Scale of 1 to 7, with 1 being little understanding and 7 being very good understanding.						

Table 2: Inter-organizational information system differences

Type of Information Exchanged	Info Type	Frequency	Adequacy	Direction	Formality	Informality	Media Richness
Problem resolution	c	a	c	c	b	b	c
On-time delivery	a	a	a	a	b	c	a
Product quality	b	a	b	c	a	b	c
Invoice accuracy	b	a	a	a	c	c	c
Forecast supply and demand	b	a	a	c	a	c	a
Complete orders	c	c	a	a	c	c	a
Flexibility to accept order changes	c	a	c	a	c	c	a
New product development	c	a	a	a	c	a	a
Opportunities and threats	c	a	a	c	c	c	a
Price negotiation	c	a	a	c	c	a	c
Significance: a = 99% confidence; b = 95% confidence; and c = no significant difference.							

Inter-Organizational Information System

There were significant differences in the perceptions of sales and purchasing staff about most aspects of the IOIS for most information types (Table 2).

The most differences were in information systems for on-time delivery, invoice accuracy, product quality, and new product development. More specifically, on-time delivery information systems were completely different except in terms of formality. Invoice accuracy information systems were different except in terms of formality and the richness of communication media used. Product quality information systems were different except in terms of direction of information flow and richness of communication media used. New product development information systems were different except in terms of formality and whether this information was exchanged.

The detailed results of comparisons made for each aspect of the IOIS for each information type were as follows (supporting tables in Appendix 2).

To see whether customers' perceptions were different than suppliers' perceptions about the nature of the information being exchanged, chi-square tests were undertaken (Appendix 2, Table 8). There were some statistical differences in the information being exchanged. Compared to sales staff, purchasing staff were more likely to exchange information about on-time delivery, product quality, accurate invoicing, and forecast demand and supply.

Differences in perceptions about the frequency of information exchanges were assessed with chi-square tests (Appendix 2, Table 9). Sales and purchasing staff also had different perceptions about the frequency with which all information types were exchanged, except for the completeness of orders. Sales staff felt they exchanged information more frequently than did purchasing staff about problem resolution, price negotiation, and invoice accuracy. Purchasing staff exchanged information more frequently about timeliness of deliveries, forecast supply and demand, order change flexibility, product quality, opportunities and threats, and new product development.

A comparison of perceptions about whether information was exchanged as often as they considered necessary (adequacy) was examined with t-tests (Appendix 2, Table 10). Overall, sales staff members were slightly less satisfied than purchasing staff that information was being exchanged as often as necessary. The differences in perceptions were statistically significant across most types of information including delivery timeliness, order completeness, invoicing accuracy, price negotiation, forecasts, new product development, and opportunities and threats.

Differences in perceptions about the direction of information flow were assessed with chi-square tests (Appendix 2, Table 11). Compared to sales staff, purchasing staff perceived information to flow more in both directions about accurate invoicing, flexibility to accept order changes, completeness of orders, and new product development. However, purchasing staff perceived delivery timeliness information may also come upstream from suppliers one way information flow.

Differences in perceptions about the formality of the information exchange systems were also assessed with chi-square tests (Appendix 2, Table 12). As respondents could specify if there were both formal and informal systems, percentages were calculated based on the percent of possible cases for each category and chi-square tests run for formal and informal systems variables. While sales staff were more likely to have formal systems for problem resolution, purchasing staff were more likely to have formal systems to exchange information about product quality, timeliness of deliveries, and forecasts of supply and demand. Compared to purchasing staff, sales staff members were more likely to have informal systems to exchange information for price negotiations, problem resolution, product quality, and new product development.

Comparison of the richness of the communication used to convey different information types was examined using chi-square tests (Appendix 2, Table 13). Following Daft and Lengel (1986), the media was ordered from most (1) to least rich (3): 1—face to face; 2—telephone; and 3—written e-mail, fax, invoice, or report. Compared to purchasing staff, sales staff perceived they used more rich

Table 3: Sales and purchasing staff satisfaction with the inter-organizational information systems

	Sales		Purchasing		Diff in	
	Mean	S. D.	Mean	S. D.	Means	Sig
Timely and up to date	5.0	1.2	5.6	1.0	-0.6	a
Accuracy, reliability, and completeness	5.1	1.1	5.6	1.0	-0.5	a
Usefulness and relevancy	5.3	1.1	5.5	1.1	-0.3	a
Depth and range of content	4.7	1.2	5.2	1.3	-0.6	a
Change in timeliness and up to date	4.7	1.1	5.3	1.0	-0.6	a
Change in accuracy, reliability, and completeness	4.7	1.1	5.2	1.1	-0.5	a
Change in usefulness and relevancy	4.7	1.1	5.2	1.0	-0.6	a
Change in depth and range of content	4.8	1.2	5.3	1.1	-0.5	a
Information shared has improved our knowledge	4.1	1.8	5.6	1.2	-1.5	a
Customer/supplier initiates new ideas for improvement	3.7	1.7	4.6	1.7	-0.9	a
Significance: a = 99% confidence; b = 95% confidence; and c = no significant difference.						
Scale of (1) dissatisfied or less satisfied to (7) very satisfied or more satisfied.						

face-to-face communication tools to exchange information about new product development and opportunities and threats. However, purchasing staff perceived they used more rich communication tools to exchange information about forecasts, timeliness of deliveries, completeness of orders, and order change flexibility.

An overall comparison of sales and purchasing staff satisfaction with the IOIS was tested using t-tests (Table 3). Differences were significant across all variables, with purchasing staff more satisfied than sales staff.

In conclusion, there were differences between sales and purchasing staff across most facets of the IOIS for most information types. Purchasing staff were more satisfied with the IOIS with suppliers. They exchanged more types of information and were slightly more satisfied that information was exchanged whenever necessary. Purchasing staff exchanged all information types more frequently than sales staff, with the exception of problem resolution, price negotiation, and invoice accuracy. They were more likely to perceive information flowed more often in both directions. While sales staff used richer media to exchange information about longer-term strategic issues, such as new product development, opportunities, and threats, purchasing staff used richer media for operational issues. The extent that the two groups had more formal or informal systems varied depending on the type of information exchanged. To explain why these differences arose, the nature of the relationships with customers and suppliers was compared.

Customer/Supplier Relationship Perceptions

The t-tests were used to see whether sales staff had different perceptions from purchasing staff about the nature of the relationships with customers and suppliers (Table 4). There were significant differences, with sales staff rating customers lower (compared to purchasing staff rating of suppliers) in terms of their responsiveness and willingness to change and the changes in this over the last 5 years, the overall performance compared to others in industry, their trustworthiness compared to others in industry, and how this had changed over the last 5 years. However, sales staff had a higher commitment to developing long-term relationships with customers compared to purchasing staff commitments to suppliers. Overall, in comparison to sales staff, it would seem that purchasing staff perceived they had better relationships with suppliers but did not need to be as committed to them. The reasons for these differences in perceptions may be explained by the nature of the environment in which they were doing business.

Perceptions of Business Environment

Purchasing and sales staff had significant differences in perceptions about most aspects of the business environment (Table 5). Compared to purchasing staff, sales staff perceived that they were more dependent on customers who had

Table 4: Sales and purchasing staff perceptions about the relationship

	Sales		Purchasing		Difference	
	Mean	Std Dev	Mean	Std Dev	in Means	Sig
Customer/supplier responsiveness and willingness to change	4.7	1.3	5.7	1.5	**-1.0**	a
Change in responsiveness and willingness to change	4.7	1.4	5.1	1.2	**-0.4**	a
Commitment to developing long-term relationships	6.8	0.6	6.1	1.3	**0.6**	a
Change in commitment to developing long-term relationships	4.8	1.3	4.8	1.4	0.0	c
Overall performance compared to others in industry	5.3	1.1	5.7	1.0	**-0.4**	a
Change in overall performance	5.1	1.2	5.0	1.2	0.1	c
Trustworthiness compared to others in industry	4.6	1.3	5.4	1.2	**-0.8**	a
Change in trustworthiness	4.2	1.0	4.5	0.9	**-0.4**	a
Significance: a = 99% confidence; b = 95% confidence; and c = no significant difference.						
Scale of 1 to 7, with 1 being low and 7 being high.						

Table 5: Sales and purchasing staff perceptions about the environment

	Sales		Purchasing		Difference	
	Mean	Std Dev	Mean	Std Dev	in Means	Sig
Dependency and Power						
Choose to remain with them if alternatives available	6.4	1.2	5.4	1.8	1.0	a
Crucial to future performance	5.9	1.6	5.6	1.8	0.3	b
Difficulty in replacement	5.8	1.8	4.4	2.2	1.4	a
Importance to customer/supplier	5.6	1.8	5.7	1.6	-0.1	c
Strength of influence over us	4.8	1.5	3.8	1.8	1.0	a
Uncertainty						
Quality of supply predictability	6.5	0.7	5.8	1.5	0.6	a
Variability of production yields	2.2	1.5	3.4	1.9	-1.2	a
Level of competition	6.1	1.3	4.9	2.0	1.2	a
Rate of change in consumer preferences	4.5	1.8	3.9	1.8	0.6	a
Volume of supply predictability	5.6	1.1	5.4	1.5	0.2	c
Demand predictability	5.1	1.5	5.1	1.5	0.0	c
Significance: a = 99% confidence; b = 95% confidence; and c = no significant difference.						
Scale of 1 to 7, with 1 being strongly disagree and 7 being strongly agree.						

greater influence over their organizations and were more difficult to replace, and that they would choose to remain with them if alternatives were available. Sales staff perceived their organization was more reliable in providing customers with predictable quality and little variability in production yields. In addition, sales staff perceived customers were in a more uncertain market, with higher competition affected more by changes in consumer preferences. In summary, compared to purchasing staff, sales staff members were in a more uncertain business environment and were more dependent on their customers.

Multivariate Analysis

As a result of the statistical differences between customers and suppliers as revealed by the initial t-tests and chi-square tests, it was considered that *multivariate data analysis* might be appropriate to take account of multicollinearity. Consequently, a stepwise discriminant analysis (Klecka, 1980) was undertaken to determine, in a multivariate sense, which of the variables differed between the two groups. Using the F-statistic of the between-object to within-object variance as a measure of separation (Johnson, 1977), sales and purchasing were found to be significantly different from each other at the 0.001 level, (F-statistic 39.1 significance less than 0.001), suggesting that meaningful differences exist. Using the I^2 statistic suggested by Peterson and Mahajan (1976), it was found that the single function between the two groups explained 79% of the variation in the data. The method was 96% accurate in correctly classifying respondents, which was higher than the 60% and 30% expected by chance (95% using the leave-one-out cross-validation procedure). Following Johnson (1977) and Soutar and Clarke (1981), variables with structural correlation coefficients greater than 0.25 are usually used to interpret the functions. However, all variables had structural correlations less than 0.24. This, along with the very high I^2, indicated that while there were significant differences between purchasing and sales staff, the variables that explained these differences were included in the model. Therefore, the standardized canonical discriminant function coefficients and the means for each group were used to explain the differences between the customers and suppliers (Table 6). The results need careful interpretation, as the variables were entered into discriminant analysis in a stepwise manner. Although the best variables were entered, this may mean that multicollinear variables that do not measure the differences quite as well were eliminated, when they may assist in interpreting differences.

There were differences in the IOIS used by sales and purchasing staff. Compared to sales staff, purchasing staff were more likely to exchange information about new product developments and quality issues, and perceived quality information was exchanged whenever necessary. Purchasing staff used more formal systems for the exchange of forecast information. Sales staff used

Table 6: Discriminant analysis

Independent Variables	Discriminant Coefficient	Sales Mean	Purchase Mean	Diff in Means
New product development communicated (1 = yes)	-0.48	0.95	0.96	0.01
Quality communication (1 = yes)	-0.85	0.97	1.00	0.03
Quality relative frequency (never = 1 to 7 = when necessary)	-0.59	6.8	7.0	0.2
Price negotiation communication (1 = yes)	1.06	**0.97**	**0.97**	**0.0**
Price negotiation informal system (1 = yes)	0.46	0.94	0.93	-0.01
Order completeness informal system (1 = yes)	-0.45	0.74	0.70	-0.04
Forecast formal system (1 = yes)	-0.49	0.40	0.76	0.36
Invoice accuracy, both directions (1 = yes)	0.66	0.94	1.00	0.06
Invoice accuracy, one direction (1 = yes)	0.82	0.06	0.00	0.06
Usefulness and relevancy of information satisfaction (low = 1 to 7 = high)	0.49	5.3	5.5	0.3
Change in usefulness and relevancy of information satisfaction (less = 1 to 7 = more satisfied)	-0.68	4.7	5.2	0.6
Accuracy, reliability, and completeness information satisfaction (low = 1 to 7 = high)	-0.44	5.1	5.6	0.5
Change in accuracy, reliability, and completeness information satisfaction (less = 1 to 7 = more satisfied)	1.30	4.7	5.2	0.5
Information shared has improved our knowledge (disagree = 1 to 7 = agree)	-0.63	4.1	5.6	1.5
Choose to remain with them if alternatives available (disagree = 1 to 7 = agree)	0.66	6.4	5.4	-1.0
Difficulty in replacement (disagree = 1 to 7 = agree)	0.51	5.8	4.4	-1.4

more informal systems for exchange of price negotiations and order complete-ness. The exchange of invoicing accuracy information was more one directional for sales staff.

There were also differences in satisfaction with the IOIS. Compared to sales staff, purchasing staff were more satisfied with usefulness and relevancy, and accuracy, reliability, and completeness and this satisfaction had improved more over time. Purchasing staff perceived that information shared with suppliers had improved their knowledge.

In addition, the environment in which the business was conducted was perceived to be different by sales and purchasing staff in terms of dependency and loyalty. Sales staff were more likely to remain with customers if alternatives were available (loyalty) and perceived it would be harder to replace customers.

Inter-Organizational System Discussion-Within Organization Comparison of Sales and Purchasing Staff

The main result of this research in terms of inter-organizational systems was that purchasing staff and sales staff had different views about the information system and relationships with suppliers and customers as well as the environment in which they worked. Overall, compared to sales staff, purchasing staff were more satisfied with the information system, perceived the information shared had improved their knowledge, and exchanged more types of information and in a more formalized manner. Sales staff were more loyal to customers and per-ceived that customers were harder to replace. In evaluating why purchasing and sales staff have these differences in perception, it may be argued that it may have to do with the role of the organization as buyer in dealing with suppliers or as seller in dealing with customers. Purchasing staff as buyers tend to have more say in what goes on as they decide what to buy. Sales staff as sellers tend to have power limited to the control of scarce or nonsubstitutable goods and services. Therefore, purchasing staff have more say in initiating more information exchanges and formalizing information systems to monitor the relationships.

Other studies have found differences between buyers (purchasing staff) and sellers (sales staff). Spekman, Kamauff, and Myhr (1998), in a study of 161 respondents in different functional departments (operations, procurement, ma-terials management, or marketing) and levels (suppliers, focal company, custom-ers) in 22 supply chains, found that buyers were different from sellers. They found that buyers were less likely to view the customer/supplier as irreplaceable and essential to their future business. In addition, they found that buyers tended to be less willing to share information. While the study reported in this chapter did not examine willingness to share information, similar results were found: sales staff (sellers) were more dependent than purchasing staff (buyers).

Forker, Ruch, and Hershauer (1999), in comparisons between 181 pairs of relationships between an electronic systems manufacturer and the suppliers, found significant differences in perceptions for seven out of 16 (quality) management practices. This was notwithstanding long and close business relationships and over 20 years of involvement in supplier development programs. Forker, Ruch, and Hershauer (1999), due to this and the degree of communication, concluded it was unlikely that the perceptual differences were due to a lack of awareness. Rather, they suggested that perceptual differences were due to inconsistent priorities, motives, and methods underlying the administration of the supplier development programs. While the study reported in this chapter did not specifically measure priorities and motives, it is suggested that they could be reflected in perceived relationships and therefore provide some support for the findings presented.

Storer et al. (2002), in a study of dyadic pairs of customers and suppliers in the green-life nursery industry, found that there were significant differences in perceptions between customers and suppliers about the nature of the IOIS, environment, and relationships. To further assess the generalizability of the results presented in this chapter, a comparison of the studies was made between variables that were significantly different in both studies (Table 7). In making the

Table 7: Comparison of current and Storer et al. (2002) studies

Similarities in Results	Differences in Results
Customers/purchasing staff > suppliers/sales staff	
Type of information exchanged:	Information exchanged whenever necessary:
Quality, delivery timeliness, invoicing accuracy, forecasts	Order completeness, delivery timeliness customers/sales staff < suppliers/purchasing staff
Frequency information exchanged:	Frequency information exchanged:
Quality, delivery timeliness, forecasts, order change, opportunities and threats	Problem resolution, price negotiation, invoice accuracy Customers/sales staff > suppliers/purchasing staff
Two-directional information exchange:	
Order flexibility, invoice accuracy	
Communication media richness:	
Order completeness	
Relationship:	Environment:
Responsiveness now and change in 5 years	Remain with them Customers/sales staff > suppliers/purchasing staff

comparison, the green-life customer equates to the food processor purchasing staff, as purchasing staff were interviewed in the green-life customer dyad (plant retailers). Similarly, the green-life supplier equates to the food processor sales staff, as sales staff were interviewed in the green-life suppliers (plant nurseries).

Overall, the green-life dyadic pair study provided some support for some of the findings presented here. There were similarities in results about the types of information exchanged, direction of information flow, communication media richness, and relationships, as well as some similarities in terms of the frequency some types of information were exchanged. However, there were dissimilarities about the nature of the environment, the adequacy of information exchanges, and the frequency with which some information types were exchanged.

Specifically, in terms of similarities, both studies found that customers/purchasing staff exchanged information more frequently than suppliers/sales staff about quality, delivery timeliness, invoice accuracy, and forecasts. Customers/purchasing staff exchanged information more frequently about quality, delivery timeliness, forecasts, order changes, and opportunities and threats. Customers/purchasing staff were more likely to have two-directional information exchange about order flexibility and invoice accuracy. In addition, customers/purchasing staff perceived their suppliers were more responsive now and had become more responsive over the last 5 years.

However, the pattern of customers matching up with purchasing staff was not consistent between all significant variables common to both studies. Compared to customers and sales staff, suppliers and purchasing staff were more likely to perceive that information was exchanged when necessary about order completeness and delivery timeliness. Customers and sales staff exchanged information more frequently about problems, pricing, and invoice accuracy. In addition, customers and sales staff were more likely to agree they would remain with their suppliers/customers.

Before concluding that the differences in the results between the two studies affect the validity of the findings, difficulties in making comparisons between the studies must be noted. There were differences in which variables were significantly different between the groups in each study, so comparisons could not be made for some variables. This may be due to the smaller sample size of the dyadic pairs study, with only 30 supplier and 34 customer responses and fewer significant differences between the customers and suppliers. Alternatively, this may be due to the customers/suppliers study being done in the green-life nursery industry and the sales/purchasing study being done in the food industry. While both industries deal with perishable products, the sizes and scales of the industries were different. The food industry organizations were larger national and multinational companies, with more formalized systems and more specialized staff. The nursery industry organizations were smaller regional and national companies, with less formal systems and fewer staff who were multiskilled. Further studies are needed to see if the results can be replicated.

Conclusion

In summary, based on the results of this food processor survey, the comparative pairs analysis method was successful in highlighting that views of downstream customers were significantly different from views about upstream suppliers. Despite the difficulties in making close comparisons to previous studies, one major finding was that purchasing and sales staff had differences in perceptions. These inherent differences between purchasing and sales staff have implications for conducting chain research and comparing results of different studies. Many studies have only looked one way in the chain by examining organizations' views of either suppliers (upstream) or customers (downstream). When comparing the results of chain studies, it would be necessary to compare upstream studies with upstream studies and vice versa. In addition, it is suggested that when conducting chain research, a better view of each counterpart in the chain can be achieved by using comparative pairs data collection methods, by getting the views of both purchasing and sales staff.

In terms of validity testing, individual respondents were able to differentiate about the IOIS, relationships, and environment for one organization where they dealt in different food categories. The consequences are that when collecting data about IOIS and relationships with other third parties, it is important to specify which product category is being examined. This would be especially important when multiple respondents are being surveyed within the one organization. In addition, individual respondents were able to differentiate about the IOIS, relationships, and the environment for pairs of organizations. This means that asking about pairs of organizations is a valid means by which to get rich qualitative data during the surveying process to explain differences in responses.

In terms of conducting research, collecting information about pairs of organizations simultaneously from each respondent is very powerful. Primarily, it allows respondents to clarify how their differences in perception were based on a variable by variable basis. This gives insights into how respondents think and aids in explaining differences overall. In addition, it allows the researcher to understand what is going on at each data collection instance. It also allows the researcher to revise the data collection instruments if the explanations given are not covered by structured questions asked of all the respondents. Often, these insights are not gained until the data is being analyzed, and the research is left to hypothesis what may have happened if data were collected about other issues.

In the food processor research project, it became clear after 10 interviews that differences in information satisfaction may relate to the added knowledge that the information exchanges generated as well as if it had improved the business. As a result, additional questions were included to ask all respondents about this. Not only were these additional questions asked, but also their explanatory power was explored with each interview. Further insights were gained about why they explained some respondents' perceptions but were not very useful for others. Subsequent data analysis will be conducted to test the explanatory power of these questions.

The main advantage of comparative pairs data collection and analysis is that explanations can be gained before the data is analyzed. For many industry research projects, the population of interest is small (e.g., sales managers or computer software users in an organization), and each group being analyzed may have less than 50 potential respondents. As a result, detailed statistics such as t-tests, discriminant analysis, and regression analysis are not appropriate. This data collection method allows for an investigation of explanation of reasons for differences in opinions without detailed statistics. Data can be collected until a general consensus of views is reached to get a qualitative assessment of an explanation.

While many may see comparative pairs data collection and analysis as only of interest to researchers, managers can also use it. When looking for an explanation about why a process is not working well, stakeholders can be asked to make a comparison to another process they think is working well and explain the differences. Similarly, the performance of two customers, two suppliers, two products, two services, two managers, etc., can be compared.

References

Ancona, D. G., & Caldwell, D. F. (1992). Bridging the boundary: External activity and performance in organizational teams. *Administrative Science Quarterly, 37*(4), 634–665.

Anderson, E., Lodish, L., & Weitz, B. (1987). Resource allocation behavior in conventional channels. *Journal of Marketing Research, 24*(1), 85–97.

Anderson, J. C., Håkansson, H., & Johanson, J. (1994). Dyadic business relationships within a business network context. *Journal of Marketing, 58*(4), 1–15.

Anderson, J. C., & Narus, J. (1990). A model of distributor firm and manufacturer firm working partnerships. *Journal of Marketing, 54*(January), 42–58.

Andraski, J. C. (1998). Leadership and the realization of supply chain collaboration. *Journal of Business Logistics, 19*(2), 9–11.

Batt, P., & Rexha, N. (1999). Building trust in agribusiness supply chains: A conceptual model of buyer–seller relationships in the seed potato industry in Asia. *Journal of International Food and Agribusiness Marketing, 11*(1).

Benedict, C., & Margeridis, H. (1999). Chain reaction. *Charter*, March, 46–49.

Bensaou, M. (1997). Interorganizational cooperation: The role of information technology. An empirical comparison of U.S. and Japanese supplier relations. *Information Systems Research, 8*(2), 107–124.

Bensaou, M. (1999). Portfolios of buyer–supplier relationships. *Sloan Management Review, 40*(4 Summer), 35.

Bensaou, M., & Venkatraman, N. (1995). Configurations of inter-organizational relationships: A comparion between U.S. and Japanese auto-makers. *Management Science, 41*(9 September), 1471–1492.

Borgen, K., & Ohren, O. (1999). The logistics of information in collaborative organizations. Paper read at *11th NOFOMA - Annual International Conference on Nordic Logistics Research*, 15–16 June 1999, Lund, Sweden.

Bowersox, D. J., & Closs, D. J. (1996). *Logistical management: The integrated supply chain process*. New York: McGraw-Hill.

Choo, C. W. (1996). Towards an information model of organizations. In E. Auster, & C. W. Choo (Eds.), *Managing information for the competitive edge*. New York: Neal-Schuman Publishers.

Christopher, M. (1997). *Marketing logistics, The Marketing Series*. Oxford, UK: Butterworth-Heinemann.

Cunningham, C., & Tynan, C. (1993). Electronic trading, inter-organizational systems and the nature of buyer–seller relationships: The need for a network perspective. *International Journal of Information Management, 13*(1), 3–28.

Daft, R. L., & Lengel, R. H. (1986). Organizational information requirements, media richness and structural design. *Management Science, 32*(May), 554–571.

Daft, R. L., & Lengel, R. H. (1996). Information richness: A new approach to managerial behavior and organizational design. In E. Auster, & C. W. Choo (Eds.), *Managing information for the competitive edge*. New York: Neal-Schuman Publishers Inc.

Dansereau, F., & Markham, S. E. (1987). Superior–subordinate communication: Multiple levels of analysis. In F. M. Jablin, L. L. Putnam, K. H. Roberts,

& L. W. Porter (Eds.), *Handbook of organizational communication: An interdisciplinary perspective*. Newbury Park, CA: Sage Publications Inc.

Doney, P. M., & Cannon, J. P. (1997). An examination of the nature of trust in buyer–seller relationships. *Journal of Marketing, 61*(2 April), 35–51.

Ellinger, A. E., Daugherty, P. J., & Plair, Q. J. (1999). Customer satisfaction and loyalty in supply chain: The role of communication. *Transportation Research Part E-Logistics & Transportation Review, 35*(2), 121–134.

Farace, R., Monge, P., & Russell, H. (1977). *Communicating and organizing*. Reading, MA: Addison-Wesley Publishing Company.

Forker, L. B., Ruch, W. A., & Hershauer, J. C. (1999). Examining supplier improvement efforts from both sides. *Journal of Supply Chain Management, 35*(3), 40–50.

Ganesan, S. (1994). Determinants of long-term orientation in buyer–seller relationships. *Journal of Marketing, 58*(2 April), 1–19.

Gassenheimer, J. B., & Scandura, T. A. (1993). External and internal supplier influences: Buyer perceptions of channel outcomes. *Journal of the Academy of Marketing Science, 21*(Spring), 155–160.

Gifford, D., Hall, L., & Ryan, W. (Eds.). (1998). *Chains of success: Case studies of international and Australian food businesses co-operating to compete*. Canberra, Australia: Agribusiness and Commodity Branch, Department of Primary Industries and Energy.

Gundlach, G. T., Achrol, R. S., & Mentzer, J. T. (1995). The structure of commitment in exchange. *Journal of Marketing, 59*(1 January), 78–92.

Hair, J. F. J., Anderson, R. E., Tatham, R. L., & Black, W. C. (1998). *Multivariate data analysis* (5th ed.). Sydney, Australia: Prentice Hall International Inc.

Heather, B. (2001). *Buyer seller relations: Retail supplier relations in the horticultural industry*. Honours Thesis, Muresk Institute of Agriculture, Curtin University of Technology, Bentley, Western Australia.

Hines, P. (1998). Supply chain management: From Lorries to Macro-Economic Determiner. Paper read at *Proceedings of the Logistics Research Network Conference 1998*, 10–11 September 1998, at Cranfield University, United Kingdom.

Hines, P., Rich, N., & Hittmeyer, M. (1998). Competing against ignorance: Advantage through knowledge. *International Journal of Physical Distribution & Logistics Management, 28*(1), 18–43.

Holland, C. P. (1995). Co-operative supply-chain management: The impact of interorganizational information systems. *Journal of Strategic Information Systems, 4*(2 January), 117–134.

Huber, G., & Daft, R. (1987). The information environment in organizations. In F. M. Jablin, L. L. Putnam, K. H. Roberts, & L. W. Porter (Eds.), *Handbook of organizational communication: An interdisciplinary perspective.* Newbury Park, CA: Sage Publications Inc.

Johnson, R. M. (1977). Multiple discriminant analysis: Marketing research applications. In J. N. Sheth (Ed.), *Multivariate methods for market and survey research.* Chicago, IL: American Marketing Association.

Kanflo, T. (1998). *Information in transportation chains.* Licentiate, Department of Transport and Logistics, Chalmers University of Technology, Goteborg, Sweden.

Klecka, W. R. (1980). *Discriminant analysis, Sage Series.* Thousand Oaks, CA: Sage Publications.

Kohli, A. K., Jaworski, B. J., & Kumar, A. (1993). MARKOR: A measure of market orientation. *Journal of Marketing Research, 30*(4), 467–477.

Kumar, N., Stern, L. W., & Achrol, R. S. (1992). Assessing reseller performance from the perspective of the supplier. *Journal of Marketing Research, 29*(2), 238–253.

Leuthesser, L., & Kohli, A. K. (1995). Rational behavior in business markets: Implications for relationship management. *Journal of Business Research, 34*(3), 221–233.

Mohr, J., & Nevin, J. R. (1990). Communication strategies in marketing channels: A theoretical perspective. *Journal of Marketing, 54*(4 October), 36–51.

Mohr, J. J., & Sohi, R. S. (1995). Communication flows in distribution channels: Impact on assessments of communication quality and satisfaction. *Journal of Retailing, 71*(4), 393–416.

Mohr, J. J., Fisher, R. J., & Nevin, J. R. (1996). Collaborative communication in interfirm relationships: Moderating effects of integration and control. *Journal of Marketing, 60*(3 July), 103–115.

Morgan, R. M., & Hunt, S. D. (1994). The commitment–trust theory of relationship marketing. *Journal of Marketing, 58*(3 July), 20–38.

O'Brien, J. A. (1999). *Management information systems: Managing information technology in the internetworked enterprise* (4th ed.). Boston, MA: Irwin/McGraw-Hill.

Peterson, R. A., & Mahajan, V. (1976). Practical significance and partitioning variance in discriminant analysis. *Decision Sciences, 7,* 649–658.

Samuel, D., & Hines, P. (1998). Designing a supply chain process: A food distribution case. Paper read at *1998 Logistics Research Network*

Conference, 10–11 September 1998, at Cranfield University, United Kingdom.

Sharma, N., Young, L., & Wilkinson, I. (2001). The structure of relationship commitment in interfirm relationships. Paper read at *The 17th Annual IMP Conference: Interactions, Relationships and Networks—Strategic directions*, at Holmenkollen Park Hotel Rica, Oslo, Norway.

Soutar, G. N., & Clarke, Y. (1981). Lifestyle and television viewing behaviour in Perth, Western Australia. *Australian Journal of Management*, June, 109–123.

Spekman, R. E., Kamauff, J. W. J., & Myhr, N. (1998). An empirical investigation into supply chain management: A perspective on partnerships. *International Journal of Physical Distribution & Logistics Management*, 28(8).

Stank, T. P., Emmelhainz, M. A., & Daugherty, P. J. (1996). The impact of information on supplier performance. *Journal of Marketing Theory & Practice*, 4(4 Fall), 94–105.

Storer, C. E. (2001). Inter-organizational information feedback systems in agribusiness chains: A chain case study theoretical framework. Paper read at *2001 International Agribusiness Management Association World Food & Agribusiness Symposium*, 25–28 June 2001, at Sydney Hilton, NSW.

Storer, C. E., Soutar, G., Darrington, M., & Rola-Rubzen, M. F. (2002). Buyer & seller reflections on inter-organizational information systems: Implication for chain data collection methods. *Journal of Chain & Network Science*, 2(2), 117–133.

Tashakkori, A., & Teddlie, C. (1998). *Mixed methodology: Combining qualitative and quantitative approaches*. Thousand Oaks, CA: Sage Publications.

Trienekens, J. (1999). *Management of processes in chains: A research framework*. Den Haag, The Netherlands: CIP-Data Koninklijke Bibliotheek.

Van der Vorst, J. G. A. J. (2000). *Effective food supply chains: Generating, modelling and evaluating supply chain scenarios*. Ph.D. thesis, Wageningen University, Wageningen.

Van Hoek, R. I. (1998). Logistics and virtual integration postponement, outsourcing and the flow of information. *International Journal of Physical Distribution & Logistics Management*, 28(7).

Vijayasarathy, L. R., & Robey, D. (1997). The effect of EDI on market channel relationships in retailing. *Information and Management*, 33(2 December 5), 73–86.

Womack, J. P., Jones, D. T., & Roos, D. (1990). *The machine that changed the world: Based on the Massachusetts Institute of Technology 5-million dollar 5-year study of the future of the automobile.* New York: Rawson Associates.

Appendix 1- Questionnaire

Experience and Understanding

How many years have you been working with this organization?

How many years have you been working in the Industry?

How many years has your organization been doing business with these *customers/suppliers*?

How well do you understand these *customers/suppliers*?

How well do you understand the *customers/suppliers* in this industry generally?

I do not understand it					I understand it very well	
1	2	3	4	5	6	7

How **responsive** do you feel these *customers/suppliers* are to your requirements, and how willing are they to change relative to others in the industry?

Not at all responsive & willing to change		Somewhat Responsive			Highly responsive and willing to change	
1	2	3	4	5	6	7

How responsive do your feel these *customers/suppliers* are to your requirements, and how willing are they to change relative to others in the industry now compared with <u>5 years ago</u>?

Much less responsive and willing to change		No change			Much more responsive and willing to change	
1	2	3	4	5	6	7

If some change, ask "Why?"

How **committed** do you think your organization is to developing long-term relationships with these *customers/suppliers*?

Not at all committed long-term		Somewhat committed long-term			Highly committed long-term	
1	2	3	4	5	6	7

How committed do you think your organization is to developing long-term relationships with these *customers/suppliers* now compared to <u>5 years ago</u>?

Not at all committed long-term		Somewhat committed long-term			Highly committed long-term	
1	2	3	4	5	6	7

If some change ask, "Why?"

How would you rate the overall **performance** of these *customers/suppliers* compared to others in the industry?

Worst performance in industry		Mediocre			Best performance in industry	
1	2	3	4	5	6	7

Do you perceive the overall performance of the *customers/suppliers* is better or worse now than 5 years ago?

Much worse			No change			Much better
1	2	3	4	5	6	7

If some change, ask "Why?"

Do you find these *customers/suppliers* more or less **trustworthy** than others in the same industry?

Less trustworthy			Average			More trustworthy
1	2	3	4	5	6	7

Do you perceive these *customer's/supplier's* trustworthiness is better or worse now than 5 years ago?

Much worse			Same			Much better
1	2	3	4	5	6	7

If some change, ask "Why?"

Environment
Could you please indicate if you agree or disagree with each of the following statements:

Strongly Disagree			Neither agree nor disagree			Strongly agree
1	2	3	4	5	6	7

Dependence and Influence
These *customers/suppliers* are crucial to your future performance.
It would be difficult for your organization to replace these *customers/suppliers*.
Your organization is important to these *customers/suppliers*.
These *customers/suppliers* exert a strong influence over your organization.

Predictability
Demand by *this customer/your organization* is predictable.
Volume of supply by *this supplier/your organization* is predictable.
Quality of supply by *this supplier/your organization* is predictable.
Production yields from *this supplier's/your product* are highly variable.

Uncertainty
The level of competitive activity in *this customer's/supplier's* market is high.
Consumer's preferences in *this customer's/supplier's* markets are changing.
If other alternative customers/suppliers are available to you, your organization would choose to remain with these *customers/suppliers*.

Inter-organizational Information Feedback System
Do you exchange information with *customer/supplier 1/2* about:

Problem resolution	Invoice accuracy
Product quality	Profitability, costs, and prices
On-time delivery	Forecast demand and supply
Completeness of orders	New product development
Flexibility to accept order changes	Opportunities and threats

If yes, ask the following for each:

i. With whom do you exchange this information? *(record position title)*
ii. Do you discuss this information with anyone else? *(probe for details of flows to/from customers/suppliers for internal sources)*
iii. How do you exchange the information?
   (phone, fax, e-mail, face-to-face meetings, letter, report, invoice/credit note, telex, EDI/intranet, newsletter, radio)
iv. In what direction does the information flow? (upstream, downstream, both directions)
v. Is the information exchanged as part of a formal process or only on an ad hoc basis as perceived necessary?
vi. How often is information exchanged, on average?
   (several times a day, daily, several times a week, weekly, several times a month, monthly, several times a year, yearly, never)
vii. Indicate whether you consider that you exchange this information as often as necessary?

Not as often as necessary			Most of the time		Whenever necessary		Do not know	
1	2	3	4	5	6	7	8	9

To what extent are you **satisfied/dissatisfied with the information** you share with these *customers/suppliers* in terms of…*(read list)*?
Timely and up to date
Accuracy, reliability, and completeness
Usefulness and relevancy
Depth and range of content

Extremely Dissatisfied			Neither dissatisfied nor satisfied			Extremely satisfied	Do not know
1	2	3	4	5	6	7	8

Probe for details if not already discussed

To what extent are you more or less satisfied with the information you share with these *customers/suppliers* compared with <u>5 years ago</u> in terms of…*(read list)*?
Timely and up to date
Accuracy, reliability, and completeness
Usefulness and relevancy
Depth and range of content

Much less satisfied			No change			Much more satisfied	Do not know
1	2	3	4	5	6	7	8

Could you please indicate if you agree or disagree with each of the following statements:

Strongly disagree			Neither agree nor disagree			Strongly agree
1	2	3	4	5	6	7

The information you share with these *customers/suppliers* has improved your organization's **knowledge** of this industry.

These *customers/suppliers* initiate **new ideas** to improve the category/business.

Appendix 2 - Within Organization Comparison of Inter-organizational Information System Between Sales and Purchasing Staff

Table 8: Types of information exchanged by sales and purchasing staff

Type of Information Exchanged	Sales Staff %	Purch Staff %	Total %	Pearson Chi-Square
Problem resolution	100	100	100	0.0 c
On-time delivery	94	100	96	11.7 a
Product quality	97	100	98	5.4 b
Accurate invoicing	97	100	98	5.4 b
Forecast demand and supply	92	97	93	4.5 b
Complete orders	91	95	92	2.4 c
Flexibility to accept order changes	90	95	92	3.2 c
New product development	95	96	96	0.1 c
Opportunities and threats	97	98	97	2.4 c
Price negotiation	97	97	97	0.0 c

Percent calculated out of a total possible count of 176 purchasing staff and 297 sales staff.
Significance: a = 99% confidence; b = 95% confidence; and c = no significant difference.

Table 9: Frequency of different types of information were exchanged by sales and purchasing staff

Type of Information	Sales Staff			Purchasing Staff			Pearson Chi-Square
	Weekly or More Often	Monthly or Several Times a Month	Several Times a Year or Less Often	Weekly or More Often	Monthly or Several Times a Month	Several Times a Year or Less Often	
Problem resolution	73	21	6	59	18	24	45.5 a
Completeness of orders	45	21	34	40	21	39	1.8 c
Price negotiation	41	37	22	6	6	87	188.1 a
Timeliness of deliveries	29	23	48	49	12	39	20.3 a
Forecast supply and demand	20	33	47	40	17	43	26.0 a
Order change flexibility	17	20	63	40	20	40	30.8 a
Product quality	13	23	63	30	29	41	26.6 a
Opportunities and threats	13	28	60	13	44	43	14.4 a
New product development	2	13	85	15	18	68	31.0 a
Invoice accuracy	0	43	57	6	29	65	20.3 a
Percent who responded (total possible count of 30 suppliers and 34 customers).							
Significance: a = 99% confidence; b = 95% confidence; and c = no significant difference.							

Table 10: Sales and purchasing staff perceived adequacy of information exchanges

Information Type	Sales		Purchasing		Diff in	
	Mean	S. D.	Mean	S. D.	Means	Sig
Problem resolution relative frequency	6.9	0.5	7.0	0.3	-0.1	c
Quality relative frequency	6.8	0.9	7.0	0.2	-0.2	b
Delivery timeliness relative frequency	6.4	1.6	7.0	0.0	-0.6	a
Order completeness relative frequency	6.3	1.8	6.7	1.3	-0.4	a
Order flexibility relative frequency	6.4	1.7	6.7	1.3	-0.3	c
Invoice accuracy relative frequency	6.8	1.0	7.0	0.0	-0.2	a
Price negotiation relative frequency	6.7	1.0	7.0	0.5	-0.2	a
Forecast relative frequency	5.0	2.2	6.1	1.9	-1.1	a
New product relative frequency	6.1	1.7	6.5	1.5	-0.4	a
Opportunities and threats relative frequency	6.1	1.5	6.6	1.2	-0.4	a
Significance: a = 99% confidence; b = 95% confidence; and c = no significant difference.						
Scale of 1 to 7, with 1 not as often as necessary and 7 whenever necessary.						

Table 11: Sales and purchasing staff perceived direction of information flows

Type of Information	Sales Staff		Purchasing Staff		Pearson
	One way %	Both ways %	One way %	Both ways %	Chi-Square
Accuracy of invoicing	6	94		100	10.0 a
Flexibility to accept order changes	6	94		100	8.3 a
Completeness of orders	8	91		100	10.8 a
New product development	7	93	3	97	19.1 a
Delivery timeliness		100	7	93	21.4 a
Price negotiation		99	3	96	5.4 c
Forecast supply and demand	2	98	5	95	0.8 c
Product quality		100		100	0.0 c
Problem resolution		100		100	0.0 c
Opportunities and threats		100		100	0.6 c
Percent who responded (total possible count of 176 purchasing staff and 297 sales staff).					
Significance: a = 99% confidence; b = 95% confidence; and c = no significant difference.					

Table 12: Sales and purchasing staff perceived formality of information systems

Type of Information	Formal		Pearson	Informal		Pearson
	Sales Staff	Purchase Staff	Chi-Square	Sales Staff	Purchase Staff	Chi-Square
Price negotiation	94	93	0.5 c	86	61	38.4 a
Problem resolution	90	82	6.4 b	98	94	4.5 b
Product quality	84	93	1.7 a	96	91	6.0 b
New product development	85	80	1.5 c	86	76	6.6 a
Timeliness of deliveries	73	84	6.4 b	92	87	2.6 c
Completeness of orders	74	70	1.0 c	87	87	0.0 c
Opportunities and threats	69	70	0.0 c	95	90	3.7 c
Flexibility to accept order changes	55	64	3.7 c	90	89	0.1 c
Invoice accuracy	54	53	0.0 c	96	95	0.1 c
Forecast supply and demand	40	76	58.0 a	87	82	2.5 c
Percent of cases for each category (total possible count of 176 purchasing staff and 297 sales staff).						
Significance: a = 99% confidence; b = 95% confidence; and c = no significant difference.						

Table 13: Sales and purchasing staff perceived richness of communication media

Type of Information	Sales Staff			Purchasing Staff			Pearson
	Most Rich—Face to Face %	Rich—Phone %	Less Rich Media %	Most Rich—Face to Face %	Rich—Phone %	Less Rich Media %	Chi-Square
Opportunities and threats	97	2		87	13		20.0 a
New product development	94	4	2	85	14	1	18.7 a
Problem resolution	91	9		89	11		0.5 c
Product quality	81	18	1	80	19	1	0.8 c
Price negotiation	87	13	1	83	15	2	1.6 c
Forecast supply and demand	55	42	4	59	31	11	11.7 a
Timeliness of deliveries	34	64	1	46	47	7	19.5 a
Completeness of orders	33	53	14	40	59	2	18.1 a
Order change flexibility	25	69	6	36	62	2	9.7 a
Invoice accuracy	18	70	11	19	72	9	0.6 c
Percent who responded (total possible count of 176 purchasing staff and 297 sales staff).							
Significance: a = 99% confidence; b = 95% confidence; and c = no significant difference.							

Chapter XIII

Empirical Evidence on How Information Technology Encourages the Creation of Strategic Networks

Jose A. Medina-Garrido
University of Cadiz, Spain

Sebastian Bruque-Camara
University of Jaen, Spain

Jose Ruiz-Navarro
University of Cadiz, Spain

Abstract

This chapter analyzes how information technology fosters and supports the creation of strategic networks. First, we shall establish an eclectic theoretical framework that can appropriately explain the reasons why firms form strategic networks. We base our analysis on the theories of transaction cost economics and the resource-based view. Second, we shall analyze, from this theoretical perspective, how information technology can affect the factors of value and cost that influence the formation of strategic networks. Finally, we shall empirically test if theory predictions actually occur in practice, by studying the role that information technology has played in the formation of a network by a Spanish firm.

Introduction

Networks of firms, to give these structures just one of their names, have been very widely studied (by, for example, Thompson, 1967; Contractor, 1988; Hennart, 1988; Kogut, 1988; Hamel, Doz, & Prahalad, 1989; Powell, 1990; Hamel, 1991; Williamson, 1991; Parkhe, 1993; Ring & Van de Ven, 1994; Gulati, 1995), and there has been some work on the importance of information technology (IT) in these networks (Cash & Konsynski, 1985; Porter & Millar, 1986; Rackoff, Wiseman, & Ullrich, 1985). But there is little in the literature that explains in detail the role of IT in the formation of inter-organizational networks (see Clemons & Row, 1992). There are gaps with respect to what IT actually does, and how it makes possible, or at least facilitates, the operation of the network. This work attempts to fill this important gap, in a literature where IT appears to be very important for inter-organizational relations, but the reason why is anecdotal.

The aim of this chapter is to look in detail at the reasons why strategic networks are formed, developing a theoretical framework that can explain these reasons adequately and that allows us to analyze the role of IT in their formation and maintenance. The propositions we put forward will be tested against a case study, which, as well as being illustrative, will allow us to make a theoretical generalization (Yin, 1984; Bonache, 1999).

Background: Reasons for Network Formation

The reasons given in the literature for the formation of strategic networks can be grouped into two types: value creation and cost savings (Tsang, 2000). However, these two reasons are controversial. On the one hand, much of the literature focuses exclusively on the potential of inter-organizational relations for generating value (see Varadarajan & Cunningham, 1995; Hamel, 1991; Eisenhardt, 1996). On the other hand, some authors see strategic networks as a means of saving on various costs (see Jarillo, 1988, 1993; Williamson, 1991; Clemons &

Row, 1992; Gerybadze, 1995). Nevertheless, both views are incomplete when taken separately (Tsang, 2000). We shall now review the value-creation and cost-savings explanations for network formation. Both views will then be combined into an eclectic model.

Value Creation

Firms participating in strategic networks can create value in various ways. Among the advantages that the literature ascribes to networks are that they provide faster market penetration, the sharing of financial risks (Gulati, Nohria, & Zaheer, 2000), encouragement of innovation, access to knowledge valuable for competing (Hitt et al., 2000), and the reputation required in the market (Sharman, Gray, & Yin, 1991). In short, they make it easier for firms to gain access to the resources and capabilities that they need but do not possess, and for them to learn new capabilities (Kogut, 1988; Ireland et al., 2001).

From the perspective of the resource-based view, firms form strategic networks in order to gain value, an aim that can be broken down into three general objectives: obtaining, exploiting, and developing resources and capabilities.

Obtaining resources and capabilities can be directed at (1) gaining know-how (Powell, 1987; Kogut, 1988; Gulati, Nohria, & Zaheer, 2000); (2) looking for complementary resources and capabilities from other network members (Poppo & Zenger, 1995; Dyer & Singh, 1998; Harrison et al., 2001), which may not be in the market (Oliver, 1997); (3) creating specialized resources and capabilities in combination with those from another firm (Klein, Crawford, & Alchian, 1978; Teece, 1987) to generate Ricardian rents (Rumelt, 1987); or (4) externalizing resources and capabilities (Gulati, Nohria, & Zaheer, 2000) that the firm wants to get rid of in order to concentrate on its core ones (Prahalad, & Hamel, 1990; McGee, 1999).

As far as the exploitation of resources and capabilities is concerned, firms may have the aim of (1) using resources and capabilities in the network that were until then dormant (Baden-Fuller & Volberda, 1996, 1997; Baden-Fuller & Stopford, 1994; Garud & Nayyar, 1994); or (2) making better use of their core resources and capabilities (Arndt, 1979; Tsang, 2000) in other markets or other industries (Varadarajan & Cunningham, 1995; Kumar & van Dissel, 1996; Gulati, Nohria, & Zaheer, 2000).

Finally, the development of new resources and capabilities may lead to the use in the network of unused resources and capabilities to keep them "alive," thereby providing an option for generating dynamic capabilities when the environment changes (Teece, Pisano, & Shuen, 1997; Eisenhardt & Martin, 2000; Fiol, 2001).

The firm Fourth Shift Corp. is an example of how a firm tries to obtain from other firms resources and capabilities complementary to its own. It combines them to produce specialized resources and capabilities, which are consequently difficult to imitate and which are more easily exploited in new markets. Fourth Shift Corp. (based in Minneapolis) supplies applications in ERP (enterprise resource planning), CRM (customer relationship management), and financial management. This firm formed an alliance in 2000 with the consultants Grant Thornton. Both firms had the aim thereby of increasing their portfolio of clients. Thus, Grant Thornton focused on providing e-business consulting, while Fourth Shift centered on implementing e-business software (previously recommended by its alliance partner to clients requesting e-business consultancy).

Another interesting alliance was formed by the bank Chase Manhattan with ShopNow.com, through its Internet banking project Chase.com. ShopNow.com had experience in electronic shopping centers. The result was ChaseShop.com, an electronic shopping center earning revenues in three areas: by customers using credit cards from Chase; by selling advertising space on their Web page; and by charging for developing and hosting clients' online stores. Again, here we can see that firms have sought to create value by accessing the complementary resources and capabilities made available in an inter-organizational relation.

Cost Savings

With regard to costs, opting for forming a network rather than conducting transactions in the market would depend on the ability of certain firms within the network structure to reduce transaction costs in the market (Clemons & Row, 1992; Kumar & van Dissel, 1996; Tsang, 2000), without incurring excessive transaction costs in the network or additional production costs. Moreover, for the network to make sense, its transaction and production costs must not be higher than those incurred in an integrated firm (hierarchical situation) (Jarillo, 1993).

Jarillo (1993) provided a model of what the economic conditions should be for it to be reasonable to construct a strategic network. The model includes the internal costs of implementing an activity (IC), the price charged by an external supplier for carrying out that activity (EP), and the market transaction costs (TC_M). Thus, the necessary but not sufficient condition for forming a network is that $EP < IC$. But this would lead a firm to opt for the market structure, too. The sufficient condition would be that, in addition to the above, TC_M would satisfy $TC_M + EP > IC$, with which the firm would opt for vertical integration, unless it was able to reduce network transaction costs (TC_N) to the point of satisfying $TC_N + EP < IC$.

According to Gerybadze (1995), there are three ways of reducing external costs ($TC_M + EP$) with respect to the internal costs (IC) within the network form of organization. First, the transaction costs can be reduced by transacting with only a reduced number of market members who are well-known and trusted, thanks to the specialization of the interchanges that occur and the building of fluent channels of communication. Second, a successful network leads to the efficient reduction of production costs by benefiting from specialization and scale. Third, a discipline of cost control is introduced that may not occur in an integrated organization with captive internal markets (Jarillo, 1988).

It is particularly important to clearly define what transaction costs affect strategic networks. Williamson (1989) divided transaction costs into information costs, negotiation costs, and guarantee (or safeguard) costs. However, these costs refer to transactions carried out in the market, which are only temporary, and which are unlikely to be repeated. This makes his taxonomy inappropriate for stable network relations. In a strategic network of firms, it is not necessary to look for information or to negotiate continually, and there are safeguards inherent in the operation of the network (because stable relationships permit the parties to penalize previous opportunistic behaviors).

In this sense, it would seem to be preferable to adopt the taxonomy used by Clemons and Row (1992), for whom the transaction costs of firms operating in networks are broken down into coordination costs and transaction risks. The latter refers to the possibility that network members may behave opportunistically and against the spirit of the contract.

Finally, with respect to production costs, the literature points out that the formation of strategic networks leads to economies of scale (Arndt, 1979) and scope that would be impossible to achieve internally in an hierarchical firm (Clemons & Row, 1992; Gulati, Nohria, & Zaheer, 2000). Moreover, strategic networks allow better coordination with suppliers (Konsynski, 1993; Van der Heijden et al., 1995), which leads to improvements in terms of production costs, stock, production times, delivery times, etc.

The Benetton network (dedicated to producing and distributing colorful knitwear) is a clear example of how a firm creates a network when the production costs of other companies are lower than its own internal costs, and how the firm takes advantage of the situation cutting its market transaction costs. This network-based model revolves around granting franchises with the exclusive right to distribute products, strictly controlled by Benetton (the brand owner). There is a dispersed production system involving more than 200 "independent" subcontractors. In this way, Benetton obtains a very flexible production system, being able to react rapidly to unpredictable market situations and changes in customer preferences.

Benetton's information system plays an important role in the response of the company to market variations detected in its franchised stores. These shops communicate directly with the head office in Ponzano (Italy). The firm's ability to adjust its production levels rapidly to changing sales is made easier by the fact that it produces its garments with colorless wool, and only subsequently dyes them in accordance with customer tastes.

Organizing activities through a network has led to important cuts in production costs, due to the highly specialized and flexible subcontractors and the direct control the managers of each subcontractor exercise over their parts of the activity of the network.

Moreover, the fact that the relationship between the firms in the network is permanent eliminates the typical transaction costs that firms incur when engaging in one-off or unstable relationships. In this sense, there are practically zero search costs for finding new suppliers; and there are no contracting or negotiation costs. Although stable relations only require contracts to be signed the first time, Benetton goes further. The degree of confidence it inspires is such that the firms in the network do not sign formal contracts at all. This fact would theoretically increase perceptions that the central firm in the network can engage in opportunistic behavior, thereby increasing perceived transaction risks. However, such an increase in the transaction costs does not occur, because of various practices of Benetton and the nonopportunistic reputation it has gained. This prevents transaction risks from rising, so obviating the need to incur guarantee (or safeguard) costs.

With regard to the above-mentioned practices that reduce the perceived transaction risks, we might mention that the firm finances specialized investments in the network subcontractors, either totally or partially. The companies dependent on Benetton (the central firm) are thereby not obliged to invest important sums on specific assets that can only be used within the network; Benetton's investment will convince firms that they are unlikely to be exploited by the central firm. Moreover, the central firm will find it less likely that its subcontractors engage in opportunistic behavior, as they invest to a greater or lesser extent in resources and capabilities that are complementary (and normally also specific) to the investment made by Benetton. These investments not only involve physical assets, but also knowledge, know-how, and the development of organizational routines.

An Eclectic Model

Transaction cost economics is complemented by the resource-based view. From the resource-based perspective, resources and capabilities on which the firm depends for its current or future competitive advantages are never externalized for strategic reasons, even if this were recommendable from the perspective of transaction cost economics because of costs. In fact, occasionally, alliances are formed that involve increased transaction and production costs in the short term, in the expectance of adding value in the medium to long term. Moreover, it is also frequent for strategic networks to be formed in which there is no added value, as far as cost reductions are concerned. In this sense, the complementary orientations toward value and costs of each one of these theories (Conner, 1991; Zajac & Olsen, 1993; Teece, Pisano, & Shuen, 1997) make it evident that an eclectic perspective is required that integrates both theoretical approaches.

Thus, it is not logical to analyze cost reasons and value reasons separately, because the formation of the network may be due to the combined effects of both factors. For example, cost reasons may cancel out value reasons if the value achieved by the network does not compensate the costs incurred; or equally, the cost savings may be less than the added value provided by the other forms of governance (hierarchy or market). The network would not be formed even though it adds value in the first case and reduces costs in the second.

Hence, in order to justify the formation of a strategic network, the combined effect of cost and value reasons must be analyzed in relation to the market option as well as to the option of vertical integration.

Jointly taking into account the conditions of value and cost, we can say that opting for joining a network is advisable, compared to acting freely in the market, when:

$$(V_N - V_M + TC_M) > (TC_N + PC_{N-M})$$

where:

V_N = value obtained when the firm works in the network

V_M = value obtained when the firm undertakes transactions in the market

TC_M = transaction cost incurred when organizing the activity in the market

TC_N = transaction cost incurred when organizing the activity through the network

PC_{N-M} = difference in production costs between the network case and the market case

The network will be formed and maintained if the net value obtained from it, and the transaction costs saved by not operating in the market, are not outweighed by the additional transaction and production costs generated by the network.

Moreover, it will be better for a firm to join the network than to be integrated in an hierarchy (a firm) when the following expression holds:

$$(V_N - V_H) > (TC_N + PC_{N-H})$$

where:

V_N = value obtained when the firm works in the network

V_H = value obtained when the firm works in a hierarchy (as an integrated firm)

TC_N = transaction cost incurred when the activity is organized through the network

PC_{N-H} = difference in production costs between the network case and the hierarchy case

In short, the reasons for forming a network rather than opting for hierarchical governance are that the added value provided by the network is greater than the transaction costs plus the increase in production costs within the network. In reality, the production costs in a network tend to be lower than in an integrated firm, and thus, there are normally reductions in production costs in the network rather than increases.

It can be seen that the transaction costs within the hierarchical form (TC_H) are not considered in the last equation. Although Demsetz (1988) argued that transaction costs are not removed by producing within an integrated firm, due to the firm having to buy inputs from other firms, here we do not consider any TC_H, not because they do not occur, but because they are much lower than the other transaction costs (Tsang, 2000). It is fair to point out that there are occasions in which transaction costs within an hierarchy are greater than the external transaction costs (Eccles & White, 1988). However, this is not common.

The Role of IT in Network Formation

According to the equations proposed above, and from the value perspective, it should be assessed if IT favors the formation of networks, because it can add value to the networks or reduce the value of the hierarchical or market forms. But it seems unlikely that IT could reduce value in hierarchical and market systems of governance. In fact, the reverse is much more likely (for example in the electronic markets based on the Internet that have created new business opportunities in the market system). Thus, our analysis should focus on the role of IT in creating or adding value in networks. Specifically, we will look at the complementary role of IT in networks. This complementarity can be understood as the ability of IT to leverage the value generated by the networks, supporting their operations and helping firms to achieve the objectives that were behind the formation of the network in the first place. This complementarity fits the definitions of Teece (1986), Amit and Shoemaker (1993), and Milgrom and Roberts (1995).

As far as the "transaction cost" variables (TC_M, TC_N) are concerned, we shall study how IT can reduce the transaction costs of the network structure, in view of the fact that increasing the transaction costs in the whole market is not very probable. This increase can occur in exceptional cases in which market intermediation is monopolized and the firms of the market bear high transaction costs due to the abusive use of this monopoly[1], and the high cost of changing suppliers. Although these practices are possible, they are normally only temporary, either because of antimonopoly legal action or because firms try to avoid falling captive (Mata, Fuerst, & Barney, 1995) or because of the search for network externalities (Shapiro & Varian, 1999).

In order to study the role of IT in reducing transaction costs of networks, we shall analyze the role of IT in reducing coordination costs and transaction risks (Clemons & Row, 1992), the aforementioned components of transaction costs in stable inter-organizational relations.

Thus, breaking down the transaction costs of the network into coordination costs and transaction risk ($TC = CC + TR$) in the two expressions above that justified the formation of the network as opposed to the hierarchy or market form, the following expressions are obtained:

$$(V_N - V_M + TC_M) > (CC_N + TR_N + PC_{N-M})$$
$$(V_N - V_H) > (CC_N + TR_N + PC_{N-H})$$

The literature recognizes that IOISs can reduce coordination costs (Child, 1987; Malone, Yates, & Benjamin, 1987; Rockart & Short, 1989), such that information relations can reduce the costs of control and coordination in the network. This allows firms to subcontract without losing efficient control over the operation of the contractual relation (Sanchez, 2001). There has been less said about transaction risks, although some authors have ascribed to IT an influence on these through its effect on information asymmetries, transaction-specific capital investment, and loss of control over information resources made available on the network (Clemons & Row, 1992).

IT can also reduce "production costs" (PC_{N-M}, PC_{N-H}), through the use, for example, of design tools and computer-aided production or engineering (Arjonilla & Medina, 2002). In principle, the reduction in production costs would affect networked structures as much as the other structures. There are occasions, however, where savings in production costs are due to the network, because the firms can concentrate on their core resources and capabilities and join forces with the best firms for externalized activities (McGee, 1999).

The "value" variable may include the benefits accruing from becoming associated with firms with reduced production costs or by lower production costs due to network synergies. In view of the obvious difficulty of untangling the value created in a network from the reductions in the production costs of the network (Demsetz, 1988), we opted not to analyze the production costs independently, and to take these improvements as value added by the network. From this perspective, IT plays a complementary role here too in generating this value.

In the following section, we propose some propositions relating to the question of whether IT can favor the formation and maintenance of networks by adding value, reducing coordination costs, or reducing transaction risks. If this is the case, IT favors the option of working in a network against that of operating in the market or hierarchy system, as shown in the following expressions:

$$(\uparrow V_N - V_M + TC_M) > (\downarrow CC_N + \downarrow TR_N + \downarrow PC_{N-M})$$
$$(\uparrow V_N - V_H) > (\downarrow CC_N + \downarrow TR_N + \downarrow PC_{N-H})$$

Propositions

In coherence with the above reasoning, we propose various propositions on IT's role as an engine for the formation of strategic networks. These propositions will be based on the relations displayed in Figure 1. In this model, IT is seen as improving transaction costs by reducing both coordination costs and transaction risks. Moreover, IT plays a complementary role that allows it to leverage the value created by the strategic network. As we have seen, we consider that the reduction in production costs in networks is equivalent to greater added value.

Whatever the combination of cost and value reasons, the network is a better system of governance than the market or hierarchy systems, if the net benefit with respect to these systems, produced by the variations in value and transaction costs, is positive.

Figure 1: A preliminary theoretical model

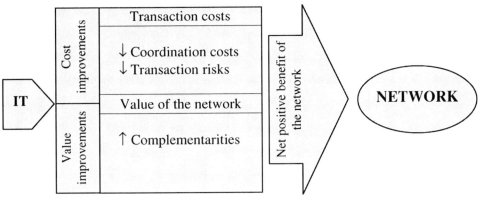

Complementarity

The complementary role of IT is expressed in Proposition 1.

Proposition 1 - IT complements in a contingent way the management of firms that operate within a network.

This first proposition can be broken down into several secondary propositions describing the function of IT in networks in more detail. These propositions analyze the ability of IT, acting as a complementary resource, to increase the value created by the network. This is expressed in Propositions 1.1 and 1.2. Other propositions derived from Proposition 1 show that the support role of IT may be contingent on various circumstances, which leads to four contingent propositions (from 1.3 to 1.6), focusing on the role of the type, geographic distance, physical or information character of the activities, and the compatibility of the IT systems of the distinct members of the network. Our interest in studying this contingent effect lies in that it impacts on the role that IT plays as "lever" of the value generated by the network.

In Proposition 1.1, we extrapolate from the individual firm to the strategic network the support that IT lends to the following functions: the planning (Davis & Olson, 1989; Monforte, 1995; Arjonilla & Medina, 2002), implementation (Porter & Millar, 1986; Arjonilla & Medina, 2002), and control of activities (Davis & Olson, 1989). As Grandori and Soda (1995) pointed out, the processes of planning and control in the individual firm are not very different from those required in strategic networks.

Proposition 1.1 - IT complements the management (planning, implementation, and control) of the activities of firms that operate in networks.

Networks play an important role in the processes of learning and interchange of knowledge between different firms (Kogut, 1988; Hitt et al., 2000; Gulati, Nohria, & Zaheer, 2000). Communication and connectivity support collective behavior, foster the creation of a common knowledge base, and accelerate learning curves (Winch et al., 1997), as well as improve the absorptive capacity (Medina & Ruiz, 1999). IT applications in this area can be used to store knowledge, improve knowledge communication, and identify and contact people with specific knowledge. Therefore, Proposition 1.2 can be expressed in the following synthesized form:

Proposition 1.2 - IT favors the creation of a common knowledge base in networks, and accelerates learning curves.

It is widely recognized in the literature that there are differences in the IT used depending on the organizational activities that it supports (Monforte, 1995; Gil-Pechuan, 1996; Arjonilla & Medina, 2002). Similarly, Porter and Millar (1986) stressed the use of different information technologies for the different activities in the value chain. Proposition 1.3 suggests that the types of activities shared in the network also influence the type and complementarity of IT used.

Proposition 1.3 - The complementarity and type of IT used in strategic networks depend on the types of activities shared.

The geographical distance of the activities in a network makes the coordination of the firms that form it difficult. Under these circumstances, it would be reasonable to expect that the use of IT would be more intensive, because it improves (or makes possible) coordination, control, communication, and working in groups, in spite of distances. In view of this, we put forward Proposition 1.4, which also assesses the possibility that the type of IT used differs according to the distance:

Proposition 1.4 - The intensity and type of IT used in a network depend on the geographical distance separating the firms.

For Porter and Millar (1986), the physical component of activities comprises the physical tasks carried out, and the information component comprises the capture, processing, and transmission of the information required for the activities to be carried out. These authors stress how, in the past, technology had improved only in its support of the physical component. However, they argued that the situation has now changed, in that it is the information component of activities that is now enjoying exponential improvements thanks to the new technologies. This can also be seen in Edwards, Ward, and Bytheway (1997), in their study of the source of benefits accruing from the application of IT to the external value chain. In this sense, we propose Proposition 1.5 that suggests that the intensity and type of the IT used in network activities depend on the physical and information components of these activities.

Proposition 1.5 - The intensity and type of IT used in a strategic network depend on the physical and information components of network activities.

Finally, Proposition 1.6 expresses the importance of the coherence between the information systems of the firms in the network. According to Dyer and Singh (1998), in order for a firm to achieve complementarities with other members of the network, it is necessary for it to develop a certain organizational complementarity. It needs to make sure that the ITs used in the different firms that make up the network are compatible, because IT is fundamental in the systems of control and information.

Proposition 1.6 - Compatibility between the IT systems of the firms in networks improves the benefits of the relation.

Coordination costs

As we saw above, these costs form part of the transaction costs that firms incur when transacting with others (Williamson, 1975, 1985; Clemons & Row, 1992), and the literature recognizes the ability of IOISs to reduce them (Child, 1987; Malone, Yates, & Benjamin, 1987; Rockart & Short, 1989). In this sense, we put forward the following generic proposition:

Proposition 2 - IT reduces coordination costs in strategic networks.

Extending to networks the structural elements of coordination sufficiently well-known in individual organizations (see Mintzberg, 1979; Galbraith, 1973), we can see that coordination of the networks can be based on the following mechanisms: (1) the mutual adaptation between the different members of the network, in which lateral relations play an important role (Winch et al., 1997); (2) the planning and control that standardizes the results obtained; and (3) inter-organizational routines.

IT plays an important role in the application of these mechanisms. Thus, the literature recognizes the function of IT in reducing coordination costs, because it improves coordination, control, communication, and working in groups (Rockart & Short, 1989; Clemons & Row, 1992; Kumar & van Dissel, 1996), allowing for faster communication in decision making involving liaison staff and in overcoming problems of distance or time. IT has also been shown to support planning (Davis & Olson, 1989; Monforte, 1995), facilitating the gathering of internal and external information for complex calculations, simulations, and models (Arjonilla & Medina, 2002). Moreover, IT also helps in the communication of the agreed plan to the agents affected. With regard to its support role in control, IT is used for producing normal and ad hoc reports (Davis & Olson, 1989); for combining or breaking down variables of interest, in spite of the distance between points being controlled; for calculating more complex control indicators; and for quickly finding deviations and their causes (Arjonilla & Medina, 2002). In this way, there is more efficient detection and solution of problems. Moreover, occasionally the need for explicit control is relaxed due to organizational routines (Nelson & Winter, 1982), or in this case, inter-organizational routines. The critical resources of firms can cross over company limits and become incorporated into inter-organizational routines and processes (Dyer & Singh, 1998). IT can also become incorporated into these routines and can, in fact, improve them. This reasoning leads us to break down Proposition 2 into the following secondary propositions:

Proposition 2.1 - IT reduces coordination costs by fostering mutual adaptation and lateral relations between firms coordinating their activities in the network.

Proposition 2.2 - IT reduces coordination costs in networks by improving the planning of shared or related activities.

Proposition 2.3 - IT reduces coordination costs in networks by improving the control of shared or related activities.

Proposition 2.4 - IT reduces coordination costs by supporting inter-organizational routines.

It can be seen that Propositions 2.2 and 2.3 are similar to Proposition 1.1, relative to IT complementarity. This is, in fact, no accident. Many of the functions carried out using IT have a dual effect in improving value in the network and reducing coordination costs. As we saw above, it is difficult to separate the variables of cost and value (Demsetz, 1988).

Transaction Risks

Even if IT reduces coordination costs between firms, this does not immediately lead firms to opt for the network form of governance if this would lead to an increase in the probability of opportunistic behavior, where members of the network are exploited within the relation. As is expressed in Proposition 3, the question of whether IT reduces transaction risks (or at least does not increase them) must be addressed:

Proposition 3 - IT reduces transaction risks in strategic networks.

Authors have identified three possible sources of risk in transactions: (1) transaction-specific capital investment that has little value outside the relation (Williamson, 1975; Klein, Crawford, & Alchian, 1978; Milgrom & Roberts, 1993); (2) information asymmetries that prevent the control of the behavior of the network members (Clemons & Row, 1992); and (3) the loss of control over resources placed at the disposal of the relation, fundamentally information, which is used by firms in competition with the original owner (Williamson, 1991; Loebecke, Fenema, & Powell, 1999; Tsang, 2000). Thus, testing this proposition requires us to analyze the impact of IT on transaction-specific capital investment, on information asymmetries, and on the possibility of losing control over shared resources.

Regarding transaction-specific capital investments, it is significant that firms are increasingly tending to use standard IT for coordination between firms (Zenger & Hesterly, 1997), technologies that are still useful if a member wishes to leave the network, and that allow firms to benefit from the externalities they provide. Porter (1990) confirmed that every specialized resource loses specialization in time. The more the standard technologies develop, the less investment in transaction-specific IT will be made, and the easier it will be to establish new relations with suppliers and customers (Sanchez, 2001). Thus, as is reflected in Proposition 3.1, standard IT discourages opportunistic behavior. Complementary to this proposition, Proposition 3.2 suggests that some firms may avoid belonging to networks that require them to invest in transaction-specific IT, due to the fact that this investment increases transaction costs (Cainarca, Columbo, & Mariotti, 1993; Zenger & Hesterly, 1997).

Proposition 3.1 - Standard IT reduces the transaction risks in networks caused by transaction-specific capital investment, and so encourages network formation.

Proposition 3.2 - Costly and transaction-specific capital investment in IT hinders participation in networks by increasing transaction risks.

With regard to the second source of transaction risk, IT can expose member behavior, reducing information asymmetries and thereby reducing opportunistic behavior. All this will lead to a reduction in transaction risks (Rockart & Short, 1989; Kumar & van Dissel, 1996). As is reflected in Proposition 3.3, this information transparency allows firms to control the behavior of the other members, which will lead to increasing confidence that no firm will attempt to exploit the others in the network, and that the benefits of operating in the network will be shared equitably. The relation will thereby have more chance of being long lasting.

Proposition 3.3 - IT reduces the transaction risks in networks deriving from information asymmetries.

Nevertheless, IT may increase transaction risks by making it easier for firms to lose control of resources placed at the disposal of the network, fundamentally those resources based on information and know-how (Clemons & Row, 1992). The problem of loss of control over resources, when, for example, one of the network members attempts to learn more from another than was initially agreed (Tsang, 2000), is exacerbated by easy access to information stored electronically. It is a problem that can be ameliorated, in part, by greater control of, or, what amounts to the same thing, by reducing information asymmetries (see Proposition 3.3). In this sense, it is necessary to express this in a proposition:

Proposition 3.4 - IT increases the transaction risk that derives from the possibility of firms losing control of resources.

As we have seen, IT may have a dual effect in terms of transaction risks, because it can both reduce these risks (Propositions 3.1 and 3.3) and increase them (Propositions 3.2 and 3.4). This paradox requires a more detailed analysis, which we shall develop in the following sections.

A Case Study Analysis

We shall now analyze a case in a first approximation at empirically testing the theoretical propositions above. We have opted for the method of the case study. This method is appropriate for answering "how" and "why" questions (Yin, 1984), and the central questions of this chapter are "how" and "why" IT influences in network formation. Moreover, when the expected results are not tangible (for example, obtaining knowledge from another member of the network, or gaining from its reputation), it is clear that we have to develop a qualitative study (Rouse & Daellenbach, 1999). The relations between firms are so complex and abstruse that qualitative methods must be used in order to understand the key concepts and their interrelations (Parkhe, 1993).

The option of the case study is also recommended by Eisenhardt (1989), Bonache (1999), and Lee (1999), who pointed out that this method is appropriate for creating and exploring new theoretical frameworks. In this sense, Borch and Arthur (1995) argued that generating new theory in complex and dynamic systems, such as networks, requires a methodology that contributes to increasing the contextual analysis. These authors recommend the case study method in particular for researching strategic networks.

According to Bonache (1999), the case study methodology for explanatory studies (1) does not separate the phenomenon from its context (Yin, 1984); (2) is based on a preliminary theoretical model, and has the objective of building theory and obtaining a more complete explanatory model; (3) chooses the cases for reasons of theory rather than for statistical representativity; (4) looks for objectivity via triangulation (Yin, 1984), with more sources of evidence than quantitative studies; (5) allows the researcher to be more flexible in the research process (Stoecker, 1991), which is useful in the process of constructing and refining the theory (Sutton, 1997); and (6) leads to theoretical deductions from the fieldwork using analytical induction, rather than using statistical generalizations for a population. In this chapter, we do not aim for a statistical generalization, rather we attempt to generalize the theory, that is, we want an analytical generalization (Yin, 1984).

The Case

We shall analyze the strategic network to which Intec-Air, a firm in Cadiz (southern Spain), belongs. This firm, trading since 1988, belongs to the aeronautical sector, manufacturing various parts of the fuselage of planes and helicopters, both commercial and military. Its principal market is in Europe. At present, the firm works for the main aeronautical manufacturers in the world (Airbus, Boeing, and EADS, among others). The sector chosen is appropriate, because its manufacturing and marketing processes involve a very large number of firms. Moreover, the technical complexity of aircraft assembly means that the firms interact intensely among themselves, a situation that favors the creation of strategic networks and the use of IT.

Sources of Evidence

We used four sources of evidence in this research: as a secondary source of information, the analysis of documentation; and as primary sources of information, observation, questionnaires, and semistructured interviews. The use of diverse sources of evidence allows us to triangulate the data and improve the internal validity of the study (Yin, 1984).

Questionnaires and interviews were carried out with all management staff that had responsibilities or knowledge concerning the inter-organizational relationships of the firm or the use of IT in these. The validation of the questionnaire and of the script followed in the semistructured interviews made it necessary to undertake a pilot case study in another firm[2] and to consult with a panel of experts.

The questionnaires calculated the degree of agreement (measured using a 5-point Likert scale), with various assertions relating to the propositions we proposed earlier. The transcripts of the interviews were tabulated using the technique of template analysis (King, 1998; Crabtree & Miller, 1992).

Analyses

We now test the three generic propositions that we outlined above, through their derivatives, against the evidence that we collected.

Complementary Role of IT

Although the survey provides moderate scores with regard to the support role of IT in the implementation and control of activities, the support of IT in planning is recognized to a greater extent. However, the interviews make it clear that managers agree that IT helps them not only in planning their network activities, but also in the control of member behavior. The recognition of managers is even greater in terms of IT's contribution when carrying out activities, specifically in receiving manufacturing orders from customers, sending designs and production specifications, sending the finished products, and subsequent invoicing and payment. In conclusion, the evidence confirms the role of IT in the planning, implementation, and control of activities of interest to strategic networks. Thus, Proposition 1.1 holds.

Proposition 1.2 also holds after observing the high scores given to IT regarding its role in storing knowledge useful to the network, as well as in providing tools for sharing knowledge useful for network activities, or identifying and contacting people on the network who possess knowledge useful for network activities.

The interviews with managers of Intec-Air demonstrate that they identify these knowledge bases in the files stored in their own system as well as those accessible by FTP in the systems of their customers. The systems allow them to graphically manipulate the products they are manufacturing, find out their specifications, and establish the processes to implement and the manufacturing sequences. The content of these knowledge bases not only includes information provided by the customers but has been extended by Intec-Air by the practical experience of processing earlier orders. This has allowed managers to adapt graphical designs in 3D to their manufacturing processes and to design their own manufacturing sequences.

In regard to the use of IT for sharing knowledge and identifying and contacting people, the company staff members mostly use technologies as basic as the telephone or fax, or at most electronic mail.

Referring to Proposition 1.3, the survey does not place much importance on the fact that the IT applied in different activities may differ. However, the interviews and observation made it clear that the type of IT was contingent on the types of activities. Thus, for example, CAD and CAM tools were used in engineering and production, respectively, while managers managed the invoicing processes using a computerized control of order receipts, electronic funds transfer, and online bank consultation. Moreover, it was recognized that IT was more useful in some activities than in others. In short, Proposition 1.3 also holds.

In the survey, the managers of Intec-Air had the opinion that IT was used more in the case of firms that were geographically distant. They also agreed that the type of IT used was not the same in function of the geographical location of the firms. However, the interviews and observation contradicted this. In contrast to the result of the survey, the diversity of IT used did not appear to bear any relation to distance between firms. For example, relations with all of the customer firms were established through some system, more or less sophisticated, for dealing with orders. Production specifications and graphic design files in standard CAD format were usually sent via e-mail and FTP; and the use of the telephone and fax was common whatever the geographical location of the firm. On the other hand, the nearest firms frequently sent staff physically to the Intec-Air factory with their orders, and problems were often resolved by personal contacts, thus reducing the intensity of IT use in these cases compared to more distant firms, according to survey results. All this partially supports Proposition 1.4, because the geographical distance is not contingent in terms of IT type, but it is in terms of the intensity of use of IT.

The moderate scoring in the survey relating to the question of whether IT was similar in type or intensity when it is used to support the information or physical component of the activities does not allow us to affirm this point, and the reverse cannot be proved. However, the interviews are clearer on this point: the managers claimed to use IT more intensively, as well as different ITs, for information purposes than for directly carrying out their manufacturing. This phenomenon is perhaps related to the system of production organized in workshops characteristic of Intec-Air. This is necessary due to the diverse nature of the production of the firm, and the subsequently small batches, a situation that does not allow for automatic production. Whatever the reason, this shows that the type and intensity of IT use depend on the information and physical component of the activities, which supports Proposition 1.5.

The managers of Intec-Air agree clearly that if the IT systems used by different firms are compatible, this improves their collaboration with the other firms. It is of note that the company is continually striving to adapt its systems to sectorial standards and to those of its customers with a view to achieving better compatibility with the systems of the firms in its network. Proposition 1.6 therefore clearly holds.

In short, the interviews with managers, along with the evidence from observation and documentation, prove that Proposition 1 holds.

In this sense, the complementary role of IT in the planning, implementation, and control of the activities within the network is clearly proved (Proposition 1.1). Equally proven is that IT fosters knowledge and learning within the network (Proposition 1.2). Moreover, it is believed that this complementarity is contingent on the types of activities shared (Proposition 1.3), on the physical or information component (Proposition 1.5), and on the compatibility between the systems of the firms in the network (Proposition 1.6). However, the belief that the type of IT used is contingent on the geographical distance of the firms (Proposition 1.4) only partially holds. In this sense, although it seems that IT is used more intensely with distance, it also seems that the type of IT used does not depend on that variable.

Improvements in Coordination Costs through IT

In the surveys, the Intec-Air managers do not agree strongly that IT improves mutual adaptation; they stress in the interviews the importance of direct contacts and personal visits in resolving problems. However, they are more convinced that IT can form routines of work and communication that support the work of inter-organizational lateral relations, thereby improving coordination in the network. This means that Proposition 2.1 partially holds.

The survey accepted that IT helps in the planning of shared or interrelated activities in the network, as well as that the planning was useful in reducing any unexpected behavior by network members. Thus, the role of IT in the planning and the role of planning in the coordination of the total network behavior are shown. In this sense, the interviews agreed that the information provided by IT allows managers to plan their behaviors in advance with a view to coordinating their compliance with their roles within the network structure. Thus, Proposition 2.2 holds.

Although in the survey managers scored moderately the support that IT gives to the control of the operation by network members, in the interviews, it was clearly shown that this support is significant. Managers commented that the installation of IT equipment, standard as well as specific, allowed their main customers to observe the development of their orders and to find out at what stage of manufacture their orders were. It was also noted that IT allows managers to estimate the probability of hitting delivery deadlines by allowing access to the warehouses of other firms, helps to check that customers have received their orders properly and if they have been invoiced, and facilitates error detection in the invoicing process. This leads us to support Proposition 2.3.

The managers of Intec-Air surveyed confirmed that IT supported inter-organizational routines, and that it even formed part of them. This was corroborated in the interviews, in which managers detailed how IT formed part of routines in dealing with orders, sending orders and manufacturing specifications, and announcing delivery of the finished batches. Thus, Proposition 2.4 holds.

Proposition 2 attempts to prove that IT reduces the coordination costs of the firms in networks. This has been proved by the support IT provides to the lateral relations (Proposition 2.1), planning (Proposition 2.2), control (Proposition 2.3), and inter-organizational routines (Proposition 2.4). But we cannot prove that IT facilitates mutual adaptation (Proposition 2.1), a means of coordination that seems to be limited to informal personal contacts. Despite this, the evidence is sufficient to support Proposition 2.

Reduction in Transaction Risks through IT

The survey does not support the view that standard IT is preferable to specific (made-to-measure) IT in forging new relations, or that standard IT is growing in contrast to specific IT. The view that once a firm possesses standard IT that working with other firms will be encouraged is only partially held.

Managers made it clear in the interviews that they preferred to use standard IT in their relations. However, this desire, and the reduction in transaction risks arising from standard IT use, do not appear to provide a sufficient condition to establish new relations or to reject relations that require specific IT, without considering first how valuable the relationship is.

Furthermore, in the interviews, it became clear that the large variety of standards (for EDI applications, systems of production management, CAD applications, etc.), with none being particularly predominant, makes it equally necessary to invest in new IT for each new relation. This IT will often not be of use for the subsequent relation. Thus, investment in standard IT may also increase transaction risks for the simple reason that it is expensive. This evidence clearly means that Proposition 3.1 does not hold.

With regard to Proposition 3.2, the responses to the survey do not appear to prove that specific investment increases transaction risk and thereby discourages a firm from joining a network. The interviews also provided evidence in the same line. Managers argued that they assessed any investment in specific IT in function of the value provided by the new relation. It did not matter whether the IT was standard or specific, but that the investment was necessary to be able to compete. In short, Proposition 3.2 does not hold.

The evidence allows us to support Proposition 3.3. Although the survey scored poorly the ability of IT to supervise the behavior of the other firms, the interviews made it clear that IT facilitates such control. In this way, IT leads to a reduction in transaction risks that derive from information asymmetries. Managers stressed that IT allowed them to check that goods had been received by the customers, that these were paid, and whether there had been any mistake in the invoice.

The evidence concerning the influence of IT in the loss of control of resources (Proposition 3.4) is contradictory. Managers recognized in the survey that IT makes it easier for business practice and knowledge to leak, thereby increasing the risk that the information ceded is misused. Nevertheless, the interviews point in another direction. Although managers did not deny that IT facilitates the loss of control of resources, they argued that the risk did not increase transaction risks because of contractual safeguards, which are common and sufficient to dissuade other firms from opportunistic behaviors. Therefore, Proposition 3.4 does not hold. This is positive for the generic Proposition 3 in terms of the reduction, and not increase, in transaction risks.

The propositions we analyzed lead us to partially support Proposition 3. Specifically, we observe that the potential reduction in transaction risks that may arise from investment in standard IT (Proposition 3.1), or the increase in the case of investment in specific IT (Proposition 3.2), are not determinant in the participation of the firm in the relation. It is more important for the firm to forge valuable, new relations whatever the IT required. In terms of the ability of IT to reduce information asymmetries (Proposition 3.3), the balance is more positive, thereby leading to a reduction in the transaction costs. Moreover, the threat that IT increases these risks by facilitating the loss of control of information resources (Proposition 3.4) is limited by contractual safeguards. In short, we can conclude that IT reduces transaction risks through its role in information asymmetries and that it does not particularly influence in the case of specific investment or threat of loss of control of resources.

Catalyzing and Moderating Variables

Throughout our analysis of the propositions in the case we presented, diverse variables that were not initially considered came to the fore and proved to be catalysts of value creation (Proposition 1) and coordination costs (Proposition 2), or moderators of transaction risk (Proposition 3). These variables were related to long-term relations, the importance of reputation, investment among members of the network, contracts, the value of the relation, and the firm's position in the network.

With regard to the establishment of long-term relations, it became clear that the complementarity of IT when it supports inter-organizational relations is greater when these relations are stable. When the relations are long lasting, information systems are established that allow the firms to concentrate on the activities central to the relation and not worry about the details of the communication process. Equally, the role of IT in improving coordination costs is more important in long-term relations, because the development of mutual understanding takes a long time. Finally, long-term relations influence the third generic proposition. Here we observed the reduction in transaction risks (incurred when a firm invests in specific IT or by the threat of losing control of information resources), when it was certain that the relation being forged would be long term—a relation in which trust is developed, which will continue into the future, and which is valuable and worth investing in. When the relation with other firms was only to be temporary, the firm did not make costly investments in transaction-specific IT, resorting to more rudimentary technologies or using the services of subcontracted technologies.

The managers of Intec-Air also highlighted that the good reputation of the firm with which a relation is desired favors the investment in specific IT without increasing transaction risks (or at least the managers' perception of the probability of opportunistic behavior). On the other hand, operations were frequently rejected because of the poor reputation of the other firm (in terms of compliance with deadlines, planning capability, confidence that it would complete the project, etc.). Managers also mentioned firms that express interest in products simply to find out what the costs will be and how the company works. The response to this interest is not as open as it is to firms that have solid reputations.

With regard to investment among network members, the managers believed that trust increases, thereby reducing transaction risks, if the other firms invest in specific IT in order to work with Intec-Air, or if these firms finance transaction-specific IT investment in these technologies in Intec-Air installations.

We expected that the ability to transfer information easily and quickly, and occasionally anonymously, would increase the probability of a loss of control of information sensitive to the firm, thereby increasing transaction risks (see Clemons & Row, 1992). However, the case we studied shows that although managers are aware of this risk, there are contractual and legal safeguards thought to be sufficient to dispel it. Thus, another variable appeared that catalyzed transaction risk: contracts.

As we observed earlier in our analysis of Proposition 3.2, investment in specific IT, that in theory would increase transaction risks, was, in fact, encouraged by the opportunity to forge a valuable relation with other firms. The value of the relation is, therefore, another factor that is a catalyst of transaction risk. This does not mean that managers do not recognize that standard IT would allow them to relate to other firms more easily and in greater number. But although desirable in that respect, whether the IT was standard or specific was secondary in decision making on IT investment.

Finally, a position of power within the strategic network was also a determinant in the transaction risk of IT investment. This position allows a firm to promote standard IT (or specific IT that it already possesses) within its network, in order to avoid transaction risks.

In short, although we expected that investment in transaction-specific IT and the threat of a loss of control of resources would increase transaction risks, the evidence is against this. The paradox thrown up in the development of Proposition 3 has not therefore been fulfilled. This analysis permits us to conclude that IT reduces transaction risks, and that Proposition 3 holds when these moderating variables are present.

Conclusions

As can be seen in Figure 2, there has been an evolution from the initial propositions to a preliminary theoretical model, which was developed from a theoretical generalization of the results obtained from the case under study. This model still recognizes the ability of IT to leverage the value of operating in a network, that is, its complementary role, supporting the management in the network (planning, implementation, and control of network activities) and knowledge management. It also identifies the contingent factors that determine when technologies can provide more, and when less, to these networks. These contingent factors coincide with those that appear in the initial propositions, except that geographical distance is considered contingent now only with the intensity to which IT is used, and not with the type of IT used. The long-term relations, moreover, help to improve the synergies of the complementary resources and capabilities of the network firms. These resources and capabilities include IT and the ability to use it appropriately.

With regard to coordination costs, as can be seen in Figure 2, the support that IT provides to lateral relations, planning, control, and inter-organizational routines, as well as the catalyzing role of long-term stable relations, led to reductions in coordination costs. However, the expected support for mutual adaptation disappears from this model, considering that it is a coordination mechanism that to a large extent requires the personal contact that IT cannot provide.

The contribution of IT to the reduction of transaction risks is fundamentally based on the reduction of information asymmetries, because investment in standard IT

Figure 2: The role of IT in the formation of networks

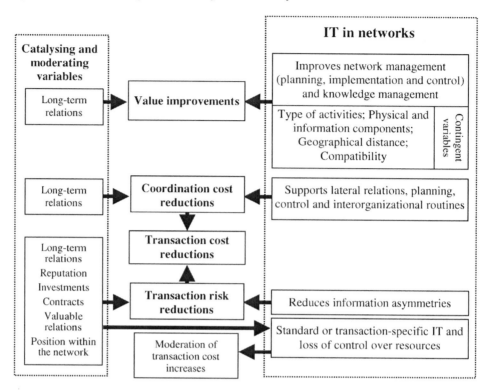

does not appear to have the expected risk-reducing effect. On the other hand, specific IT and the probability of loss of control of information resources do not increase the transaction risk as was thought. This is due to the intervention of various moderating variables, such as the value provided by the relation and the position of power in the network, in the first case, and contractual safeguards in the second. In short, the paradox that was threatened in the initial propositions does not occur.

In addition to these new variables—the value of the relation, the position in the network, and the contracts—we also detected the long-term relations based on mutual confidence, the reputation for behaving fairly in relations, and specific investment among firms in the network.

This work has some limitations, which may be due to the study's qualitative nature. Thus, with regard to the fieldwork, it is inevitable that the facts observed in an external reality are reflected from the researchers' perspective (Rorty, 1979). This disadvantage has been methodically combated as far as was possible (through the use of triangulation of the sources of evidence and by comparing the results with the opinions of the managers involved), in order to obtain the truest reflection of reality, that is, internal validity. However, and although this may not be much consolation, problems of subjectivity are not exclusive to qualitative methods but also affect quantitative methods (Bonache, 1999).

We might mention some future research directions. It would be interesting to find alternative or complementary explanations to those given here by using other theoretical frameworks. For example, Population Ecology (Aldrich & Pfeffer, 1976; Hannan & Freeman, 1977; Aldrich, 1979) could analyze if the network structure, and the use of IT in it, has allowed firms to survive. The Resource Dependence Theory (Pfeffer & Salancik, 1978) could study if IT is useful in controlling network members. Institutional Theory (Meyer & Rowan, 1977; DiMaggio & Powell, 1983; Powell & DiMaggio 1991) may be able to explain the imitation of networks as a form of governance, and the use of IT in this, in a firm's search for institutional legitimacy. Finally, the sociological perspective may help us to understand the social complexity behind some inter-organizational networks (Boisot, 1986; Hamilton, Zeile, & Kim, 1990). Clearly, a more multidisciplinary treatment would have improved the analysis presented in this chapter, but it would hardly have been feasible, because combining too many approaches would have vastly increased its complexity.

Finally, the model presented here will be useful for analyzing stable strategic networks. But this model could also be extended to include dynamic networks: those in which firms work together for a specific project or product and then separate at the end to form new networks, subsequently. Some authors call this type of network *virtual corporation* (see, for example, Nagel & Dove, 1991). Such structures require the firm to possess capabilities of collecting information and looking for new firms with which to transact, negotiating with them and building in safeguards or guarantees of some kind (all these generators of transaction costs that were not considered for stable networks), as well as the capabilities to coordinate and manage the network. The model presented in this work would be affected by the particular characteristics of dynamic relations, and IT would also be a key factor.

References

Aldrich, H. (1979). *Organization and environment.* Englewood Cliffs, NJ: Prentice Hall.

Aldrich, H. E., & Pfeffer, J. (1976). Environment of organizations. *Annual Review of Sociology, 2,* 79–105.

Amit, R., & Schoemaker, P. (1993). Strategic assets and organizational rent. *Strategic Management Journal, 14,* 33–46.

Arjonilla-Dominguez, S. J., & Medina-Garrido, J. A. (2002). *La gestion de los sistemas de informacion en la empresa.* Madrid: Ediciones Piramide.

Arndt, J. (1979). Towards a concept of domesticated markets. *Journal of Marketing, 43*(4), 69–75.

Baden-Fuller, C., & Volberda, H. (1996). Strategic renewal in large complex organisations: A competence based view. Working paper, *16th Strategic Management Society Annual Conference,* November, Phoenix, AZ.

Baden-Fuller, C., & Volberda, H. (1997). Dormant capabilities, complex organizations and renewal. Working paper, *American Academy of Management,* Boston, MA.

Baden-Fuller, C. W., & Stopford, J. M. (1994). *Rejuvenating the mature business* (2nd ed.). Londres: Routledge.

Boisot, M. H. (1986). Markets and hierarchies in a cultural perspective. *Organization Studies, 7*(2), 135–158.

Bonache, J. (1999). El estudio de casos como estrategia de construccion teorica: caracteristicas, criticas y defensas. *Cuadernos de Economia y Direccion de Empresas, 3*(enero–junio), 123–140.

Borch, O. J., & Arthur, M. B. (1995). Strategic networks among small firms: Implications for strategy research methodology. *Journal of Management Studies, 32*(July), 419–441.

Cainarca, G. C., Columbo, M. G., & Mariotti, S. (1993). Computer-based automation and the governance of vertical transactions. *Industrial and Corporate Change, 2,* 73–90.

Cash, J. I., & Konsynski, B. R. (1985). IS redraws competitive boundaries. *Harvard Business Review, 63*(2), 134–142.

Child, J. (1987). Information technology, organization and the response to strategic challenges. *California Management Review,* (Fall), 33–49.

Clemons, E. K., & Row, M. C. (1992). Information technology and industrial cooperation: The changing economics of coordination and ownership. *Journal of Management Information Systems, 9*(2), 9–28.

Conner, K. R. (1991). A historical comparison of resource-based theory and five schools of thought within industrial organization economics: Do we have a new theory of the firm? *Journal of Management, 17*(1), 121–154.

Contractor, F. J., & Lorange P. (1988). *Cooperative strategies in international business.* Lexington: Lexington Books.

Crabtree, B. F., & Miller, W. L. (1992). A template approach to text analysis: Developing and using codebooks. In B. F. Crabtree, & W. L. Miller (Eds.), *Doing qualitative research.* Newbury Park, CA: SAGE Publications.

Davis, G. B., & Olson, M. H. (1989). *Sistemas de informacion gerencial.* Mexico: McGraw-Hill.

Demsetz, H. (1988). The theory of the firm revisited. *Journal of Law, Economics, and Organization, 4*(1), 141–161.

Dimaggio, P. J., & Powell, W. W. (1983). The Iron cage revisited: Institutional isomorphism and collective rationality in organizational fields. *American Sociological Review, 48,* 147–160.

Dyer, J. H., & Singh, H. (1998). The relational view: Cooperative strategy and sources of interorganizational competitive advantage. *Academy of Management Review, 23*(4), 660–679.

Eccles, R. G., & White, H. C. (1988). Price and authority in inter-profit center transactions. *American Journal of Sociology, 94*(Supplement), S17–S51.

Edwards, C., Ward, J., & Bytheway, A. (1997). *Fundamentos de sistemas de informacion.* Spain: Prentice-Hall.

Eisenhardt, K. M. (1989). Building theories from case study research. *Academy of Management Review, 14*(4), 532–550.

Eisenhardt, K. M. (1996). Resource-based view of strategic alliance formation: Strategic and social effects in entrepreneurial firms. *Organization Science,7*(2), 136–150.

Eisenhardt, K. M., & Martin, J. A. (2000). Dynamic capabilities: What are they? *Strategic Management Journal, 21*(10–11), 1105–1121.

Fiol, M. (2001). Revisiting an identity-based view of sustainable competitive advantage. *Journal of Management, 6,* 691–699.

Galbraith, J. (1973). *Designing complex organizations.* Reading, MA: Addison-Wesley.

Garud, R., & Nayyar, P. R. (1994). Transformative capacity: Continual structuring by intertemporal technology transfer. *Strategic Management Journal, 15,* 365–385.

Gerybadze, A. (1995). *Strategic alliance and process edesign.* Berlin; New York: Walter de Gruyter Press.

Gil-Pechuan, I. (1996). *Sistemas y tecnologias de la informacion para la gestion.* Madrid: McGraw-Hill.

Grandori, A., & Soda, G. (1995). Inter-firm network: Antecedents, mechanisms and forms. *Organization Studies, 16*(2), 183–214.

Gulati, R. (1995). Social structures an alliance formation patterns: A longitudinal analysis. *Administrative Science Quarterly, 40,* 619–652.

Gulati, R., Nohria, N., & Zaheer, A. (2000). Strategic networks. *Strategic Management Journal, 21*, 203–215.

Hamel, G. (1991). Competition for competence and inter-partner learning within international strategic alliances. *Strategic Management Journal, 12*(Winter Special Issue), 83–104.

Hamel, G., Doz, Y., & Prahalad, C. (1989). Collaborate with your competitors and win. *Harvard Business Review, 67*, 133–139.

Hamilton, G., Zeile, W., & Kim, W. J. (1990). The network structure of East Asian economies. In S. R. Clegg, & G. Redding (Eds.), *Capitalism in contrasting cultures* (pp. 105–129). Berlin: De Gruyter.

Hannan, M. T., & Freeman, J. (1977). The population ecology of organizations. *American Journal of Sociology, 83*, 929–964.

Harrison, Hitt, M., Hoskinsson, R. E., & Ireland, D. (2001). Resource complementarity in business combinations: Extending the logic to organizational alliances. *Journal of Management, 6*.

Hennart, J. F. (1988). A transaction costs theory of equity joint ventures. *Strategic Management Journal, 9*(4), 361–374.

Hitt, M. A., Dancin, M. T., Levitas, E., Arregle, J. L., & Borza, A. (2000). Partner selection in emerging and developed market contexts: Resource-based and organizational learning perspectives. *Academy of Management Journal, 43*, 449–467.

Ireland, R. D., Hitt, M. A., Camp, S. M., & Sexton, D. L. (2001). Integrating entrepreneurship and strategic management actions to create firm wealth. *Academy of Management Executive, 15*(1), 49–63.

Jarillo, J. C. (1988). On strategic networks. *Strategic Management Journal, 9*, 31–41.

Jarillo, J. C. (1993). *Strategic networks: Creating the borderless organization*. Great Britain: Butterworth-Heinemann.

King, N. (1998). Template analysis. In G. Symon, & C. Cassel (Eds.), *Qualitative methods and analysis in organizational research* (pp. 118–134). London: SAGE Publications.

Klein, B., Crawford, R. G., & Alchian, A. A. (1978). Vertical integration, appropriable rents, and the competitive contracting process. *Journal of Law and Economics, 21*(2), 297–326.

Kogut, B. (1988). Joint ventures: Theoretical and empirical perspectives. *Strategic Management Journal, 9*(4), 319–332.

Konsynski, B. R. (1993). Strategic control in the extended enterprise. *IBM Systems Journal, 32*(1), 111–142.

Kumar, K., & van Dissel, H. G. (1996). Sustainable collaboration: Managing conflict and cooperation in interorganizational systems. *MIS Quarterly,* (September), 279–300.

Lee, T. (1999). *Using qualitative methods in organizational research.* Thousand Oaks, CA: SAGE Publications.

Loebecke, C., Van Fenema, P. C., & Powell, P. (1999). Co-operation and knowledge transfer. *Database for Advances in Information Systems, 30*(2), 14–25.

Malone, T. W., Yates, J., & Benjamin, R. I. (1987). Electronic markets and electronic hierarchies. *Communications of the ACM, 30*(6), 484–497.

Mata, F. J., Fuerst, W. L., & Barney, J. B. (1995). Information technology and sustained competitive advantage: A resource-based analysis. *MIS Quarterly, 19*(4), 487–506.

McGee, J. (1999). Knowledge dynamics and corporate restructuring: Deconstructionism as a new paradigm? *2nd International Workshop on Organization of the Future in the "Information Society": Managing Change, Human Resources and Structure*, Cadiz, Spain.

Medina-Garrido, J. A., & Ruiz-Navarro, J. (1999). Information system and information technology as a source of dynamic capabilities. *4th International Conference on the Dynamics of Strategy.* 22–23 April 1999, University of Surrey, UK.

Meyer, J. W., & Rowan, B. (1977). Institutionalized organizations: Formal structure as myth and ceremony. *American Journal of Sociology, 83,* 340–363.

Milgrom, P., & Roberts, J. (1993). *Economia, organizacion y gestion de la empresa.* Barcelona: Ariel Economia.

Milgrom, P., & Roberts, J. (1995). Complementarities and fit: Strategy, structure and organizational change in manufacturing. *Journal of Accounting and Economics, 19*(2/3), 179–208.

Mintzberg, H. (1979). *The structuring of organizations.* Englewood Cliffs, NJ: Prentice Hall.

Monforte, M. (1995). *Sistemas de informacion para la direccion.* Madrid: Ediciones Piramide.

Nagel, R., & Dove, R. (1991). *21st Century manufacturing enterprise strategy.* Lehigh: Iacocca Institute of Lehigh University.

Nelson, R. R., & Winter, S. G. (1982). *An evolutionary theory of economic change.* Cambridge, MA: Harvard University Press.

Oliver, C. (1997). Sustainable competitive advantage: Combining institutional and resource-based view. *Strategic Management Journal, 18,* 697–714.

Parkhe, A. (1993). Messy research, methodological predispositions, and theory development in international joint ventures. *Academy of Management Review, 18*(2), 227–268.

Pfeffer, J., & Salancik, G. R. (1978). *The external control of organizations: A resource dependence perspective.* New York: Harper & Row.

Poppo, L., & Zenger, T. (1995). Opportunism, routines, and boundary choices: A comparative test of transaction cost and resource-based explanations for make-or-buy decisions. *Academy of Management Journal* (Best Papers Proceedings), 42–46.

Porter, M. E. (1990). *The competitive advantage of nations.* London: The MacMillan Press.

Porter, M. E., & Millar, V. E. (1986). Como obtener ventajas competitivas por medio de la informacion. *Harvard Deusto Business Review, 25,* 3–20.

Powell, W. W. (1987). Hybrid organizational arrangements: New forms or transitional development? *California Management Review, 30*(1), 67–87.

Powell, W. W. (1990). Neither market nor hierarchy: Network forms of organization. In B. M. Staw, & L. L. Cummings (Eds.), *Research in organizational behavior,* 12, 295–336. Greenwich, CT: JAI Press.

Powell, W. W., & Dimaggio, P. J. (1991). *The new institutionalism in organizational analysis.* The University of Chicago Press.

Prahalad, C. K., & Hamel, G. (1990). The core competence of the corporation. *Harvard Business Review, 68*(3), 79–91.

Rackoff, N., Wiseman, C., & Ullrich, W. (1985). IS is for competitive advantage: Implementation of a planning process. *MIS Quarterly, 9,* 285–294.

Ring, P. S., & Van de Ven, A. H. (1994). Developmental processes of cooperative interorganizational relationships. *Academy of Management Review, 19*(1), 90–118.

Rockart, J. F., & Short, J. E. (1989). IT in the 1990s: Managing organizational interdependence. *Sloan Management Review,* Winter, 7–17.

Rorty, R. (1979). *Philosophy and the mirror of nature.* Princeton, NJ: Princeton University Press.

Rouse, M. J., & Daellenbach, U. S. (1999). Rethinking research methods for the resource-based perspective: Isolating the sources of sustainable competitive advantage. *Strategic Management Journal, 20,* 487–494.

Rumelt, R. P. (1987). Theory, strategy, and entrepreneurship. In D. J. Teece (Ed.), *The competitive challenge* (pp. 137–158). Cambridge, MA: Ballinger.

Sanchez Fernandez, J. (2001). *Sistemas de informacion en las organizaciones.* Madrid: Ediciones Piramide.

Shapiro, C., & Varian, H. R. (1999). *Information rules: A strategic guide to the network economy.* Boston, MA: Harvard Business School Press.

Sharman, M. P., Gray, B., & Yin, A. (1991). The context of interorganizational collaboration in the garment industry: An institutional perspective. *Journal of Applied Behavioral Science, 27,* 181–208.

Stoecker, R. (1991). Evaluating and rethinking the case study. *Sociological Review,* 88–112.

Sutton, R. I. (1997). The virtues of closet qualitative research. *Organization Science, 8*(1), 97–106.

Teece, D. J. (1986). Profiting from technological innovation: Implications for integration, collaboration, licensing and public policy. *Research Policy, 15,* 285–305.

Teece, D. J. (1987). Profiting from technological innovation: Implications for integration, collaboration, licensing and public policy. In D. J. Teece (Ed.), *The competitive challenge: Strategies for industrial innovation and renewal* (pp. 185–219). Cambridge, MA: Ballinger.

Teece, D. J., Pisano, G., & Shuen, A. (1997). Dynamic capabilities and strategic management. *Strategic Management Journal, 18*(7), 509–533.

Thompson, J. D. (1967). *Organizations in action: Social science bases of administrative theory.* New York: McGraw-Hill.

Tsang, E. W. K. (2000). Transaction cost and resource-based explanations of joint ventures: A comparison and synthesis. *Organization Studies, 21*(1), 215–242.

Van der Heijden, H., Wagenaar, R., Van Nunen, J., & Van den Bosch, F. (1995). Redesigning process control mechanisms using EDI: An agency theoretic perspective. In R. Sprague, & J. Nunamaker (Eds.), Proceedings of the *28th Annual Hawaii International Conference on System Sciences* (pp. 388–397).

Varadarajan, P. R., & Cunningham, M. H. (1995). Entering China: An unconventional approach. *Harvard Business Review,* (March–April), 130–140.

Williamson, O. E. (1975). *Markets and hierarchies: Analysis and antitrust implications.* New York: Free Press.

Williamson, O. E. (1985). *The economic institution of capitalism.* New York: Free Press.

Williamson, O. E. (1989). Transaction cost economics. In R. Schmalensee, & R. D. Willig (Eds.), *Handbook of industrial organization* (pp. 136–182). Amsterdam.

Williamson, O. E. (1991). Comparative economic organization: The analysis of discrete structural alternatives. *Administrative Science Quarterly, 36*, 269–296.

Winch, G., Gyllstrom, H., Sauer, F., & Seror-Märklin, S. (1997). The virtual neural business system: A vision for IT support for network form organization. *Management Decision, 35*(1), 40–48.

Yin, R. K. (1984). *Case study research: Design and methods.* Newbury Park, CA: SAGE Publications.

Zajac, E. J., & Olsen, C. P. (1993). From transaction cost to transactional value analysis: Implications for the study of interorganizational strategies. *Journal of Management Studies, 30*(1), 131–145.

Zenger, T. R., & Hesterly, W. S. (1997). The disaggregation of corporations: Selective intervention, high-powered incentives, and molecular units. *Organization Science, 8*(3), 209–222.

Endnotes

[1]   A well-known case is that of American Airlines, which increased the transaction costs of the airlines that posed a threat to it, increasing their costs or hindering their use of its widely used computer system for reservations, the program SABRE, which connects an airline's electronic ticket sales with travel agencies.

[2]   The firm that took part in the pilot case study belongs to the sector manufacturing high-precision electronic components for cars.

About the Authors

Sean B. Eom is a Professor of Management Information Systems (MIS) and had been appointed as a Copper Dome Faculty Fellow in Research at the Harrison College of Business of Southeast Missouri State University during the academic years 1994–1996 and 1998–2000. He received his PhD in Management Science from the University of Nebraska–Lincoln in 1985. His other degrees are from the University of South Carolina at Columbia (MS in international business), Seoul National University (MBA in International Management), and Korea University (BA). His research areas include decision support systems (DSS), expert systems, and global information systems management. He is the author/editor of five books (published or forthcoming) including *Encyclopedia of Information Systems*, published in 2002 by Academic Press. He has published about 50 refereed journal articles and more than 60 articles in encyclopedia, book chapters, and proceedings of such conferences as International Conference on Information Systems, International Conference on Enterprise Information Systems, DSI Age 2002 (An IFIP TC8/WG 8.3 Open Conference), Decision Science Institutes, International Conference on Information Systems Development and Association for Information Systems.

*   *   *   *   *

Sebastian Bruque-Camara is lecturer of Business Administration on technological firms. He is currently working at the Department of Business Administration, Accounting and Sociology in the University of Jaen (Spain). His main research interests are IT use and competitive advantage, the IT productivity paradox, and the impact of cultural differences on IT management. He has published articles in: *The Journal of High Technology Management Research, Technology Analysis and Strategic Management Journal, Internet Research Journal and Technovation*, and *International Journal of Informa-*

tion Technology. He has been a visiting researcher at the Nijmegen School of Management in The Netherlands.

Janice Burn has had a 30-year career in information systems, and she is currently Foundation Professor and Head of School of Management Information Systems at Edith Cowan University in Perth, Western Australia, and a Director of the We-B research center—Working for e-Business. She previously held senior academic posts in Hong Kong and the United Kingdom with visiting positions in Australia and Canada. She is a member of the Australian Research Council and an adviser to the Australian Government on IT and National Research Priorities. Her research interests relate to information systems strategy and benefits evaluation in virtual organizations, with a particular emphasis on social, political, and cultural challenges in an e-business and e-government environment. She is recognized as an international researcher with over 150 refereed publications in journals and international conferences.

Wendy L. Currie is professor and director of the Centre for Strategic Information Systems (CSIS) at Brunel University. She has recently won three research grants from the EPSRC, ESRC, and EU for studies on e-business models, focusing specifically on application services provisioning, Web services and e-logistics, and supply-chain management. She has wide experience within business and IT strategy, with numerous books and articles within the fields of IS strategy, outsourcing, e-business, and the global software and computing services industry. Her recent books include *The Global Information Society*, *New Strategies in IT Outsourcing in the U.S. and Europe*, and *Rethinking MIS*. She published in the following journals: *OMEGA, BJM, EJIS, JIT, LRP*, and others. She is an associate editor of *MIS-Q* and is on the editorial boards of the *JSIS, JIT*, and *JCM*. A member of the US-AIS and the UK-AIS, she is a visiting fellow at Oxford University and associate faculty at Henley Management College.

Jill Drury is a usability engineer and researcher with an interest in evaluating collaborative computing systems; she is an Associate Department Head in the Collaboration and Multimedia Department of The MITRE Corporation and an Adjunct Assistant Professor in the Computer Science Department of the University of Massachusetts, Lowell.

Bonnie C. Glassberg is currently an assistant professor at Miami University/Ohio. She has a Ph.D. from the University of South Carolina, an MBA from Indiana University, and a B.S. degree from Cornell. As an assistant professor at the University at Buffalo (1997–2001), she taught information systems at the graduate and undergraduate levels. Bonnie has 10 years of industry experience as a senior analyst with a Fortune 100 chemical giant. She has been involved in the planning, design, implementation, and management of major corporate systems. She has served as a reviewer for *JMIS*, *CACM*, and the *Mid-America Journal of Business*.

Marcel Gogolin is a researcher, lecturer, and PhD candidate in the Department of Information Systems at the University of Muenster, Germany, from which he also holds an MSc degree in Information Systems. Mr. Gogolin has participated in various European and national research projects. His research interests include ICT impact on industry structures and inter-organizational arrangements, electronic business, and IOS development.

Matthew W. Guah is a researcher at the Centre of Strategic Information Systems, Brunel University. He is currently investigating how an ASP vertical model can be applied to the United Kingdom's National Health Service, building on previous IT research. He also has a more general interest in the cognitive, material, and social relationships between science, technology, and business as well as their implications for present-day understandings of creativity and innovation. He comes in academia with a wealth of industrial experience, spanning more than 15 years within Merrill Lynch (European HQ), CITI Bank, HSBC, British Airways, British Standards Institute, and the United Nations. His recent journal publications include *International Journal of Healthcare Technology and Management, Issues of Information Systems, Journal of Information Technology Cases and Applications*, and others. He is a member of UKAIS, IAIS, BMiS, BSC, among others.

Ilyoo B. Hong is currently a visiting scholar in the Anderson Graduate School of Management at UCLA, and is also Professor of Management Information Systems at Chung-Ang University in Seoul. He holds a BS in Management from Indiana University, a MS in Management from the University of Illinois, and a Ph.D. in MIS from the University of Arizona. His current research interests include Internet-based inter-organizational systems, Web site evaluation methods, and strategic planning of Web site information systems. He has published in such journals as *Decision Sciences, Information and Management*, and other international scholarly journals. Dr. Hong has recently founded Korea Website Institute to promote research on Web site strategies.

Shashidhar Kaparthi is Associate Professor of Management Information Systems at College of Business Administration, University of Northern Iowa,

Cedar Falls, IA. He received a PhD in Management Systems in 1993 from the State University of New York at Buffalo. His research interests are in decision support ystems, applications of artificial neural networks, and Internet technologies. He is the senior editor of the book titled *Macromedia ColdFusion*. He has several publications in journals such as *Decision Sciences, Journal of Decision Systems, International Journal of Production Research, European Journal of Operational Research, Journal of Intelligent Manufacturing, Computers & Industrial Engineering,* and *Discrete Applied Mathematics*.

Stefan Klein is the John E. Sharkey Professor of Electronic Commerce at the MIS Department, University College Dublin, Ireland, on leave from his position as Director of the Department of IS at the University of Muenster, Germany. He has held teaching or research positions at the Universities of Linz, Austria, Koblenz-Landau, Germany, and St. Gallen, Switzerland, at Harvard University, the German National Research Center for Computer Science (GMD), and the University of Cologne. His research interests include ICT impact on industry structures and inter-organizational arrangements, electronic business strategies, and information management. Dr. Klein has been program committee member or track chair of international IS conferences (ICIS, ECIS, ENTER, Bled International Conference on Electronic Commerce) and is a member of the editorial board of *Die Betriebswirtschaft*, the *Electronic Journal of Organizational Virtualness, EM – Electronic Markets, e-Services Quarterly, International Journal of Electronic Commerce,* and *Information Technology & Tourism*.

Hope Koch is an assistant professor of information systems at the Hankamer School of Business, Baylor University. She received her PhD from Texas A&M University. Hope spent 5 years in industry as a Certified Public Accountant for McLane Company, a Wal-Mart subsidiary. Her primary research interest is critical success factors for business-to-business electronic commerce marketplaces. Her publications are in the *Information Resources Management Journal* and the *Journal of Electronic Commerce Research*.

Choong Kwon Lee is an assistant professor of Information Technology at Georgia Southern University. He received a PhD from the University of Nebraska–Lincoln. He worked as a systems analyst in Korea Aerospace Research Institute. His research interests are in the areas of IT skills, networking, and IT strategy. His articles have appeared in *SAM Advanced Management Journal* and *Management Decision*.

Jose A. Medina-Garrido is lecturer at the University of Cadiz, Spain. His research interests include the enabling role of information systems for strategic networks, and dynamic capabilities development. He was Visiting Fellow at the University of Warwick, has contributed to two books on IT, and published articles in the *International Journal of Information Technology*, the International Conference on the Dynamics of Strategy (University of Surrey), European Academy of Management International Conference, and the AEDEM and ACEDE conferences. He is a member of Regional Entrepreneurship Monitor in Andalusia (Spain), part of the GEM (Global Entrepreneurship Monitor) international project, developed by Babson College and the London Business School.

Athanasios Nikas is a PhD candidate in the Department of Management Science and Technology at the Athens University of Economics and Business. He holds a bachelor's degree from the Department of Financial and Banking Administration at the University of Piraeus (2000) in Greece and an MSc degree in the Analysis, Design and Management of Information Systems obtained at the London School of Economics and Political Science (2001). His research interest is focusing on studying the social and organizational dynamics that underlie recent technological and work developments in networked organizations. He is also a research officer in the Electronic Trading Research Unit (ELTRUN).

Joseph B. O'Donnell is currently an assistant professor at Canisius College. He has a PhD and MBA from the State University of New York at Buffalo and an undergraduate degree from the University of Notre Dame. Dr. O'Donnell, a CPA, has 6 years of experience as a systems consultant and auditor with an international accounting firm. He has publications in the *Journal of Data Warehousing* and *Encyclopedia of Information Systems* and has presented papers at Decision Sciences Institute Conferences and the Americas Conference of Information Systems. His research interests include e-commerce trust, valuing IT, inter-organizational information systems, and continuous financial reporting.

Dimitris Papakiriakopoulos is a Ph.D. candidate in the Department of Management Science and Technology at the Athens University of Economics and Business. He holds a Computer Science degree from the Athens University of Economics and Business (1998) and an MSc degree in Information Systems from the same university (2000). Since 1999, he has been working in the Electronic Trading Research Unit (ELTRUN), and participated in various European and national research projects. His research interest is focusing on management control systems in collaborative business environments, emphasizing the development of nonaccountant methods for monitoring organizational performance.

Federico Pigni graduated cum laude from Università Carlo Cattaneo–LIUC in Business Administration in 1998. Since 1999, he has been working as a research assistant at CETIC, and since 2001, he is lecturer of Multimedia Management at the Catholic University in Milan. He is a PhD student in "MIS and supply chain" at Cattaneo University. His current research concerns the organizational impact of ICT adoption within SMEs and the role of enterprises' aggregations in this context. Other research interests are in the field of ERP systems and e-business.

Angeliki Poulymenakou is an assistant professor in the department of Management Science and Technology at the Athens University of Economics and Business. Prior to that, she worked as a lecturer in Information Systems at the London School of Economics and Political Science. She holds a first degree in Mathematics (Athens), and MSc and PhD degrees in Information Systems (London School of Economics and Political Science). Her current research focuses on information technology enabled organizations capability development, where she studies, in particular, organizational processes related to knowledge management adoption. Overall, her published research work addresses three areas of interest: analysis practices for knowledge-intensive systems, the management of ICT projects (and the study of project failure), and the socioeconomic impact of ICTs, with a specific emphasis on ICT-enabled organizational change and electronic commerce. She has served as a member of the scientific committee of four international conferences in information systems (ICIS, ECIS, IFIP 8.2 and 9.4) and has acted as a referee in several international journals in the field.

Daniel J. Power is a professor of Information Systems and Management at the College of Business Administration at the University of Northern Iowa, Cedar Falls, Iowa. Professor Power received a PhD in Business Administration from the University of Wisconsin–Madison. His research interests include the design and development of decision support systems and how DSS impact individual and organizational decision behavior. He is also the author of the book titled *Decision Support Systems Concepts and Resources for Managers*. Dr. Power has published more than 40 articles in journals like *Decision Sciences*, *Decision Support Systems*, *Journal of Decision Systems*, *MIS Quarterly*, *Academy of Management Review*, and *Information and Management*. Currently, he is the editor of the World Wide Web site DSSResources.COM at URL *http:// DSSResources.com*.

Mohammed Quaddus received his PhD from the University of Pittsburgh, MS from University of Pittsburgh and Asian Institute of Technology. His research interests are in information management, decision support systems, group decision and negotiation support systems, multiple criteria decision making, systems dynamics, business research methods and in the theories and applications of innovation diffusion process. Dr. Quaddus has published in a number of journals and contributed in several books/monographs. In 1996 he received "researcher of the year" award in Curtin Business School, Curtin University of Technology, Australia. Currently he is an associate professor with the Graduate School of Business, Curtin University of Technology, Australia. Prior to joining Curtin, Dr. Quaddus was with the University of Technology–Sydney and with the National University of Singapore. He also spent a year at the Information Management Research Centre, Nanyang Technological University, Singapore.

Aurelio Ravarini graduated from Politecnico di Milano in Management Engineering in 1994. From 1996 to 1999 he received a research grant at LIUC in the Information System department. In 1998 he attended the Master Training Trainers (ISMO, Milan). He is an assistant professor at Cattaneo University, CETIC, since 2000. Since 1996 he has been researching in the field of information systems, with a specific focus on issues related to the adoption and use of ICT within SMEs. At the moment, his research interests cover the topics of Internet technologies and inter-organizational processes, e-learning management and knowledge management systems.

Kai Riemer holds a 1-year position as a visiting lecturer in the Department of Information Systems at the University of Melbourne, Australia. He is also a researcher, lecturer, and PhD candidate at the Department of Information Systems at the University of Muenster, Germany, from which he also holds a degree in Information Systems. Mr. Riemer has participated in various European and national research projects. His research interests and publications cover the areas of e-commerce and interfirm networking, and his current research focuses on the organizational impact of ICT in inter-organizational arrangements, in particular, the role and management of social capital in interfirm relationships and virtual organizations.

Jose Ruiz-Navarro is Professor of Management and Dean of the Faculty of Business Administration at the University of Cadiz (Spain). He has been visiting professor at Purdue University Kranner School of Management. Dr. Ruiz-Navarro has been a consultant for the Chamber of Industry and Commerce in Cadiz, as well as for the following industries: automotive (Ford), aeronautic (Construcciones Aeronauticas, now EADS), food, and shipping. He has been

CEO at ZUR (a Promotion Office of the Spanish Ministry of Industry), Gestion 1 (Consultancy), Free Zone Port of Cadiz, INI (Spanish Industrial Public Holding), and Astilleros Españoles, S.A. (Shipyard Industry). His articles and conferences have been published by *Long Range Planning*, Eastern Academy of Management, International Conference on the Dynamics of Strategy (University of Surrey), EGOS (European Group of Organizational Studies), Strategic Management Society, Conference of Management and Organizational Cognition, and *Strategic Management Journal* (forthcoming). He is an Expert Evaluator of the European Commission DG XII. He was reviewer of the International Congress of Academy of Management—Organization and Management Theory Division, 2000; Iberoamerican Academy of Management, 1999; I, II, and III Workshops on Human Resources and Strategy (Spain); and Revista Europea de Direccion y Economia de la Empresa.

Jean Scholtz is a computer scientist with an interest in evaluation of interactive systems and human–robot interactions; she is a research scientist in the Information Access Division of the Information Technology Laboratory at the National Institute of Standards and Technology.

Donatella Sciuto received her PhD in Electrical and Computer Engineering in 1988 from University of Colorado, Boulder. She is currently a full professor at the Dipartimento di Elettronica e Informazione of the Politecnico di Milano, Italy. She is a member of IEEE, IFIP 10.5, and EDAA. She is a member of different program committees of EDA conferences, and associate editor of the *IEEE Transactions on Computers* and the *Journal Design Automation of Embedded Systems*, Kluwer Academic Publishers. Her research interests cover mainly the methodologies for co-design of embedded systems and the analysis of the impact of information and telecommunication technologies on business.

Geoffrey N. Soutar has an Economics Degree from the University of Western Australia and a PhD from Cornell. He was Foundation Professor of Management at Curtin University (1994) and Executive Dean of the Faculty of Business at Edith Cowan University before becoming Director of the Graduate School of Management at the University of Western Australia in 2000.

Christine E. Storer is a lecturer in agribusiness at Muresk Institute, Curtin University of Technology in Western Australia. Research interests include information communication systems and management; inter-organization, chain, and network research; consumer and buyer behavior and attitudes; small business; and market analysis. Research has been published in the *Journal of*

Chain and Network Science, Journal of Supply Chain Management: An International Journal and the *Australasian Agribusiness Review.*

Carlo Angelo Zanaboni graduated from Università Carlo Cattaneo—LIUC in Business Administration in 2002. From 2002 to 2003 he worked as a research assistant at CETIC dealing with the organizational impact of ICT adoption within SMEs and the role of enterprises' aggregations in this context. At the moment, he works as a freelance e-business consultant and collaborates with Politecnico di Milano in some of its major e-business projects.

Index

supply chains 249
supranets 80
synchronous collaboration application
      272
synchronous collaborative awareness
      and privacy 268
system support level 59

T

task analysis 273
technology issues 10
transaction costs theory 140
trust 47
typology for an IOIS 8

U

ubiquity 93

V

value-added networks (VANs) 91
value creation 330
VBScript 253
vertical linkage 267
virtual association platform (VAP) 144
virtual private network (VPN) extranets
      82

W

web-based DSS 237
web development and server
            technologies 249
workflow management systems 77
workflow systems 88

X

XML 39, 253

CPSIA information can be obtained at www.ICGtesting.com
Printed in the USA
BVOW021659091212

307621BV00006B/188/P